We Are Not Able to Live in the Sky

We Are Not Able to Live in the Sky

THE SEDUCTIVE PROMISE OF MICROFINANCE

Mara Kardas-Nelson

METROPOLITAN BOOKS

HENRY HOLT AND COMPANY

NEW YORK

Metropolitan Books
Henry Holt and Company
Publishers since 1866
120 Broadway
New York, New York 10271
www.henryholt.com

Library of Congress Cataloging-in-Publication Data

Names: Kardas-Nelson, Mara, author.
Title: We are not able to live in the sky: the seductive promise of microfinance /
Mara Kardas-Nelson.
Description: First edition. | New York: Metropolitan Books: Henry Holt and Company,
2024. | Includes bibliographical references and index.
Identifiers: LCCN 2023055945 | ISBN 9781250817228 (hardcover) | ISBN 9781250817259
(ebook)
Subjects: LCSH: Microfinance—Sierra Leone. | Women—Sierra Leone—Finance, Personal.
Classification: LCC HG178.33.S5 K37 2024 | DDC 3323.09664—dc23/eng/20240105
LC record available at https://lccn.loc.gov/2023055945

Our books may be purchased in bulk for promotional, educational, or business use. Please contact
your local bookseller or the Macmillan Corporate and Premium Sales Department at (800) 221-7945,
extension 5442, or by e-mail at MacmillanSpecialMarkets@macmillan.com.

First Edition 2024

Designed by Meryl Sussman Levavi

Map by Gene Thorp

Printed in the United States of America

1   3   5   7   9   10   8   6   4   2

For Theresa Tengbeh

*Go walk around and see
what it's like yourself.*
—KADIJA TURAY

Contents

Part 2: Trouble the Water

We Are Not Able to Live in the Sky

Key Sites in the History of Microfinance

Bay Area, California, U.S.
Home of tech staffers and executives who first became interested in for-profit microfinance around the early 2000s.

New York, U.S.
Headquarters of several banks supporting microfinance, including Citigroup, Morgan Stanley, and JP Morgan Chase. Also home of Michaela Walsh, one of the founders of Women's World Banking.

Boston Area, Massachusetts, U.S.
The headquarters of Accion, a major early microfinance lender. Also home to the Massachusetts Institute of Technology, where Abhijit Banerjee and Esther Duflo helped to popularize the use of Randomized Controlled Trials in international development.

MEXICO
Where the 1975 United Nations conference on women was held to commemorate International Women's Year. Also the headquarters of Compartamos microlender.

Washington, D.C.
Where President Harry S. Truman gave his 1949 inaugural speech, which kicked off modern international development. Also the site of significant lobbying for microfinance in the 1980s; where Bill and Hillary Clinton and Muhammad Yunus had lunch in February 1983; the 1997 Microcredit Summit; and headquarters of USAID, the Center for Financial Inclusion, the Consultative Group to Assist the Poor, and FINCA.

EL SALVADOR
Site of the 1932 La Matanza Massacre; FEDECRÉDITO credit union; and early FINCA lending efforts.

COLOMBIA
John Hatch's Peace Corps placement.

BOLIVIA
Where FINCA gave its first microloan in 1983. Also where nonprofit lender ProDem converted to BancoSol, one of the first successful commercial microlenders.

BRAZIL
Site of first Accion loan.

SIERRA LEONE
See detail

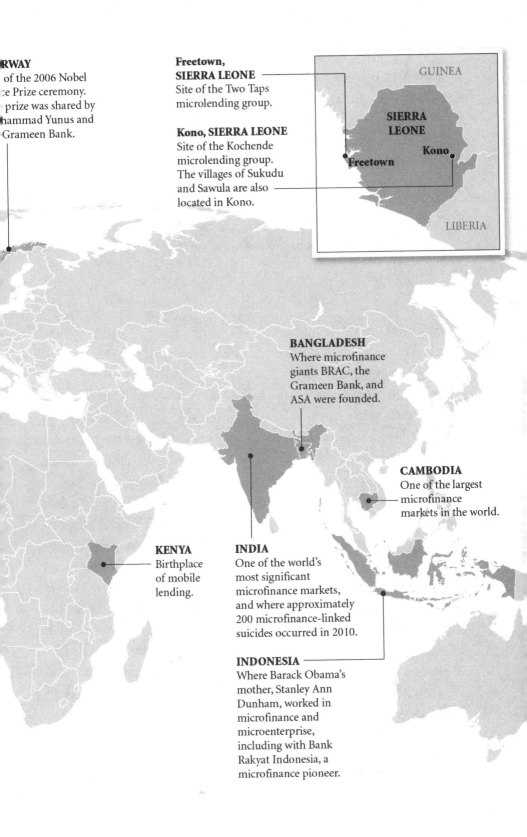

RWAY
of the 2006 Nobel
ce Prize ceremony.
prize was shared by
hammad Yunus and
Grameen Bank.

**Freetown,
SIERRA LEONE**
Site of the Two Taps
microlending group.

Kono, SIERRA LEONE
Site of the Kochende
microlending group.
The villages of Sukudu
and Sawula are also
located in Kono.

GUINEA

**SIERRA
LEONE**

Kono

Freetown

LIBERIA

BANGLADESH
Where microfinance
giants BRAC, the
Grameen Bank, and
ASA were founded.

CAMBODIA
One of the largest
microfinance
markets in the world.

KENYA
Birthplace
of mobile
lending.

INDIA
One of the world's
most significant
microfinance markets,
and where approximately
200 microfinance-linked
suicides occurred in 2010.

INDONESIA
Where Barack Obama's
mother, Stanley Ann
Dunham, worked in
microfinance and
microenterprise,
including with Bank
Rakyat Indonesia, a
microfinance pioneer.

Map by Gene Thorp

Gone

Old Post, Koidu, Kono, Eastern Sierra Leone

Several years back,
no one can remember when exactly.

YABOM WAS LUCKY. SHE HEARD ONE FLAT TONE, THEN AN ABRUPT POP. A moment of silence, then the flat tone again. *Thank God*, she thought. The phone was ringing.

She hadn't been certain that her friend Musu's phone would be on. It was already reaching late afternoon, and Yabom guessed electricity would be off just a few blocks away at Old Post, the neighborhood where she lived with her kids at the edge of Koidu, the largest city in the district of Kono, eastern Sierra Leone. Old Post had been there for as long as Yabom could remember. It had been built by the government back in "colonial times," when the British were keen to house workers who would dig the region's impressive diamond deposits. Those who first lived at Old Post hoped the huge mine that loomed over the settlement would provide income for them and their families for generations. But jobs dried up as diamond deposits were depleted and illegally leaked from the country. Although a colossal, industrialized mine run by a foreign company now overlooked Old Post, most of the miners who lived here were "artisanal" miners. While the phrase suggests an ancient activity conducted by artisans who transform rough material into precious, hand-crafted wonders, it actually denotes informal, often poorly paid work done in deep red pits by mud-caked laborers who make anywhere from $1 to $4 a day.

With little formal employment, Old Post morphed from a work camp to a low-income community at the close of Sierra Leone's eleven-year-long civil war, which spanned from 1991 to 2002. Old Post was desirable in that it was close to the center of town and unimaginably cheap—diamond workers hadn't been charged anything to live there, and now residents were charged just a few dollars a year by the local government. But it was undesirable in that the mine could produce blasts so forceful that rocks fell on residents' houses.

Yabom knew that even though the mine had power 24/7, it was on a separate electricity system from the rest of the city. The town of Koidu's electricity, on the other hand, was sporadic, always cutting out when the heat was most oppressive. Like it was now. From her spot at the police station, Yabom could almost see the afternoon's humidity clinging to the station's low ceilings. Beads of sweat formed on the blue walls; the damp encouraged scabs of peeling paint to separate from the concrete. The ceiling fans looked nice, at least, even if they didn't move.

The police officers didn't seem to mind the heat. They still marched around in their tight blue uniforms, felt berets, and high black boots, passing through the station's front doors with straight backs, as if they were puppets on strings. The few officers who did look hot sat in the front doorway, their uncurled legs bridging the divide between the floors of the station and the dirt of the parking lot outside.

None of the officers seemed to notice Yabom. Her small body cowered over the phone she cupped in her hand.

Another ring, silence, ring. The static coming through the phone sounded tin can-y, as if the person she was trying to reach was far away. If Yabom had just been allowed to step outside and walk to Old Post, she would have been able to reach the neighborhood in just a few minutes. But the officer dealing with her case had told her she couldn't leave, not even to ask a friend for a favor, not even to tell her kids what had happened. Yabom had crossed a line. She owed too much money, had waited too long to pay it back. Hers was a criminal matter now. If she didn't have the money today—and, clearly, she didn't—they'd have to investigate the case. She would remain in their custody while they did.

Yabom knew not to argue. She had tried that before and was slapped with fines she didn't understand or have the means to pay. This time, she gave a "yes sir" and asked if she could use a phone for just a minute. She had to figure out what to do with her kids.

* * *

On her way into town earlier that morning, Yabom's friend Musu had brought her small black cell phone to the charging station around the corner from her house. When Musu placed it down on the wooden kiosk, the man who operated the shop looked up from his own phone in silent greeting. He needed 20 cents to charge the phone for the day, or for as long as the electricity would last. Musu plugged the phone into a black charger attached to a long white power strip. Its battery bars blinked, then began to swell.

Satisfied, Musu walked down the dirt road that led out of Old Post and toward the center of Koidu, where diamond shops lined Post Office Road, a main thoroughfare. Even though the shops are not as plentiful as they once were, the town is still famous for the minerals, which made the region a critical and violent site of the country's civil war. Throughout the conflict, the district was intermittently controlled by rebels, then recaptured by the Sierra Leone Army, both of whom killed, raped, and maimed businesspeople, local chiefs, government officials, diamond sellers, mothers, and children. Thousands of people left Kono, most often to relatively safe Freetown or to neighboring Guinea. Some who stayed were forced to mine, sifting through wet buckets of earth for rocks whose profits further fueled the war. When it all finally ended, Kono emerged destroyed and shrunken. Whole villages had been displaced. Farms had been neglected for years. Homes and schools had been destroyed.

People like to tell stories about what Koidu was like before all that. They talk of bustling commerce that attracted visitors from across West Africa. Robust farms, thriving private doctors' practices, grand houses, pool parties attended by the town's wealthy elite. "They used to call Koidu the Paris of West Africa," one older Kono man told me as we sat in the city's worn out downtown. "Maybe it will be like that again one day. But it won't be in my lifetime."

Musu knew these streets well. She walked them most days, selling whatever she could get her hands on. Today, it was pineapples; she could smell the fruit from their place in the bucket on top of her head. The scent told her that one was perfectly ripe. It gave off a soft, light sweetness that just barely reached her nose. The other had a stronger smell, a twinge of alcohol. She would have to sell that one first, and offer a discount, lopping 50 cents off.

The businesswoman wouldn't be happy. Musu was acting as the big woman's agent today, a mobile human extension of her stall at Gbense Market, the main market in town. Only established businesspeople who had enough money and clout set up there, those who could afford to rent a stall and buy goods to fill it. Women like Musu had to sell their wares outside the market, while walking around or—a less successful tactic— waiting for customers to come to their homes. Musu and the big woman had agreed that Musu would get a flat $2 in exchange for her selling all the pineapples. No matter how long it took, no matter how well Musu haggled.

This wasn't Musu's preferred vocation. She wanted to start a business selling used clothes, generally referred to as "junks" in Sierra Leone. She thought it would be lucrative to sell men's underpants to her husband's colleagues over at the diamond mines. Musu had watched them over the years and observed what she considered an overlooked universal truth: men always buy more clothing than women, despite allegations to the contrary. While women had learned to manage with whatever they had, men were vain, the first to spend extra cash on a new T-shirt or cologne. Musu was sure that if she could just carry junks around, instead of this rotting fruit, she could make $3, $5, $10 a day.

For now, though, she was in a sweet spot for the day's pineapple job: far enough away from the main market to stave off any serious competition, but close enough to the heart of town to find the people with money. She walked down Post Office Road, stretching her legs wide over the open cracks in the sidewalks. When someone tssked or called her by the name of the fruit on her head—"Pineapple, pineapple!" "Hey, pineapple!"—the basket swiveled toward the crier faster than Musu's eyes could, her goods disconnected, momentarily, from the body that carried them.

After a few hours of pacing, all the pineapples had finally sold. Musu saw that the shadows on the verandas of the diamond offices were growing longer. She briefly thought of her husband. Every day, a bucket and shovel in hand, he left Old Post to sift through wheelbarrows of earth. He never came up with much—"He's still waiting for his big diamond," as Musu liked to say—and in the meantime the work had ruined his body. "He has so much pain," Musu explained. "I have to warm water to put on his back. I rub medicine on it every night." She had learned to be grateful for whatever little money he gave, whenever he gave it. Lowering her hopes kept her mind at ease, even if it meant that she could have no expectations at all. "He never hides any money from me. We do all right. My husband and I, we don't fight at all."

She placed the bucket, now empty of pineapples, back on top of her head and started to walk home.

Back at the charging station, the phone rang soon after Musu pulled it from its cord. "Hello?" Musu's voice rose with the "o." To Yabom on the other end, Old Post sounded so tantalizingly close. She could hear the high-pitched squeals of kids, the rooster who only crowed when the time wasn't right, spoons scraping the bottom of emptying pots. She could see from her spot at the police counter that it was that in-between hour, when the hustle of the day had died down but the night's had not yet begun. Finally, it would be cool enough for the boys at the soccer pitch to play but still warm enough for the bars to put on some music and entice the few people with money to buy beers.

But Yabom needed one more thing done today. "Please," she said into the phone to Musu. "I'm begging you."

Years later, Musu wouldn't be able to remember how much information Yabom had offered on the call: whether she knew where she was going or for how long. Maybe Yabom had known and just hadn't told Musu the details. "She just called me to ask me to take care of the kids. That's it. I don't know if Yabom went to Freetown or went to the Barracks. All I know is that the two kids are here with me. I've never seen her again."

Introduction

It is not that money is "just" a relationship. It is that all that we are, as social beings, is "just relationships." These relationships include our moneys.

—BILL MAURER, *HOW WOULD YOU LIKE TO PAY?*

I FIRST HEARD ABOUT MICROFINANCE WHEN I WAS ABOUT SIXTEEN YEARS old. I had recently become interested in HIV and AIDS, by then a clear global crisis. This was the early 2000s; an estimated five million people were infected by the virus in 2004 alone. Treatments were technically available but often priced out of reach. While I was completing high school, over three million people died of AIDS.

I began volunteering with my local Planned Parenthood in Olympia, Washington, and, with the help of an energetic mentor, learned about movements to expand access to HIV treatment both in the United States and internationally. I was desperate to learn more about the broader world, how and why it functioned as it did, or more specifically how and why it could be so acutely, unjustly, dysfunctional. I read *Mountains Beyond Mountains*, Tracy Kidder's chronicle of Paul Farmer's health care efforts, Stephanie Nolen's writing about HIV in Africa, novels set in Cape Town and Nairobi; I followed the impressive activism of South Africa's Treatment Action Campaign. My mentor suggested that if I was interested in "global issues" I read something else, too: *Banker to the Poor*, by a Bangladeshi economist named Muhammad Yunus.

I had never heard of Yunus, or microcredit, the term he used to describe lending small amounts of money to poor women, a way to help them become self-sufficient. Yunus insisted that microcredit could end poverty. By giving women just a few dollars, they could start small businesses, then use those profits to take care of themselves and their families. Focusing on women would not only bring one of the most marginalized groups into the economy. Thanks to their sense of duty as caregivers, their success would also mean the success of their children, their communities. Yunus also argued they were more responsible than men, more likely to use the money well and repay on time. Through something as simple as a small loan, Yunus argued that gender equality could be achieved, economies and neighborhoods strengthened. My mentor, a staunch feminist, insisted that this was an idea that was changing the world.

She seemed to be right. Within a few years, Muhammad Yunus and the Grameen Bank he set up would share the Nobel Peace Prize "for their efforts to create economic and social development from below." In 2010 alone, it was estimated that over two hundred million families were impacted by a microfinance loan. I began to notice the word "microcredit" everywhere: in newspaper headlines, in fundraising pleas from the international organizations I had recently become interested in, who now promised to give loans alongside health care so that the women they worked with could become economically independent. Throughout the early 2000s, microfinance seemed to be everywhere, even if mentioned only briefly: in college economics and international relations courses, by presidents,* at rock concerts, in interviews with celebrities,† at my family's summer BBQs (the only time I heard any economic development program, let alone an international one, mentioned at such a gathering).

---

* Bill Clinton highlighted microfinance in his 2007 book, *Giving: How Each of Us Can Change the World.* In 2009, Barack Obama gave Muhammad Yunus the Medal of Freedom. "President Obama Names Medal of Freedom Recipients," The White House, Office of the Press Secretary, July 30, 2009, https://obamawhitehouse.archives.gov/the-press-office/president-obama-names-medal-freedom -recipients.

† For example, Natalie Portman highlighted her work with FINCA, a major microfinance organization, at a 2007 talk at the Stanford Graduate School of Business. Margaret Steen, "Natalie Portman: Microfinance Lifts Families out of Poverty," October 1, 2007, https://www.gsb.stanford.edu/insights/natalie -portman-microfinance-lifts-families-out-poverty.

And then, suddenly, around the year 2010, I stopped hearing so much about microfinance. It was as if the program that had promised to uplift millions had quietly died.

Microfinance remained an afterthought until I moved to Sierra Leone, West Africa, in 2015, when I took a job with a health organization just as the country was emerging from the largest Ebola outbreak in world history. A couple of years into my stay, while talking with a colleague about her previous job at a Sierra Leonean legal aid organization called AdvocAid, she mentioned that AdvocAid had documented women being taken to the police and to prison for failure to pay their microfinance loans. She explained that the law in Sierra Leone enabled this because it penalizes debtors of all kinds, allowing for criminal cases to be pursued against them.

I have a vivid memory of how surprised I felt: of course, that women were finding themselves entangled in the criminal justice system for small unpaid debts. But also: that microfinance still existed, that people—many people, according to my colleague—were still taking out these loans, which, from my American viewpoint, formed by reading the news and conversations with academics and people who worked in international NGOs based back home, had fallen far out of favor. I remember saying something to the effect of, "I kind of forgot about microfinance!" My colleague, appropriately, snapped back, "Go ask anyone here, many people take it."

Later that afternoon, I walked across the street to the fruit and vegetable vendor I often bought cabbage, mangoes, pineapple, and coriander from, asking her if she knew of anyone who had taken out such a loan. She, too, looked at me like I was an idiot. "Yes. I've taken out many. Many! Every few months. In fact, I have a few right now." I asked her whether she had ever heard of anyone going to the police when they couldn't pay back. She hesitated. She insisted she had never had a problem herself but had heard of other women who had, those who, as she put it, "weren't very careful." Back at the office, I asked a colleague whether he knew anyone who had taken out microfinance loans. "Yes!" he said. "My wife!"

Somehow, I had missed all of this, apparently blind to the circumstances around me. I had only paid attention to one side of the equation: those who designed and funded and talked up the astounding promises of new anti-poverty programs like microcredit. I had completely ignored the other side: the people who experienced those programs in their day-to-day lives, who lived with them long after books and celebrity campaigns promoted them. I wanted to know more. To understand how and why microfinance became so popular in the West, how its narrative changed—why it is I suddenly stopped hearing about the tiny loans—and how these changes continued to impact the lives of borrowers around the world, long after so many of us had forgotten about Muhammad Yunus's promise that they would end poverty.

* * *

Microfinance, in its current form, came into being in the 1970s and 1980s, as "international development" transformed from a concept whose pro-grams were designed and dominated by government wonks, to a booming global industry. Microfinance would not have been so successful were it not for the rise of this industry. And international development—now a broad umbrella term used to describe a tangle of programs and policies generally meant to make a country more economically prosperous—would not have felt so tangible to people in relatively wealthy countries—people like me—were it not for microfinance. To understand how and why Sierra Leone seemed blanketed in loans, I realized I would need to start not in the streets of Sierra Leone, but the halls of institutions like USAID and the World Bank.

I spoke with dozens of people who worked in the "early days" of mod-ern international development and microfinance: with policymakers, bankers and investors, lawyers, academics, former Peace Corps volun-teers, and consumer rights advocates. In total, I interviewed over 350 peo-ple for this book, from Sierra Leonean tomato sellers to USAID staffers. While I had email correspondence with Muhammad Yunus, who is now in his mideighties, he did not respond to several requests for an interview, although I did have extensive interviews with several people who worked closely with him. (In my research I learned that my mentor, the woman who had first given me *Banker to the Poor* when I was sixteen, had, for a time, run RESULTS, an organization that, as we'll see, was essential to

the popularity of Muhammad Yunus in the United States and globally.)
I read his published books, including his PhD dissertation. In one email,
Yunus suggested that, because memories and recollections can be unreliable, I focus on documents instead, which I have done wherever possible,
combing through old microfinance manuals, the Sierra Leone national
archives, newsletters and policy notes that date back decades, as well as
histories of debt, international development, feminist movements, and
trade and economic development in West Africa and elsewhere, among
others.*

As I dug into the history of microfinance, I realized that, in many ways,
this was as much an American story as it was a Sierra Leonean or Bangladeshi one, with American policymakers, activists, feminists, and funders
helping to create the conditions for my fruit and vegetable vendor, and
those two hundred million other families, to take out a microfinance
loan. To learn about the history of microfinance, I needed to learn about
the history of American economic policy, both at home and abroad, to
reconsider how we understand and explain our own approach to poverty
and inequality, and what the American government, American institutions, and Americans themselves think we should do about it. I wanted
to know what it was about these tiny loans that so interested Peace Corps
volunteers and USAID staffers and, later, Silicon Valley investors and
philanthropists, wanted to know how their viewpoints and experiences
shaped one of the most lasting and impactful foreign interventions of the
last fifty years, one that has morphed into a multibillion-dollar industry.
What were they reading, who were they talking to, what was the political
discourse at the time that made an idea like microfinance feel simultaneously exciting and new, something many advocates felt like only they
could truly understand and believe in, and at the same time obvious,
even inevitable, an idea that major Western institutions would come to
back? It will be easy to criticize this book for being too deeply rooted

---

* My focus on documentation was hamstrung in one important way. In Sierra Leone, many prison files
are destroyed after three years; police files can be destroyed more regularly. If I could not find documentation that someone was taken to the prison or police, I would corroborate their story with at
least two other people, ideally including the police and/or microfinance company allegedly involved,
if they would talk to me and if doing so would not put the borrower at risk. I also spoke to Sierra
Leonean lawyers, paralegals, and judges to help me understand whether a story was plausible.

in a Western, particularly American perspective, but that is the point. This viewpoint has, in many ways, affected the lives of millions of people borrowing small amounts of money, millions of people trying to get by. (In the same breath, as you'll see in these pages, in many other ways it hasn't changed the main texture of their lives, just some of their particularities.)

My aim was not to cover every actor or historic moment in microfinance, to expose those who make money off the for-profit aspect of the industry, or even to argue whether microfinance works or doesn't—as we'll see, determining if a loan is "successful" becomes very complicated when you actually talk to people taking on the debt. Those who know the history of microfinance well will no doubt complain that I missed many people and events in this book, and that is absolutely true. Microfinance is so broad, stretching far back into history and with a wide geographical reach, that it would be immensely difficult to capture everything. My goal was broader: to explore how different people and different ideas in different parts of the world influence one another, often in ways they are unaware of, and to examine the lasting, sometimes unintended imprint of that influence.

Mostly, I wanted to know how women themselves understand these loans. So, in the summer of 2019, by this time having moved back to the United States and having fully transitioned to journalism, I returned to Sierra Leone. I started by interviewing the staff at AdvocAid, the Sierra Leonean legal aid organization my colleague had worked with, which helped women who were taken to police stations and jails because of unpaid debt. I pored through years of data they had collected. I followed their paralegals to court cases and women's prisons across the country. Through AdvocAid, and just by hanging around police stations and market stalls, I met women who were awaiting trial or in jail for unpaid debts or other petty crimes, or those who had already been in prison for unpaid debts, sometimes for years, often without an official trial. To make sure I was understanding the breadth of the problem, I also attended court cases and interviewed prisoners independently from AdvocAid (visits were sometimes facilitated by the Legal Aid Board, a government body). I interviewed judges, lawyers, police officers, legal advocates, journalists, and whatever microfinance staff would speak to me, mostly loan officers and mid-level managers. I spent weeks at the Sierra Leone national archives learning about the history of debt and small-scale trade in the country.

And I spoke to as many women who had taken out microfinance loans as possible. I wanted to know so much more, not just about entanglements with the legal system but about how the debts functioned in the local economy and their lives. I went to markets across the country, asking what must have seemed like inane questions to fruit vendors and sellers of used clothes. Where do you get money for business? How much do you sell this T-shirt for? Why did you set that price? How did you decide which microfinance company to borrow from? Where did you borrow from before? How do you use money? Where do those mangoes even come from? I spoke to over a hundred market women that summer. The majority had taken out microfinance loans. Their experiences varied widely, but all were built on hope, a series of "ifs." If I had money; if I had a bigger business; if I had a fixed location to sell my wares from, rather than my house; if I could buy goods from China and bring them directly here; if I could buy cheaply from rural areas to sell in town. If, then life would be better.

For some of the women, the ifs had borne out. Out of the hundred I interviewed, I met three who said with certainty that they had been able to expand their businesses thanks to a microfinance loan—several others said more substantial help came from family or political connections, or conceded they succeeded because they already had a steady business, with the loan just offering a cherry on top. Of the three changed by microfinance, one had a particularly dramatic story. She said the only reason she was able to leave her husband, who became abusive after he learned she was HIV positive, was the freedom a microfinance loan offered. She used the money to start a successful fish business, eventually remarried, and by the time we met had enough money to comfortably take care of herself and her kids. The second successful woman sold plastic jewelry in the country's main market and took out a $60 loan to expand the wares on her table, facilitating more sales. The third was an incredibly elegant woman, who gave off the scent of a newly opened perfume bottle; she had bundled together multiple microfinance loans to buy a plane ticket to China, bringing back suitcases full of beauty supplies to sell out of a hair salon in Sierra Leone's capital, Freetown. (I later learned that she not only had several microfinance loans but also loans from a commercial bank, and even, she said, a credit card—the first businesswoman I met who had one.)

But I met many more women who complained about the loans. That they were too small to do anything substantial with, that the repayments were too high and came too fast or that they ate into their profits, essentially nullifying any business growth. I noticed that these women were visibly poorer than the ones who said they were successful, with clothes worn thin and stalls that were less impressive. To help make payments, many had taken out multiple loans, one to pay off another, from multiple sources: different microfinance companies, their husbands' bosses at work, another trader—a balancing act that seemed at once to be working, in that they were staying above water, but was also immensely stressful. Every single one was clear-eyed about the risks of debt. They had seen friends go to jail, neighbors or family members who had left their homes and communities when they could not pay off a loan. But they also described tangible benefits. Not of launching successful businesses that propelled them out of poverty, as Muhammad Yunus promised, but more basic wins like covering school fees and annual rent. Many of the women said they were "managing," a word used in Krio to suggest they were getting by, but only just.

I could not outline the story of one hundred women in these pages. Instead, I decided to focus on two groups of borrowers who might help me, and hopefully you, learn a little bit about how microfinance functions in a place like Sierra Leone. Their stories, which take place over several years, are interspersed here, in between a history of modern microfinance.

One of the groups is in Freetown, a sprawling city of just over one million people on the Atlantic coast, and another in Koidu, Kono, the largest town in the country's diamond district, a rural area in Sierra Leone's lush eastern hills. The Freetown women live in Two Taps, a poor but not acutely impoverished neighborhood hidden beneath some of the city's most spectacular pockets of wealth. The houses here are sturdy, some people have jobs, many of the women I met are married, have TVs, and send their kids to private school. Yet sewage still flows through the streets and corrugated iron roofs still leak with each monthslong rainy season. In Kono, I met a group of women in Old Post, a neighborhood on the outskirts of town, in the shadow of one of the city's largest mines. These women are considerably poorer than those in Freetown. Only a few are married, none have TVs, and all send their children to free government schools. By following these two groups of women over several years—one relatively rich by Sierra Leonean standards, although poor by any other comparison, another deeply impoverished—I hoped to better understand how microfinance works, or doesn't, in one of the poorest countries in the world.

A few comments on wording: This is a work of nonfiction. However, certain names have been changed. In these pages, I use the terms "nonprofit" and "NGOs" to describe private organizations that officially function outside the government. The ones I refer to here are often, but not always, based in or have offices in America and Europe, with programs focused on poorer countries; for reasons we'll go into, these organizations dominate narratives, economies, basic services, and government policy in places like Sierra Leone. I use these terms interchangeably, even though sometimes nonprofits do make a profit or have a profit-making arm and even though "Non-Governmental Organizations" often work on government-affiliated programs, shape government policy, and rely on government funding. I interchangeably use the terms "microcredit" and "microfinance" to describe small loans given to poor people with the stated intention that they will use them for business. "Microcredit" was primarily used in the early days of such programs, with "microfinance" becoming more prominent after 2005 or so. Although they are deeply flawed, reductive, and limited, I use the terms "developed countries" and "developing countries" to denote countries that are currently wealthier and those that are currently poorer, primarily because these are terms used by those I interviewed and in the books and documents I reviewed. Sometimes, I talk about "the West" as a shorthand for these relatively wealthy countries, namely Canada, the United States, and Western Europe. I use "international development" to denote policies and programs that broadly attempt to set a country and its citizens on a "wealthier" trajectory. When citing interest rates for microfinance loans,

I indicate whether the rate is for the length of the loan or an annualized interest rate (although as we'll see, loans are often extended if a borrower is late, which can push up the interest rate). To calculate dollar amounts for the Sierra Leonean chapters, I used a ten-thousand-to-one leone to dollar conversion, given that the exchange rate fluctuated greatly over the period of reporting (2019–2022).

Finally, a note on the tempo of the women's stories: Because the women you'll meet here, even the relatively wealthy ones, are impoverished by international standards, their lives are not full of movement and action. Bound by societal expectations, childcare, the need to tend to little stalls of goods they've set up in their living rooms, and—most important—without money to go anywhere or a job to go to, they are largely confined to their homes and neighborhoods. They find ways to pass each day by trading stories and dreams and memories from porches and plastic chairs. While many aspects of their experiences are immensely stressful, their minds busy and their internal lives complicated and expansive, their ability to move around—whether to buy groceries at the local market, visit their daughter down the road, or see their family hundreds of miles away—is severely limited by their circumstances. While Western narratives are dominated by action, drama, and tension, the women I met are characterized by long periods of waiting, punctuated by moments of hope and planning and violence and fear. I urge you to set aside your expectations of a neat traditional narrative, and allow yourself to enter, very briefly, their worlds. If nothing else, I hope this book encourages readers to be humble enough to recognize the limits of their knowledge and curious enough to explore, openheartedly, that which they don't know.

PART 1

The Rise

Economy and religion, to their believers or knowers, provide master principles, master narratives, and master metaphors for making sense of the world.

—Parker Shipton, *Credit Between Cultures: Farmers, Financiers, and Misunderstanding in Africa*

CHAPTER 1

Twenty-Seven Dollars
to Forty-Two Women

IN 1992, MUHAMMAD YUNUS, AN ECONOMIST FROM BANGLADESH, WAS about to become famous. His rising recognition was helped when Bill Clinton, then governor of Arkansas and a prominent presidential hopeful, told *Rolling Stone* that year: "Muhammad Yunus should be given a Nobel Prize."

Yunus and Clinton had met several years before, in the mid-1980s; a friend of Bill's wife Hillary had made the initial connection. Clinton, whose presidential campaign hinged on reforming—and later gutting—welfare, was on the lookout for alternatives to an economic system that many voters felt was rigged, a feeling that had become particularly acute during the early '90s recession. (Famously, his unofficial 1992 campaign slogan was "It's the Economy, Stupid.") In their meeting, Clinton and Yunus found they had a lot in common. Clinton was "blown away" by Yunus's commitment to promoting "independence, not dependence," to making "enterprise work." They agreed that a reliance on the free market to create jobs and solve poverty was better "than creating a bureaucracy to hire a bunch of full-time people to give somebody a check." Clinton hoped to empower America's "dependent" communities—which he called "economic basket cases," where income only came "from the government or from drugs"—by using, among other things, "a different sort of banking system," such as the one that Yunus had set up.

At the time of the *Rolling Stone* interview, Muhammad Yunus had already gained recognition among philanthropists, people working in international aid, and the occasional banker interested in doing good.

The Grameen Bank, which Yunus had founded a decade before, had already been funded by the World Bank and the Ford Foundation, the second-largest private foundation in the United States. Yunus had even been invited to speak to the U.S. Congress.

But outside of special committees and niche finance and international development circles, few people had heard of Grameen or Yunus or his concept of microcredit. One of the journalists interviewing Clinton remarked that he seemed to be one of the only people who knew of the guy.

That was about to change. The world was on the cusp of learning the same story that Yunus told Bill and Hillary Clinton, the World Bank, the Ford Foundation, and American statesmen: how a few dollars, lent to a few women, could change the world.

It went something like this.

In the early 1970s, thirtysomething Muhammad Yunus found himself heading the Economics Department at Chittagong University in Chittagong, Bangladesh. He was new to the post but familiar with the busy seaport city on the Bay of Bengal, having spent his childhood nearby. Yunus grew up well-to-do, in a two-story house at Number 20 Boxirhat Road, situated, he writes in his autobiography, *Banker to the Poor*, "in the heart of Chittagong's old business district," on a "busy one-way lane." The bottom half of the building was reserved for his father's jewelry shop— Yunus says his dad was "the foremost local manufacturer and seller of jewelry ornaments for Muslim customers." His father had so much jewelry that he kept "three iron safes, each four feet high, built into the wall at the back of his store behind the counter."

The family lived on the second floor, above the shop. From up there, Yunus writes that he could hear the constant clang of entrepreneurial efforts. "When toward midnight the calls of passing street vendors, jugglers, and beggars finally subsided, the sounds of hammering, filing, and polishing in my father's workshop took over." From the rooftop, Yunus and his siblings "often idled away our time watching the customers downstairs or the gold artisans at work in the back room, or we would just look out at the endlessly changing street scenes."

Yunus paints his father as strategically frugal, willing to spend money on life's most important things—for example, Islam requires that Muslims who can afford it take a pilgrimage to Mecca, something his father did three times. But otherwise he kept "an extremely simple household." Yunus respected his father's prudence and work ethic, but it was his mother, Sofia Khatun, who he says had "probably the strongest influence on me." Like his father, she also came from a well-off family, made up of merchants, traders, and landowners. Still, she centered her attention on the well-being of the poor. She had her own little jewelry business and gave away the profits "to the neediest relatives, friends, or neighbors who came to her for help." Yunus describes her as "a strong and decisive woman . . . full of compassion and kindness."

Yunus was a bright student. He performed so impressively in college that his alma mater offered him a post as an economics teacher just after he graduated, at the age of twenty-one. In the mid-1960s, Yunus further pursued economics while on a Fulbright, first at the University of Colorado in Boulder and then at Vanderbilt University in Nashville, Tennessee. He initially enrolled in a master's program but says he found the workload too light, so opted for a PhD instead. Outside of class, he was drawn to the most American things America had to offer: *I Love Lucy*, *Gilligan's Island*, *Hogan's Heroes*, and square dancing. He was impressed by the rebellious, freewheeling students he met, surprised that women were just as likely to argue over ideas as men. He quickly "learned to enjoy the personal freedom of the United States." He even married an American. After finishing his PhD, he took a teaching post at Middle Tennessee State University in Murfreesboro, just southeast of Nashville.

Just three years in, he gave it up, to nurture a country only just born.

From 1947 to 1971, the country now known as Bangladesh, which sits in an eastern pocket of India, was called East Pakistan. Before that, the countries now known as India, Pakistan, and Bangladesh made up much of the British Raj, one of the most lucrative colonies in the British Empire. By one estimation, Britain drained the equivalent of $45 trillion from the British Raj in just 150 years through a complicated system of tax and trade, fueling lavish British estates, the monarchy, British businesses, and further colonial expansion. Sick of exploitation and colonial rule, independence movements, most famously led by Mahatma Gandhi, Jawaharlal Nehru, and Mohammed Ali Jinnah, called for an end to British taxation and for legal and economic self-determination. Gandhi and Nehru were Hindu, Jinnah was Muslim—he envisioned not only a non-British state but also one that would explicitly protect Muslims, who were a minority. In 1947, after years of political agitation and negotiation, independence was won at the same time the subcontinent was split. In a process overseen by British bureaucrats, the former British Raj was divided into two separate, self-governing dominions through a process known as Partition, which divided the region into two separate countries that intersected in a confusing, overlapping puzzle: West Pakistan to the west, India in the middle, East Pakistan to the east. After Partition—a bloody, messy affair that tore communities apart—Hindu-majority India was surrounded by Muslim-majority West and East Pakistan.

Now, instead of the British dictating formal laws and overseeing the formal economy, relatively wealthy and powerful West Pakistan wrote East Pakistan's legislation, planned its economy, and ran its largest businesses. Albeit with a different ruler, East Pakistan was again relegated to the status of colony, with local administrators left to decipher and implement plans made thousands of miles away.

Yunus grew up knowing that the outline of his life and the fate of the people and places he loved were determined by out-of-touch bureaucrats. And he hated it. So when, in late March 1971, the Bangladeshi independence movement declared the country free from Pakistan, Yunus, a newly minted PhD teaching at Middle Tennessee State University, threw in his support. From across an ocean, he decided, "My choice is Bangladesh . . . Those who do not join Bangladesh, I will consider Pakistani and an enemy of my country."

Pakistan's response to the independence movement was swift and brutal. Pakistani forces destroyed roads, bridges, and machinery, crippling vital sectors like tea and jute, a type of fiber central to Bangladesh's economy. According to a piece in *Time* magazine, "a special team of inspectors from the World Bank observed that some cities looked 'like the morning after a nuclear attack.'"

Back in America, Yunus helped to fundraise for the independence movement. He helped to publish a newsletter about the struggle for the new nation, organized teach-ins across the United States, and lobbied on Capitol Hill, encouraging other countries to support Bangladesh.

On December 16, 1971, just over six months after the independence declaration, Pakistani forces retreated. In the course of the conflict, over six million homes had been destroyed; over a million farmers were dispossessed of their land, tools, and animals; and hundreds of thousands of Bangladeshis were killed. Ten million people fled to India. When they left, Pakistani-owned businesses emptied the newly independent country of its resources—one airline was left with just 117 rupees ($16) in its account. Bangladesh's newly formed Planning Commission estimated the country needed "$3 billion just to get the country back to its 1969–70 economic level." "By the time the war was over," Yunus later wrote in *Banker to the Poor*, Bangladesh was a "devastated country. The economy was shattered. Millions of people needed to be rehabilitated."

A few months later, in early 1972, Yunus gave up his position at Middle Tennessee State University and moved back to Bangladesh to help the new country rebuild. He easily slipped into the elite circles he had grown up in and was given a position with a "fancy title" at the government's Planning Commission. Although he had been a vehement supporter of the independence movement and was excited to help his country, he was disappointed to find the new government just about as inept and disconnected as the Pakistani rulers he had grown up resenting. In his autobiography, Yunus describes ineffective bureaucrats who were uninspired and underworked but overwhelmed with foreign consultants who had flocked to the country post independence. Foreign engineers and policymakers offered ideas about how to fix roads, how to help women "develop skills," how to grow the country's natural gas sector, how and where and why to build new textile mills and power stations. One academic framed international efforts in Bangladesh at the time as fevered yet haphazard and unfocused, "a Herculean effort of uncertain outcome . . . a kind of humanitarian experimentalism that has pervaded Bangladesh's national development project."

The country was born during the frenetic adolescent years of what is now broadly referred to as "international development," which first took shape in the 1940s. In 1948, the U.S. Congress passed the Economic Cooperation

Act, better known as the Marshall Plan, a dramatic package of loans and grants to help Europe rebuild after World War II and encourage western Europe to look toward American, not Soviet, influences. The billions in aid would be used to rebuild infrastructure and factories and towns that had been destroyed, while also providing an outlet for American companies looking to find new markets. The World Bank, only recently set up in 1944, also to support post–World War II rebuilding, offered a pathway for money to flow and technical advice on how to use it. A sister organization, the International Monetary Fund, was also set up in 1944, with three clear goals: "promot[e] international monetary cooperation, support the expansion of trade and economic growth, and discourag[e] policies that would harm prosperity." It was envisioned that by offering some sort of cohesive global economic order through the Bank and the IMF, with funding and guidance from the U.S., another economic depression and conflict could be avoided.

These early efforts focused almost exclusively on Europe. That left a huge gap: not just the hundreds of other countries in the world, but specifically the three dozen that achieved some sort of independence from their European rulers between 1945 and 1960. Even though many had also been battlegrounds in World War II, and also contributed resources to the fight, those that had been under British and other colonial rule— including Pakistan, Bangladesh, and India—were excluded from the Marshall Plan, despite the Indian subcontinent having sent 2.5 million men to fight in the conflict.

In his 1949 inauguration address, U.S. President Harry S. Truman offered a vision for countries that had "been stirred and awakened . . . by the spread of industrial civilization, the growing understanding of modern concepts of government, and the impact of two World Wars." Truman framed such newly independent countries as poorer and less advanced than the United States, lamenting that "more than half the people of the world" had economic lives that were "primitive and stagnant." Americans should care that millions of people were "living in conditions approaching misery" because "their poverty is a handicap and a threat to both them and to more prosperous areas." Poor, hungry people could fall prey to ideology—just consider Germany's descent into fascism, or Communism's looming global threat. More practically, pervasive poverty meant these countries didn't offer healthy markets for American goods. If there was to be stability and peace and economic growth, not just in Europe but globally, things had to change.

Truman painted a bleak picture, but his tone was optimistic. "For the first time in history," he proclaimed, "humanity possesses the knowledge and the skill to relieve the suffering of these people." America, "preeminent" in "industrial and scientific techniques," would lead the way. In Truman's rendering, poor countries were somehow instrinsically starting at a lower baseline; he didn't seem to dwell on the histories of how they had become so impoverished. They simply needed a boost. Development was about providing an additive to some sort of unfortunate but fundamental way of being, a way to put poor countries on an upward path toward progress that the United States had paved.* As one scholar put it, such countries would "catch-up with the [W]est by replication and imitation."

To facilitate this, Truman would borrow the basic architecture from the Marshall Plan. Capital would again be used to fund a very specific kind of industrial development: the building of roads, dams, factories. Highly planned projects would be the foundations of modernity, and new infrastructure would at once spur and indicate economic progress. Countries' ascent would be measured by Gross National Product, or GNP, a figure first used in the United States in the 1930s to capture the sum of economic activity. GNP would become so important that the IMF would soon explicitly tie its support to countries' plans to increase their GNP.

Through the Marshall Plan, the United States had committed $13 billion—between $150 billion and $200 billion in today's dollars—to Europe. Truman was now talking about using a similar model in dozens of countries, many far poorer than postwar Germany or Italy. With concerns over the price tag, and with magnanimity wearing off as World War II shrank farther back in Americans' minds, Truman considered it essential that the newly "awakened" countries pay for the bulk of the

---

* Before Bangladesh achieved independence, some development economists had seen Pakistan as their "laboratory" in which to test out new ideas, including the theory that "functionalist inequality" would raise GDP and spur industrialism, thanks to an abundance of cheap labor. Michelle Murphy, *The Economization of Life* (Durham, NC: Duke University Press, 2017), 40.

efforts themselves. Poorer countries would be expected to commit their own human, financial, and technical resources to realizing plans shaped in the West. Grants, but particularly loans, would be offered through the U.S. government, as well as the World Bank. The focus on loans lowered the price tag while also working to instill a culture of fiscal responsibility—a country's success, Truman argued, would "depend in part upon savings habits, willingness to work, and the adaptability of the indigenous peoples."

Truman's enthusiastic inaugural address kicked off the modern era of Western-led international development, marked by technology-heavy, capital-intensive industrial development projects largely conceived of in and financed by North America and Europe and deployed elsewhere. By the time Bangladesh gained independence, entire government agencies and private companies had been set up to put countries on a prescribed path of progress. Bangladeshi politicians, planners, and bureaucrats received trainings, technical advice, ready-made policy plans, and cash from foreign engineers, policymakers, scientists, and economists, who all had a clear vision for what the region could become.

* * *

When he returned to Bangladesh in the early 1970s, Yunus found himself as unimpressed with international development as he was with his new colleagues at the government's Planning Commission. In *Banker to the Poor*, he points to a study suggesting that most of the foreign assistance given to Bangladesh "was spent on equipment, commodities, and consultants from the donor country itself." He lambasted "rich nations" who "use their foreign aid budget mainly to employ their own people and to sell their own goods, with poverty reduction as an afterthought."

On a more granular level, Yunus found some programs bogged down with "perennial management problems and technical breakdowns." Just as had been the case when politicians in West Pakistan determined the lives of those in East Pakistan, the funders and technocrats in DC and Dhaka were woefully disconnected from the lives of everyday Bangladeshis. Even though the development consultants he met were controlling—Yunus complained "the assumption is that the recipient countries need to be guided at every stage of the process"— foreign consultants and government officials had neither the time nor the ability to consider the "people-centered problems . . . technology brought with it." Lackluster, paper-pushing bureaucrats in the Bangladeshi government were left to carry out ill-fitting, cookie-cutter programs created thousands of miles away.

Tucked under larger critiques of Bangladesh's ill-functioning bureaucracy and the Western governments that helped to fund it was a more personal gripe. His job at the Planning Commission "was a bore," he recalls in his autobiography. "I had nothing to do all day but read newspapers." He resigned and took a job heading the Economics Department at Chittagong University.

In 1974, soon after he started his new post, Bangladesh faced a crippling famine. Despite the United States pushing governments to adopt agricultural tools and techniques used in the West, promising these would invigorate newly independent economies and feed the world, much of Bangladesh remained food insecure. On top of that instability, rice prices rose steeply, thanks to Bangladeshi government policies that encouraged food rationing (some scholars argue that speculative price bubbles were also to blame). To make things worse, as the famine was brewing, the United States halted food donations to the country in protest over Bangladesh's trade with Cuba. Then, an already dire food shortage was worsened by floods.

Yet again, Yunus was underwhelmed by the response from his country's government, which he described as consisting primarily of inadequate "gruel kitchens. But every new gruel kitchen ran out of rice." International support also sputtered, contingent on policy changes. While twenty-two nations acknowledged that Bangladesh would need $12 billion to get through the crisis, the *New York Times* wrote that many made their help "conditional on a devaluation of the Bangladesh currency, which is highly overrated, and measures to increase industrial production, particularly in the jute industry."

Yunus watched the famine unfold in the villages around Chittagong. Poor, landless, rural laborers were hit hardest. Photographs of stick-thin children, their faces contorted with pain and fear, made global headlines. Over a million people died.

Yunus says it was his mother and "her concern for the poor and disadvantaged" that had initially prompted his interest in "economics and social reform." Now, surrounded by mass starvation, the formal economic discipline felt callous and disconnected. In *Banker to the Poor*, he wrote, "I started to dread my own lectures. What good were all my complex theories when people were dying of starvation on the sidewalks and porches across from my lecture hall?" The poor people in the villages around Chittagong seemed to exist in something of their own world, detached from what Yunus had been taught, from institutions that economists like him had built and propped up. They grew most of their own food, made their own furniture and clothing, didn't borrow from or save with banks—existing outside of the formal economy, none of their work, not to mention their daily lives, would be captured by Gross National Product, the measure of productivity economists had become obsessed with. Yunus wanted a change. He decided, "I am going to go into the village and learn economics from the villagers."

In 1976, in a village called Jobra, Yunus met a twenty-one-year-old mother of three named Sufiya Begum* working from her home. He found Begum "squatt[ing] on the dirt floor of the verandah, a half-finished bamboo stool gripped between her knees . . . totally absorbed in her work." She was "barefoot on the hard mud. Her fingers were callused, her nails black with grime."

At first, Begum didn't let Yunus and his colleague in the house, given that there was no male family member around. Still, they got to talking about her stools. Yunus learned that she borrowed five taka—about 22 cents—from local middlemen she bought the bamboo from. At the end of each day, the same middlemen bought her stools for the same five taka, putting a mere fifty poysha, or 2 cents, on top. Borrowing from those she bought from and sold to seemed to put Begum at a serious disadvantage; working all day for 2 cents shocked Yunus. But Begum said she preferred it over going to a local moneylender, who would charge up to 10 percent interest per day.

Yunus watched Begum's "small brown hands plaiting the strands of bamboo as they had every day for months and years on end." Even with all her hard work, she could barely feed her family. He reasoned that "Sufiya's status as a bonded slave would only change if she could find that five taka

---

* Her name is sometimes spelled "Sufia."

for her bamboo." He could just give her the money; "that would be so simple, so easy." But he resisted the urge, since "she was not asking for charity. And giving one person twenty-two cents was not addressing the problem on any permanent basis." A loan, he believed, "could bring her that money. She could then sell her products in a free market and charge the full retail to the consumer."

But there was a problem: there was "no formal financial structure . . . to cater to the credit needs of the poor." Getting a loan from a bank was out of the question since Begum was a woman, and besides, government and international development programs only gave loans to relatively wealthy farmers and landholders, who had the right connections and collateral. The truly impoverished didn't make the cut.

Yunus decided he would do what the banks would not, and what moneylenders only would for a hefty charge. He would lend to poor, asset-less, landless women like Sufiya Begum, who had been deemed uncreditworthy. He would focus on women because they were society's most vulnerable, left out of the formal economy, formal banking sector, and formal development sector.

With a small team of research assistants, Yunus made a list of Jobra villagers who relied on middlemen or moneylenders. He lent a total of $27 to forty-two different women, an act that would be recounted numerous times over the next several decades: in the New York Times, the Guardian, the BBC, in academic papers, at conferences; by Bill Clinton, Barack Obama, European nobility.* At Oslo City Hall on December 10, 2006, when he accepted the Nobel Peace Prize, Yunus told princes, kings, queens, and the hosts of the evening, Sharon Stone and Anjelica Huston, "I offered . . . $27 from my own pocket to get these victims out of the clutches of those moneylenders. The excitement that was created among the people by this small action got me further involved in it. If I could make so many people so happy with such a tiny amount of money, why not do more of it?"

Yunus was thinking big. His research assistant, Maimuna, was a bit more pragmatic. When he gave that first $27, she asked him, "When should they repay you?" He replied, "Whenever they can. Whenever is

---

* Depending on the source, the amount is sometimes $26.

advantageous for them to sell their products. They don't have to pay any interest. I am not in the money business."

* * *

Despite how famous the story of Muhammad Yunus's first loan would become, soon after giving the $27 to forty-two women, Yunus considered the action "ad hoc and emotional." The right thing to do, and a good proof of concept, but a bit like firing from the hip. Next, he thought, "I [need] to create an institutional answer that these people could rely on."

So Yunus began a multiyear effort to get Bangladeshi banks to lend to women directly. It started quite badly. When he approached Janata Bank, one of the country's largest government banks, the manager complained that the women were illiterate and had no collateral. Yunus countered that collateral was useless since the poor were so desperate. "That is the best security you can have—their life."

Still unconvinced, the Janata manager suggested the women have a guarantor, "a well-to-do person in the village who would be willing to act on behalf of the borrower." The guarantor would vouch for the poor woman, offering a sort of social collateral when material collateral was absent. If she couldn't pay, that guarantor would be responsible.

Yunus offered to act as guarantor himself. The manager agreed, and a small lending program was born.

Although initially enthusiastic, Yunus's writings betray annoyance at the arrangement—among other things, signing off on loan requests interrupted international travel to the United States and Europe. Yunus toyed with ways to make the loan process easier for everyone. He instituted a daily payment, low enough that the "borrowers would barely miss the money" while also keeping payments on track. In place of one well-to-do guarantor, he put borrowers in groups of five. Money would be given individually but members could only keep borrowing if everyone paid back. The group members would essentially act as each other's guarantors, providing a mix of "support and protection" and "subtle and not-so-subtle" peer pressure. Each member also had to attend a seven-day training, after which they were quizzed on the bank's policies. Peer pressure worked here, too. Yunus wrote that if one group member failed the exam, she risked being chastised by a fellow member, who would say, "For God's sake, even this you can't do right! You have ruined not only yourself but us as well."

Yunus would later be criticized for cultivating "submissive" clients—despite his insistence that poor women should be trusted with money, it seemed they also needed to be told how to use it—but he defended these practices. The groups and exams ensured that only "needy" and "serious" members would join. "We want only courageous, ambitious pioneers . . . Those are the ones who will succeed."

Although Yunus hadn't charged the initial forty-two women any interest, borrowers who took out loans through the Janata arrangement would pay 20 percent for their loans (loans often lasted just a few months). Although interest is forbidden in Islam—and although Bangladesh is a majority-Muslim country—banks got around the rule by claiming that they weren't charging usurious, profit-oriented interest rates, just enough to cover inflation and their costs. The higher cost was needed to protect Janata from a higher risk of default they said was inherent with poorer women and to cover the higher relative cost of overhead per tiny loan, since operational costs were the same whether the bank was lending $5 or $500. And although 20 percent was far above the heavily subsidized rates banks offered to wealthier clients, Yunus argued that it was still a steal compared to moneylenders, who could charge over 100 percent per year. Members would also set aside savings. In addition to helping them squirrel away some much-needed cash, their deposits could be used to lend to others and to support operational costs.

After working with Janata Bank, Yunus pitched a similar version to a different government bank, Bangladesh Krishi Bank. Yunus had better luck this time—the bank was interested right away. It might have helped that he knew the bank's manager, who allowed Yunus to set up his own mini lending system with Krishi, with his own rules, procedures, and staff.

In 1977, just a few years after the devastating famine, Yunus's team was supporting around five hundred borrowers. In 1979, after being provoked by a banker who claimed the lending program only worked because Yunus was a native of Chittagong District, Yunus opened another branch, this time in the district of Tangail. Soon, there were nineteen branches in Tangail, six in Chittagong, plus the one he had initially started back in Jobra. By the end of 1981, less than a decade since Yunus had moved home, the effort had lent $13.4 million. In 1982 alone, with the support of the American-based Ford Foundation, the International Fund for Agricultural Development (a UN body), and the government's central bank, another $10.5 million was lent. By November 1982, there were twenty-eight thousand borrowers.

In 1983, looking to expand even further, Yunus negotiated another deal with the Central Bank of Bangladesh, the country's most powerful financial institution, to set up a new bank that only lent to the poor. The partnership came with some serious strings attached, most notably that the government would become the majority owner, a condition Yunus agreed to despite his reservations about inept government programs. But he insisted that the remaining 40 percent be overseen by borrowers. Yunus felt strongly about this condition. He wanted whatever the bank made to go back to the borrowers themselves, not to bank owners or private share-holders. Still, despite this provision and even with all his kvetching about lazy bureaucrats and corruption, his experiment would effectively "become a government-owned bank," a scenario he accepted begrudgingly. "Like it or not, the Grameen Bank"—which means "of the village"—"was born."

Restless

Freetown, Sierra Leone

End of 2020

AMINATA SAT ON HER PARLOR FLOOR, PICKING OFF THICK FLAKES OF THE pink nail polish she had layered on her toes a few days before. She didn't feel much like looking pretty. Even though it was almost noon, Aminata hadn't washed, eaten, or put on a shirt. Her lapa, a brightly colored African-print fabric decorated with flowers whose colors were inverted—grass green for the petals, yellow for the stems—was tied loosely around her waist. Her hair escaped the bun she had encouraged it into the night before. Her earrings, resembling thick bands of gold hugging a pearl, were still on. They stood out as the only bright thing around.

Aminata lay down on the cold concrete floor, tilting what was left of her bun toward the ceiling. With puffy eyes, she stared toward the front door. It was still locked. She didn't care about making any sales today and ignored the knocks and calls of "Aminata, is there any water?" "Any ginger beer?" "Yogurt?" Her customers' bodies caught the sun, their shadows spilling into her house through the large cracks, like so many crooked teeth, in the wooden door. She let out a tsssk, then rolled over. "I don't feel like doing this today," she said. She stretched her legs toward the wall. "Not today."

It had been exactly three years and seven months since Aminata had come to Freetown from Pendembu, her natal village in northern Sierra Leone, an important cultural and historical locale that, at least when she was growing up, was so dense with rice swamps and forests it was easy for a person to get lost in them. One of Aminata's first memories is of bodies piling up at the bottom of Pendembu's well. "The rebels killed them all. My auntie, my mom's younger sister, they killed her. I didn't really understand what was happening until everyone ran away. My village, it's beautiful, but it wasn't a nice place to grow up."

For much of Sierra Leone's eleven-year civil war, rebels attacked towns across the north, including Pendembu. When they entered her village, they took "everything, except the dogs. We called the dogs 'agents of darkness' because they were such good security dogs. But the rebels took everything else. They took my grandfather's cows, sheep, and goats. They destroyed all our food. After that, we only had cassava, which we boiled with a little salt and oil. That's how we survived, for six or eight months." When the war finally ended, in 2002, Aminata was eight years old. Her family emerged from the conflict with few crops, no livestock, no house.

The family trudged along after that, piecing together what they could, but they never managed to make up for what they had lost during the conflict. Aminata was an exceptionally bright student, studying through lunch to perfect her English and distract herself from hunger pains, but her mother ran out of money to pay for school fees when Aminata was in high school. She suggested marriage was the next best—maybe Aminata's only—option. Her mother arranged a meeting with the son of one of the most respected and oldest men in the village. Aminata only had a few opportunities to meet her fiancé, a man named Idrissa, before the wedding. Aminata didn't dislike him. Like her, he also valued education above all else. He had even been a teacher before becoming a driver for a big international organization in Freetown, a position that paid significantly more. He felt bad that her school days had been cut so short, felt bad that he hadn't yet been able to go to college. They both harbored dreams of studying further, whenever time and money allowed it.

But Aminata strongly resisted the idea of marriage. She still felt too young, more like a schoolgirl than a bride. Her mother insisted, telling her this was God's plan. Aminata cried throughout the whole wedding, greeting guests and unwrapping gifts with blurred vision. The next day, she left for Freetown with Idrissa, her cousin Mommy, and her adopted daughter, Doris, who she considered her own, joining soon after.

When Aminata moved in to Idrissa's three-room house in Freetown's Two Taps neighborhood, she figured it would only be a few months before she could save enough cash to pay the $20 round-trip transport to visit her family back in Pendembu. But now, three years and seven months later, Aminata had been in Two Taps long enough to know its unpaved, pedestrian roads by heart. She swore she could walk them in the dark, with her eyes closed. The neighborhood, a maze of small concrete houses topped with corrugated iron roofs, is tucked among a few of Freetown's quieter, cushier streets, on the side of a winding hill that leads to an expansive view of the Atlantic Ocean, on which UN agencies rent gated compounds and a night in a palatial hotel costs more than Aminata's husband's monthly salary.

"The benefit of being near the big ones," Idrissa explained over dinner one night, pushing his nose up toward the mansions surrounding them, "is that we get light, when it comes"—he pointed his spoon toward the cluster of wires above connecting their house to their neighbor's, their neighbor's to someone else's, and so on—"and the quiet."

"Unless they decide to have a party," Aminata said and flashed a smile. "Then we're up until morning."

That length of time weighed on her. "I've been here three years and seven months," Aminata repeated while picking the pink off her toenails, as if it were a mantra. "Three years and seven months." It was her mother who she missed most. Through relatives, Aminata heard she hadn't been doing so well lately. Her mother's ailment was ambiguous but persistent, explained in snippets by family members who called almost every day: lots of headaches, not a lot of appetite, feeling tired but unable to sleep. Her father worked in "country medicine," selling herbal remedies packaged in modern-looking pills and powders. Her mom would have tried those, but the police had recently confiscated his supply, slapping him with a fine because he hadn't officially registered as an herbalist. Aminata's mother could go to the nearby mission hospital, about an hour's drive away. Although it was understaffed and often didn't have the medicines a person might need, it was still by far the best hospital in the area, and at least the treatment was free. Getting there would cost quite a bit, though, an expense compounded by the fact that someone would need to go with the ailing woman to make sure she had enough to eat, given that hospital food was notoriously unreliable.

To save up for the trip and for her mom's care, Aminata kept whatever cash came her way in a small metal box that sat on a bookcase in the living room in Two Taps. The bookcase was packed with the few books and notebooks that her daughter, Doris, used at school, along with piles of folded clothes, old, broken cell phones, and some culinary basics Aminata kept in big plastic jars—salt, sugar, lime powder.

The bookshelf was kitty-corner from a TV that was almost as wide as her outstretched arms, placed directly below the only framed photo in the house. A full-body shot of her husband, Idrissa, peered out from it, taken from a time before they had met. The man in the image appeared noticeably thinner than the man she lived with now, with fewer lines on his face. He was also, uncharacteristically, unsmiling, as if he were trying to appear stern and gruff and serious, a true patriarch. The man she knew always wore a grin, even after eighteen-hour days shuttling his bosses around town on both official and personal business. Idrissa even smiled when their aging neighbor, whom everybody called Grandpa, insisted on talking politics. Idrissa and Aminata were staunch supporters of the All People's Congress, or APC, one of Sierra Leone's two major parties. Grandpa was a lifelong supporter of the APC's only real opposition, the Sierra Leone People's Party, or SLPP. The political rivals now shared a wall, a landlord, a bathroom, and, effectively, given that they lived so close together, a front porch. It was impossible to avoid Grandpa when the family ate dinner outside, the man shouting greetings and political slogans over the Congolese music he played from his radio every evening.

Idrissa's stern-faced photo sat across from the family's newest and most important asset, the means through which Aminata planned to pay for her trip to Pendembu and the reason she was in a depressive state on this day: a huge white refrigerator, low and long and big enough for Aminata to lie down in if she had wanted to. Idrissa had recently bought it for her. It had cost him around $250, almost double what he made in a month.

Rather than pay particularly competitive salaries, the organization he worked for offered low-interest loans to their employees. Idrissa eagerly took one, paying off bit by bit through automatic payments docked from his already slim paycheck. Considering the debt, he and the family had to survive on less than $50 a month.

But the fridge meant everything to Aminata. She had a lot riding on this hulking white giant. It was her savings account, her insurance. A way to make something of herself, to give shape to her days. Her mother's medical care, her daughter's school fees. Her ticket to Pendembu.

* * *

After marrying Idrissa and moving to Freetown three years and seven months ago, Aminata figured that although she would miss Pendembu, at least her life would become lively. She pictured parties and business opportunities that would keep her so busy she would barely sleep.

Instead, with Doris at school and Idrissa at work and little money to go anywhere or do anything, Aminata and her cousin Mommy spent most of their time at home. To pass the time, Aminata tried napping on the living room couch, but it was so old that it sank into itself, sucking her into cushions that had become damp in Freetown's persistent humidity. For the few hours the electricity worked she and Mommy watched the news. Mostly, they were dead bored. They spent a lot of time sitting on the front veranda, waiting for something to happen, although most days nothing really did.

Aminata didn't like relying so much on Idrissa, who paid their bills and had known everyone in Two Taps for ages before she came around. "I want to stand on my own, because when you depend on a man, and then he doesn't give you anything, you're going to really struggle," she reasoned. Without a high school degree, getting a full-time job felt out of the question. The only people in Two Taps who had official posts—with titles, paychecks, and ID cards that let them into offices—were the few men who were drivers, like her husband, plus that one lucky girl down the street who had graduated from a private high school, spoke perfect English, and worked in an air-conditioned supermarket on the main road. The girl's job was so important she even had a uniform.

Aminata wasn't so lucky. The only job she had ever been offered was to go to Saudi Arabia to work as a cleaner. The local mosque had apparently worked out a deal with the support of the Sierra Leonean government, or so her neighbor Grandpa said. The old man trusted the imam, plus of course the ruling SLPP, currently in power, so his daughter immediately signed up for the gig. Grandpa heard she would make a few hundred dollars a month, quadruple what Grandpa had made during his long career as a security guard. She'd just be away for two years, sending back whatever she could.

Aminata considered the offer, but saw working for someone else to be inherently risky, especially if it meant going out of Sierra Leone. She had heard stories of women who traveled overseas for "cleaning jobs," then forced into sex work or some sort of slavery: their cell phones and passports taken, their days spent locked indoors, their wages garnished to cover whatever they ate. She turned the imam down. "It's difficult here, but at least there's freedom."

The only thing Aminata could think to do instead was to start a small, informal business from her house. She was motivated by contingencies she expected to arise: emergency surgery for her mother, Idrissa losing his job, her daughter, Doris, needing tutoring help. She hoped to save enough money to make such unavoidable exigencies feel manageable. Tucked behind those worries, she harbored a vision of growing herself, too. She planned to put something aside for catering classes, maybe even a private high school graduation exam so that she could pursue her dream of becoming a nurse. Really, the details of what she studied didn't matter. "I just want to go to school."

Hence the new, gleaming white fridge, watched over by Idrissa's serious photo. He had bought it for her so that she could start a yogurt business. She was a good cook, knew how to make yogurt that was perfectly smooth, with no unsavory chunks of milk or flavoring. While Aminata sold the goods from the house, her cousin Mommy could walk around the main road at the base of Two Taps, selling plastic sachets of yogurt from a cooler on top of her head.

Idrissa also longed for Aminata to be more independent. Perhaps having something to do would stymie the griping he had become accustomed to hearing in the evenings: about how bored Aminata was, about the vapidness of their neighbors, about how she missed all the space back in Pendembu and her mother's cooking. There were also the economics of coupling to attend to. Before the wedding, Idrissa was barely getting by on his $150-a-month salary, about $30 of which went to taxes. Now that they were married, he had not just one extra person in the house, but three, Doris, Mommy, and Aminata coming as a package deal. Aminata needed to work if they were going to make rent—which could go up anytime, at the whim of their landlord—pay Doris's private school fees, and feed themselves each week. "That fridge," he said, "is our only hope. That is what we will eat and drink."

Soon after he bought the fridge, Aminata made a few batches of yogurt, as well as ginger beer and bissap, a sweet maroon-colored hibiscus drink. But even though all sold quickly, Aminata didn't make enough money to buy another set of materials, milk and stabilizer and vanilla and sugar, which she estimated would amount to about $200. When she told Idrissa she needed more money to get the business off the ground, he left the house in anger. He hadn't even finished paying off the loan he'd taken to buy the fridge, and already she was asking for more.

So Aminata lay down on the floor, resigned to waiting. For nothing, maybe. For the day to be over, and another one to start.

CHAPTER 2

An Epiphany

PART OF THE ALLURE OF MUHAMMAD YUNUS'S STORY IS THE SEEMING singularity of his ingenuity. As it is told in Yunus's autobiography, *Banker to the Poor*, and innumerable times before and since, Yunus's decision to give $27 to forty-two women was powered by a mix of critical observation, empathy, and creativity unique to him: only he, the son of a successful entrepreneur, trained in economics in the capitalist West but whose true north was his mother's devotion to the poor and who had his eyes opened to the harsh reality of the country he loved, could have imagined such a solution to poverty. Only he could have "invented"* microfinance.

It's easy to argue that Yunus has done more to proselytize small loans and their poverty-defying power than anyone else. For many of us, if we know anything about "microcredit," we conjure an image of his smiling face. He's undoubtedly the icon of an idea. It's just that he didn't come up with the idea alone.

* * *

Just a few months after Yunus was born in Chittagong, Bangladesh, nearly seven thousand miles away and across an ocean, Winslow Roper Hatch, a botany professor at Washington State University, braved a freak snowstorm in Pullman, Washington, to get his wife, Dita Keith, to the hospital. She was going into labor with their second son, whom she would name John in

---

* As the publisher of *Banker to the Poor*, PublicAffairs Books, claims.

honor of her father, a successful Costa Rican banker known for his magna-nimity and charity.

Little John Hatch did not initially live up to the expectations his name suggested. The only compliment he remembers hearing from a teacher is, "John sings sweetly." But he took to history and writing, propelled by sto-ries of his family. On his father's side, he traced his ancestry to Governor Josiah Winslow of the Massachusetts Bay Colony, who was himself the son of a *Mayflower* passenger and Pilgrim leader, and on his mother's, to Spanish conquistadors. "I love that my mother's family is half pure-blood Spanish, and it's half Inca," he told me. "That's my blood, too." Centuries later, Hatch's great-uncle on his mom's side, Minor C. Keith, helped to oversee Costa Rica's first railroads. Keith had bankrolled part of the effort by setting up banana plantations up and down the railway line. The rail-way was something of a disaster, but the plantations took off and bananas became one of Costa Rica's main exports. Within a few decades, Keith would help to launch the United Fruit Company, which would go on to monopolize commercial banana growing throughout much of Latin America and the Caribbean, dominating the region's politics, with the company supporting political and worker repression and bloody coups. It was the fruit's influence on the export-oriented, commodity-reliant economy—and ultimately the undemocratic politics of countries in the region—that gave them the moniker "banana republics."

John Hatch relied on his love of history and sharp storytelling to get into Johns Hopkins University, where he majored in history. During summer breaks, Hatch worked for his maternal uncles—one in Costa Rica, one in Colombia—while learning Spanish. Although his family was well-to-do, he found it was impossible to ignore the poverty around him. Equal parts entranced by the romance of the tropics and moved by the desperate situa-tions of those he met, Hatch set his heart on leaving the States before he had even completed college.

He saw his chance in 1961, during his junior year, when John F. Kennedy came into office.

It was just over a decade since Truman's "newly awakened countries" speech. Kennedy liked the basic premise of extending American aid abroad but considered the country's international development programs "fragmented, awkward and slow"—and, as it happened, not particularly popular. In an effort to rebrand, Kennedy's administration set up the Agency for International Development (A.I.D., now referred to as USAID), which would become America's primary means of deploying money and technical resources to poorer countries. Speaking to Congress at the beginning of his presidency, and sounding an awful lot like Truman, Kennedy championed the new agency, claiming, "The economic collapse of . . . less-developed nations . . . would be disastrous to our national security, harmful to our comparative prosperity and offensive to our conscience."

In addition to launching USAID, Kennedy's flagship international program was the newly formed Peace Corps, which he announced just after he took office. Kennedy envisioned that through the Corps young people freshly graduated from college would "serve, shoulder to shoulder, with citizens of newly emerging countries . . . devoting part of their lives to peace and to strengthening the ties that bind men together."

The Peace Corps proved immensely popular, with thousands signing up for two-year stints volunteering abroad before the program was even officially launched. The Corps attracted a certain type of American: young, college educated, ambitious, idealistic, concerned about the fate of their nation and the world and convinced they could change both. Also, often, but not always, they were white and male, in part a reflection of who could attend university and then afford to take two years off. The Peace Corps ultimately created a sort of breeding ground for USAID staffers, with hundreds of young Americans, now with a few years' experience under their belt, ending up at the young agency. One longtime USAID staffer, who joined the agency after serving in the Peace Corps, told me that Kennedy "created an atmosphere in government where we thought that we could change the world for the better."

Hatch felt that way, too. "I thought that [the Peace Corps] was the most interesting thing since sliced bread," he told me. "The idea of fighting poverty in Latin America, oh my God! There was no doubt in my mind that it was exactly what I wanted to do." The A he received for his senior thesis, written on his uncle Minor C. Keith and his railroad and banana exploits in Latin America, lifted his GPA just high enough to graduate.

* * *

In July 1962, Hatch was assigned to live for two years in Hoyo Sapo ("Toad Hole"), a neighborhood on the outskirts of Medellín, Colombia. When he arrived, he felt like a rock star. "To a twenty-one-year-old, it was a very glamorous occupation," he told me. "The people adored me because when had an American come to the community and wanted to help? It was just this wonderful, magical way to start a career."

Hatch had been sent with a rather nebulous mission: "organiz[e] the community to improve its own standard of living through community action and cooperation." The hope was that the people of Hoyo Sapo could "organize themselves to solve their problems." During the day, Hatch helped to build community halls, schools, sports fields, aqueducts, sewers, and women's clubs. His evenings were more lonely, mostly spent on his typewriter, penning letters to a girl back home.

The correspondence meant that Hatch took regular trips to the post office in Medellin. One day, in a rush to get to town, he came across a little boy in the road. The kid—Hatch guessed he was around three—was clearly unwell. He was "totally naked, and he was rising from having been squatting on the path and he had left this whole lake of diarrhea. He looked bad. I knew he had symptoms of severe malnutrition." But Hatch was in a rush to get to the post office, and in something of a mood—the girl's letters had been coming less frequently of late—so he quickly walked past the sick boy. "I said, 'if I stop and get involved with this kid, I'm going to miss my bus to the city and I'm not going to get my letter from my girlfriend.'" (The letter didn't come anyway. Hatch soon stopped writing.)

Two days after encountering the boy in the road, Hatch "saw a group of neighbors walking by my house with a little white coffin. The little boy had died. I felt so ashamed. I was devastated." Even though he's still not sure what exactly he could have done to help the boy, this young American with no real skills to speak of, he felt, "I had allowed that little boy to die. I was just totally, totally, totally distraught. It was one of the worst moments in my life." Hatch says he "went down on my knees and I just begged God for forgiveness for this incredibly poor decision on my part. I said, 'I swear I'm going to dedicate my life to do everything I can to help people in severe poverty." This is how I'm going to atone for this horrible, horrible decision."

Reformed, Hatch spent most of his second Peace Corps year simply observing the women and children around him. It was obvious that they were the poorest in Hoyo Sapo. The sports fields and community halls he had helped build the year before felt trivial now, disconnected from what the community really needed. If he was going to fulfill his promise to "help people in severe poverty," he should start here.

At the end of his two-year term, Hatch submitted his Peace Corps termination report, which he titled "Peace Corps and over-involvement." "I said the whole concept was misconstrued, because what we were doing was coming into these communities and leading projects and developing projects." Hatch felt Peace Corps volunteers risked "going over the [heads] of existing local leadership. It was about us being the good guys, the saviors."

Hatch's report somehow made its way to the assistant director of the Peace Corps. Hatch expected a reprimand, but the director apparently told him, "That's the best damn termination report I have ever read." Hatch soon took a job as regional director for the Peace Corps. Now based in Peru, he oversaw American volunteers in the region, dozens of whom had been placed with local credit unions. The American government had begun dabbling with local financial institutions, hoping that loans and bank accounts would offer an attractive antidote to Communist and Socialist movements sweeping the region, fund investment from the bottom up, and recruit private industry to the work of nation building.

Upon seeing the credit unions, Hatch recalls thinking, "What an interesting instrument for helping people progress! Mobilizing savings, wow, that's good, getting small loans, that's good, starting little businesses, that's good!" But Hatch also observed what he considered a fundamental gap: The credit unions were only lending to men. Without women, they "weren't getting to the really poor"—the people he had committed to spending his life serving.

Hatch soon left the Peace Corps to pursue a PhD in economic development.* Straight out of graduate school, he got a job within a new, pow-

---

* At the University of Wisconsin–Madison.

erful cadre in the increasingly complex international development sector: professional development consultants. The idea was that these private consultants would be more efficient and objective than government or World Bank staffers, given that they weren't official bureaucrats but instead trained professionals with a corporate mindset, driven by measurable results. Perhaps they could help institutions like USAID plan, implement, and evaluate programs better than the government itself could.

Hatch says he started taking on part-time freelance work for Development Alternatives, a newly formed American consulting firm founded "to do economic development on a competitive, cost-effective basis that was self-sustaining because it was profitable" and who did work on behalf of USAID. Hatch found himself largely unimpressed by the USAID projects he reviewed. Like Yunus, he also viewed USAID as divorced from the realities of the communities the agency was meant to help, its programs designed by technocrats better at pushing papers than getting meaningful results. If, in meetings with USAID, Hatch was asked his opinion— a rare occurrence—he always offered the same advice: programs should "get down to the poorest of the poor." He says his suggestion was never taken up.

Hatch's criticisms reflected a larger shift that was brewing, away from top-down, big-ticket, Western-led development programs that stemmed from the Truman era, toward grassroots efforts. Anti-colonial thinkers like Walter Rodney called for a more critical eye to history that focused on colonial repression and extraction—Rodney suggested that the reason his home country, Guyana, was "underdeveloped" was precisely because the British had spent centuries stealing from it. He viewed wealthy European countries as "overdeveloped" due to their brutality, their leeching off others, a kind of grotesque excess that newly independent nations shouldn't aim to emulate. A variety of other thinkers and movements rejected the idea that Western ideology and programs were appropriate for every context, including anti-colonial leaders like Mahatma Gandhi and his movement for Indian self-sufficiency, the Black Panthers' free breakfast programs and other mutual aid efforts, and out-of-the-box thinkers like economist E. F. Schumacher, who called for small-scale, context-specific interventions. One small Bangladeshi organization* described the skepticism of outside determination and the turn to grassroots, bottom-up development this way: "man must be given the opportunity to think for himself, speak for himself, work for himself and even make mistakes for himself."

Such criticisms were bolstered by academics and researchers, including those in the West, who worried that international development efforts were becoming an embarrassing debacle. There were reports of communities flooded by new dams and displaced by new roads; of half-built schools without textbooks and clinics without medicine; of waste, mismanagement, nepotism; of money going to the already enriched. Even with Kennedy's efforts to reform aid, America's international efforts remained clunky and unpopular both at home and abroad. His Alliance for Progress, a sort of Marshall Plan for Latin America—albeit with a far less impressive budget—did little more than build schools and hospitals, give out free books, and offer military assistance to counter Communist sympathizers; it did not radically change the region's economic landscape. Even in official U.S. government reports, the program is painted as a phenomenal failure.

Inept projects seemed even more unfortunate considering how much debt poor countries were taking on to fund them.† Independence and post-independence leaders expressed indignation at having to whittle down already limited budgets to pay off foreign loans that hadn't seemed to have done much. In the 1980s, Thomas Sankara, the Marxist-Leninist and Pan-Africanist president of Burkina Faso, saw a direct link between debt and an attempt at foreign control, "a cleverly managed reconquest of Africa," a type of "neocolonialism," as Kwame Nkrumah, Ghana's first prime minister and president, described expensive, ill-fitting, foreign-made development plans. Sankara observed, "The origins of the debt date back to the origins of colonialism. Those who lent us the money, they are the ones who colonized us. They are the same people who managed

---

* Proshika.

† By the late 1980s, the West African nation of Gambia would incur so much debt that it would take nearly a century to pay off—that is, if it didn't take on more. Parker Shipton, "How Gambians Save and What Their Strategies Imply for International Aid," Policy Research Working Paper Series 395, World Bank, Agriculture and Rural Development Department, April 1990.

our states and our economies. It was the colonizers who led Africa to contract loans with creditors of the North . . . We are strangers to this debt. Therefore we cannot repay it." Julius Nyerere, the president of Tanzania from 1964 to 1985, implored the country's creditors, "Must we starve our children to pay our debts?"

By the last third of the twentieth century, there was a prevailing sense—as likely to be uttered in Washington, DC, boardrooms as in leftist reading groups—that expensive, top-down development projects had failed. Many skeptics gravitated toward a new approach—slow and small, with communities in the driver's seat and programs designed with the poorest in mind. This grassroots sentiment resonated across the political spectrum. Those on the political left were inspired by social movements that demanded broader social, economic, cultural, and political sovereignty—drawn to a "third way" that rejected top-down government and put power in the hands of individual people and communities instead. Many on the political right were also critical of big government programs, which they saw as inherently characterized by largesse; they were motivated by a belief in unbridling individual freedom. The increasingly popular bottom-up focus infiltrated U.S. policy. In the 1960s, the U.S. Foreign Assistance Act was amended to "recognize the differing needs, desires, and capacities of the people of the respective developing countries and areas." A few years later, Congress asked USAID to shift "away from technical and capital assistance programs" that had dominated international development and focus instead on programs that centered on everyday needs of the poor.

* * *

There were also concerns about what all those ill-fitting, ineffective development programs did for America's international reputation. John Hatch told me he wasn't just worried that USAID programs weren't reaching the truly poor. He was also embarrassed by the disconnected diplomats and USAID bosses who supposedly represented his country. He wasn't alone. In 1958, Joseph Blatchford, a young tennis star, found himself wondering about America's place in the world when then vice president Richard Nixon's car was attacked by a mob during a state trip to Venezuela. What could provoke such ire? The next year Blatchford took a trip to the region himself, where he developed a strong critique of the American business-men and diplomats who lived in the "American section" and didn't bother to learn Spanish, and the American government, which didn't seem to have any problem propping up repressive elites. Despite his criticisms, Blatchford still deeply believed in American-style democracy and ideals, but thought they should be promoted with a lighter touch: more carrot, less stick, and without explicit government involvement. So, a few years later, when Blatchford was studying law at UC Berkeley, he and a few classmates decided to start an international "self-help group," a way to support poor people around the world as they "start[ed] their own lives, as opposed to relying on charity"—something of a mix between John Hatch's nebulous Peace Corps mission to help people help themselves and Muhammad Yunus's anti-charity approach. Blatchford and his friends launched a new organization they dubbed Americans for Community Cooperation in Other Nations, or Accion. In 1961—the same year Ken-nedy announced the Peace Corps—Accion sent a few dozen recent grad-uates from UCLA, Berkeley, and Stanford to Venezuela to volunteer.

Although Blatchford was "rather critical of American foreign policy and American ways of doing things in [other] countries," Accion's method was quintessentially American: offer a hand up, not a handout. An early pro-motional video explained that "the Accion worker" would be "in the bar-rio" to "observe, guide and advise," to encourage neighborhoods to "accept community responsibility" rather than waiting for the government. "It is a new approach to development," the video explained, "based on the concept of self-help and the effective and imaginative use of outside resources and technical assistance."

To ensure they were not seen as agents of the increasingly criticized American government, Blatchford did not want to rely on official U.S. government funds—Accion soon became known as a "private" version of the Peace Corps. Instead of asking for government money, Blatchford approached private companies for help. Howard Bowen, an economist at Grinnell College, had recently published *Social Responsibilities of the Businessman*, which argued that companies should not only act ethically within their business but also more broadly in society, a message that resonated within the burgeoning environmental and feminist movements and the civil rights era. Companies with a hold in Latin America, including General Motors, Ford, Mobil Oil, Shell, Bayer, and Abbott Laboratories, enticed by a reputation for doing good, would donate to Accion. Its board of directors would soon include Donald M. Kendall of PepsiCo., Inc., Henry R. Geyelin from Chase Manhattan Bank, and Rodman C. Rockefeller—an American businessman and philanthropist and great-grandson of Standard Oil cofounder John D. Rockefeller, one of the richest men of his era—who had founded the International Basic Economy Corporation, which focused on encouraging "competitive businesses" in developing countries.

Despite Accion's spectacular fundraising success, the programs themselves were not particularly effective. It became clear, pretty quickly, that sending bright, young, well-educated but largely untrained Americans to work in complicated situations wasn't all that helpful. William "Bill" Cloherty, who went to Venezuela with Accion in 1965, recalls realizing, "'Gee, maybe I'm learning something about Latin America, but what am I actually contributing?' . . . The only lives that were profoundly being changed were our own."

So when, in 1969, Blatchford was recruited by now president Nixon to run the Peace Corps, the Accion staffers and volunteers who remained held a conference to discuss the organization's future. They reconsidered the work they had been doing—the help with building schools and latrines and water wells, their broad, general "community guidance." One Accion member remembered thinking, "If we just gave the money directly to the community, they would be better off."

Soon, they saw an opportunity to do just that.

* * *

In 1972, a report from the International Labor Organization, a UN body, first used the term "informal sector" to describe the millions of people whose work was not captured by Gross National Product and other measures used to track economic progress premised on a country's growing production and consumption. By one estimate, up to 70 percent of the urban labor force in poor countries was involved not in the "official" economy, but in small, off-the-books activities such as fruit vending and tailoring. The breadth of such informal activities in part reflected a geographic shift. Many poor people now lived on the margins of cities, which were growing at an exponential rate. As economies moved toward manufacturing and export-oriented resource extraction and opened their doors to cheap imports, often at the behest of the World Bank and IMF, which promoted an interconnected global economy, agrarian sectors withered in the face of international competition. Rural migrants were drawn to urban areas by the promise of industrialization. But the jobs didn't always materialize. As more people flooded to cities such as Lagos, Mexico City, Caracas, and Nairobi, researchers estimated that hundreds of millions of people would need to rely on small businesses to get by instead of traditional farming or official employment. The shift from rural to urban and toward the informal sector was so remarkable that in 1969, the U.S. Congress, whose members represented sometimes fractious cities, which themselves were changing with migration, civil strife, and "white flight," asked USAID to create an Urban Development Office and attempt to understand and support very small enterprises taking place in cities around the world.

Recognition of the informal sector acknowledged, in the words of one Accion staffer, that the butcher, the baker, and the candlestick maker were important economic contributors, too. To have a comprehensive economic policy, economists and policy makers realized they should focus not only on the top—on big government and big businesses—but on the middle and the bottom, too. One American researcher observed that squatters in Port-au-Prince, Haiti, although desperately poor, were mostly "employed" in that they were busy every day, making and hawking goods or selling their labor. What if these little entrepreneurs could be made even more productive? Could they then earn more than just pennies a day? And if they did, would that fix some of the problems that large-scale development programs had not?

Muhammad Yunus was excited about the informal sector,* which he called the "people's economy." He didn't see people clutching at, in the

---

* Yunus did want the Grameen Bank to explicitly focus on rural areas, although "rural" in Bangladesh, one of the world's most population-dense countries, means something quite different than in a place

words of one anthropologist, "ephemeral opportunities" as they were shut out from both the formal economic system and traditional activities their forebearers relied on. Instead, he saw millions of people slinging mangoes or sewing clothes as a demonstration of their ingenuity and innate entrepreneurial ability. "Microeconomic theory . . . is incomplete," Yunus would argue in *Banker to the Poor*. "It views individual human beings as either consumers or laborers and essentially ignores their potential as self-employed individuals." Self-employment was not "a symptom of underdevelopment" as some economists had claimed. Instead, it "represents the people's own effort to create their own jobs." The shift could be emancipatory. "If all of us started to view every single human being . . . as a potential entrepreneur the old wall between entrepreneurs and laborers would disappear."

Accion, rethinking their approach, also saw an opportunity here. The organization primarily worked in Latin American cities, where, one staffer observed, "there were many entrepreneurs in the barrios." They were getting by, but just barely. Just as Yunus had when he met Sufiya Begum, the stool maker in Jobra, the staffer also thought that "a real obstacle to unlocking talents" of those working in the informal sector "was the lack of capital."

There are a few explanations of how exactly Accion landed on loans as a solution. However it happened, Accion insists it happened organically, without the influence of Grameen. "We certainly started this before Muhammad Yunus did," an Accion staffer named Bruce Tippett said, noting that Accion started a small lending project in 1971, half a decade before Yunus gave $27 to forty-two women—before he had even returned to Bangladesh, in fact. "Accion was there first, in terms of microlending."

The Accion effort began in Brazil, where Accion hired twenty-seven-year-old Pedro Paes Leme to help provide technical, managerial, and credit assistance to small businesses. Paes Leme was the son of a banker, and part of his job was to try to convince banks to lend to the poor directly—the same tactic Yunus had initially tried. When Paes Leme

---

like Ethiopia. The other parts of Yunus's idea—the focus on small shopkeepers and ice-cream makers—were consistent with the focus on the urban poor.

visited a director he knew at a large Brazilian bank,* he found his friend
in a distressed state: he was about to fire the bank's eleven-person cleaning crew, having decided it would be cheaper to contract out instead. Paes
Leme stayed around for the sacking—his friend wanted moral support—
and saw an opportunity when one employee asked his boss, "Will you
contract us, instead of an unknown company?" Paes Leme convinced the
director to lend start-up money to his now former employees—all men—
with Accion acting as guarantor and providing administrative support.
Paes Leme considered it a perfect win-win. The bank had found a cheaper
solution to its HR problem, and Accion had its first entrepreneurs.

* * *

Despite his disenchantment with international aid, John Hatch continued
working as a development consultant for years. The job provided a healthy
enough paycheck and allowed him to stay in Latin America, a region he
continued to love. Then, in 1983, half a decade into his consulting work—
and the same year that Yunus officially set up the Grameen Bank—while
drinking a double bourbon on a bumpy flight over the Andes, Hatch had
what he describes as "an epiphany. It was like a warm draft coming over
my body. I just grabbed a napkin and started writing down ideas. I haven't
had anything like it before or since. It was just meant to be, and it just
came, as they say, out of the blue. It felt like a very spiritual experience."

Hatch's bourbon-fueled epiphany was that he would start a small lending program. In our conversations, he told me he may have been vaguely
aware of Accion's work, maybe of Grameen's, too—he might have read
something of Yunus's, he can't quite remember—but he says the idea
primarily came from thinking about the little boy back in Hoyo Sapo,
Colombia, whose death he was still trying to repent for. Maybe if his
mother had resources, Hatch reasoned, he wouldn't have died. Thinking about the boy and his family, Hatch decided that loans should be
offered primarily to women, the poorest of the poor he had been implor-
ing USAID to work with for years. To ensure that the loans reached the
very poor, three-fourths of the borrowers would be illiterate (the literate

---

* Banco Economico. Email with Pedro Paes Leme.

quarter would help with the bookkeeping). There would be no collateral required; instead, the women would be put in groups of thirty, effectively guaranteeing loans for one another. Hatch says that on that flight, "I just locked into the methodology, and that was it!" He decided he would call his program "village bank."

Hatch began lending $50 a pop to poor women in Bolivia, with a grant from USAID (improbably, given Hatch's open criticism of them). Over four months, borrowers offered weekly payments on their principal, plus some interest—around 3 percent. Borrowers also put some money toward a small savings fund, which could then be used to lend to others. This, Hatch hoped, would encourage a thrifty mindset and make the program self-sustaining once the USAID grant ran out. Within months, Hatch told me, the experiment reached four hundred villages—far more than Accion had reached in a matter of years, given that they had focused on larger loans to individuals who ran more established businesses. Hatch told me "we had 100 percent repayment"—a success he attributes to a mix of desperation and gratitude. "[The borrowers] had never had a chance to do something like this."

USAID was less impressed. After a staffer learned that borrowers were offering in-kind repayments by way of potatoes, sheep, carrots, fruit—cash was scarce given a currency crisis—the agency reviewed the program. The results were scathing. Hatch's program seemed chaotic and haphazard, and USAID couldn't figure out how the money was being spent, or whether it really helped borrowers. USAID took back the grant money they had given Hatch, including the machinery, vehicles, and typewriters he had bought. Dejected and defiant, Hatch says that he and his assistant "decided we can't ever let this happen again. We're going to start our own foundation, raise our own money."

To keep on with his "village banking," Hatch launched FINCA, or the Foundation for International Community Assistance, a year later, in 1984.* In lieu of U.S. government funding, FINCA limped along on funds from his brother's church. Hatch, meanwhile, continued to do consulting work, getting by on paychecks often ultimately funded by USAID,

---

* "Finca" also means "farm" in Latin American Spanish and is generally used to refer to coffee farms.

the agency he now despised. On the upside, the consultancy trips helped him to spread his idea. Every time he visited a project, he would contact three or four nonprofits and give his pitch. "I would say, 'I've got this idea for village banking. If you can come up with $5,000, I'll give a seminar on Saturday, and then on Sunday we'll go out and create a bank.'" Again, loans would be given $50 at a time, in groups, collateral free, mostly to illiterate women. While Accion had by now homed in on small businesses in need of a boost, and Grameen was reaching nearly thirty thousand borrowers, John Hatch says he "was like a Johnny Appleseed, spreading the idea all over Latin America." All three would soon converge to make microfinance a household word.

Back Home

Old Post, Koidu, Kono, and Sawula, Kono, Eastern Sierra Leone

2014–2019

IN THE SPRING OF 2014, ABBIE'S HUSBAND HAD JUST SETTLED INTO HIS job as a cleaner at Koidu Government Hospital, a couple of miles down the road from their home in Old Post, the neighborhood on the outskirts of the mining town of Koidu, Kono, when her neighbors called the government hotline, complaining that the man looked sick. Jingles on the radio and posters around town warned about the signs of Ebola, which was spreading quickly throughout Sierra Leone and the region. The neighbors thought the man's symptoms matched what they had been told to look for. He seemed weak, maybe had reddish eyes, and besides, he worked at the place where everyone was dying from the virus. When Abbie saw the ambulance coming around to load her husband in the back, she knew that she would never see him again.

After he died, Abbie took her kids back home to Sawula, a village in Fiama Chiefdom, Kono, several hours' drive from bustling Koidu. The village was made up of a few dozen houses, surrounded by all manner of greens: the light, psychedelic hue of young bananas, the darker shade of cassava leaves. Abbie recalled an idyllic childhood in Sawula. She spent her mornings selling the soap her aunt Finda made from charcoal. Each ball looked like a dark little moon, slippery and soft in the palm of her hand. She then helped Auntie Finda farm in the afternoons, tending beans and a small kitchen garden. Nights were the most fun. She and Finda "would sleep in these little huts in the field, way out in the bush," making sure no one disturbed the cows. Finda was more of a mother to her than an aunt, teaching Abbie everything she knew: about business, about how to survive in a small town with little more than the land to sustain them. The days engraved themselves on Abbie's young body. Dirt gathered under her fingernails and her nose tingled when nearby fields were burned into submission for the next planting season.

Sawula was home, but the village could not provide the same opportunities as Koidu. Even though the biggest city in Kono was no longer the Paris of West Africa, Koidu was livelier than Sawula, which had no electricity and where school ended at age thirteen. By the time she hit puberty, Abbie knew that if she wanted to grow, she had to leave. Finda encouraged her to do so. Abbie was bright and pretty, with a solid head on her shoulders. Her auntie didn't want the girl to just sell soap for the rest of her life.

So Abbie went to live with her uncle in Old Post. She found a hardness everywhere in her new home. Unlike the mix of raffia and mud they used back in Sawula, every building in Old Post was made from concrete, in varying shades of white and gray. Some of the houses were hoisted on platforms to protect them when the nearby mine sporadically flooded.

Abbie enrolled in school. She found that her early days selling soap helped her to excel in business studies and math. She hated English but passed the National Primary School Examination anyway. She advanced to Form 3, farther than any of the other women in her family had ever gone.

She was fifteen, still in school, when Abbie noticed that some of the women from Old Post had begun clustering themselves into groups, then going to NGO offices and coming back with cash. The women said they were involved with something called microcredit. Abbie remembers thinking it must be a good thing, even though her uncle grumbled about men being left out. "The women were talking about it and saying they were able to push themselves a little bit with the money."

At the end of the year, Abbie saw that the borrowers, in their small groups, went to a multistoried nightclub, guesthouse, and event center at the edge of Old Post for an annual prize ceremony one of the microcredit lenders put on. The "microcredit ladies," as Abbie had begun to think of them, showed up looking exquisite, wearing tailored African-print dresses and matching head wraps. Abbie rested her shoulder on the cold metal of the club's blue gate and watched the women walk by arm in arm, giggling like little girls. At the ceremony, the groups that had repaid their loans quickly were called to a stage and congratulated with one big bag of rice. The slower ones didn't get anything but a plate of food. Still, Abbie thought, not nothing.

A few months later, her mother stopped sending money from the village for Abbie's school fees. Her uncle didn't have the means to pay either, and Finda, with nothing but her soap business, was of no use. So Abbie dropped out. Abbie says the decision pained her—the whole point of going to Koidu was to go far, to do something she couldn't have done back in Sawula, and now she was leaving school just a few years later than she would have at home. But she also shrugged when recalling this, as if it were an unfortunate but not unexpected event. "I didn't come from a rich family, I didn't have connections for government scholarships. What could I do?" Abbie soon met the man who would become her husband and became pregnant at an age she remained, deep into adulthood, embarrassed to disclose. Her life, it seemed, would now be centered here, in Old Post, away from Finda and her beans and soap and the quiet nights Abbie still remembered. But she didn't resist "God's plan," which seemed set and determined. She simply settled into it.

* * *

Even though it had been years since she had lived in Sawula as a child, Abbie found it easy to settle back into life in the village after her husband's death. She stayed with her family, first for a few months, then for years. They still got by harvesting beans along with hot peppers, which the family would trade for rice or oil, or which Abbie would bring to Koidu to sell on the edge of Old Post. But soon came the question of her eldest daughter Princess's education. The girl, a spitting image of her mother, was reaching the age that Abbie had been when she left Sawula. Abbie had placed the same expectations on her that she had had for herself: to complete high school, maybe even to qualify for an office job one day, at the very least go farther in school than her mother had. For that to happen, they would have to leave again. Back to Old Post.

To start over in Koidu, Abbie needed cash. She remembered the "microcredit ladies" at the end-of-year event at the nightclub, with their fine clothes and matching head wraps, their carefree attitudes, their bags of rice and plates of food. Abbie already had an outline for a business she could start, buying shoes in Koidu and then selling them for markup in Sawula. She considered it an excellent idea. When she was growing up, her mom and Auntie Finda complained about not being able to find shoes they needed for special occasions, strappy sandals or a chunky heel. Miners and farmers complained about not having good work boots. These things were plentiful in Koidu, and cheap compared to Sawula, where everything was at a premium thanks to the distance.

Abbie soon heard about something called LAPO, or the Lift Above Poverty Organization, a Nigerian organization that gave out loans across Sierra Leone, including in Kono. A loan officer told her she could take out what amounted to about a $60 loan, so long as she was able to put together a borrowing group. Abbie walked to her neighbor down the road, a woman named Ramatu. Ramatu was a few years older than Abbie and considered herself innately cosmopolitan, a status she demonstrated by regularly rotating through a series of long fake eyelashes, bright nail polishes and lipsticks, and thick chains. Ramatu lived with her daughter, Janet, in a house near the front of Old Post. She had made it up as best she could, over the years slowly building on a front stoop, a covered veranda, and wooden-shuttered windows. There was no electricity, but Ramatu's brother down the road offered an illegal hookup, linking wires from his house to hers. Ramatu was most proud of her bedroom, big enough for a sinking queen-sized mattress that was always freshly made up, with several large stuffed bears and some red paper hearts resting on the headboard. The remainder of the bedroom was filled with dozens of hats, bags, and shoes. A full-body mirror leaned against the wall, decorated with photos of Janet and Ramatu. Silver, blue, and red tinsel, Christmas decorations Ramatu never took down, draped from the ceiling.

To Abbie, on the hunt for someone she could start a microfinance group with, Ramatu seemed money-wise, street-smart, sophisticated: the shoes, the house, the swagger. But it was her connections that really made her blessed.

On her mother's side, Ramatu was part of the Jabba family, something of a political dynasty in Kono. Although the family was no longer particularly powerful, the name was still highly respected—Ramatu thought she even had distant relatives in Parliament. Even more important, Ramatu had recently befriended an older man, himself from a powerful political family, who lived on a big farm on the outskirts of Koidu. The farmer had a brother in the United States, and friends in America and the UK. They all sent him money—sporadically, and never enough, but still. Sometimes, Ramatu would go over to his place and come back with more cash than Abbie had seen in days.

The man had been pursuing Ramatu for years, motivated by multiple interests. First, to sleep with her. Then, to change her, from what he saw as a materialistic, image-obsessed girl tainted by modernity, to a focused, humble, diligent woman. Finally, to marry her. The two of them, he imagined, could pursue a traditional Kono homestead together.

Ramatu appreciated his attention, the way he stopped by the house most days to check in on her and her daughter, Janet, who considered the farmer something of a father figure. And she appreciated his support. Sometimes, he would bring a bag of rice or a plate of food from a restaurant in town.

But she didn't appreciate that with the gifts came unsolicited advice: about how she should spend her time and, particularly, with whom. He was jealous of all the men who visited her, even though, she insisted, she just had a large family, with lots of brothers. Weary of possessiveness and protective of her freedom, Ramatu kept the farmer close enough to be helpful but not enough to be significantly influential. Even though he had become a regular visitor to Old Post—everyone knew about their relationship— Ramatu rarely mentioned him by name, and when she did, she always put a "Mr." in front of it, a way to denote both respect and distance. Like other women she knew, Ramatu rarely spoke of any of the men in her life. They could offer cash but weren't ultimately responsible for big economic decisions, weren't the ones dealing with the daily ins and outs of managing a house on no money. The farmer man was material, but ultimately peripheral. If he happened to be around, and could help, great. If he wasn't, Ramatu would get by as she always had, piecing what she could together.

Abbie knocked on Ramatu's front door, then pushed it in before she heard an answer. Although it was already midmorning and hot outside, the parlor was still cool and quiet. Ramatu wore a pink lapa that hung down to her knees, held up by a tight knot fastened at her chest.

"My sister," Abbie said. "We need to talk." Ramatu raised an eyebrow and tilted her head, then pulled out a plastic chair for Abbie to sit down in.

CHAPTER 3

Copycats

IN THE LATE 1970S, INTERNATIONAL DEVELOPMENT DONORS LIKE USAID wanted to "confirm," in the words of one staffer, the newfound focus on grassrootism and the informal sector. At this point, the Grameen Bank wasn't on the radar—Muhammad Yunus had only recently met Sufiya Begum, the stool maker in Jobra who inspired his $27 loan to forty-two women, and hadn't yet teamed up with the Bangladeshi Central Bank to officially launch the Grameen Bank. But USAID *did* know of Accion's new lending efforts, having funded some of their earlier community develop-ment work in "the barrios" of Latin America.* So the agency contracted the organization to lead a study on lending programs for small businesses around the world. Did lending to small businesses, as hoped, improve productivity? Increase income? Create jobs? Did investing in the infor-mal sector really make sense? Was this the development solution they had hoped for?

A new Accion staffer named Jeff Ashe was put in charge. Following JFK's nod to internationalism, Ashe had done a stint with the Peace Corps upon graduating from UC Berkeley in the mid-1960s, where "beatniks were morphing into hippies and the student revolutions were getting underway." In 1965, three years after FINCA founder John Hatch landed in Hoyo Sapo, Colombia, Ashe found himself in Ecuador. Officially, his initial job was to support credit unions like the ones Hatch had encoun-tered in Peru. But, inspired by Brazilian thinker Paulo Freire's work on

---

* USAID became a funder despite Joseph Blatchford's earlier insistence that the organization not rely on government funding.

grassroots education and the broader turn to bottom-up development, Ashe found himself more drawn to "campesinos revolucionarios"—revolutionary farmers—who were "demanding their share of the estate" that their families had worked for generations, pushing back against monopolized cash-crop agriculture like the kind that Hatch's great-uncle Minor C. Keith and his United Fruit Company had helped to forge a century before. Taking his cue from Freire's *Pedagogy of the Oppressed*, Ashe says he spent most days asking these "revolutionary farmers" about their lives and desires and their plans for change. After the Peace Corps, Ashe stayed in Ecuador to work on agrarian reform. He then joined Accion in 1975.

For the USAID study on lending to small businesses, Ashe and his colleagues were tasked with reviewing dozens of small credit programs in Latin America, Asia, and Africa. It didn't take long for Ashe to realize that around the same time Accion was encouraging banks in Brazil to lend to small businesses, dozens of other organizations were also experimenting with small loans to the poor. In addition to Yunus and Hatch, there was a group in the Philippines, where local leaders helped to identify and vouch for those in need of cash—a version of the "guarantor" concept. There was the Self-Employed Women's Association, an unemployed women's union founded in 1972 in Gujarat, India, which had recently begun giving loans to newly unemployed fabric producers. Ashe learned about a bank in Java that offered credit to rural Indonesians, employing a system that was remarkably like the one Muhammad Yunus was honing: the loans were short-term, with relatively high interest rates, and required savings but no collateral.

But Ashe was surprised to find many more small-scale lending efforts that preceded all this—sometimes by several centuries. While many had also been set up by "reformers" concerned with social welfare—akin to John Hatch or Muhammad Yunus—many others were overseen by poor people themselves.

Some of the efforts felt uncannily similar to the small-scale lending efforts springing up around the world in the 1970s. Perhaps the most familiar took place at the turn of the twentieth century, when Albert Filene, founder of the American department store Filene's Basement, had an experience that was a near mirror image to those Muhammad Yunus, John Hatch, and Accion staffers would describe having decades later. While traveling around the world, Filene was "shocked by the poverty he witnessed in India and the Philippines" and "appalled that [people] had to borrow money at very high interest just to pay for special occasions, such as weddings," Mehrsa Baradaran, an American law professor specializing in the history of banking law, writes in *How the Other Half Banks*. Filene was equally distressed that few of America's poor could access a bank account or loan without relying on loan sharks or pawn shops.

Filene saw an answer in the British agricultural cooperative banks, which took their inspiration from the German cooperative movement of the mid-nineteenth century, offering farmers an alternative to high-priced moneylenders and a way to purchase land as feudalism waned. Cooperatives pooled and then lent members' money to one another; any profits were plugged back to the members themselves. Baradaran writes that, convinced through his travels that "poor villagers needed adequate credit and the ability to own land," Filene spoke with President Theodore Roosevelt about these observations; several influential journalists and a bank commissioner promoted the idea of cooperative credit, too. Using the European movement as a model, in 1908, America's first credit union—a nonprofit financial institution that targeted lower-income people—was opened in Manchester, New Hampshire, by Canadian immigrants, with members' savings used to fund loans to other relatively low-income people. As credit unions spread, many of the loans focused on consumer credit, not business efforts—a way for the poor to buy things like washing machines and later automobiles, as well as to cover the rising cost of basics like rent and food. Still, there was no shortage of idealism. Baradaran writes that small-scale banking efforts like credit unions were understood to favor "the common good above profits, communities over institutions, and mutual control over hierarchy," with tight-knit group dynamics associated with high repayment rates: remarkably similar to the uncollateralized group loans pitched by Yunus and Hatch.

There are more similarities, reaching even farther back and across many other movements. Baradaran writes that small-scale lending and savings efforts existed throughout the eighteenth, nineteenth, and twentieth centuries, as governments, philanthropists, and bankers—in Ireland, America, Indonesia, and elsewhere—sought to "meet the needs of the poor" by offering alternatives to high-priced loan sharks.* Several examples, such as America's Morris Banks from the early twentieth century, also didn't require collateral, relying on guarantors instead. Like Yunus, Arthur Morris, a Virginia lawyer who started the banks and "first coined the phrase 'democratization of credit,'" insisted that those who received the loans were "'not a recipient of charity.'" Rather, "The Morris Plan helps people help themselves." Credit unions were also "adamantly not charities," a stance that "fit nicely into the post–World War I ideology of self-reliance and 'welfare capitalism.'"

Eighteenth- and nineteenth-century European and American savings banks—precursors to the credit union—focused on women. With their assumed propensity for frugality and caretaking roles, they were seen as a vehicle to instill "middle-class morality" among the poor. Other marginalized groups were included in programs that could have, in Baradaran's words, "heavy paternalistic tones." In nineteenth-century Britain, to save was not only a financial act, but "a social policy, a moral and a religious good, and a way of maintaining social order" since a "'small saver' . . . 'would be less likely to depend on public assistance, turn to crime, or engage in revolution.'" America's Freedman's Savings Bank, a private bank chartered by Congress in 1865, focused its efforts on freed Black people who "struggled to adapt to the forces of capitalism." Baradaran writes that the Freedman's Savings Bank sought "to instill into the minds of the untutored Africans lessons of sobriety, wisdom, and economy, elements integral to 'the economic and industrial development of a people.'"

---

* Some of the basic tenets in Muhammad Yunus's early work may have gone back farther. Yunus writes in *Banker to the Poor* that as he was coming to grips with how to help small farmers during the 1974 Bangladesh famine, he launched Three Part Farm, a tripartite effort in which he provided the capital, landowners their land, and sharecroppers their labor—the parties would then split the profits. (It was through the experiment that he observed, "the poorer the worker, the smaller her share," a realization that prompted him to focus on the "really poor.") Although Yunus writes about this effort as though it was his own innovation, in *Debt: The First 5,000 Years*, anthropologist David Graeber describes a practice that's strikingly similar. Graeber writes that in communities influenced by Islamic tradition—Bangladesh is majority Muslim—there were partnerships "where (often) one party would supply the capital, the other carry out the enterprise. Instead of fixed return, the investor would receive a share of the profits. Even labor arrangements were often organized on a profit-sharing basis." David Graeber, *Debt: The First 5,000 Years* (Brooklyn, NY: Melville House, 2011), 276.

In his research, Ashe found himself particularly drawn to savings and lending groups still widely used across Africa, Latin America, the Caribbean, Asia, and parts of Europe,* and in many diasporic communities around the world. Operating under a variety of names, with a variety of methods, and influenced by a variety of self-help practices that go back centuries, such savings and lending groups are often clumped together under the acronym ROSCA, short for Rotating Savings and Credit Association. The basic setup is simple. Members offer fixed contributions to a shared pot, maybe the same amount every day, or every week; it doesn't matter so long as each member gives an equal share. From the combined pot, money is parsed out to group members, one at a time. To give an example, members could give $10 a week, with those contributions bundled together and distributed: $100 for this person, then $100 for that person, and so on. Sometimes, money is also lent to outsiders. Sometimes there's interest, sometimes there's not. More than just acting as a lending mechanism, ROSCAs are often seen by their members as a type of savings account. Members offer money today, to be used in a few weeks or months, whenever the rotating "pot" comes around to the person, a handy way to squirrel away cash that would otherwise get eaten up by daily costs. And because contributions are grouped together, the amounts are often far more than an individual would be able to save at any one time.

Western anthropologists, sociologists, and early development workers began documenting ROSCA-type practices in the early-to-mid-twentieth century. Some were specifically searching for local financial institutions that could spur capitalist growth and promote monetization—an antidote to rising Soviet influences. (Similar sentiments spurred the American government to promote credit unions internationally, including through the Peace Corps.) In Western academic circles, the American anthropologist Clifford Geertz helped to popularize ROSCAs in 1962 when he suggested that individual savings could counteract the inflation associated with the substantial cost of development programs, which threatened to "frustrate

---

* One method was documented in Korea in the ninth century. There was at least one ROSCA-style group in Italy in the seventeenth century. F. J. A. Bouman, "ROSCA: On the Origin of the Species / ROSCA: Sur l'origine du phénomène," *Savings and Development* 19, no. 2 (1995): 117–48, https://www.jstor.org/stable/25830410.

all efforts towards the realization of such" programs. "Unless the basic savings habits of the people of a country can be altered," he wrote, "the prospects for sustained economic growth are dim indeed." Globally, the use of ROSCAs has grown since the 1960s, as increasingly monetized societies and economies have spurred a greater need for cash.

In West Africa, ROSCA-style groups are generally referred to as susus or osusus. They may have started in what is now Nigeria, with Yoruba people using such practices as far back as 1600. Susus survived the transatlantic slave trade, with similar practices still used across the Caribbean and the United States today. In Sierra Leone, such groups were observed in the late eighteenth century. Today, they are ubiquitous across the country. Every microfinance borrower I spoke to—and, for that matter, just about every person I have spoken to in several years of living and reporting from there— has been or is part of an osusu. Members often use their share to save up for a big life event: weddings, school fees, funerals, emergencies. I have a friend who paid for his annual university fees when his "osusu pot" came around. Another covered a trip to Ghana with his church. The women I met in Kono were less ambitious but equally reliant on osusus. They would use the chunk of cash to buy provisions in bulk, like rice and palm oil. Sometimes, osusus are used to fund businesses. Other times, the money is used to pay off debt, including microcredit loans. (I met one woman who had created a dizzying but effective merry-go-round of osusu contributions and microfinance loans. She contributed to several osusus, and when it was her turn in each osusu, she used the money to pay off her loans. Then, she used money from the loans to contribute to more osusus. And so on.)

Communities around the world have also—and continue to—save, lend, and borrow through nonmonetary means. Goods, labor, and favors act as a sort of currency, with obligations exchanged and accounted for in complicated, intermingling webs of debt and reciprocity that can stretch back generations. In some cases, people prefer to store their wealth through nonmonetary means, using land, animals, houses—and even loans to others—as a way to save for the future. A large asset, or an unpaid debt, offers a way of investing in future financial security without the hassle, or temptation, associated with saving cash.

Power can also be exerted through the act of lending. Until the early twentieth century, and in many cases still today, many poorer Sierra Leoneans relied on chiefs and other well-to-do community members for basic necessities such as food during lean times, a way for "big men" to express and exert their largesse through patron-client relationships. In many communities, informal loans, given not by banks or formal institutions but through social networks, still dominate. Although moneylenders are regularly painted, by everyone from novelists to microfinance advocates, as fat leeches who suck the life out of the poor, in many cases and communities, local lenders are farmers, businessmen, shopkeepers, politicians, and fellow family members. In much of East and West Africa, moneylenders, at least as popularly understood, largely don't exist, with borrowers relying on a tapestry of relatively wealthy community members, family, religious institutions, and ROSCAs to get by.

Informal lending and borrowing remain commonplace in Sierra Leone, not only in ososus but among traders and within like-minded groups like churches and mosques. There's a common form of lending that takes place both between traders and with their customers in which people can take out goods on "trust," promising to pay for products when money eventually comes. Sometimes, a small tip, akin to interest, is expected. Often, these loans are interest free, attached instead to a different type of expectation, often unspoken but implicitly understood: of favors, reciprocal "trust," customer loyalty. (In the early days of her business, Aminata often gave a sachet of water to a thirsty neighbor even when they didn't have money on hand, hoping that they would then choose to buy from her in the future.) Trade and barter remain an essential part of the Sierra Leonean economy, too, with neighbors, traders, family, and friends offering a cup of beans, say, in exchange for a cup of rice. Sometimes, whatever is owed is only paid back weeks or months later. Even though these transactions are informal, and almost never written down, they are committed to memory and treated as very tangible loans with a specific value. One of my conversations with a microfinance borrower was interrupted by a visit from her neighbor, who was hoping to pay off two liters of palm oil she had borrowed several weeks earlier with a quarter bag of charcoal. Her lender was unimpressed with the offer, saying it didn't match what she was owed and telling the woman to come back again later with something better.

These informal but complex financial systems work as a sort of connective tissue that can solidify social and family ties. In borrowing from someone, you are binding yourself to them. "'Informal' systems are actually highly formalized," Bill Maurer, an anthropologist who studies money and exchange, told me. "People have to be highly financially literate to be able to balance multiple lending and borrowing."

Yet these practices *have* been consistently deemed secondary to "formal" ones, particularly those exported from the West. In Sierra Leone, under British rule, any trade or barter practice that did not involve cash, interest, savings, capital accumulation, or private property was seen as "inferior" by colonial administrators, who were skeptical of "informal," nonmonetized trade and debt. British capitalism was considered "the most evolved way of doing business"—even though, in the words of one historian, British capitalism is "itself a culture as much as . . . 'traditional' barter commerce is." Around the world, "money"—the way it was used, by whom, for what purpose—"was an integral part of social and religious programs for training, disciplining, and oftentimes controlling the poor in the name of modernity," writes the anthropologist Maurer. In Sierra Leone, the insistence on formal credit was part of a larger effort to Britishize Freetown, a sort of assimilation-by-debt, molding the colonized to believe that to be civilized was to be in debt.

Wittingly or not, these traditional lending methods influenced at least some elements of modern microcredit. Jeff Ashe observed that Accion staff were often members of "tandas or susus or pasanaqus"—different types of ROSCAs. Across the Indian subcontinent, such groups have been going for generations; they may have even inspired Muhammad Yunus. In the early days of Grameen, members decided which fellow group members would get a loan each week—the most desperate first, and then, if she paid off, the others—a riff on the "rotating" part of ROSCA. Grameen borrowers could also take an interest-free loan from a group fund they had contributed to, just as many ROSCA members do.

Microfinance advocates also use some of the same rationales and methods of the moneylenders they aimed to replace. The anthropologist Nicolas

Lainez explains that moneylenders in Southeast Asia are, in many communities, widely accepted—even with their high interest rates and difficult requirements—"because they filled a void left by credit institutions and informal credit sources." Yunus, in turn, argued that the Grameen Bank's interest rates, while higher than commercial banks, would be tolerated because borrowers had no other option and because they had been "shut out" from formal financial systems. In lieu of collateral, some moneylenders require a guarantor—just as Yunus did for early Grameen borrowers and many microfinance lenders still do today. Moneylenders require regular payments—in Lainez's telling, daily; for most microcredit institutions, daily or weekly.

It's not clear that Yunus, Hatch, Ashe, and others directly gleaned ideas from moneylenders, or even knowingly from traditional savings and borrowing groups. Perhaps these practices have become so firmly baked into the financial ecosystems poor people use that they just *appear* to be common sense. Or perhaps it really *is* just common sense that having someone like a guarantor is the only real option when lending to low-income people without collateral.

Regardless, the microcredit efforts of the 1970s and 1980s looked remarkably like the many variations that had come before them, even offering more or less the same loan amounts. Erin Beck, an anthropologist who studied microfinance in Guatemala, has observed "policymakers and funders may be prone to amnesia," noting that old "technologies or approaches often reappear as 'new' development in the eyes of the 'experts.'" Maybe that's why poor people around the world seemed so comfortable taking up these "innovative" microcredit programs: because they felt so familiar. Only now, instead of being looked down upon for being "informal," they were endorsed by national banks and the international development sector.

* * *

Jeff Ashe stepped away from his research genuinely surprised by the depth of historical lending practices. "It turns out," he told me, "that microcredit had been going on for years and years. I even found some reference to a

Roman administrator talking about the need to stimulate small business development."

But he was largely unimpressed by most of the newer lending programs he encountered, those run by nonprofits and small banks that were popping up around the world. "The vast majority of the programs were just pure junk," he recalls—prone to graft, expensive, disorganized, or too small to take notice of. "But out of the detritus, there were a few good ideas."

Ashe was especially taken by one. In 1980, he homed in on "grupos solidarios"—solidarity groups—overseen by a credit union in El Salvador called FEDECRÉDITO. The program was built on the same architecture that the Grameen Bank and John Hatch's FINCA would rely on—small loans given in groups, fueled by members' savings, focused on businesses. But whereas Grameen and FINCA and Accion's efforts were still relatively nascent, FEDECRÉDITO had been using these methods for decades.

The model came from Rochac Zaldaña, a prominent, politically connected Salvadoran philanthropist who, in 1935, wrote a paper titled "Rural Credit." Gleaning inspiration from lending and borrowing groups that had been instituted around the world, Zaldaña argued that to make credit more accessible, it should be given in a community setting, not a bank. Borrowers should be assessed not by bankers but by their neighbors, friends, and colleagues, who would be better able to speak to their creditworthiness. Zaldaña even argued that women should be included in such schemes, even though they couldn't yet vote. Zaldaña, himself a very wealthy man, had a strategy here. He hoped that democratizing credit could help to quell growing dissent in one of the most unequal countries in the world, a divide that was deeply rooted in large-scale, export-oriented coffee farming—by the 1930s El Salvador was known as the "Coffee Republic"—made possible by the private enclosure of land that had once been communally held. As Indigenous peasants lost access to traditional farms, they became cheap labor for wealthy coffee growers. To engender further dependence on low-wage work, some plantation owners even uprooted food-producing trees like mango and avocado, forcing laborers to rely on plantation owners' measly food provisions instead.

Zaldaña's "Rural Credit" paper was read by General Maximiliano

Hernández Martínez, then president of El Salvador. General Martínez's administration was undergoing something of a rebranding at the time, an attempt to recover from a state-led massacre known as La Matanza. A few years before, on January 22, 1932, Martínez had ordered the military, police, national guard, and the "civic guard"—essentially a militia made up of aristocrats—to quash a revolt led by Indigenous peasants and members of the Communist Party who were protesting poor working conditions and political repression. In a matter of hours, tens of thousands of Salvadorans were killed. Most of them were Indigenous people.

Now yearning for a legacy beyond the brutal repression he had become known for, General Martínez tried instituting social reforms. Taking inspiration from Zaldaña's "Rural Credit," Martinez asked Zaldaña to help set up credit unions across the country. He hoped that loans offered to poor, rural farmers might act as something of a salve to soothe the deep wounds inflicted by the massacre and smooth tensions born out of the country's deep-seated inequality. Even though the uprising had been quelled, that didn't mean there wouldn't be another one, which could threaten the country's government and economy. Even El Salvador's wealthiest families were aware of how tenuous the situation was, not only for peasants but for their own stability, too. Reforms could help to nip unrest in the bud.

In 1943, at the tail end of General Martínez's decade-plus reign, FEDE-CRÉDITO was founded with the objective of "protecting and improving the work of small producers and merchants," to "strengthen the people's relations with the home, land and national wealth, through cooperative organization." In the early 1950s, the credit union launched a "solidarity group" with twelve market vendors. The experiment was immediately considered a success. Borrowers used the money to buy daily goods that were otherwise out of reach; they also paid off their loans. Emboldened, FEDECRÉDITO offered similar programs across the country.

When Jeff Ashe came across the solidarity groups in 1980, he knew nothing of this messy history, stumbling upon them as if they were brand-new. Missing the complex social, political, and economic context, Ashe found himself "blown away about how brilliant this concept was. Each solidarity group . . . made the decisions, not the bankers." Ashe was also impressed by the "mutual assistance" he observed in the groups: members helping one another out, approving each other's loans, holding each other accountable. "It was the most revolutionary concept that I had seen through the whole study. It was a total breakthrough—simple, replicable, low cost, highly effective with great repayment rates," he remembers. Although he had initially been drawn to international development work because of his conversations with "revolutionary farmers" and the specificity the field allowed—working with one community or one person at a time, supporting them to articulate and address their needs—he now felt solidarity groups could work for many people, maybe millions. "For me it was the first time you could effectively reach down to truly microenterprises at scale"—to reach many people, with one program, without a lot of money.

Finally, Ashe had an answer for USAID. He realized, "This could be cookie cuttered all over the world."

Easy Money

Freetown, Sierra Leone

Early 2021

ONE MORNING AT THE HEIGHT OF SIERRA LEONE'S DRY SEASON, THE SKY hazy with Harmattan sands, Aminata turned her Two Taps parlor into a yogurt factory. She brought pot after pot of water to boil over a propane tank the size of her torso, then stirred in milk powder, water, stabilizer, vanilla, and banana flavoring, pouring the hot liquid through a sieve held high above a round plastic bowl so big it took over half the parlor floor. Aminata took great pleasure in watching the mixture fall through the mesh of the sieve, shimmying stubborn chunks of milk into submission.

To make the yogurt, she had spent $95 for a big bag of powdered milk as high as her waist, $25 for condensed milk, $15 for sweet milk, $25 for flavoring, and $20 for sugar, plus whatever else for all the little bits and pieces she needed to make her business look professional: napkins, food dye. She also bought $18 worth of soap, which she could sell to her neighbors, an extra little side hustle. In total, she estimated she spent around $200.

Aminata had paid for most of the provisions with money from a loan given to her by the Sierra Leonean arm of ASA Microfinance, one of the world's largest and oldest microfinance companies. Started in 1978 in Bangladesh, ASA had a growing presence in Sierra Leone, boasting nearly fifty thousand clients across fifty-four offices. Two were within walking distance from Aminata's house: one up the hill, another down near the ocean.

Aminata had heard about ASA from her neighbor Kadija, a woman about a decade older than Aminata who was married to Abdul, Aminata and Idrissa's landlord. As the son of the woman who founded Two Taps, Abdul had grown up with relative wealth, but Kadija had been dirt poor before she met him, several years before, when she was living in a friend's shack at the edge of Two Taps. She already had three kids by then and got by hairdressing. Abdul had kids of his own, too. He told her he was drawn to how independent she was, doing all that child-rearing and business management on her own, although she imagined her beauty helped. Even now, as she neared forty, her cheeks retained a deep, subtle plum-purple, alight on burnt-caramel skin. She knew she was one of the most beautiful women in Two Taps.

Soon after they met, Kadija became pregnant and moved in with Abdul. She found herself in one of the nicest homes in the neighborhood. About four times the size of Aminata's, it had an open-air parlor and a private concrete courtyard with a covered awning. It even had a private bathroom, which meant that Kadija didn't have to shower in the communal one Aminata shared with dozens of other residents.

But Kadija soon learned that although Abdul appeared rich, he was stingy. Even though he had a full-time job working as a driver for a local women's rights organization, he only gave Kadija money for the one biological child they shared, Ada. He refused to support any of her other kids, including her daughter Rose, even though she was just a young teenager and lived with them, too. All of Rose's school fees, her clothing, everything was on Kadija.

The girl's education would have been expensive enough if she had gone to a public school. Although government schools are nominally free in Sierra Leone, teachers regularly demand unofficial fees to make up for their paltry salaries. Combine these extra costs with supplies, transportation, school uniforms—a requirement in Sierra Leone—and food, and "free" education can add up to hundreds of dollars a year, a significant weight on families where the GDP per capita is $480,* one of the lowest in the world. Even when families can scrounge up the money, public education is often lacking, with a limited number of trained teachers, few basic supplies like books and chalk, and a curriculum focused on rote learning.

* As of 2021, the most recent year available. "GDP Per Capita (Current US$)—Sierra Leone," The World Bank, https://data.worldbank.org/indicator/NY.GDP.PCAP.CD?locations=SL.

UNICEF, the UN's children's agency, estimates that only one quarter of Sierra Leonean students complete high school.

In large part because it's so bad, education has become something of a national obsession. With an adult literacy rate of 48 percent, and given that the country's few well-paying jobs are limited to those who have passed the final high school exam, there's a dual appreciation for just how paltry education opportunities are and just how important they can be. Encouraged by government and international campaigns that champion education as the key to success,* many caretakers see it as their main duty, and a deep source of pride and fulfillment, to be able to put kids through school. At the same time, precisely because the government and big international organizations tout education as essential to both personal and national development, families can experience significant guilt, shame, and social stigma if their kids don't go to school or don't go far. Families will prioritize education even if it means significant sacrifices, even if the education is so poor that it may not be worth going.

Kadija was determined to give her daughter the best life she could, far better than the one she had. Both of Kadija's parents had been killed during the war and Kadija had been fending for herself ever since. She had made it through primary school but could only write one word: "Kadija." Her last name, "Turay," still eluded her. It felt essential that Rose have the opportunities she did not. Kadija was deeply skeptical of government schools, where, she said, "I'll pay all this money and [Rose] would learn nothing." So she enrolled her daughter in private school instead. Investing in the girl was something of an insurance policy, a way to make sure Kadija would be taken care of when she got older. She imagined a not-too-distant future when Rose worked in an office job, maybe even overseas, sending money to her mother, who could spend her days watching the Nigerian soap operas she loved. "You know, my own life has been destroyed, but with her, if she's lucky, I'm also lucky," Kadija explained.

She had seen firsthand how such luck could manifest, if only a mother

---

* In November 2022, President Julius Maada Bio told the *Guardian*, "We are throwing all our resources, all our energy into education. We cannot develop without improving education. I see it as an existential issue." Tom Collins, "Sierra Leone's President Defends Large Education Budget as 'Necessary Risk,'" *Guardian*, November 23, 2022, https://www.theguardian.com/global-development/2022/nov/23/sierra-leones-president-defends-large-education-budget-as-necessary-risk.

pushed her children hard enough. One of Kadija's closest friends had found a way to pay for her own daughter's private education by taking out a series of microfinance loans, borrowing in the hundreds of dollars, often from multiple places at once. When the woman's daughter graduated from high school, the girl's English and math skills were strong enough to land her a job inside a lush, air-conditioned supermarket down on the busy main road. The shop was one of the nicest in the city. It had parking assistants and sold imported gin and whiskey alongside bright plastic-wrapped snacks from India, Lebanon, and the UK.

The girl's new position at the supermarket was an accomplishment her mother had dreamed of but barely dared to voice. It really was something of a miracle: she was now one of the only women in Two Taps with a full-time, salaried job. To thank her mother, the girl used some of her salary to buy her an official electricity connection and a refrigerator. "That is why I pushed her so hard in school," the girl's mother explained to Kadija. "I knew that if God blessed her, I would also benefit."

To help pay for Rose's private school fees, Kadija had begun selling cheap gin, kush—a synthetic cannabinoid—and tramadol—an opiate—from the covered porch outside Abdul's house while he was away at work. At any given time, about half a dozen Two Taps residents, mostly men, smoked and drank on a cement bench that was affixed to a cool yellow wall in the courtyard. Kadija was an adept manager, intermittently flirting with her customers and offering advice on how to make their lives better, then sympathy when things stayed the same. She had one of those smiles, bright and warm, that made a person feel like it was only for them, and she knew how to use it. Her business flourished. On a very good day, she could net about $10, more than many Sierra Leoneans made in a week, some even in a month.

Despite her success, Kadija, an intensely religious woman, had never named her "bar," lest it seem too permanent. "This isn't a real business," she insisted. "I just do it because I need money." She never referred to her goods by name, offering a handwave or a "this stuff" or "my business" or "whatchamacallit" instead. To curb any holy wrath, she restricted her sales to one tab of tramadol per person per day—a serious concession, given that this was by far the most popular and profitable item she sold. "And I only give it to those who look strong," she added. When customers stumbled away from the back of her house, she wished that each one be "blessed" or "safe," calling out, "You take care of yourself, okay?"

Although Kadija had spotted arguably one of the best business opportunities in Two Taps—at least considering economics, morals aside—she found she needed even more cash to cover Rose's private school fees. It seemed no amount of tramadol would pay for three $100 terms each year. Kadija didn't remember things being so expensive before. "Even though our own party is in power"—Kadija had long supported the Sierra Leone People's Party, currently in office—"we don't like this president. He has soaked his hand with blood. People are dying, people are suffering, people are so hungry."

By observing the friend whose daughter now worked at the fancy supermarket, Kadija had become convinced in the power of microfinance. She was determined to start a borrowing group herself. She had decided on the lender ASA simply because it had an office nearby. "We can get money there, easily," Kadija told Aminata. "I've seen so many women take it."

Aminata was desperate for money but deeply hesitant. She had first learned about microfinance when she was a young girl, growing up in Pendembu. One day, soon after the war, people from overseas came to her village. They were offering money. The foreigners explained "that this was a loan, for businesspeople," remembers Aminata. "It wasn't free money, a person would have to pay it back." Since her mom sold cloth, rice, and palm oil to help the family get by, the people said she could take it. Her mother did, not knowing that this would make her ineligible for other support programs—to help the country rebuild, there were several cash grants being offered across Sierra Leone at the time. But the foreigners told Aminata's mom that since she could stand on her own two feet now, what with her loan and her business, "she couldn't have any free money anymore, because now she had microcredit." Aminata's mother, intensely religious after having somehow made it through the war, said, "No problem. I'll make do with what I have. Whatever is meant to be, God will make it possible."

In the twenty years since, Aminata's mother had borrowed from each of the country's major microfinance institutions, several times over. She relied on the loans when she needed large amounts of cash that she didn't otherwise have: to hire laborers to ready the land for rice planting, to purchase goods in bulk so that she could get significant discounts from wealthier market women. After a big purchase, Aminata's mom would stuff piles of flip-flops and long rolls of fabric into the corners of her house. Each stash was a wish, a vision for the future. She planned to sell the goods when things got particularly tight, or when she needed another chunk of cash before the loan cycle was up.

But Pendembu was poor, and small. Sales never flew. Nearly everything Aminata's mother made went to paying off the debt. By the time she did, she would be so broke that she'd need to take out another loan, then another. She began to see microcredit as a sort of second income, a way to make up for consistent shortfalls in the first. Aminata watched her mother achieve a sort of precarious balance, as if she were hopping from stone to wobbly stone in a long river. She briefly felt the airiness of wealth with every new loan, then experienced scarcity so severe she would give up meals to make her payments. The woman got wet but never drowned. But she never really swam either.

Aminata explained to Kadija that she wasn't sure she wanted to be like her mother, reliant on and hamstrung by microdebt. Kadija understood Aminata's reluctance—she heard the loan was expensive, with up-front fees and high weekly payments. "If it wasn't for my daughter's education, I wouldn't take it," Kadija explained. "The things we do for our children"—Kadija clicked her tongue against the roof of her mouth—"you have to sacrifice for them." Aminata thought about the refrigerator Idrissa had bought her, her dreams of a yogurt business—and about Kadija being married to her landlord. It may have been coincidence that all the women in Kadija's microfinance group either rented from her husband or his brother. Perhaps just circumstance, given that the men owned most of Two Taps. But the leverage might have helped. It was something of an honor to be asked by Kadija to participate. It showed she considered the other, poorer women to be in her orbit, even if in subordinate positions. Maybe she would put in a good word to Abdul for them. Maybe it wouldn't be such a big deal if the rent was a week or two late. Kadija also applied more direct pressure. "She said unless I join [the group], they're not going to give them any money," Aminata recalled. "So I agreed."

When Aminata accompanied Kadija to the ASA office, she was struck by a mix of disdain for and envy of the women who worked there, with their tight pencil skirts, their button-down shirts, their technicolored business suits and sturdy heels. She told them about the yogurt business she had been trying to start, about the fridge her husband had bought for her. One of the pencil skirts wrote down her answers wordlessly, didn't ask her any more questions, then went on to Kadija. She would expand a drinks business, Kadija said, offering no details about what kind of "drinks" she sold. It didn't seem to matter; the woman didn't probe. When one of the pencil-skirted loan officers came to do a spot check of Aminata's house—"they wanted to see if I was lying about anything and see what I had"—Aminata noticed that the tips of her stilettos were wet with the sewage that ran through one of the adjacent pedestrian streets. Aminata felt pleased: a little moment of justice.

CHAPTER 4

Cookie Cutter

In the early 1980s, Accion's Jeff Ashe walked into a conference room just outside Washington, DC, armed with a sales pitch. USAID had asked the Accion research team Ashe was leading to give a presentation on what they had found about lending to small businesses in the informal sector. More excited than nervous, Ashe was convinced that the FEDE-CRÉDITO solidarity groups he had seen in El Salvador should act as a blueprint for programs worldwide. If USAID wanted to help poor people, this, he determined, was the way to do it.

Ashe had tested out the pitch a year before. After returning from El Salvador, he tried to convince Accion to launch a version of the solidarity groups. It didn't go well. "There was total skepticism," recalls Ashe. "They said, 'This is the stupidest idea I've ever heard of, this is completely ridiculous.'" The idea of lending in groups unnerved Accion—ever since Pedro Paes Leme convinced his Brazilian banker friend to lend to his former employees, the organization had promoted one-on-one lending, often to larger, more established businesses. Accion didn't think group members would actually hold one another accountable for paying off their loans.

This time, Ashe came to the USAID boardroom armed with case studies about a variety of small lending projects around the world. One claimed that lending programs "had significant economic and social impact on the participants," sometimes doubling the income of borrowers. Another said that borrowers had become empowered to "chang[e] their lives," that they had become "noticeably more self-confident." Across all the projects studied, a majority of the borrowers were women. Repayment rates were as high as 90 percent.

Then, Ashe gave his pitch. He talked about how "blown away" he'd been by the FEDECRÉDITO model. He was surprised to find that USAID was open to the idea. Small loans, in groups, seemed like a low-cost way to reach more people, without requiring a lot of staff time. The agency agreed to fund two new projects to further test the concept.

Ashe recalls only one dissenter. "Some guy said, 'Well, you're the flavor of the week, but I wouldn't expect us to remember this for another few months. It's a flash in the pan, just like everything else.'"

Two major changes in international development would prove that man very wrong.

* * *

In the early 1970s, Dale Adams, a young American economist, got a break that would change his career and alter the course of the international development sector.

In line with Truman's vision that poorer countries follow the trajectory of richer ones, in the mid-twentieth century, development agencies encouraged countries to adopt Western agricultural tools and techniques. Technologically heavy farming and harvesting methods, including the use of fertilizer, pesticides, and "new attitudes" were promised to invigorate large-scale farming and feed the world. There was so much excitement about the approach that in 1968 a USAID administrator predicted that the era would be remembered for being "as significant and as beneficial to mankind as the industrial revolution of a century and a half ago"—a kind of "Green Revolution."

Just as credit had been at the heart of national development efforts since the Truman era, loans also formed the bedrock of many agricultural programs. If farmers had cash, the logic went, they would be able to pay for these new technologies, boost output, and then pay the loans back. Such international programs were near replicas of those offered to American farmers during the Depression; in fact, many were created and managed by those who had overseen American agricultural finance just a few decades before. Since they were designed primarily to keep farmers afloat during precarious circumstances, the Depression-era American credit programs had been heavily subsidized, offering loans far below commercial rates. So, when the blueprint was plucked from the wheat fields of Kansas and plopped onto the coffee plantations of El Salvador, the subsidies remained. Credit was suddenly cheap, and it was plentiful.

Subsidized credit programs popped up around the world, with interest rates so low they were sometimes even below inflation. By the 1960s, agricultural credit schemes dominated much of USAID's work, accounting for half of the agency's spending in Latin America. Subsidized credit was also supported by the World Bank and several European government donors, some of whom helped to set up local agricultural development banks, which would offer small credit. Billions of dollars were pumped through.

In the 1960s, USAID funded Ohio State University to research how agricultural credit schemes really worked, not just in theory but on the ground. In 1966, Dale Adams was hired, partnering with other researchers from Ohio State and staffers from the World Bank to help USAID write a series of papers that would become known as the "Spring Review of Small Farmer Credit." Despite the innocuous title, the studies, which interrogated agricultural policies in about sixty countries, had significant ramifications for international aid. Most important, the studies' conclusions directly paved the way for Western support of small, high-priced loans focused on poor entrepreneurs.

The "Spring Review" had a few key findings, all of which eviscerated the rationale for low-cost credit underpinning agricultural lending programs. Adams and his colleagues argued that because the subsidized credit was so cheap, farmers had an incentive to keep borrowing, even if they didn't really need a loan. Too many loans to people who didn't need them created massive defaults: in some cases, less than half of the loans were repaid. But, seeing that the money kept coming from donors overseas anyway, intent as they were on fueling the promised Green Revolution, the local banks that oversaw implementation of the loans had little incentive to chase after debtors or limit the reach of the lending programs.

Overborrowing and nonrepayment, often two sides of the same coin, underlay a second major finding: the credit schemes were completely unsustainable without outside support. The programs had such poor recovery rates, and had generated almost no independent revenue, that without cheap money from donors they would almost immediately fizzle.

Third, and perhaps most concerning to Dale Adams, the loans weren't going where they were intended: to poor farmers.

Earlier, colonial-era credit schemes had, by design, concentrated land in the hands of a few. Cheap government credit offered to coffee plantation owners in El Salvador is one example, but there are many others. In Kenya, loans offered by the British colonial government reshaped an area that became known as the White Highlands, so named because white farmers were the only ones allowed to settle the land and receive loans from the colonial administration. Here, as in many cases, land that had been collectively utilized by the indigenous people was cordoned off into private estates to grow coffee and tea.

Given the history of unequal credit and its links to land privatization and dispossession, some in international development hoped the revamped mid-twentieth-century agricultural loan schemes could finally help smallholder farmers buy and develop land their families may have worked for generations but didn't formally own. Perhaps this could be something of a quiet political revolution, a way to ease the pain engendered through decades of institutionalized inequality. At the same time, the loans would encourage more productive use of land, at least in the eyes of Western consultants and planners, by turning subsistence plots into commercial ones.

But Dale Adams and his colleagues discovered that there *was* no quiet agricultural revolution. Instead of going to small farmers, some of the loans went to politically connected landed elites, who it turns out, sometimes used the money to buy up smaller farms. The subsidized agricultural credit hadn't undermined concentration of land. It had furthered it.

Adams was appalled that even though the loans were subsidized, they were largely going to what he called the "non-poor." The actual poor—which is to say, most farmers—still relied on high-priced loans or no loans at all. They still sold their crops at fixed prices to wealthier middlemen, who now had an even greater leg up. Overall, Adams says, "there was little evidence that credit programs were boosting agricultural production *or* significantly easing poverty." Decades of programs and billions of dollars seemed to have failed.

* * *

The "Spring Review" findings, at first revelatory, soon seemed like common sense. Bolstered by an academic, USAID-approved study, staffers at development agencies who funded cheap agricultural credit programs now felt emboldened to complain that they had long known such programs were expensive, administratively burdensome, and had a limited reach. Some at USAID confessed that they had seen almost no impact in their years of work.

Academics and practitioners outside of international development had critiques, too. Some in the growing international feminist movement complained that the agricultural credit schemes excluded women, since in many countries, laws, often enacted under colonialism, explicitly barred women from formally owning land. Even when there was an effort to give smallholder farmers land titles that they had been previously denied, women were again left out. One representative to the UN Commission on the Status of Women observed that "African women are responsible for 60–80 percent of the agriculture work," yet "agricultural extension services, loans and marketing assistance do not reach [them]."

What feminists *did* espouse was the newfound focus on the previously unseen informal sector. Because Truman-esque development had focused on strengthening the formal economy, such programs had naturally gravitated toward those who were employed or employable: namely, men. This focus on increasing formal employment, some argued, actually *increased* women's domestic duties—with one party gone to work in factories or building roads, there was simply more work to be done at home. A narrowing in on formal work also undermined and undervalued traditional and essential "women's work"—things like child-rearing and food-making—by placing a higher relative value on out-of-the-house wage work. (Some feminists argued that to rectify this, "women's work" should be waged, too.) Others pointed out that many women *were* in fact engaging in paid, if not officially salaried, work, by selling food and goods they made at home or in a local market. When economists and policymakers only considered the formal economy, all of this was missed. But in the more expansive informal economy, such women could be recast as enterprising businesswomen, essential to a community's wellbeing.

These characterizations of women as innate mothers, caregivers, homemakers, and entrepreneurs risked essentializing. But these framings did encourage policymakers to see women, sometimes for the first time, as formidable political and economic actors worthy of specific attention and resources. In 1973, the U.S. Foreign Assistance Act was amended to "give particular attention to those programs, projects and activities which . . . integrate women." A year after that, the administrator of USAID proclaimed that women were "a vital human resource in the improvement of the quality of life in the developing world," contributing "directly to national social and economic progress." By the late 1970s, tens of millions of dollars had been earmarked for programs that supported "women as equal partners in the development process in the developing countries"— particularly programs that increased their economic production.

Politicians were rewarded for plugging women's programs not only thanks to the rise in feminism, but also because support for women had become broadly synonymous with support for population control, namely through family planning. In the late 1950s and early 1960s, growing concerns about overuse of natural resources and environmental degradation became wrapped up in an underlying anxiety about the rising numbers of humans on Earth. If the population kept expanding, economists and environmentalists warned, there would be a point in the very near future when the world wouldn't be able to sustain life. If population remained low and consumption limited, however, families could save, economic prosperity would be achievable, and the environment could be salvaged. "Empowering women" not only suggested empowering them to be economic actors, but to take control of their reproductive lives. In both cases, they would be in the service of their nation's—and the world's—development. The link between a country's stability and how many babies a woman had was understood to be so fundamental that a 1958 report penned under President Dwight D. Eisenhower's administration called for economic aid to be explicitly tied to "population control." A decade later, President

Lyndon B. Johnson favored family planning programs over other types of aid. The future of humanity, it seemed, rested on women, whose behavior the development sector was eager to mold.

* * *

In 1975, after decades of campaigning by feminists for greater recognition of women's rights, Mexico City hosted the first-ever United Nations conference on women, to commemorate International Women's Year. Michaela Walsh, an ambitious young woman from Kansas City with a background in banking, flew in from New York. She attended as a new employee of the Rockefeller Brothers Fund, a philanthropy set up by members of the wealthy Rockefeller family. At least externally, Walsh did not present as a firebrand feminist: she was more interested in hobnobbing on Wall Street than marching for equal rights. But she *was* interested in breaking glass ceilings.

A few years earlier, when she was twenty-six, Walsh had moved to Beirut, Lebanon, to be one of the first employees of Merrill Lynch International at "the beginning of global finance," when banks were first opening interconnected branches around the world. Merrill Lynch initially refused to transfer Walsh to Lebanon—too dangerous, they argued, for a young woman on her own. So she paid her own way, showed up at the office, and talked herself into a job.

Walsh describes her five years in Beirut as a sleepless blur, spent dancing all night and working all day. Her time abroad instilled in her a love of international travel, and discussions with Lebanese colleagues and friends helped her to reconsider "that the American way was the only way."

When she moved back to New York, Walsh worked in venture capital when the field was still in its infancy, volunteering in school antidrug programs in her spare time. It was her unique background in finance and social projects that led her to the Rockefeller Brothers Fund. They sent her to Mexico City to see what she could learn about women and the economy as this focus was gaining steam in international development circles.

At the conference, Walsh was presented with a dizzying array of statistics. She learned that "women performed 65 percent of the world's work, yet they earned only 10 percent of the income and owned less than 1 percent of the world's property." She met women from around the world who were just as ambitious as she was and just as incensed about gender inequality. Walsh was particularly taken with Dr. Esther Ocloo, a Ghanaian entrepreneur who had come to the conference on behalf of the Ghanaian first lady. She had a message from the country's market women. "They said their needs were simple," Walsh would later recall. "Once they had credit, they could use that to generate the funds they required to satisfy all other needs." Walsh also met Ela Bhatt, a leader of India's Self-Employed Women's Association, which Jeff Ashe had learned about in his research on small lending programs around the world. The organization had been originally envisioned as a union for self-employed women who were unprotected by state law. Some had lost their jobs in Gujarat's textile industry when automation and foreign competition forced factories to close, pushing thousands of people out of work. But SEWA had recently begun giving out loans, too. Its leader, Ela Bhatt, took inspiration from Mahatma Gandhi's philosophy of self-reliance. If the women couldn't rely on employers, they would have to go it alone by setting up their own enterprises to support themselves and their families.

When Walsh met Ocloo and Bhatt, everything suddenly congealed: her background in finance, her interest in women's empowerment, her belief in a woman's ability to be independent. She recalls an intoxicating, tangible sense of a global feminist awakening. "For me," Walsh would later write, "the Mexico City experience was a whirlwind of energy and color. Colors of skins, colors of garments, colors of speech. . . . Our meetings had the color of emotion, of passion, of disagreement. We listened, we worked, we ate, and we danced and sang; we were driven by hopes for our children and our world. . . . When I saw conference delegates clad in magnificently colored African dresses and Asian saris instead of black suits, it was clear to me that the world was changing."

Soon after the conference, Walsh, Ocloo, Bhatt, and about a dozen other women launched a "committee to organize Women's World Banking," conceived of as something of a World Bank just for women. Walsh says this idea was entirely independent of Accion and John Hatch and Muhammad Yunus, which is conceivable: FINCA and Grameen didn't officially launch until the early 1980s, nearly a decade later, and at the time of the Mexico City conference Accion's lending project was so small as to be virtually unknown. Once formed, Women's World Banking soon reached out to banks and philanthropists across Europe and North America, with charismatic and enthusiastic Walsh, Bhatt, and Ocloo helping to popularize the idea of women as trustworthy and loan-worthy—an idea that is more often credited to Muhammad Yunus, even though, according to Jeff Ashe,* Grameen only made the full switch to lending to women in the mid-1980s, a claim also asserted by Bangladeshi academic Lamia Karim. (An early video from Grameen's nascent microfinance efforts shows men chanting the Grameen motto alongside women, suggesting men may have been borrowing then, too.) Women's World Banking argued that lending to women was not only in the service of women's empowerment but also secured their children's future, their community's future. "It is the women who are the leaders in change," Bhatt would later observe. "Without their participation, poverty can never be removed."

This reframing offered a unique opportunity for donors. Through a single loan, they could claim to be addressing women's empowerment, overpopulation, the informal sector, bottom-up democracy, culturally appropriate programs, and "community development," all in one fell swoop. Programs that focused on women would soon prove to be remarkably good fundraisers, as photos and stories of poor women working fields, meeting in groups, having discussions over water wells, counting money, and caring for their families conjured ideals that Western funders were eager to tap into: of women-led, bottom-up development that supported prosperous, stable, and industrious societies. (To capitalize on this frenzy, some enterprising small-scale, mixed-gender community groups even began rebranding themselves as "women's groups," even though their meetings were led by men.)

Women's World Banking and efforts like it ensured that loans would remain central to the evolving field of international development, as they had for decades—this time, though, by targeting individual female entrepreneurs, not large-scale efforts run by men. But there would be one sig-

---

* Accion had started its lending efforts by focusing on men, too.

nificant change from the agricultural loans that had dominated just a few years before: interest rates would be much, much higher. That was in part thanks to Dale Adams and his fellow "Spring Review" authors, who advocated for hiking up interest rates to at least market rates or above. This would, they argued, rectify some of the problems they had identified in the corrupt, inept programs that primarily served the elite. With higher interest rates, long-term, locally controlled, self-sustaining programs could be created, with loans only going to those who really needed them; if someone was desperate for credit, they would find a way to cover the extra cost. Decades after the "Spring Review" was published, Adams described the study as having "put a stake in the heart of subsidized credit."

Women would now get loans. They would just have to pay a lot for them.

* * *

This idea of a self-sustaining program that the poor would pay for themselves fit perfectly with the blossoming neoliberal, market-led, individual-first era, which reached fever pitch with the election of Margaret Thatcher in 1979 and Ronald Reagan in 1981. Both argued that welfare programs encouraged laziness and graft, a fear encapsulated in Reagan's spectacularly dramatic story of a "welfare queen," a Black woman who allegedly defrauded the federal government of hundreds of thousands of dollars. Reagan claimed that it was "now common knowledge that America's welfare system has itself become a poverty trap" because it was "a creator and reinforcer of dependency." Instead of being reliant on the government to meet their basic needs, Thatcher and Reagan felt that individuals should be responsible for meeting those needs themselves.

In the United States, the United Kingdom, and around the world, efforts once based on charity or state support were exchanged for those reliant on market forces. "Government," Reagan argued, "does nothing as well or as economically as the private sector of the economy." Government funding for basics like health care, education, and food was cut, government agencies culled, and services privatized.

Such neoliberal ideology and policy extended into the development sector. Although USAID had always supported the private sector, under Reagan it revved up this focus. The year he was elected, the agency, in its own words, "overlaid a predominant 'private sector' rationale" on the projects it supported. Across all its programs, USAID now ensured that "market-based principles" were used to "restructure developing countries' policies and institutions." Individuals were expected to thrive in this newly unleashed market. International development became dominated by what anthropologist Erin Beck calls "bootstrap development," characterized by a belief that "the poor could lift themselves out of poverty." They would do so through their own "enterprise," a word that became ubiquitous across aid agencies and "seemed to," in the words of anthropologist Parker Shipton, "encapsulate everything good, everything hopeful, about energy, imagination, and free market activity." "Enterprise" conjured deep-seated American ideals: "the Emersonian self-reliance beloved of Yankee individualists, the bootstrap populism favored by Reagan Republicans, and that favorite North American ideal that transcends region, party, or period: growth and success from humble origins." Perhaps most important, Shipton noted, "it seemed to avoid everything that had come to look bad about governments."

In the mind of Accion's Jeff Ashe, inspired by grassrootism and liberation theology and deeply skeptical of top-down government programs, the focus on the individual represented an important shift in international development. His belief in this approach was not so much grounded in neoliberal ideology. Rather, Ashe was committed to rejecting paternalism. He believed that only an individual, based on their own experience, background, and knowledge, could know what was best for them, not economic planners or "experts" thousands of miles away.

But this well-intentioned focus also obscured the more complicated structural reasons for poverty that lay far beyond an individual's life or purview: decades of land privatization, economic extraction, ineffective if not downright harmful policies, and low wages. The focus on individual responsibility at the expense of greater historical understanding meshed well with broader shifts in Western political thinking. "It's much better to tell the story of the self-made man or woman who bootstrapped her way out of poverty than 'we need to create a social system for everyone,'" Philip Mader, who researches debt and development at the UK's Institute of Development Studies and has written extensively on microfinance, told me.

Loans fit the times perfectly: a way to stimulate economic production without a large government hand, perhaps even a way to replace expensive government efforts, all while embodying American-style capitalism that focused on individual efforts. Rather than encouraging lending through large government banks, as had been done with agricultural loans a few decades before, credit was primarily given through private actors such as banks or NGOs. (Dale Adams and his "Spring Review" team also played a role here, arguing that government banks had proven, at least at times, capable of siphoning off funds and rewarding political allies.)

In pushing for microcredit just as neoliberal ideologies were taking hold, Yunus and others would come to parrot some of the key claims that Reagan made. Of the emphasis on the private sector, Yunus wrote in *Banker to the Poor* that Grameen advocates for "the least government feasible," with the government not "getting involved in running businesses or in providing services." He believed "the public sector has failed. Or at least it is on the way out despite our best efforts. Bureaucratization cushioned by subsidies, economic and political protection, and lack of transparency is killing it off. It has become a playground of corruption. What started out with good intentions became a road to disaster." Like Reagan, he didn't believe that unemployment benefits were "the best way to address poverty," since charity "robs [poor people] of [their] incentive, and more important, of self-respect." In the 1990s, Yunus told PBS, "Giving money to people doesn't solve anything, because it doesn't make the person responsible for that money." One microcredit training manual, from the 1980s, told its readers that "poor people . . . will only climb out of poverty when they realize that they can change their situation." In 2018, Yunus told the publication QZ, "The welfare system never produced any entrepreneurs. Systems should be geared toward us creating activity, creating entrepreneurship rather than dependence. Taking risk. That's what human beings are for."

* * *

By the time Jeff Ashe made his pitch to USAID in that Washington, DC, boardroom in 1981, the critique of subsidized agricultural credit alongside the rise of entrepreneurial feminism and market-first policies had significantly increased the appetite for the agency to focus on small loans. In our conversations, Dale Adams reflected that if it hadn't been for the "new paradigm" built off his study—high interest loans through private institutions—small-scale lending would have been, as the USAID staffer had warned Jeff Ashe, "a flash in the pan." Instead, the changes allowed for "realistic interest rates." Subsidies were traded in for "sustainability." Those who had once been "beneficiaries" were now "clients," whose enterprise would keep them afloat.

After USAID gave him the go-ahead to test out the FEDECRÉDITO solidarity group concept, with borrowers taking out loans together, Accion launched two projects, one in the Dominican Republic and one in Costa Rica. Borrowers were mostly tricicleros (tricycle cart vendors), seamstresses, or other small businesspeople, who leaned more middle class than poor. Most were given loans for one year, a couple hundred dollars each. Fitting with the goal of creating sustainable programs that covered their own costs, the loans came with 24 percent annual interest, just above Yunus's 20 percent rate.

The results, which came a few years later, were overwhelmingly positive. Ashe and his team claimed incomes increased by as much as 40 percent; they also claimed that this approach improved cohesiveness among group members and borrowers' self-esteem. For the most part, borrowers paid off their loans. That, coupled with the higher interest rates, meant that repayments could cover operating costs—a shocking conclusion in the wake of agricultural credit programs that, it was now understood, had never been able to pay for themselves.

By now, USAID staffers had largely come to expect underwhelming findings—there was a running complaint that in the international development field "nothing ever happens," with ready-made projects deployed with now predictably unimpressive results. They were stunned by what Ashe claimed. Elisabeth Rhyne, who oversaw the agency's microenterprise development in the 1990s, remembers thinking, "I don't believe this guy. I don't think it's true." While small business loans themselves weren't innovative, the method and the scale Ashe proposed was "so different. It was a huge leap away from what everybody had been doing." If Ashe's findings were correct, in this new lending model, donors like USAID would only be responsible for start-up costs. Once a project was up and running, lenders could use their profits to continue operating. USAID hoped this could achieve several aims: Create programs that were financially self-sufficient, as Reagan had asked. Support both women and small businesses in cities, as Congress had mandated. And, if those businesses grew, address poverty, given that more robust businesses could help families to meet their basic needs. Thomas Dichter, who worked in microfinance for decades, has reflected that the idea "almost has an irresistible magic to it. A low-cost, if not no-cost investment, and boom! Poverty is solved."

Ashe, already a believer, now became a full-blown evangelist. "Jeff became Mr. Microfinance," recalls John Hammock, his boss at Accion. "He was out there as an evangelizer pretty quickly." Despite Accion's initial skepticism of the solidarity group model, Hammock had been convinced, too. "It was taking off everywhere, we were raising money for it, people were paying off their loans, we could make the claim that we were generating jobs, we were proving that poor people could make money," says Hammock. By the mid-1980s, "it was clear that this microcredit thing was the one to bet on."

Kochende

Old Post, Koidu, Kono, Eastern Sierra Leone

Early 2019

AFTER RAMATU LISTENED TO HER NEIGHBOR ABBIE LAY OUT HER PLAN for getting money from the Nigerian microlender LAPO, she sat back in her chair in her cool, airy parlor and shrugged. Ramatu wasn't against the idea of opening a business. The farmer man had always said she should become a caterer, or maybe open a restaurant. He claimed she cooked the most delicious bean stew in town, a statement Ramatu couldn't argue with. When she cooked a full meal, which was rarely—the ingredients were getting too expensive—she took great comfort in settling in front of the coal pot in her parlor, watching the onions slowly sizzle before pouring water and palm oil in. Although generally easily distracted—by her neighbors, her daughter, WhatsApp, whoever stopped by—these were Ramatu's most focused, calm moments. She would shut the front door and quietly wait for the stew to tell her it was ready.

Still, Ramatu had never been particularly interested in *becoming a businesswoman*. She wanted to *do business*—a subtle distinction. She told Abbie, "I want to make money. To solve two or three problems in my life." For example, she wanted a bit of extra cash to pay for her daughter Janet's school fees, with enough money left over to make real dinners for herself, maybe not bean stew—too expensive—but at least rice with some seasoning. Lately, when her friend the farmer didn't stop by, she subsisted on gari, ground cassava root that went for 20 cents a bag.

Ramatu also needed money for plans that extended beyond Old Post. She wanted to visit her dad's family several hours away in the neighboring district of Kailahun. He had died when she was young, at the beginning of the war, just before Ramatu fled to Guinea to wait out the conflict. Ramatu remembered almost nothing about him. She regretted never having learned to speak his language, Mende. "But they say I look like him." To check, she examined an old photograph her uncle sent to her brother via WhatsApp. It was too small and blurry, black-and-white, to see any resemblance, but she retained a tenderness. "My mom says that my dad really loved her." She smiled. "He was a good man."

Ramatu thought she'd need around $100 for the visit. Abbie warned that they'd probably get more like $50 from LAPO, since it was their first loan as a group. So Ramatu altered her ambition, figuring that the trip and a restaurant were both too expensive. She had seen other women getting by selling cool drinks from their house—things like plastic sachets of water and homemade ginger beer. She figured since she lived on one of Old Post's main pedestrian streets, near one of Koidu's key thoroughfares, she might as well do the same.

Now microcredit partners, Ramatu and Abbie walked back toward the quiet part of Old Post, corralling Ramatu's mom to join their group. Even though she was in her fifties, Ma Jabba was the hardest-working woman either of them knew, always up before the rest of the neighborhood. But though she was tireless, Ma Jabba's body had been worn down by a spinal condition that bent her sideways like a squiggly C. Her body made her job chopping and selling charcoal a difficulty and a pain. So, after very little convincing, Ramatu's mom decided she would take a loan and buy a big wooden table to put in front of her one-room house that sat at the back of Old Post. She could break the charcoal there, not stooped over on the ground. She would then leave the bags on the table for people to buy throughout the day.

Now a team, the three walked over to see Adama, a woman with a stomach that had been hardened into a washboard by years of breaking, then selling chunks of large gray rocks discarded from the big mine behind Old Post. Adama was cheery and spry, but the quarry work showed on her hands, which had become swollen and calloused. They resembled puppet hands, engorged and out of proportion with her otherwise slight body. Blood sometimes dripped down her fingers.

Ramatu and Abbie agreed that Adama was by far the poorest woman in Old Post. Her husband had left to find work some years back and never returned—Adama wasn't sure where he was, but she wasn't about to go look for him. To support her five kids, she sold the broken rocks for 10 to 20 cents a bucket to people who had enough money to build their own homes. The sales were sporadic and competitive. Adama had to jostle with dozens of other rock sellers who ran up to the cars and SUVs that parked outside the quarry, all knocking hard on the windows to get a chance to show their wares. Each bucket of rocks was more or less the same, all sold for the same price, so a sale was netted primarily thanks to the zest, charisma, and luck of the seller. If she didn't get there fast enough, Adama could miss her only sale of the day. In addition to needing at least a dollar or two a day for food, she also needed around $10 a week to pay the laborers who brought down a fresh supply of rocks from the top of the mountain for her and the other women to break. If she didn't have the cash—and she often didn't—she didn't have rocks, and her business and income would stall.

So she told Ramatu and Abbie yes, she would join. She planned to use a loan to cover some of these larger payments and keep her business afloat.

Next Ramatu and Abbie went to Musu, the woman who had taken Yabom's kids a few years ago, after she "went off" from the police station. Musu slowly pieced together what had happened. She heard that Yabom had been taken to the station because of unpaid microfinance debt. She knew her friend had been struggling to pay off a loan but didn't know how serious it was. By the time she realized that she may not be coming back, "I wasn't able to go chase her. I don't know her whereabouts. Some say she's in Peyima"—a former mining boomtown a few hours away— "some say they hear about her some other place, some say she died. Those two kids of hers, they're my responsibility now."

Now Musu would be the one to try her hand at microfinance. She had wanted to sell used clothes for years, considering herself to have a knack for salesmanship, with wide smiles and compliments at the ready. With the responsibilities that came with Yabom's two children, she felt a renewed urgency to start something new.

Abbie and Ramatu continued winding their way through the narrow streets of Old Post. They brought together nearly half a dozen women, then went to LAPO, telling them they had formed a new microfinance group. Abbie had blessed it with a name: Kochende. "It means 'Good Thing,' in Kono," she said.

A loan officer told them each person would get around $60, paying back $3.50 a week over six months, totaling around $84—officially a 40 percent interest rate for a six-month loan, but nearly 100 percent if you calculated all the fees: $3.50 for a LAPO booklet, $4 for membership photos, a little something for a "starting fee." They also had to put about $10 into a savings account. "Oh, then 'die man' money," recalled Abbie. "When a person dies, LAPO comes to see the body, and then they won't ask for that person's money again. So you have to pay a little bit for that." To her, the message was simple: "They just said we had to pay money, before we got our own." Weekly loan payments would be tracked by a loan officer, who would write each payment in a bright blue booklet. On the inside of the front flap was the company's motto: "To borrow is good, to repay is better, to use it well is best."

CHAPTER 5

The Poorest of the Poor

WHILE ACCION'S JEFF ASHE WAS OFF "EVANGELIZING" FOR THE EXPANSION of microcredit, John Hatch, the founder of FINCA, was living a quiet life back in the United States. He was nursing wounds from a divorce and figuring out next steps for FINCA, which had been limping along since his bourbon-fueled epiphany launched the small lending project mostly thanks to his unflinching enthusiasm. Somewhat in limbo, he had taken a short-term job with an event called Hands Across America, a 1986 effort to create a human chain across the country. The event was sponsored by the organization U.S.A. for Africa, best known for producing the 1985 song—meant to be inspirational but often mocked—"We Are the World." The song was part of a larger effort to get the music and arts industry involved in fundraising for famine relief in Ethiopia, a tragedy officially ascribed to drought even as political repression against minority groups led to tens of thousands of deaths. Sales of the song ultimately raised $60 million.

After "We Are the World," celebrity remained central to the organization's efforts. As part of the domestically focused Hands Across America campaign, 6.5 million people paid to save a spot in the human chain, including Ronald and Nancy Reagan, Bill Clinton, and Yoko Ono. Money raised went to America's hungry and homeless, whose numbers had swelled under Reagan as housing subsidies and low-cost rental units declined.

Hatch's job was to oversee the chain in a nearly two-hundred-mile stretch, from Gallup, New Mexico, to Flagstaff, Arizona. To show solidarity with the poor of America, five FINCA borrowers from Bolivia had been flown in courtesy of Hatch's brother, who was helping him fundraise. The

Bolivians joined the chain near a group of students brought in from Tucson by a teacher named Marguerite, who went by Mimi. She and Hatch got to chatting, and he learned that in her free time Mimi volunteered with an organization known as RESULTS.

Short for Responsibility for Ending Starvation Using Legislation, Trimtabbing, and Support, RESULTS had been created a few years earlier, in 1980, by a Miamian named Sam Daley-Harris. (Trimtabbing refers to trim tabs, small movable surfaces on a boat's larger steering device, such as a rudder, that allow a captain to steer. The reference was meant to be a metaphor for individual empowerment and the ability of individuals to exert influence on larger political systems.) Daley-Harris, a former teacher and musician, radiated a passion for advocacy on hunger and poverty. He felt strongly that individual Americans had a responsibility to influence national and international policy. Daley-Harris took inspiration from the 1971 Concert for Bangladesh, held in Madison Square Garden and organized by musicians George Harrison and Ravi Shankar to raise funds for refugees fleeing the war between West Pakistan and East Pakistan—the conflict that would cause Muhammad Yunus to proclaim his allegiance to Bangladesh and move back home. By the time Hatch met Mimi at the Hands Across America event, Daley-Harris was hosting regular trainings and spearheading a network of RESULTS chapters across the country (there would even soon be one in my hometown of Olympia, Washington, which organized annual events at the state capitol and sent delegates to Washington, DC).

Then, around the time that "We Are the World" hit the airwaves, Daley-Harris and other RESULTS volunteers saw a video that suggested a radical and alluring new way to fight poverty.

The film, produced by the International Fund for Agricultural Development, a UN agency, begins with a close-up shot of a Bangladeshi woman holding a young baby. Looking to the right of the camera, she gives her name—Nazma—then her story. "I was married at thirteen. My husband treated me just as badly as my father did. My father is dead." Nazma begins to cry.

Nazma explains that after her husband left her, she borrowed from the Grameen Bank. She was reluctant at first, worried about how she would pay off the loan, but spoke to other borrowers and mulled it over for a year. "Now," a male narrator explains, "Nazma is her own boss," selling goods in her neighborhood and using the profits to build her own house, which cost $7. Nazma eventually helped to lead a Grameen lending group. The video shows women being told by a stern-faced Nazma to stand up and down and recite the Grameen Bank's "16 Decisions." Instituted the year after the bank was officially formed, the Decisions encouraged borrowers to "not live in dilapidated houses," "grow vegetables all the year round," to build and use pit latrines, drink safe water, not participate in dowry or child marriage, to exercise, to send their children to school and "keep . . . families small." The video explains that the borrowers' declarations and calisthenics demonstrate their "discipline and solidarity."

As for Nazma, she had big plans: for her group to buy a rice mill, a sewing machine, for her children to go to school. Grameen had big plans, too, the narrator explained: "To eradicate poverty in Bangladesh through a real bootstrap operation, perhaps the best method of tackling the structural problems of this country." The video claimed Yunus had said, "Either I'm mad, or I'll change the economic structure of this country." By now, the mid-1980s, his efforts were picking up steam. With support from the International Fund for Agricultural Development, the Ford Foundation, and the Central Bank of Bangladesh, Grameen was opening roughly one hundred branches each year. The video proclaimed that eighty-four thousand people had "built up an independent existence thanks to this bank."

Daley-Harris and other RESULTS volunteers found themselves incredibly moved by the film. "We had never seen such a thing," recalls Daley-Harris. "It focused on more than just saving lives . . . it focused on bringing dignity." Even though RESULTS had primarily advocated for big government programs in the United States—expanding the reach of food stamps and nutritional programs for kids through Head Start, for example—the group was taken with Yunus's notion that, at least internationally, big aid funneled through big government was essentially a waste, driven by American paternalism. One volunteer was excited that a "dramatic change could be achieved with no dumping of Western largess on the infrastructure which serves only the wealthier classes." Another was convinced that "a poor person, newly empowered with a little credit to buy her own tools and to reach a market, would raise herself out of poverty." The political climate may have influenced the group, too. Under Reagan, there was pressure to meld social justice and the marketplace. "Microfinance fit that bill," another volunteer remembers. "It appealed to those who were typically free market and to those who were pro-poor, pro-women, with more of a progressive ideology. It had something for everyone."

Daley-Harris and RESULTS, already focused on congressional advocacy in Washington, soon began working on legislation that aimed to funnel millions of American dollars into microcredit programs targeting the world's poorest women. Rather than ask for a new pot of funding—never a winning strategy, particularly in the wake of the 1980s recession and amid budget cuts—it was instead proposed that a portion of funds that had been traditionally *donated* to foreign countries be *lent* instead. When governments repaid, the money would be used to fund microcredit programs, meaning that national debt would essentially fuel individual debt. RESULTS hoped this would have several effects: slim down a reliance on foreign grants, something the Reagan administration was keen to do, while also fueling new individual-focused, bottom-up programs that promoted self-sufficiency. If it passed, the legislation would "slowly shift tens and eventually hundreds of millions of dollars in foreign assistance . . . to . . . microenterprise poverty lending programs," Daley-Harris later wrote.

The bill checked progressive boxes—pro-poor, pro-woman, pro-internationalist, pro-grassroots—and conservative ones, too—pro-individual and pro-business, anti–big government. Microcredit seemed to offer a tantalizing third way that rejected top-down thinking, expanded economic opportunities without relying on big government programs, and gave poor people the power to help themselves. The legislation received bipartisan support, including from would-be political rivals, such as civil rights leader John Lewis and Georgia Republican Pat Swindall. Republican representative Clay Shaw of Florida reportedly told the *Fort Lauderdale News* that the idea "'hits at the basis of Republican philosophy . . . to give people a hand up rather than a handout.'"

By now, USAID was already firmly on board with funding small businesses in the world's poorest countries, thanks in part to Jeff Ashe's advocacy and to a certain extent John Hatch's work, despite his self-professed "hatred" of USAID. But it was Muhammad Yunus's story that became essential to RESULTS' legislative advocacy. In 1986, at a congressional hearing on world hunger, Yunus told the story of Sufiya Begum, the stool maker, the $27 to forty-two women. Well-spoken and impeccably dressed, with a bright smile and charismatic presence, Yunus gave off an alluring air of friendly indignation—warm, righteous, wise, approachable, maybe a bit holier-than-thou. One observer described him as "a very ambitious Buddha." He was at once familiar—spoke perfect English, had studied in America—and foreign, hailing from a country that most Americans probably primarily knew for its poverty, if they'd heard of Bangladesh at all. He donned traditional Bangladeshi clothing made up of checkered shirts and slim button-up vests, a handsome look that was sharp and distinctly non-Western. Most captivating, he was unwaveringly confident in his solution to poverty—a simple one, tailored to the problems of his poor country, problems that had evaded international consultants and Western governments for decades. Although Jeff Ashe had learned that Yunus almost certainly did not come up with the idea of giving loans to poor people alone—not to mention other essential components such as group monitoring and lending to women—he certainly seemed to be the one to articulate it best. When he spoke, "the clouds lifted, in terms of his clarity," Daley-Harris told me. One of the congressmen pushing for microcredit legislation said that efforts would not have gone forward without the Grameen Bank.

Jeff Ashe also spoke to Congress, to far less fanfare. Giddy with his research findings, he proclaimed, "almost inconceivably small amounts of credit—from $10 to $500 . . . can lead to significant increases in income, production and employment, and importantly, an upsurge of hope for the future." Although USAID's interest had been piqued by Ashe's work, they didn't exactly agree with the "inconceivably small amounts of credit" part. USAID worried that this approach was off-target. While traditional lending groups like osusus are essentially recirculating money that is already in a community, external loans could inject new cash into impoverished communities, creating new business opportunities. While it was narratively compelling to say that a poor woman could spring herself out of poverty with a $10 loan and cover interest payments to boot, the focus on market-rate, minuscule loans to very poor people who ran cottage businesses didn't seem to radically shift the equation. Instead, staffers argued that more substantial resources were needed to really make a difference. USAID had a different proposal: fund bigger loans of up to $1,000 to small, but not tiny, businesses, including those that were already up and running. The hope was that the businesses would expand and employ others, engendering a robust economy at the bottom of the pyramid.

Yunus flatly rejected USAID's approach. It completely missed the point. Millions of people around the world *were* self-employed. That *was* how they survived, and there was no reason to believe they would suddenly become employable or that there would be enough jobs to employ them. There simply weren't enough factories, not even enough tiny motorcycle repair businesses, for this to be achieved, especially for poor, illiterate women. Rather than hoping that economic expansion would eventually trickle down, Yunus advocated "lending to the poor directly." And because they were very poor, it stood to reason that they would only need small loans, like the few dollars he had given the women back in Jobra; anything too large and they would soon go underwater. To ensure a poverty-focused approach, the RESULTS-backed legislation included a cap not of $1,000 but of $300. The lower amount would guarantee that loans went to the "poorest of the poor."

USAID thought the cap was "ridiculous," in the words of one former staffer. The agency didn't want to be hamstrung by Congressional mandates that would confine their programs, they fundamentally believed in larger loans to larger businesses, and they worried that offering poor people debt, especially if it came with high interest rates, was a fantastic way to ensure they would fail. The risks felt especially tangible given that microcredit was essentially unregulated, falling outside the gamut of banks and government institutions. Eric Chetwynd, who worked on early microcredit initiatives within USAID, explains the agency worried that "Muhammad Yunus's program was too unidimensional. The problem was more complicated." It required not only a micro approach but macrolevel changes, too, things like market analyses, training for businesspeople, and altered trade policies. USAID wanted to help *small* shopkeepers but not necessarily the *smallest* shopkeepers; one USAID staffer told the *Christian Science Monitor* that the very poor were so destitute "they can't run a business." The agency advocated that the truly impoverished, women like Nazma and Sufiya Begum, rely not on loans but on separate social programs instead. So when a version of a bill with the $300 cap was introduced in the Senate, USAID explicitly opposed this "poorest of the poor" approach, with the staffer telling the *Christian Science Monitor* that it was "unsound, and contrary to [USAID's] mandate."

By now, RESULTS had amassed a small army of volunteers who believed deeply in Yunus's version of microcredit: tiny loans, to women, the poorest of the poor. They saw USAID's skepticism of Yunus not only as an insult to Grameen but morally repugnant and actively anti-poor, a stance that was hardened when a USAID official was anonymously quoted in the *Christian Science Monitor* saying, "A lot of people are poor because they don't have the talent, skills, or IQ to get out of poverty." RESULTS advocates had become adept at haranguing elected officials and regularly lobbied the Hill. One USAID staffer recalls suddenly getting calls from "all these people I had never heard of," who were pushing for the $300 limit. The staffer found it ironic that USAID was accused of being blind to tiny enterprises, given that the agency had been funding experimental lending programs like Jeff Ashe's "solidarity groups" for a decade. He scoffed, "and now they were demanding that USAID do something."

* * *

Back in Arizona, Mimi called up John Hatch to explain about the goings-on in Washington. RESULTS thought he would be a solid ally in their legislative work, given his background in U.S. international development efforts, his focus on group lending and women, and the formidable storytelling skills he had honed since childhood. The group wanted his help drafting policy language and testifying on the Hill. Mimi asked Hatch to move to Tucson, where he could set up an office rent-free. Mimi, despite being a full-time teacher, would offer her accounting service—at no charge—and straighten out his books. "I couldn't refuse an offer like that," Hatch says. Hatch moved to Tucson and started making trips to DC to bolster RESULTS' congressional lobbying.

To dismiss concerns that the loans would be too small to have any significant impact, John Hatch told a forum held on Capitol Hill, "I'm an economist. I look for economic results. I can give you case after case of net income generated of 100 percent, 150 percent, 200 percent from a $50 loan." Even with these impressive results, borrowers, he said, "rarely mention economic benefits. Instead, they say things like 'my family is more united,' 'our community works together,' and 'I feel like somebody.' Empowering people—that's the real benefit of these loans." He referred to the legislation as "potentially the most important foreign policy initiative since the Marshall Plan."

It was too optimistic a vision for Congress and journalists to ignore. RESULTS' promises, and their persistent advocacy, were more spectacular than USAID's pragmatic stance. Dozens of members of Congress supported the pro-poor legislation, and Yunus's framing was solidified in the public narrative: "microcredit" now meant small loans, to poor women, to help them get out of poverty, not larger loans to middling businesses. USAID had lost the argument. Yunus and Daley-Harris had won.

Still, despite support from many in Congress, the legislation floundered. Instead, at the end of 1987, an appropriations bill earmarked $50 million of USAID's budget for small business loans. An accompanying report suggested that 80 percent of those earmarked funds go to the poorest 50 percent of a country's population, with an emphasis on women-owned businesses. USAID was now being forced to facilitate loans to the poorest of the poor—the exact group they thought would be most harmed by credit.

Now, after years of despising USAID, John Hatch finally had his shot at vindication. From the earmarked money, FINCA was awarded a multimillion-dollar grant that launched the organization from a small-scale weekend effort to one of the darlings of a growing microcredit industry. Hatch's leap of faith, in joining Mimi in Tucson, had paid off.

In May 1988, Hatch and Mimi were married. In Tucson, they spent their weekends driving to the Mexican border to set up his "village banks." They put together a manual so that others could copy the program, too. Mimi offered to quit her job and follow Hatch wherever his lending efforts took him.

Soon, the couple moved to El Salvador to start a lending program. They arrived amid a bloody conflict that had begun several years earlier, around the time Ashe had stumbled upon the FEDECRÉDITO solidarity groups he so admired. A leftist coalition had formed under the banner "Farabundo Martí National Liberation Front" (FMLN), a movement that traced its lineage back to the Communists and peasants who had been killed in the 1930s La Matanza massacre overseen by General Maximiliano Hernández Martínez. Just as they had half a century before, Salvadorans called for land reform, an end to the country's oligopoly, and an end to political repression.

The civil war lasted more than a decade. The FMLN and their sympathizers clashed with the military, which received training and tens of millions of dollars in support from the United States. Over the twelve-year conflict, nearly one hundred thousand people were killed, including by American-backed "death squads."

Predictably chipper and undeterred by the FMLN fighters who surrounded their "nice little house in a quiet *cul de sac* at the edge of town," Hatch was pleased to find that a FINCA-style program appealed even during war. Perhaps that was because it felt so familiar. FINCA's model was strikingly similar to FEDECRÉDITO's, which had been organized in the wake of La Matanza. They both included lending to small groups, with no collateral, to help small businesses—and a mission to soothe and uplift the poor.

The City Hustle

Freetown, Sierra Leone

Ramadan 2021

RAMADAN WAS A PERIOD MARKED BY OPPOSITES: BOREDOM THEN excitement, long periods of waiting then intense spurts of activity. Hunger then satiation. During the month, Aminata spent even more time at home than usual. She rarely went shopping because the price of everything was jacked up in anticipation of the upcoming Eid al-Fitr feast. Plus, why waste precious energy when you're fasting, haggling for prices, and hauling bags in the heat. In between naps, Aminata sold a few drinks and yogurt, went to the mosque to pray, then started preparing dinner long before she needed to, the smell of food helping to ease her want of it.

About halfway through the holy month, her mother called from Pendembu, reminding her to visit her aunties and uncles across Freetown. Aminata's relatives fanned across the eastern part of the city, tucked into its more affordable outskirts. Such neighborhoods had grown as people fled conflict during the country's long war and then pursued opportunities in its wake. By 2023, about 15 percent of Sierra Leone's roughly nine million people lived in the capital.

One bright morning, Aminata traded in her lapa and high-top bun for black leggings, rhinestone sandals, and a white and green hijab. From the parlor floor, she grabbed a huge cloth bag with "Walmart.ca" printed on its side—a purchase from a junks stall—filling it with a squat pot of rice and stew, a watermelon, and an oblong platter topped with plantains, fish, fried onions, and potatoes. As she walked out the front door, she called out to her cousin Mommy, "Give from the fridge if anyone comes while I'm gone."

Aminata was feeling optimistic about her business. Sales weren't going too well, but that was to be expected during Ramadan what with everyone eating less. And she was making a bit of money. Some adults liked to cut their fast with her yogurt; the kids too young to fast relied on Aminata's ginger beer to keep them full for much of the day. There had only been a few weeks when she hadn't been able to make her loan payments—her husband, Idrissa, helped then, even if he complained about it. Overall, Aminata felt like things were finally moving forward, for once. Whenever she could, she put the few bills she had to spare in her cashbox. It felt like progress, even if it only amounted to a few dollars.

Aminata wound her way down to the main road, the ends of her hijab trailing behind her. The heavy Walmart bag tilted her body to the right, pulling her gait into an uncomfortable lilt. At the intersection, she waved by taxis and kekes—rickshaw taxis. Too expensive. Taking a poda poda—a minibus—would save her 5 cents. She chose one that wasn't yet over-crowded. As she sat down, the driver turned to her, pointing to his face mask, which was pulled just below his nose. "Do you have one?" he asked. "The police are checking today."

Aminata huffed. She found the COVID pandemic to be an awfully con-venient emergency for President Julius Maada Bio, the leader of the SLPP party Aminata detested. The country had received millions of dollars from donors like USAID for over-the-radio tutoring lessons and a slow rollout of the Chinese and British versions of the vaccine. To demonstrate that the government was taking COVID seriously, despite surprisingly low official infection rates, police now made a show of setting up checkpoints around the city, where officers with masks wrapped around their chins ensured that everyone else was complying. Aminata remembered that govern-ment coffers had also filled up a few years before during another public health emergency, Ebola. Her beloved APC party had been in power then. Aminata much preferred the approach of the former president, Ernest Bai Koroma, who she swears used the Ebola money to give out handfuls of cash to help everyday Sierra Leoneans get by, an act the current president, Maada Bio, and donors called wasteful and corrupt but Aminata thought efficient: if poor people needed money, why not just give it to them directly? "This," she waved her hand aimlessly at the road, imagining government coffers filling up again, "is their own Ebola." Aminata told the poda poda driver that yes she had remembered her mask, although it wouldn't have been a problem if she hadn't. Half a dozen street sellers, spotting a business opportunity, now surrounded the vehicle, hawking disposable masks for sale. A tall man in the front seat wordlessly waved a 20-cent note out the front window, grabbing one just before they reached the checkpoint.

Aminata put her own on just before a female police officer approached the van. She took a quick look at the masked passengers and then waved the vehicle on.

The driver had been ready for a fight. "This country," he moaned. "Police can do whatever they want." A woman in the back seat chimed in, telling everyone in the poda poda that her son had been taken to the police by his employer, who accused him of stealing. An officer told her she had to pay $10 if she wanted him to avoid the jail cell. She didn't have the money, so he was locked up. "A son, for $10. Imagine!" Aminata grunted in sympathy.

The driver turned up the radio, and a man's voice, calm and self-assured, filled the vehicle. He offered a rationale for why things like rice, eggs, and sugar were nearly double what they were a year before. There was no one to blame, nothing the government could do. People in rich countries just didn't want to work the ports due to COVID, he said. Products weren't getting on ships. Sierra Leone relied on outside countries for almost everything. Since the supply was down, the prices were going up. All they could do was hope that things would get better. Aminata shrugged when she heard the man's rationale. "Okay."

A bit farther down the road, Aminata pointed to a cluster of shops on the left side of the street. Each was small, maybe big enough for ten people to fit inside, made of the same corrugated iron that covered Aminata's house. Just a few weeks before, the shops had sold tea, chips and snacks, sugar, milk, and eggs. Now, what remained of their crinkle-cut walls had been pushed out to the side, the material all askew, like a mouth with punched-out teeth. Doors had been pulled off their hinges. "Looks like the City Council has been here," remarked Aminata. To formalize trading, in an effort to clean up Freetown, the Council had recently been cracking down on small unlicensed sellers whose spots they deemed inappropriate. "They tell them they have to move if they don't have an official shop, if they don't have the right papers." Many didn't. Getting registered took time and money and regular payments to the City Council that some vendors didn't have. Signs were plastered onto the walls near the broken shacks, proclaiming that the land had been reappropriated by the government.

In principle, Aminata supported this City Council; it was one of the few arms of government still led by her APC. But she knew several people who had their business destroyed, their wares confiscated. "They did that to my auntie," she said. "Threw her table on the ground, scattered her things all over the street, told her she could only trade inside the market. She lost so many things that day."

In the center of town, traffic churned so thick that walking seemed the most efficient choice. Aminata left the irritable driver and his mangled windshield and entered PZ, the city's busiest market, which was quickly filling up with hundreds of merchants selling all manner of things: rainbow-colored children's sandals, cold drinks, plaid shirts, wrap dresses, African-print fabric, pineapples. Peeling off her face mask, Aminata slipped into the hurried flow, making her way forward with efficient elbow jabs.

Aminata's first visit was to Samuel, her elder cousin, who she considered her uncle, who sold onions and potatoes at the end of PZ. She knew that he had taken out microfinance, too, but only once: in 2007, when he was just starting his business, he borrowed about $120. He remembers that the interest rate was 32 percent, plus the usual up-front fees, which he saw as "bribes."

That was his only monetary loan. Now he was indebted in other ways. Over the years, Samuel had cultivated a relationship with two Lebanese importers who worked from a big office at the end of PZ. The importers offered him onions and potatoes from their warehouse, directly off the boat from Europe. They never demanded cash up front—they only expected payment after Samuel made his sales, no interest charged. He paid for the goods and nothing else. Potatoes and onions in hand, Samuel then negotiated with market women he sold to, charging a small 50-cent markup per bag. Like his dealings with the Lebanese importers, these transactions were also done entirely on "trust": goods to the women first, money to Samuel later, interest-free. It was a constantly churning cycle, Samuel always, at the same time, owed and owing. But the cyclical nature of the debt also meant he always had cash in hand, and the relationships felt less threatening and more predictable than taking out a loan from a foreign lender. Over the years, Samuel had even saved up enough to build a new house in the far east end of the city. He expected to be moving in any day. Aminata felt a sense of pride to see someone in her family become so successful.

After she handed Samuel the stew, asked after his family, and inquired about the plans for his home, Aminata waved goodbye. As she walked toward the end of PZ, Aminata was met by the unsmiling face of the current president, Julius Maada Bio, whose poster was plastered on all four sides of a large clock tower at the end of the road, just past Samuel's stall. She scoffed, then found a bus going farther east.

Aminata took a seat underneath a blown-out window. It turned out to be drenched from the previous night's rain, but by the time Aminata realized her smock was soaked, the bus was too packed to move. She placed the Walmart bag firmly on her lap, holding its straps closed, and occupied herself by watching the TV at the front of the vehicle, a former European tour bus now reincarnated. It played videos from some of her favorite artists: Beyoncé ("Irreplaceable"), Rihanna ("Te Amo"), Chris Brown, Pitbull, Justin Bieber, Nicki Minaj. She liked Justin Bieber best.

Aminata looked out the window at a shop, its big iron doors painted rust red and bolted closed. It had an awning, a robust porch, plenty of space for sales. Aminata found herself thinking about this place a lot. She had inquired about renting it when she first moved to Freetown. Her idea was to sell what she called "touristic items" there, things like woven cloth, hand-dyed batiks, baskets that reached as high as her waist. Her mom would be able to procure them cheaply in Pendembu; Aminata figured that Sierra Leoneans from around the country, plus NGO workers, might be interested in something a little more traditional than the plastic baskets from China and used clothes from America and Europe that dominated the markets. Aminata decided that she needed a shop in the center of town for her touristic business, because who was going to pay a visit to

Two Taps' winding pedestrian-only streets for cloth? It wasn't just location she was after—it was also presentation. Of the businesspeople who had made it in Freetown, she knew the key was being unique. This was no great trade secret, not something specific to Sierra Leone, but differentiation is especially vital in a country where most vendors sell some version of a staple that someone else is also selling, sometimes just feet away and almost always at the same price: basic foodstuffs, plastic flip-flops, imported clothes. There were exceptions, of course, like the tailor who specialized in handmade silk kimonos, the supermarket that sold dog bones and yoga mats, the bar with handcrafted cocktails. But there could only be so many silk kimonos in one of the poorest countries in the world. If substantive difference could not be realized, the appearance of difference—through a unique location, a catchy name, a particularly clean storefront, longer hours—would have to do instead.

When Aminata inquired about renting the red-doored place, the owner quoted about $1,500 a year. That was almost the entirety of her husband Idrissa's annual salary, and ten times the loan amount ASA said Aminata qualified for. Aminata had heard that women who *already* had shops qualified for much larger microcredit loans, with much larger interest rates—the lenders said they were more trustworthy, and could offer collateral, so they got a better deal. She had seen how they had been able to invest these larger amounts, "to really do something." But she was in a bind. She didn't have enough start-up capital to rent a shop. Which meant she didn't qualify for a big loan. Which meant she would have to stick to an at-home business she wasn't sure would grow. She had been categorized as small, so she would likely stay that way.

* * *

After twenty minutes on the soaked seat, Aminata finally found herself outside Freetown's busy city center. She hopped off the bus, then paid another 15 cents for a bus going farther east, then another 15 cents to get all the way to Waterloo Market. Known for its fresh fish and wares that were cheaper than those sold in town, Waterloo Market was about twenty miles east of Two Taps. The final bus stopped at the mouth of a muddy parking lot, where taxis competed with trucks, crowds of shoppers, and sellers of toothpaste, okra, fresh-baked bread, and plastic sachets of water. Aminata latched onto a string of people forcing their way inside the market via a thin, unpaved walkway, her rhinestone sandals slipping on the mud. She paused for a moment in the jewelry section, listening to recordings merchants had made to lure customers. Played together, their voices merged: this product for 10 cents, that one for 20 cents, this bundle for $2.50. One implored, "Get it before the rainy season comes, when the price will go up!"

Aminata worked her way to the back of the market, where she found Idrissa's uncle, whom the family just called Sheikh, in the middle of his broad yard with his two wives. Together they inspected a few rows of thin cassava shrubs, about calf high. Each bush had a few spindly arms adorned with leaves. It was clear they were far from ready.

The old man waved his hand over the crop as he talked through the busy day ahead of him. He expected tough negotiations with City Council representatives that afternoon. In exchange for $1 a day from each of the market's thousand or so traders, the Council had promised to install a water well, a commitment that remained unfulfilled. As imam of the Waterloo Market Mosque, Sheikh's presence would add a weightiness to the conversations. On top of that, he needed to cobble something together to help his wives make their weekly payments to BRAC, one of the world's largest and oldest microfinance lenders. Originally Bangladeshi, BRAC began lending in Sierra Leone a few years after the country's civil war and now had lending offices across the country. Sheikh spoke in a breathless manner, his voice strained with effort. It was already midmorning. "The loan officers will be here soon."

Both of his wives had been taking loans for years, from both BRAC and LAPO, the Nigerian microfinance lender that also had a large presence in Sierra Leone. The women started small, around $30, but now were up to around $100 each. The loans helped the women buy and then sell rice, palm oil, and peanuts. The profits covered daily household necessities that Sheikh couldn't. A trader himself, he had a fierce, almost singular focus on giving his kids a leg up, spending whatever he made to that end. He had paid for all of them to take a private version of the final high school exam after they failed the public one, then spent a significant amount of money getting three into Oman, one to Kuwait. He wanted them to find work, save up for college. All had begged him to be able to come home. "I say to them, 'You come from a poor family. Deal with it! Maybe you'll be there six months or one year, when you come back, you'll have something. If you want to learn, you're going to have to suffer.'"

Although Sheikh's wives relied on the loans to provide the daily necessities he couldn't, he was adamant that he didn't approve of the credit and would never take on such debt himself. Being a strict adherent to Islam, which forbids both receiving and paying interest, meant he found the practice deeply immoral, not to mention impractical. "The interest is way too much," he reasoned. "No one can pay that. By the time you pay it back, there's no money left for you." He didn't seem to dwell on how his wives' microcredit helped him, and not just because money from the loans covered daily costs he couldn't. More directly, the women bought their goods from him—Sheikh was their supplier, the one they paid for the rice, palm oil, and peanuts they sold. In a not-so-distant sense, he made money off their debt.

Sheikh's cassava garden was meant as a sort of backup plan for the times when his wives' payments were elusive. The women had missed several payments already but hadn't been taken to the police. His status helped—he knew not only City Council members but local police officers, too. "I beg for them," he said.

Sheikh excused himself when the City Council people passed by. Aminata gave the watermelon and platter of food to Sheikh's oldest wife, cupped the youngest child's head in her hand, and wished them well. She snaked back through the market, stopping to buy $1's worth of dried fish, cheaper than what she could get in town. She passed by the jewelry section again. Her eyes caught a pair of round, gold-colored earrings, but she quickly moved on.

Aminata found a poda poda going back west toward Freetown. Only midmorning, the day was already getting hotter; to beat the heat, she whipped a washcloth back and forth in front of her face. As the bus pulled away, Aminata pointed to a white van parked on the side of the road. "Look," she giggled. "The BRAC vehicle!"

A few well-dressed men, young looking, in white shirts and black trousers, hopped out of the van. One instinctively picked his foot up from the ground, checking to make sure his sharp-toed shoes hadn't gotten muddy. As she watched them, Aminata found herself smiling. She seemed to take a sort of comfort in knowing that others dealt with the same things that those in Two Taps did, that her mother had for decades: the worries about payments, the cobbling together of whatever could be found. It wasn't so much that she was feeling schadenfreude. It was more a sense of solidarity. At least the joke wasn't only on her.

CHAPTER 6

Bees

IN 1988, THE AMERICAN ORGANIZATION FREEDOM FROM HUNGER BEGAN searching for alternatives to trainings, food donations, and farmers' groups they had supported for decades, which had begun to look tired in the new era of do-it-yourself "bootstrap development." They wanted to grow and reach more people, but after the 1980s recession and in the Reagan era, money felt tight.

Exploring other options, the organization reached out to Jeff Ashe, who had by now left Accion to do private consulting. He showed them the same video that RESULTS leader Sam Daley-Harris had seen a few years earlier, about Nazma, the young Grameen Bank borrower in Bangladesh. Ashe taught them about solidarity groups and the basics of self-sustaining microcredit. Interest rates needed to be high enough to cover costs; by now many rates hovered around 20 percent annually, although some, such as FINCA's rate in Uganda, were nearing 70 percent. Instead of collateral, group lending could help to keep repayments coming. Staffers would later write that Freedom from Hunger was also drawn to the group model because they were "intrigued by the possibility that [a borrower's] success with their groups could help members transform an attitude of 'I can't' to 'I can.'" Putting women in groups would also help the organization more efficiently, and cheaply, disseminate information on health and nutrition.

A few staffers then went to visit Muhammad Yunus. Kathleen Stack, who led the Freedom from Hunger delegation, found that he was "soft spoken, confident" with "a calm gentle aura, an almost guru-like persona, emanating kindness and dedication to the poor. He had this whole giving nature. He was very inspirational." She was also impressed by the dedication of the women borrowers, in their bright saris, reciting Grameen's "16 Decisions."

This dedication extended to repayment. To much fanfare, Grameen claimed that 98 percent of borrowers paid off their loans, a rate far higher than most commercial banks. This happened to be the same rate that FINCA claimed, and Accion, too, and soon other microcredit programs. The figure came to be expected in the industry, a steady fact that could be taken for granted. In *Banker to the Poor*, Yunus acknowledged that borrowers' poverty and exclusion were instrumental to high repayments. "The women who are the most desperate, who have nothing to eat, who have been abandoned by their husbands and are trying to feed their children by begging . . . They have no other choice," Yunus wrote. "They do not have any cushion whatsoever to fall back on. If they fall afoul of this one loan, they will have lost their one and only chance to get out of the rut." Equally, since women had been so dramatically excluded from financial systems, Yunus argued, they were most likely to appreciate credit. Yunus describes Grameen's loans as having an almost redemptive quality to them, a way to finally enfold a woman into a society that had forgotten her. "To her family she has been nothing but another mouth to feed, another dowry to pay . . . for the first time in her life, an institution has trusted her with a great sum of money." When the woman "finally receives the twenty-five dollars, she is trembling. The money burns her fingers. Tears roll down her face. She has never seen so much money in her life."

Freedom from Hunger was most taken with Yunus's claim that, given their role as mothers and homemakers, women would use their loans more wisely than men—an argument that had actually been made over a decade before at the 1975 women's conference in Mexico City, and then echoed in dozens of other papers and presentations (one person argued that women were more likely to send their children to school, whereas men would spend money on cockfights). "When a destitute mother starts earning an income, her dreams of success invariably center around her children," Yunus argued in *Banker to the Poor*. "A woman's second priority is the household. She wants to buy utensils, build a stronger roof, or find a bed for herself and her family." On the other hand, "when a destitute father earns extra income, he focuses more attention on himself." Even though Women's World Banking, the kernel of which started in the mid-1970s before Yunus met the stool maker Sufiya Begum, was one of the first organizations to argue that women most needed—and would best use—credit, Yunus had by now become most famous for this talking point. Freedom from Hunger hoped that by giving loans to poor women, those women would be able to increase their incomes and then spend more on their children's nutrition (they were, after all, an anti-hunger organization).

Despite his "gentle aura," Yunus was so confident in Grameen's model that he told Freedom from Hunger to "replicate it exactly as it was," recalls Kathleen Stack. Some of Stack's colleagues were unsure, particularly of the interest rates, which felt "very uncomfortable. And I think there was a skepticism about impact. Is this actually helping people?" But Freedom from Hunger went forward anyway, piecing together their own version of microcredit based on the Grameen and solidarity group models and keeping interest rates high in order to plug profits into more lending. Within just over a decade, theirs would be one of the largest microcredit programs in the world, eventually reaching millions of borrowers.

Grameen and Yunus promoted other copycat projects, too. In 1989, the Grameen Trust opened an affiliate to the bank with a goal to promote Grameen-style microcredit internationally. By 1994, it raised nearly $20 million, which would be used to launch "replication projects" in twenty-seven countries. The Grameen Trust's successes were reported in a news-letter, *Grameen Dialogue*, which was sent to a growing group of supporters outside Bangladesh such as in the United States, Europe, Australia, Japan.

But microcredit was also spreading without Yunus's help. Women's World Banking was growing, with financial support from the UN and from the Norwegian, Dutch, British, Spanish, and Canadian governments. After Hatch set up FINCA programs in El Salvador, he did the same in Mexico, Nicaragua, Guatemala, and Honduras. And after Ashe left Accion in 1986, he spent the next fourteen years as a consultant, in his words, "spreading the solidarity group methodology" to thirty-four countries. Although each called it something different—group lending (Muhammad Yunus), village banking (John Hatch), and solidarity groups (Jeff Ashe)— all offered the same underlying architecture: small loans, given in groups, to women, with frequent repayments and interest rates that were high enough to cover costs. The anthropologist Parker Shipton has referred to high-flying consultants who offered replicable, ready-made programs as "bees" who "trans-pollinated their ideas." Never mind that poverty looked and felt very different in Mexico and South Africa, with different underlying causes. If microlending worked in one struggling community, lenders and microfinance advocates assumed it must work in another.

These bees worked in a tight-knit group, cutting deals, offering advice, and sharing job and funding opportunities with one another over dinner, at conferences, at airports, on transcontinental flights. Who a person knew was essential to their success. The official creation of the Grameen Bank was only possible because Muhammad Yunus had friends in Bangladesh's finance ministry. (Although Yunus carped that "Bangladesh . . . is run entirely by a handful of people, most of whom are college or university friends," he conceded, "time and again this unfortunate feature of Bangladesh society and politics has helped Grameen overcome otherwise impossible bureaucratic hurdles.") John Hatch got his first grant because he knew the USAID team through his consulting work. Michaela Walsh was able to fundraise for Women's World Banking because, in her own recollection, no one could say no to someone connected to the Rockefellers. Accion's first loan was given because the son of a banker knew a bank manager looking for a cheaper solution to a pesky personnel problem. Jeff Ashe got the job at Accion because he knew his future boss through an agriculture project they had worked on together in Ecuador. Robert Graham, who founded Katalysis Partnership, a microfinance network created in the 1980s, got his first grant after sitting next to a USAID official on a flight to Belize. They shared drinks; later, a half-million-dollar grant was approved.

This is not to say that these people weren't qualified, or brilliant, energetic, or committed. But the connections helped. Throughout my years speaking to microcredit funders, advocates, and managers, as well as women who ultimately take out the loans, I observed a striking similarity between the two groups: both are almost wholly dependent on relationships. Women offer business and financial support to family and friends, those they know and like and trust and can get something from. The microlenders, in turn, offer each other advice, suggestions, and connections. The main difference here is scale. A connection to a larger businessperson can net a small Sierra Leonean businessperson a few hundred dollars (maybe), whereas a connection to a friendly funder could result in million-dollar microcredit grants. Another is language. For poor women, such a reliance on relationships is called nepotism. For development workers, networking.

Even though they offered something similar, all the microcredit "pioneers" I spoke to recall a sort of giddy freedom from the early days. There was a sense of discovery, of tinkering, a feeling of being on the frontier of something new, something grand and exciting. In our conversations, they described late nights, hair-raising flights, frustrating conversations, and the elation at having clinched a grant or a new connection. Several told me wild, adventurous stories. One was greeted at the airport by an official government entourage even though she was just there to audit a lending project (they assumed that she was coming to set up a brand new bank). Another learned that Sékou Touré, the president of Guinea, openly encouraged stealing from foreigners, given that foreigners had stolen from Guineans for so long, a sentiment the microfinance staffer empathized with but which nevertheless presented significant challenges for a U.S.-funded banking project. The sense of exploration may have had something to do with their age. These were people in their twenties and thirties, going to new places they knew little about, running programs when they were sometimes just a few years out of school. And, with the backing of donors, they could act fast, with much flexibility. Jeff Ashe could show up in a country and, within a few weeks, start a whole new lending project.

Rather than going through government banks, as had been done with agricultural loans, much of this newer iteration of credit flowed through private institutions such as NGOs, something Dale Adams and his "Spring Review" colleagues suggested to avoid corruption. NGOs had been integral to international development programs throughout the post–World War II era, and they became even more appealing when USAID and other donors took a firmer private-sector approach in the 1980s because they offered a way to circumvent the state while still influencing policy. Although NGOs were officially private—they were, after all, nongovernmental organizations—they often relied heavily on public funds, offering a pathway for governments to exert subtle but significant influence. More practically, NGOs' bread and butter were often small, short-term programs, easier to fund and track than long-term government programs like welfare or health care.

By the time microcredit became popular in the mid- to late 1980s, NGOs were, in the words of one group of academics, the "sweethearts of development." From the mid-1970s to the mid-1980s, Kenya saw a gargantuan 230 percent increase in the number of NGOs. By the early 1990s, there were a whopping hundred thousand NGOs in Brazil, and another hundred thousand in India (as of 2022, there were over three million in India).

These weren't necessarily locally led, grassroots community organizations that the promise of bottom-up, grassroots development might imply: they were as likely to be run by the likes of John Hatch, an American working in Bolivia, as they were by Ela Bhatt of the Self-Employed Women's Association, an Indian working in India. Much of USAID's money flowed through American-based organizations that had a presence internationally. By supporting American organizations abroad, USAID could claim not only to be in the service of Bolivia or Ethiopia but of domestic priorities, too. Their support bolstered American interests and employment— and it helped USAID. By building a constituency at home, USAID could rely on NGO staffers, their families, and their communities to lobby on behalf of the agency, which had never been anyone's budget darling. Those NGOs would have a strong incentive to do so: without USAID, they would have limited cash. As other donors looked for "professional" NGOs to fund, they also gravitated toward American- and European-backed efforts that had a foothold at home but worked overseas.

NGOs grew not only in number but in scope. As nongovernmental organizations provided both a greater number of services and more substantial services, they further diminished the role of the state, which in turn further justified the need for private organizations to provide more services. Their growth became a self-fulfilling prophecy. Advocates claimed that the rise in NGOs was not because private services had helped to undermine government ones. Rather, it demonstrated a "crisis of confidence in the capability of the state."

This dynamic was supercharged in the early 1980s. To deal with mounting national debts around the world—debts that had often been encouraged and offered by Western governments and institutions—the IMF and World

Bank promoted a series of sweeping financial, trade, and policy reforms in poor countries, generally grouped under the umbrella "Structural Adjustment Programs." Going forward, the institutions would only offer loans, which countries had come to depend on, if governments agreed to open their markets to foreign trade, lift restrictions on financial sectors, and curb government spending, even on essential programs like education. Bending to pressure, countries privatized state-run companies, reduced financial regulation, altered trade policies, and reduced price guarantees that had supported local producers, as well as price subsidies on basic goods that had kept prices low for local consumers. In some places, doctors' and teachers' wages were frozen. Basic services like health care and education were cut, privatized, or required payment through "user fees."*

As Structural Adjustment Programs winnowed government programs, private organizations were there to fill the void. By 1990, nongovernmental organizations were involved with almost half of all new projects funded by the World Bank. By the mid-1990s, as government investment in education decreased, half of all education services in Kenya were provided by private organizations. By the early 2000s, USAID funneled about a third of its funding through NGOs. Adopting the dominant market-oriented approach, some NGOs also began charging for services, which could become so unaffordable as to be inaccessible. By one count, half of all NGO revenue came from fees they charged. One writer, from a global union network, referred to NGOs, some of which embodied Western-led neoliberal values, as "the shock troops of civil society."

At least one microcredit organization was created specifically in response to Structural Adjustment Programs, a way to stem the bleeding with a private-sector approach. As the Nigerian public sector was hollowed out, hundreds of thousands of Nigerians lost their jobs. The country faced widespread unemployment, devalued currency, and anemic manufacturing and agricultural industries. Lift Above Poverty Organi-

---

* Even though the official era of Structural Adjustment Programs is technically over, these practices are still commonplace today. Over the last several years, Sierra Leone has cut several subsidies on staples like rice and fuel to make payments to the IMF and other creditors, and in a general bid for fiscal responsibility. For example, a 2011 cut in fuel subsidies, done to pay off IMF loans, led to a price increase of 30 percent. Simon Adam, "Sierra Leone Cuts Fuel Subsidy, Prices Jump 30 Pct," Reuters, May 4, 2011, https://www.reuters.com/article/sierraleone-fuel-idAFLDE74319B20110504.

zation, or LAPO, the Nigerian microlender that now has a significant presence in Sierra Leone, was started in 1987 in response to this rising poverty. Its founder, Godwin Ehigiamusoe, envisioned small loans as a way for poor people to start small businesses they would now be forced to rely on, to sustain themselves in the midst of "a sharp increase in the spread and intensity of poverty as a result of the Structural Adjustment Program."

In the face of a skeletal public system, other microlenders began providing basic services. Yunus wrote in *Banker to the Poor* that "in place of social security," Grameen offered its borrowers "shares of successful Grameen companies, non-Grameen companies, and Grameen mutual funds." Recognizing that borrowers' successes could be undermined by poor health care, Grameen also opened a private health insurance scheme, which Yunus hoped would morph "into a strong, competitive, and sustainable pro-people enterprise." Other lending programs offered health care and education alongside loans. Some borrowers said they continued to take out loans primarily to access these programs, a demand that may have spoken more to the scarcity of public resources than to the quality of the microfinance program. BRAC, another Bangladeshi lender, began selling basic medical services to their borrowers, who could use money from their loans to pay for antibiotics and pain medicine. Lindsay Wallace, an economist who helped to support BRAC's work in Uganda while working at the Mastercard Foundation, later found herself wondering: "The government of Uganda has health services, has education services. They're not great, but is this really the right way to get at that problem?" Even though she spent years promoting financial services for the poor, she recognized, "Sometimes you need public solutions. There's a limit to what private provision can do."

* * *

In the 1990s, NGOs, including those focused on microcredit, took off in countries that were somehow "post": post-conflict, post-independence, post-disaster. And, most prominently, post-Communist.

"Civil society"—a broad category that includes trade unions, churches, neighborhood associations, and nongovernmental organizations—was seen as a particularly effective vehicle through which to spread American ideals like the free market and individual liberties in societies emerging from behind the Iron Curtain. Such groups also offered another avenue by which Western governments, the United States chief among them, could fund international programs while circumventing the state.

Jeff Ashe, who had by now left Accion, found himself setting up lending programs in Angola during a proxy conflict of the Cold War that lasted a quarter century. He worked in Yugoslavia, "where everything had been blown to bits" during a protracted conflict that coincided with the breakup of the Soviet-dominated Eastern Bloc. He worked in Bosnia and Herzegovina, where nearly $100 million was reportedly channeled into microfinance institutions from the mid-1990s to the mid-aughts.

Funders hoped the little loans would unleash the entrepreneurial creativity that had been suppressed in state-controlled economies while also demonstrating the power of capital and competitive entrepreneurship in countries that had been dominated by centralized planning—a sort of hearts and minds campaign on behalf of market liberalism, privatizing economies from the ground up. In the mid-1990s, a representative from the Organisation for Economic Co-operation and Development, originally founded after World War II to administer the Marshall Plan, proclaimed, "self-employment is particularly important in the post-Socialist countries as a way of privatizing the economy." In 2002, a bill passed by both houses of Congress noted that it was in the interests of the United States to support microcredit, given that "access to financial services and the development of microenterprise are vital factors in the stable growth of developing countries and in the development of free, open, and equitable international economic systems." More practically, the influx of cash would also help to ease often painful transitions.*

The Grameen Bank also helped to set up lending programs in post-

---

* There is a parallel to the credit union movement here. In the mid-1950s, credit union leaders advocated for adoption of the model around the world. Doing so would prevent the spread of Communism by showing there was an alternative, market-oriented path, just as inclusive of the working class as Communist notions of wealth distribution. NGOs and the UN backed this idea. Mehrsa Baradaran, *How the Other Half Banks: Exclusion, Exploitation, and the Threat to Democracy* (Cambridge, MA: Harvard University Press, 2015), 73.

Communist countries. Meanwhile, at home, Yunus was accused by those on the left of hampering dissent within Bangladesh. In *Banker to the Poor*, Yunus recalls an exchange with a person he simply refers to as a "Communist Professor." "'What you are really doing,'" the professor apparently said, "'is giving little bits of opium to the poor people, so that they won't get involved in any larger political issues. With your micro-nothing-loans, they sleep peacefully and don't make any noise. Their revolutionary zeal cools down. Therefore, Grameen is the enemy of the revolution.'"

As Yunus tells it, there may have been some truth to the critiques from the "Communist Professor" (although Grameen had encouraged its borrowers to become involved in larger political issues, specifically by voting together as a bloc, a practice that was criticized by some as promoting conformity and open to manipulation by politicians, who could garner many votes by swaying just a few Grameen leaders). Many of Grameen's early workers were themselves from poor villages—some were so poor that they relied on their families to sell valuables, or even take out a loan, to pay their way to the interview. Others had been members of a militant leftist group. Yunus writes, "They had wanted to liberate the country with guns and revolution, and now they were walking around those same villages extending micro-loans to the destitute. They just needed a cause to fight for. We channeled their energies toward something more constructive than terrorism."

His was a quiet revolution. His aim wasn't to overthrow capitalism. He wanted to tame it. Years later, he would tell the *Guardian*, "Revolution is no solution. What do you do after the revolution? You have to figure out the purpose of the revolution. You don't want to go back to Communism, that didn't solve any problems."

Small loans were readily deployed in other "post" situations. After the North American Free Trade Agreement was signed, when Mexican farmers struggled to compete with cheap American corn, small loans were offered as an answer. After tsunamis, civil wars, and disease outbreaks, loan offices sprang up alongside field hospitals and refugee camps, offering loans to help survivors and refugees get back on their feet. Yunus helped to pioneer such post-disaster microfinance by offering loans in response to the 1972 famine in Bangladesh.* Then, in the wake of severe flooding in Bangladesh in the 1980s, Yunus and Grameen provided "disaster loans" alongside emergency food and water to kick-start "survival schemes" people could create themselves. Yunus reasoned, "Because national and international relief is usually late and inadequate, the only way that the victims can get through the pain, suffering, and devastation is by rebuilding what they had."

The approach was later copied in Sierra Leone. As its decade-long civil war came to a close in 2002, the government, as well as private organizations, were "trying to come up with projects that tried to address some sort of income for people who have been affected by the war," recalls Archibald Shodeke, who has worked in Sierra Leonean microfinance for decades and was the head of the Sierra Leone Association of Microfinance Institutions when we met in 2019. Shodeke says even some former child soldiers were offered loans, a way to encourage them to give up arms and reintegrate into society, one tiny enterprise at a time.†

* * *

The expansion in microlending in the 1980s and 1990s was remarkable. In 1985, in Bangladesh, there were just thirteen organizations working in small lending. Five years later, in 1990, there were roughly four times that. By 1995, the number topped three hundred. By this time, Grameen had reportedly opened a thousand branches in thirty-four thousand villages across Bangladesh, lending $370 million. Similar programs had opened in countries as varied as Bhutan, Zimbabwe, and Albania. Triumphant reports emerged: of mothers paying for their children's education with business profits; of women, newly empowered, pushing back against their husbands; of borrowers maintaining small enterprises that kept them afloat. That was true even in America. In the late 1990s, an article published by the Grameen

---

* A similar approach was undertaken by two other Bangladeshi organizations founded around the same time: BRAC was launched in 1972, initially to support famine survivors but soon operating a variety of programs, including microcredit, and the Association for Social Advancement, or ASA, was founded in 1978 to support communities still struggling from the independence war through a "bottom-up" approach, later turning to lending.

† There are many other examples. Small loans were offered in Sri Lanka after the 2004 tsunami and again as a twenty-five-year civil conflict ended in 2009. They were offered in Nepal after the 2015 earthquake and then again in Sierra Leone after the 2013–2015 West Africa Ebola outbreak.

Trust argued, "Microenterprise is now one of the most cost-effective job creation strategies in the US. Studies show that poor Americans can be launched into self-employment at a cost of less than $6,000 per job created."

Many of these efforts were supported by USAID. Equal parts convinced, through Ashe's research, coerced, through advocacy efforts like those led by Sam Daley-Harris and RESULTS, and beholden to a Congress that wanted to be seen as pro-poor, pro-women, and pro-business, the agency pumped hundreds of millions of dollars into microlending programs.* By the early 1990s, USAID considered itself at the "forefront" of the growing microlending movement. A 1990 report claimed that, thanks to their work, "poor people throughout the developing world"—who ran "vegetable stands, tea shops, bicycle repair shops, tailors, furniture makers, handicraft artisans, bakeries"—"could now create jobs and income for themselves."

The World Bank also became a strong advocate. In 1995, its president, James D. Wolfensohn, spoke with Muhammad Yunus in a meeting arranged by Margaret "Peggy" Dulany Rockefeller, philanthropist, great-granddaughter of Standard Oil cofounder John D. Rockefeller and daughter of investment banker David Rockefeller, the former chairman and CEO of Chase Manhattan Bank. Dulany was an early microcredit supporter. She had spent some of her college years in the favelas of Brazil, and then met Michaela Walsh of Women's World Banking. Later, the Rockefeller Foundation contributed to Grameen's expansion through the Grameen Trust.

After meeting with Yunus, Wolfensohn declared himself "personally, absolutely, committed to this activity." A year later, the World Bank facilitated a group of donors who would advise and help to fund microcredit programs, called the Consultative Group to Assist the Poorest—the "poorest" language nodding to the success of advocacy bent on getting loans to "the poorest of the poor."

Now that microlending had firmly caught on, aid agencies scrambled to expand it.† To reach more borrowers more quickly, growing lending

---

* In 2003, just a decade after RESULTS initially stumbled upon microfinance, President George W. Bush signed the Microenterprise Enhancement Act into law, which set aside nearly $400 million for USAID to fund small businesses. In part thanks to the continued advocacy of RESULTS, the law specifically focused on poor people and women. Sam Daley-Harris, *Reclaiming Our Democracy: Healing the Break Between People and Government* (Philadelphia: Camino Books, 1994), 248.

† There were creative ideas as to how—one person suggested "inclusion of micro-financing in the

programs homed in on urban areas. Doing so allowed for quick growth. In hyperconcentrated cities and slums, hundreds of borrowers could be reached by one loan officer, whereas in rural areas, where people lived farther apart, staff members had to travel miles, sometimes by foot, just to reach a handful of borrowers. Even though agriculture still made up the bulk of both hours invested and income for poor people around the world, farmers were now mostly neglected. Those who wanted loans were forced to rebrand themselves as entrepreneurs.

To capitalize on the funding frenzy, and responding to the dogma that successful microborrowers could take care of their own basic needs, organizations that had offered a multitude of services turned *to* microcredit and *away* from other programs. To give just one example of the shift: In 1991, ASA, or the Association for Social Advancement, a Bangladeshi organization that is now one of the largest microfinance companies in the world, with operations in Sierra Leone, discarded a broad focus on "social development" that had been central to its mission since its founding in 1978. It would now focus *solely* on microcredit. This change, ASA argued, would reduce donor dependence, increase the number of poor people they could reach, and help the organization become self-sufficient.

The hard turn to a lending-only approach was curious given that some of the most successful early small-scale microcredit programs *had* offered additional services, such as market analyses and training, auxiliaries they saw as essential to their success. Even Dale Adams and his "Spring Review" colleagues had suggested this more robust package; early studies led by Jeff Ashe suggested the same. But offering health care or education or even training was far more expensive than just getting loans out the door. And given that credit would now, apparently, help people lift themselves out of poverty, there seemed to be less of a need for more comprehensive services. Swept up by the microcredit craze, organizations intent on lending risked becoming blind to everything else. "If all you can do is lend money," one American who worked in microcredit in the 1990s observed, "then it starts to look like everyone needs a loan."

---

school curriculum." "Report on the Southern Africa Region Microcredit Summit (SARMS)," Lusaka, Zambia, September 22–25, 1998.

The Station

Old Post, Koidu, Kono, Eastern Sierra Leone

The beginning of the rains, early summer 2019

It felt uncomfortable to admit it, but a few months into paying down her LAPO debt, Abbie found she had been feeling a strange sort of nostalgia for "Ebola time," as she called it. It was awful, a time she would never ask God to return her to. But at least there was money back then.

The Kono economy always worked as a pyramid. The big people were on top—the diamond sellers, the chiefs, the ones with land or shops—with everyone else below, supplying whatever the big people needed: gold, diamonds, produce, labor. A parallel, sometimes intertwined pyramid had formed during the 2014–2016 outbreak, fueled by donors' funds. At the top were the medical workers and managers, some foreign, some Sierra Leonean. Next, those who supported them at work—drivers, community health workers, cleaners like Abbie's husband—and below that those who helped them at home—cooks, launderers, more cleaners. And then, finally, those who supported everyone: motorcycle riders, sex workers, construction workers, vegetable sellers. Thousands of people were getting sick and dying. That created a lot of work.

Soon after the country was declared Ebola-free,* it was as if someone turned on a vacuum; all the money was sucked out. Formal jobs and the informal ones that sprang up beside them were erased. Things felt especially bad during each rainy season, when roads filled with water and roofs leaked. Work was harder to come by then. Big construction projects halted, mining sputtered, motorbike riders picked up fewer rides, market

---

* On March 17, 2016. "2014–2016 Ebola Outbreak in West Africa," CDC, March 17, 2020, https://www.cdc.gov/vhf/ebola/history/2014-2016-outbreak/index.html.

stalls were less crowded. Money slowed. People turned inward, planning for what they would do during the dries.

Abbie quickly found that her business idea—buying shoes in Koidu and selling them in Sawula—didn't work with LAPO's rigid schedule. It could take days to get to Sawula and back, days in which Abbie was spending money, not making it: $6 for the bike ride to the village, $1 left at home with her young daughter for lunch, a bit of cash for her own food. Abbie came back to Koidu having spent about $10 just on travel. When she did make sales, she found that some customers said they'd take the shoes now and pay later. Others would suggest a simple swap, a pair of shoes for some local rice or palm oil.

Abbie trusted this cycle of trade and debt, built on memory, trust, a bit of pestering, and a lot "left up to God." It was what allowed her to get by when she didn't have much, to eat when there was no money to pay for a meal, and then to pay it forward when she was fleetingly, relatively, flush.

But it wasn't going to get her the $3.50 each week that LAPO required for six months. When she asked if she could pay one of her installments just a little later, Abbie learned an unfortunate detail of the loan contract. "If you are a day late paying back, they charge you 50 cents"—they'd knock that fee straight off the $10 savings she had deposited when she signed the contract. Halfway through the loan, Abbie estimated she had already lost about half of her savings to these late fees.

To make extra cash, Abbie took a job cooking and cleaning for two women at a nearby neighborhood dominated by Gambian diamond sellers that was comparatively prosperous thanks to generations of relative wealth. After a month of laundering and scrubbing, sweeping, and cooking, Abbie made $6, then got a raise up to $10 a month. She felt insulted by the tiny money and consistent harassment from her boss, who gave commands into the evening. Exhausted and disgruntled, she quit.

To cut costs, Abbie sent two of her kids back to Sawula to stay with her mom—she figured they were still young enough that inadequate schooling wouldn't really matter. She would have sent them to her beloved auntie Finda, the soap seller, but she hadn't heard from her lately and wasn't sure where she was. Princess, her eldest daughter, stayed with Abbie in Old Post.

Abbie's neighbor Ramatu was also having a rough go of it. When the water ran through Old Post, forming human-sized puddles, she put off going to the market to buy ginger and sugar for her homemade ginger beer. Drinks weren't selling now that temperatures had cooled, although even when it was warm, sales weren't flying. Her fridge turned on only sporadically, when electricity happened to come, usually in the evening, around six or seven. It stayed a few hours, long enough to get the drinks cold, but not to keep them that way until the next morning. She found lukewarm ginger beer was only so lucrative. Ramatu estimated that twenty liters of ginger beer netted 80 cents in profits.

The 50 cents or $1 she made each day went to two things: to food—30 cents for lunch to her daughter, Janet, whatever left over for dinner—and LAPO. "My life is really stressful!" she complained. "I'm not going to lie. When you have to pay money like that, you'll be worried sick."

* * *

The women of Kochende started to offer little acts of resistance to the LAPO loan officers. When they came to Ramatu's house for repayment, she kept them waiting for hours with promises that this woman or that one just needed a few extra minutes, she'd be right over, or she could just pop by tomorrow to bring the cash? The opposition was not well received. "They harassed us so much!" says Ramatu. "Every day it was a big fight. They stood right there on the front stoop and yelled, 'Where's our money? Where's our money?' Even if you're in the labor room, they'll come and ask for money."

Ramatu had intimate knowledge that being in an expectant state didn't act as an acceptable excuse, because she was about seven months pregnant. She told her friend, the farmer man who lived on the outskirts of town, that the baby was his, and although he was skeptical, he also knew it was possible and very much desired it to be true. Maybe with a baby—another, more permanent link—she would finally get serious and accept his offer.

Ramatu, stressed and desiring stability, had thought more about marriage. The farmer had a big, four-bedroom house and land so large it took about half an hour to walk its perimeter. He had pigs, beans, corn, and cassava and had built an impressive flower garden that ringed his expansive property. In the mornings, bright red birds came to feed on flower nectar. You could see the stars at night.

The farm would become her domain, he promised. She could even open a restaurant there.

Ramatu thought about the space, the fresh water from the well, the private bathroom. But she paused when she thought about the silence, fearing she would have far too much of it. There was no electricity out there—the lines didn't reach that far—which meant a restaurant wasn't really an option. Her mother wouldn't be nearby, nor her brothers and friends. There would be no hours of conversation with whoever happened to pass by, because out there, no one ever did. She knew the farmer could go days without seeing anyone.

And then there were more practical questions. How would the kids get to school? Where would she braid her hair? If she did want to sell anything, who would buy? Although his support was unsteady, she much preferred their current setup to marriage. At least she now had freedom, even if that meant she was often annoyed, swatting away his accusations of infidelity and his demands on her time. She knew she could always go to him in a pinch and he'd give whatever he could. Were they to make it official, she worried that anything she wanted—any money she wanted to spend, any person she wanted to visit—would be at his discretion.

Besides, she was becoming skeptical that the farmer man offered any real stability. Over the years, she had watched his body grow leaner, the result of thinned social connections. The beans and cassava he tended had never been enough to feed him, let alone her. The longer his brother stayed in America, the less the man remembered Sierra Leone and the less money he sent over. He had become so disconnected that he even wanted to be buried over there, a decision Ramatu found both ludicrous and telling: this was clearly not a man to depend upon. The farmer had taken to reading philosophy and had started to preach a certain type of nonattachment amid his brother's indifference, a practice he gleaned from Kahlil Gibran's *The Prophet* and Rastafarianism. Ramatu, who rolled her eyes at his wandering lectures, had learned nonattachment simply by living. She had an innate sense that material security was fleeting. You cobble together what you can, from wherever you can. But you never put too much stock in any one possibility.

So she stayed put in Old Post, developing a simple ritual for loan collection days. "I would just go to someone else's house to hide for a few hours."

* * *

Ramatu had missed a few consecutive payments when she heard the knock. The loan officer was at her door a few days earlier than expected, not in the morning as usual but in the middle of the day. A police officer stood by his side.

Ramatu was still in her lapa, not yet dressed for the day. She threw on some clothes and went to the LAPO office with her escorts. The manager demanded the money. Ramatu offered the straightest, truest answer she could think of: "I told him if I had it, I would pay it." He snapped that she was disrespectful talking like that, warned that what she was doing was wrong. Taking someone's money when you knew you couldn't pay it back was criminal in Sierra Leone, a type of "fraudulent conversion" originally outlined in a British law then woven into the country's legal system when it was a colony. She had agreed to repay, it was right there in the contract, and now she was late. Years later, Ramatu sounded both worn down and bored when she recalled the conversation. "Oh, they yelled at me so much that day!" She yawned. "All this yelling, yelling." The police officer said there was no choice; she would have to go to the station to make a statement.

Once there, she called her friend the farmer, begging for the $5 the officer said was needed for bail. She then tipped the officer another $2 to get the police to stop bothering her while she figured out a plan to repay the loan.

Several weeks later Ramatu was holding her newborn, Mark, at his first postnatal checkup at the hospital when her phone rang. Her mom was now at the police station. LAPO said she owed $12 and that she would have to stay there until she paid. Ramatu went home to grab her DVDs, sold just about but not quite enough for the $5 bail, then called the farmer again. The man gave the money, got her mom out, then yelled at Ramatu. "He said we should never take [a loan] again, because this money is so stressful. He said, 'Look at the profits they make from you! It's too much.' He told me never to go there again."

CHAPTER 7

———

New Goals

In February 1986, Muhammad Yunus had lunch at the Four Seasons Hotel in Washington, DC, with a couple from Little Rock, Arkansas, who were becoming famous.

Hillary Clinton had heard of Yunus through a friend who had worked for an American organization in Bangladesh and now worked with South Shore Bank in Chicago. The bank operated in the city's mostly poor, mostly African American South Side, which had been purposefully underdeveloped through policies like redlining, through which African American families were excluded from lending programs. South Shore, in response, explicitly gave loans to small businesses and homeowners that had been shut out from credit.

The Clintons were big fans of South Shore: a few years later, Bill would call it "the most important bank in America." And, by the time of the lunch, South Shore was already a fan of Yunus: the bank had helped Yunus formalize Grameen in its earliest days and net early funding. Two of South Shore's leaders thought the Clintons, in their quest for economic and policy alternatives, should meet Yunus, too.

Over the hour-and-a-half lunch, the couple from Arkansas and the banker from Bangladesh swapped notes. As both sides tell it, they got on like a house on fire. Although Bill's presidential bid was still a few years off, the two-term governor of Arkansas was thinking nationally, sharpening his vision for a reformed sort of welfare, one that would spark private investment in neighborhoods he would later call "economic basket cases." Like Reagan, he wanted to encourage people to forge their own way. He thought Grameenesque programs would work in the United States, specifically in his home state of Arkansas, one of the poorest in the country. Yunus was also convinced that "a Grameen-type credit program" could work "in a pocket of poverty amidst prosperity." As inequality increased, and with a nearly 10 percent unemployment rate in the early 1980s, self-employment would provide another option to poor Americans. Access to credit, Yunus proclaimed, would allow for that self-employment to be "limitless."

* * *

In September 1995, nearly ten years after the Four Seasons lunch meeting and nearly two years after Bill Clinton was sworn in as the forty-second president of the United States, the UN hosted the Fourth World Conference on Women in Beijing, China. It had been two decades since the first such meeting, in Mexico City, when dire statistics about women's inequality prompted Michaela Walsh, Esther Ocloo, and Ela Bhatt to help launch Women's World Banking. As they had twenty years earlier, attendees in Beijing learned about gender inequalities in workplaces and homes and society, inequalities that persisted despite dramatic pledges from the first conference. But this time, calls for change did not come solely from UN diplomats, NGO workers, and academics. They came from the First Lady of the United States.

The lunch conversation between Yunus and the Clintons had sparked a lasting warmth. At different times throughout Bill and Hillary's ascendancy to the White House, the couple nodded to their friendship with Yunus. The relationship demonstrated their commitment to women, to globalism, to development, to anti-poverty work, to grassroots finance— to a government more intent on encouraging entrepreneurial wherewithal than on expanding "dependency programs" (slimming such programs had remained an American obsession even after Reagan left office). As for Yunus, the connection to the Clintons would soon offer him clout and an indispensable network, helping to make him a household name.

During her husband's presidential campaign, Hillary Clinton had fought depictions of her as a "firebrand feminist." She was an easy target, not least because she was the first First Lady to have a career before taking up the position. She was widely seen as smarter than Bill, more ambitious, the breadwinner, and the true policy strategist. Her influence was so pronounced that the couple were sometimes referred to as "Billary Clinton."

But in Beijing, she leaned hard into feminism. On the second day of the conference, donning a light pink blazer and matching skirt, white shirt, and gold necklace, her shoulder-length blond hair loose and lightly curled, Hillary stood behind a lectern and proclaimed, "If there is one message that echoes forth from this conference, let it be that human rights are women's rights and women's rights are human rights." The phrase "women's rights are human rights" was then included in the conference declaration and would soon become a key rallying cry in feminist movements. (It had, in fact, been uttered by feminists for decades before Clinton said it, but now gained more mass appeal.)

Clinton offered another solution to gender inequality: credit. Back in 1975, at the first UN Women's Conference, there had been no Grameen, no FINCA, no Women's World Banking. Accion existed but was only just starting its lending efforts. The Self-Employed Women's Association, in Gujarat, India, had also only just been established.

But now, twenty years later, thousands of microcredit programs had opened, offering a ready-made solution to women's financial and social exclusion. "Credit" was mentioned twice in Clinton's speech, "loans" once, "business" once. (Together, education and schools received six mentions.) Clinton said that credit was one of the things that "mattered most" to women and their families, alongside health care. Dozens of microcredit programs, she said, had already shown to be "highly successful."

This theme ran throughout the conference. The United Nations Development Fund for Women hosted a discussion on credit for women, which Clinton attended. The International Coalition on Women and Credit put together a booth—a "Credit Corner"—"to show that poor women are bankable and to make sure that the Beijing platform for action include[s] access to finance for women as a priority." Nancy Barry, then president of Women's World Banking, and Muhammad Yunus hosted discussions at the Credit Corner. When CNN's Judy Woodruff stopped by to interview them, all three sat on bright yellow cushions on the floor.

Hillary Clinton spoke at the Credit Corner, too, recounting the time she visited the Self-Employed Women's Association. The borrowers in Gujarat told her they could now "buy their own vegetable carts. They could buy their own thread and materials so that they could make income for themselves and their families." Clinton had also visited Grameen, about six months before the Beijing conference. TV clips from the visit show Hillary and her daughter, Chelsea, both donning wide-brimmed hats, welcomed by little girls with stern faces who offered salutes. They met with potters, brickmakers, cloth makers. Clinton told the borrowers, "It's important for women to earn their own income, even when they are married," offering her own experience as proof: she had worked from age thirteen and years later earned more than her husband. Yunus, then fifty-four and wearing oversized sunglasses, stayed by their side throughout. Afterward, Clinton invited journalists who had been on the trip to lunch with Yunus and her at the Oval Room, a Washington "power dining destination" just a few blocks from the White House.

By the end of the Beijing proceedings, about a third of the conference's "platform for action" focused on "women's economic participation and power." To attain the human rights Clinton was demanding, financial equity would need to be realized, too. "If women have a chance to work and earn as full and equal partners in society, their families will flourish," she said in Beijing. "And when families flourish, communities and nations will flourish."

* * *

The Beijing affair was just one of a half dozen grand global conferences that brought together dignitaries, nonprofits, journalists, lawyers, and corporations in the 1990s. A global optimism was promoted by spectacular pledges, perhaps most notably the UN's Millennium Development Goals. Officially launched in 2000, governments together pledged to "eradicate extreme poverty and hunger," "achieve universal primary education," and "ensure environmental sustainability," among other things, within just fifteen years.* Celebrities, politicians, and philanthropists demonstrated

---

* None of these goals were achieved.

their political will through multimillion-dollar commitments and spectacular endorsements.

John Hatch of FINCA, who was now a board member of trim-tabbing RESULTS, suggested that amid these aspirational convenings, there may as well be one for microcredit. Surely the anti-poverty solution that the First Lady had pitched on the world stage in Beijing should have its own conference, too.

RESULTS' Sam Daley-Harris had remained a fervent supporter of Yunus and microcredit since seeing the Nazma video that spurred his mid-1980s congressional advocacy. With his boundless enthusiasm and single-minded focus, he, Yunus, and Hatch decided to pull together a "microcredit summit." Daley-Harris would lead in organizing. Hatch would bring his on-the-ground experience. Yunus, now also a RESULTS board member and very nearly very famous, was "the star of the show, the big draw," says Daley-Harris. Hillary Clinton agreed to be honorary cochair, a position clinched, in part, thanks to Yunus's connection to the Clintons, as well as relationships between RESULTS volunteers and Hillary's staffers.

Every summit had lofty aspirations.* Yunus and Hatch went back and forth on the goals of the microcredit conference. Yunus thought getting small loans into the hands of 200 million people by 2005 was feasible, even though at the year of the proposed Summit—1997—only around 13 million people had taken out the tiny loans, including 2.3 million from Grameen. Hatch wasn't sure that reaching 175 million people in less than a decade was feasible.

So they settled on a less ambitious, though still eye-popping target: extending credit to one hundred million of the world's poorest families, particularly the women in those families, by 2005. (The focus on "families" not "individuals" was a narrative flourish that softened the goal, given that many families consist of half a dozen people, while still aiming for the headline-catching "100 million." It also subtly allowed for men to be included, even though the rhetorical focus was still on women.) Achiev-

* Or, in the case of the UN Women's Summit in Beijing, many: "Eliminate all forms of discrimination against women and the girl child"; "Encourage men to participate fully in all actions towards equality"; "Promote women's economic independence." "Beijing Declaration and Platform for Action: Beijing+5 Political Declaration and Outcome," UN Women, 1995, https://www.unwomen.org/sites/default/files/Headquarters/Attachments/Sections/CSW/PFA_E_Final_WEB.pdf.

ing these numbers would require a nearly 40 percent annual growth rate in lending.

Daley-Harris, of course, was adamant about the "poorest" language. A decade after RESULTS' congressional advocacy, he remained incensed that USAID didn't think loans to the very poor would end poverty. In the lead-up to the microcredit conference, Daley-Harris was again warned that loans could exert "no impact" on the lives of the very poor, instead "only adding a debt burden." Even some staffers at Accion, which had backed RESULTS efforts in Congress a decade earlier, thought the poorest were not ideal customers.

But with Hatch and Yunus's blessing, the goal stuck. Microloans not only *could* go to the poor. Now, they *should* go the poor. With Hillary Clinton as honorary summit cochair, the goal implicitly received the blessing of the highest office in America.

* * *

In February 1997, twenty-nine hundred people from 137 countries gathered in Washington, DC, for the world's first ever Microcredit Summit. Hillary Clinton kicked off the festivities with a keynote speech, this time wearing a teal suit, her hair a bit shorter. "Although it is called 'microcredit,'" Clinton said, "this is a macro idea . . . microcredit is an invaluable tool in alleviating poverty, promoting self-sufficiency, and stimulating economic activity in some of the world's most destitute and disadvantaged communities." Yunus, in a beige suit and large glasses, took inspiration from Hillary's Beijing speech and her focus on "rights": Women's rights were not just human rights, to be *actualized* through the provision of credit. Yunus was more direct. "Credit," he claimed, "is a human right."

The usual players attended the Summit: Accion, Ela Bhatt of the Self-Employed Women's Association, Women's World Banking, dignitaries, feminists, and leaders of the world's largest development institutions. Throughout the two-day meeting, ideas and statements that had been polished over decades were reiterated, offered as fact: Women *must* be the poorest of the poor, since they were often asset-less, credit-less, and land-less. Given that they were more likely to pay off their loans than men, it was not only morally right to lend to them but also financially prudent. Businesses funded through small loans would allow these women to unbind themselves from tradition, oppression, and economic marginalization. And, with microcredit, incomes around the world could increase. Catholic Relief Services, an international NGO based in Baltimore, told delegates that 97 percent of Thai borrowers in one project saw their incomes rise by up to $200 a year. John Hatch's FINCA claimed that the weekly incomes of El Salvadoran borrowers increased by 145 percent.

And then, alongside microcredit stalwarts, there were the more unusual participants. The Chase Manhattan Foundation and J.P. Morgan Foundation were listed as funders of the event. Citigroup, which had given a loan to Accion back in the 1980s, joined the World Bank, the Self-Employed Women's Association, and Women's World Banking on the summit's organizing committee. At discussions and plenaries, representatives from Mobil Corporation, Monsanto, and Bank One Corporation sat alongside those from the U.S. Treasury, the Inter-American Development Bank, UNICEF, Save the Children, and the International Organization for Migration.

These atypical participants were driven to attend the summit by a few priorities. One was reputational. Journalists, activists, academics, and unions had stoked growing concerns about the now-global reach of corporations and their impact on the environment, working conditions, and labor movements. Globalization itself, as well as global TV and the rise of international NGOs, had prompted Americans to learn something of the broader world. They learned, maybe for the first time, of the factories in which their cheap clothes were made, the working conditions on the plantations on which their coffee was grown, the workshops in which their children's toys were manufactured. Microfinance exploded as global inequality increased, both across countries and within countries. For those doing relatively well and concerned about this schism, tiny loans seemed like a way to connect with and help an individual on the other side of the divide: a little glimmer into someone else's life, a way to extend a hand, even briefly.

Companies were also keen to show their concern about poverty and inequality. The 1980s had marked the era of "shareholder primacy," as it was coined by conservative free market economist Milton Friedman, who suggested that businesses should only be concerned with profits and not with larger social goals. By the late 1990s, though, corporate social responsibility was getting some emphasis, too. To shore up their reputations, companies tried to demonstrate that they were not just global *businesses*— they were global *citizens*. Throughout the 1990s and into the new millennium, Bill Clinton promoted the notion that businesses could do good while doing well, as did Kofi Annan, the secretary-general of the UN. It was no longer simply an option for a company to consider exhibiting ethics alongside a commitment to the bottom line. Now they at least had to be perceived to be doing both.

It turned out that saving the world also, conveniently, meant saving business. Speaking at the Microcredit Summit, Robert Shapiro, the chairman of Monsanto—a company most famous for creating the pesticide Roundup—warned that increasing inequality would lead to violence and chaos and would "be calamitous to all human activity, and not least for that particular human activity we call productive work." "Poverty is not only a moral tragedy," Shapiro continued. "It is also a tragic waste of the fundamental human potential to produce and contribute." Extending credit to one hundred million poor families would enable those families to afford food, clothing, health care, education—and Monsanto's products. "As families emerge from poverty," Shapiro predicted, "they can become our customers, our suppliers, our partners."*

At the same time, Microcredit Summit delegates hoped that extending the arms of capitalism to poor women could tame its worst excesses. "Women can play the lead in transforming businesses," proclaimed the executive director of the UN's agency for women, "so that [businesses] can become ecologically and socially accountable."†

There was another reason that banks and multinational corporations

---

* Three years later, an article in the newsletter of the Grameen Trust, echoed Monsanto's prediction: not only would the "world economy . . . immensely benefit if the world's poor can leave poverty behind and bring their productivity and creativity into the marketplace as producers," they would also bring "their newly acquired purchasing power to the market as consumers." *Grameen Dialogue*, no. 41, January 2000.

† An internal review of the Microcredit Summit noted that one of its biggest successes was engendering the idea that if capitalism was "invigorate[d]," it could "transform the nature of gender and class roles as well as grassroots economies in a period of rapid globalization." "Microcredit Summit Report," Microcredit Summit Campaign.

attended the 1997 Microcredit Summit, this one less semantic. If one hundred million poor families were to be offered microcredit, an additional *ninety million* poor families would need to be reached in less than a decade—again, a 40 percent growth rate *each year*. This required a massive global effort—and an estimated $21 billion. Donors like USAID were willing to foot some of that bill but made it clear that $21 billion was far beyond what they were willing to spend. And whatever donors did give couldn't be counted on in the long term; who knew what would happen with turbulent budgets and political appetites. If the summit wanted to reach the one hundred million goal, they would need to find other money.

So another goal was added. Not just to reach the poorest and to empower women but to build institutions that were "financially self-sufficient"—those that could run on their own, without injections of donor cash.

For decades now, microcredit institutions had claimed this would be easy—it was, in fact, one of their key selling points. If interest rates were high enough, and if borrowers' savings were plugged back into lending, the FINCAs and Accions and Grameens of the world could easily pay for themselves.

The problem was that, in most cases, this promise hadn't borne out. Even by the mid-1990s, most microcredit institutions still relied on donor funds. By 1997, the year of the Microcredit Summit, only 26 of the 481 microcredit organizations that received USAID funding were able to cover their lending and operational expenses. While the public narrative was that Grameen was owned by its members, with their savings used to sustain operations and facilitate further lending—a narrative that brought Yunus much praise, with its suggestion of female empowerment and grassroots capitalism—the Central Bank of Bangladesh retained a significant stake in Grameen, although Yunus, who generally bemoaned government intervention, downplayed the bank's role. (As one academic wrote, Yunus was happy to stress Grameen's "independence from 'the establishment' rather than their connections to it," rarely pointing out that Grameen was only able to rely on member savings thanks to a special act of parliament that allowed the bank to take deposits from very poor people, an exception in Bangladesh.) In its first two decades, over

$150 million in soft loans and grants had propped up the Grameen Bank, which relied on funds not only from the central bank but also on other subsidized funding into the mid-1990s.

Delegates at the 1997 Microcredit Summit wrung their hands about the fundamental quandary that arose from preaching a private-sector approach while continuing to rely heavily on donors and governments. They brainstormed ways to facilitate a shift. Lenders could raise interest rates, which many had already been doing; even though sustainability hadn't borne out in practice, by the late 1990s, an emphasis on raising interest rates to cover costs fully permeated the sector, a stance that was reiterated at the summit. (At a follow-up meeting a year later, a delegate from Mozambique referred to borrowers' willingness to pay high costs as the "Ten P's": "Poor People Progress from Poverty to Prosperity and Power, Provided they are Prepared to Pay the Price.") Microcredit lenders could focus more on savings to help cover costs and use the money to lend to others, something that FINCA and Grameen had focused on for decades and that other Bangladeshi institutions had started to do. But savings would only go so far. Because the borrowers were so poor, the funds wouldn't be enough to keep institutions afloat, a predicament that would be more acute as the institutions grew. Some advocated for offering other financial services: savings alongside or instead of loans, insurance alongside credit, training alongside a bank account—a more expansive umbrella increasingly called "microfinance" that Yunus fought against. A narrow focus on credit, he claimed, should form the linchpin of a poor person's eventual success. Everything else was superfluous and threatened to distract.*

Delegates did agree that lenders had to tap into much more plentiful private funding. They needed to borrow from banks, seek out private investors, maybe even sell shares on the capital markets to raise extra cash. With such spectacular ambitions, this was not the time for business as usual.

It seemed banks and private investors would be happy to oblige. Considering above-market interest rates and the promise of 98 percent

---

* Some had wanted the conference to be called the *Microfinance* Summit, to denote this broader package. Instead, in a nod to Yunus's strict, purist approach, it was called the Microcredit Summit.

repayment rates that were now expected in microfinance, it looked as though there was a significant, healthy market here. Private financiers, eager to show their care for the global poor, could do so while making a wise investment. Daley-Harris was aware of the potential contradiction in extending loans to very poor people and having those loans be backed by Wall Street. But he felt it was worth it if it meant that millions more poor people would be able to take out credit. "It's not like I sold my soul," he told me. This was a question of pragmatism, not principles. Daley-Harris was confident the good that would be done through expanding access to microfinance would far outweigh any risks.

At the closing plenary, John Hatch of FINCA welcomed the ambition of self-sustaining, privately financed programs for the poor. That money would help lenders like FINCA to grow. "Our microcredit movement," he said, "will someday embrace every nation of the planet." Images of a group of Indian borrowers from the Self-Employed Women's Association appeared on a large screen. They sang "We Shall Overcome" in Gujrati, joined by an in-person gospel choir who sang along in English. "The people at the Microcredit Summit, all 2,900 of them, were standing, holding hands, and singing with the choir," recalls Sam Daley-Harris. "It was quite a moment." Bill Burris, then senior vice president of Accion, called the summit a "truly historic occasion and there is no doubt in my mind that we will all look back to this moment as a watershed for the microenterprise movement worldwide."

Traffic Fines

Freetown, Sierra Leone

Mid-2021

AMINATA LIKED TO HEAR THE HUM OF HER FRIDGE. SHE FOUND THE sound calming. With the yogurt inside, she thought of it as a freshly sown field. From it, she hoped she would grow.

But the soothing noise was sporadic. When the electricity came, it came in waves, sometimes rushing and steady, sometimes choppy and small, turning the hum into more of a cat's sneeze or a weak rattling cough. Whenever there was light, Aminata made a habit of turning up the fridge to the coldest setting, hoping to freeze everything to immobility. Its contents could then slowly melt but remain unspoiled whenever the current was inevitably cut again.

Without its murmur, Aminata heard every sound in Two Taps. On this day, her older neighbor Grandpa was playing his favorite Congolese music, tin-canny on his little battery-powered radio, while frying fish. She could hear the sizzle and pop of the flesh hitting the oil. Grandpa's daughter plucked laundry off their shared line while chatting to the old man. Each item she pulled down made a soft rubbing noise, twine against fabric.

"It's too loud," Aminata muttered. "I like a quiet place." The only sound that didn't seem to bother her was the sound of her cousin Mommy's voice, curtly greeting those who passed from her spot on the porch.

Aminata was in a mood. It wasn't just the lack of electricity. Over the last few weeks, she had received a steady stream of calls from relatives in Pendembu, saying they needed money. Aminata was sympathetic. She knew about the boredom, the lack of education, the finicky harvests back home. But she also, in a way, thought life there was easier. In Pendembu, she had relied on her mother's rice and beans and local palm oil as cooking staples. In Freetown, she had to buy everything. Each meal could cost $7, almost triple what Aminata made each day from her yogurt sales. If they skimped a bit, the family could make a pot of stew last two days, bridged by a little bit of bread and tea in the morning. On one of the calls from home, when a relative implored for a visit from Aminata or at least a bit of money to be sent to Pendembu, Aminata found herself snapping back, "Everything is tight for us now."

As soon as she hung up she got a call from her husband, Idrissa. He was at the police station. The normally calculated man had made the mistake of pulling over in a busy roundabout in the rich part of town, where airy supermarkets were stocked with products from Lebanon and the UK, where foreign consultants tasked with fixing the country's education and health care ate salads and drank smoothies in air-conditioned restaurants. The neighborhood was full of money, which meant everyone was looking for an opportunity; a white SUV stamped with an NGO logo, illegally parked, was irresistible to the police officer who was stationed just around the corner. As soon as Idrissa pulled over, the officer rapped on the driver-side glass, gruffly and gleefully pointing out that he had parked illegally and moreover that the vehicle's license plates had expired. A violation of the law, he said, one that could land a person in prison. Even though Idrissa didn't own the vehicle, as the driver, he was apparently responsible—a problem that could easily be resolved, the officer explained, if he offered $80. If not, they'd confiscate his license, a devastating prospect. Without it, he couldn't drive. He'd lose his $150 a month salary. Until he had his $80, the officer explained he would need to "hold" Idrissa's license in the meantime, just in case.

When she heard the news, Aminata was incensed. "If you're a driver, your license is your weapon," she exclaimed. "Without it, you don't have anything. Nothing! What can you do without a license?"

But she was also terrified. She had seen what a tangle with the police could do to a person. Years ago, she had visited her uncle at Pademba Road. The old man had been locked up for owing $700. The country's main prison, located in the loud, sweaty heart of Freetown, was grossly overcrowded. It was built over a century earlier to house three hundred people, but by the time Aminata visited her uncle, over one thousand were inside. Inmates slept head to foot in hot, windowless cells. Prisoners were lucky if they got one thin meal a day. Fights broke out regularly, as did diseases, from diarrhea to tuberculosis. Aminata had bribed the guards to let her bring a pot of soup inside. She sat with the thin, stooped man while he ate. She found the whole thing so horrible that she never went back.

With her own loan now over her head, Aminata worried about whether she'd be taken to the police, too. She had seen it happen to her neighbor Panneh, who was visited by the police right after Aminata moved in with Idrissa. The woman was about Aminata's age, but rounder and rougher, with short hair and a tattoo of her own name in a heart on her arm. She had taken out a few microfinance loans, from a few different places. In total, Panneh owed around $500. She had been able to pay about half off before she realized she was pregnant. When her repayments stopped, the police took her to the nearby station—to "negotiate," they said. The officers told her she could go home for the evening and come back with the money the next morning—all of it, no more of this paying off little by little with weekly payments. Instead, Panneh went to her family's village for six months, waiting for the whole thing to calm down. When she came back to Two Taps, now visibly pregnant, her boyfriend left her, claiming she must have acquired the belly while she was gone.

Aminata had taken to repeating Panneh's story like it was some desperate mix of a curse, a warning, and a prayer. "They'll come right here, and they'll lock you up," she would say from her parlor. "They'll do it. I've seen them do it."

* * *

At the roundabout, Idrissa gave the police all he had, equivalent to about $15. The officer declined his offer. Her husband's boss—who refused to pay the money himself—tried talking the police down. They agreed to $40, about a third of Idrissa's $150 monthly salary.

Idrissa had called Aminata to see if she had anything in her cashbox. She told him she would check but felt embarrassed—she didn't want him to know the business wasn't going as well as she hoped. He knew almost nothing about what happened in the house while he was gone. Idrissa came home so late in the evening that he missed most of the activity in the day, and besides, after Aminata took out the loan they agreed to keep their finances separate, with Idrissa contributing money for food but Aminata having full oversight of her business. Idrissa didn't know that even though people were buying, her costs were nearly triple her profits, which she relied on to cover daily costs. Nearly everything she made went toward paying off her debt, with a few thousand leones—a few cents—left over for food and the emergency cashbox.

Part of the problem was that everything except the napkins was expensive, since it came from "outside": the flavoring from India, the milk from Malaysia. And the cost of the inputs, already expensive, was going up: inflation hit 15 percent in 2019, 13 percent in 2020, and 11 percent in 2021. Aminata knew she couldn't raise her prices; 20 cents per yogurt was already at the top of what her customers could afford. She could forgo the yogurt and focus on less expensive ginger beer and bissap, the hibiscus drink, but that was less profitable. Aminata had tried making bigger sales to wealthier people, like the time she made huge batches of yogurt for the man who owned a $100-a-night hotel up the road from Two Taps. She worked long hours, for two full days, so that he could serve it to his guests for breakfast. Months later, he still hadn't paid her.

When she opened the cashbox, she counted about $20. More than she expected but not quite enough, and the policeman didn't seem in a mood to negotiate.

Aminata had seen other Two Taps residents sell their possessions to deal with similar emergencies: to make loan payments, pay rent, or fulfill their children's school fees. Months earlier, Idrissa had acquired one of their sturdiest water containers from Panneh, the woman who had been taken to the police after falling behind on loan repayments, then fled to the village. He had given her $2 for it, a steal. Panneh then used the cash to pay down some of her debt.

Now in a pinch, Aminata followed suit, selling a few of her pots and some cloth she had set aside for such expected emergencies. She sent everything to Idrissa by mobile money, grumbling that the fees ate into the little she had.

The incident would have been annoying under any circumstances, but it was the timing that was most unfortunate. Idrissa had been taken to the police station on a Thursday. Aminata's loan payment was due on a Monday. The electricity still had not been turned back on; she worried all the yogurt inside would spoil, about $20 worth of milk and stabilizer and vanilla and sugar, wasted. She hadn't dared to open the fridge to check.

With nothing in her cashbox and a looming loan payment, Aminata began to amend her stance on what exactly microcredit, and her business, would achieve. She cut out the aspirational bits—about going to school in the future, getting a catering certificate, becoming a nurse, all things she had dreamed of when she first moved to Two Taps, then first started her business. Now, she said, "This isn't for me to grow up. This is just for me to survive with. That's all."

Aminata felt tired and weak. She didn't have an appetite. She was barely sleeping, had lost weight. Her skin hugged her shins so tightly they shone. She didn't dare plan a visit to see her family in Pendembu now. "They'll think I have some serious sickness. I'm so embarrassed. I can't go back."

CHAPTER 8

Nope

THE 1997 MICROCREDIT SUMMIT HELPED TO MAKE POVERTY-FIGHTING loans a concept millions of Americans had at least heard of, even if they still weren't very familiar with it; a few weeks after the conference, an editorial in the *New York Times* called microfinance "the world's hot idea for reducing poverty." The summit solidified and disseminated ideas that had been tossed around smaller development circles for decades. It was now common sense that tiny bits of credit could lift women out of poverty, that these loans were at once cheaper and also more effective than long-term, big-ticket programs. The conference also acted as something of Muhammad Yunus's grand debut. Thanks to his prominent role at the summit, he was no longer beloved only by do-good bankers, philanthropists, and policy wonks. Now, in the words of Jeff Ashe, Yunus was "the darling of microcredit."*

His growing recognition was swift and significant. In 1997, the year of the Microcredit Summit, Yunus was bestowed with five international awards for his work. That same year, during a congressional hearing on small-scale lending, Ileana Ros-Lehtinen, a Republican from Florida, called Yunus *the* founder of microcredit. By marrying "humanitarian instincts" with "logic and pragmatism," through "self-reliance" and "free market capitalism," Ros-Lehtinen said, Yunus offered an answer to grow-

---

* This was an analysis Yunus apparently agreed with. Years later, he said, "No other organization has done more to put Grameen Bank on the map than RESULTS and . . . the Microcredit Summit Campaign." Sam Daley-Harris, "At the Knee of Muhammad Yunus: Stories of Hope and a New Way of Seeing the World," draft essay.

ing poverty and inequality at a time when "realities force us to make tough choices"; when "budget-cutting is a necessity, we must look to new, innovative, and effective programs." FINCA, Accion, and the Self-Employed Women's Association were referenced in the congressional hearing, too—briefly. (Women's World Banking seems to have been entirely left out.) But no one called their leaders "founders" or spoke of their sweeping intelligence.* Microcredit, an approach that everyone now seemed to agree was both brilliant and essential, was almost singularly attributed to Muhammad Yunus, the smiling, optimistic banker from Bangladesh.

A year after the summit, in 1998, Yunus received six international awards, including the prestigious Indira Gandhi Prize for his "pioneering work" on microcredit. (Previous recipients included Mikhail Gorbachev, UNICEF, Jimmy Carter, and Doctors Without Borders.) The same year, PBS ran a series on microlending called *To Our Credit*, which featured a spectacular claim: that "more than half of the Grameen Bank households had come out of poverty completely." A World Bank study also featured in the PBS series offered another positive conclusion, that microcredit "alleviates poverty on a sustainable basis and makes a net contribution to local economic growth."[†] A year earlier, at the summit itself, the World Bank's president, James D. Wolfensohn, had proclaimed, "This business approach to the alleviation of poverty has allowed millions of individuals to work their way out of poverty with dignity."

Such anti-poverty claims represented a subtle but radical shift. Up until this point, most microcredit studies had focused on how much *income* a borrower could make. And as any poor person will tell you, it's possible to make an income and still be broke. Now, the claims were becoming much broader and more ambitious. It seemed that the loans not only *could* end poverty, as Yunus had long professed, but that they *did* end poverty.

Other exuberant claims soon followed. A few years later, one Nepalese organization said that, after taking out loans, nearly three-quarters of the

---

* A decade later, Hillary Clinton—who had visited the Self-Employed Women's Association before she visited Grameen, who knew of the South Shore Bank before she knew of Yunus—claimed that Yunus "invented" microfinance. Mark Landler, "A New Gender Agenda," *New York Times*, August 18, 2009.

† The World Bank expected that 3 percent of microfinance clients from three Bangladeshi institutions—including Grameen—would cross the poverty line each year. Sam Daley-Harris, "State of the Microcredit Summit Campaign Report 2007," Microcredit Summit Campaign.

women in their program reported experiencing more respect from their husbands and "an increase in their decision-making roles in such areas as family planning, children's marriages, buying and selling property and sending their daughters to school." Other studies from the time showed that small loans reduced domestic violence and abuse. As was the case with claims of poverty reduction, it seemed that female empowerment, facilitated through microcredit, was not only possible. It had been achieved.

After the PBS series aired, Yunus—with his coiffed silver hair, wide smile, and signature kurta and vest—began to be recognized in public. RESULTS' Sam Daley-Harris remembers "sitting in the back of a taxi in New York City and the taxi driver saying, 'You're that Indian guy.'"

But Yunus's final, firm breakout moment came a year later, in 1999, with the publication of his autobiography, *Banker to the Poor*. Written for a broad audience, the book is filled with inspirational, immensely quotable phrases, such as, "If all of us started to view every single human being, even the barefooted one begging in the street, as a potential entrepreneur, then we could build an economic system that would allow each man or woman to explore his or her economic potential." The book's cover shows a wooden ladder, which appears handmade, set against a red background. The red color gets lighter toward the top; the effect makes it look as though the ladder, and anyone who may climb on it, is ascending. The message was not lost on its reviewers. The *Washington Post* noted, "Hearing his appeal for a 'poverty-free world' from the source itself can be as stirring as that all-American myth of bootstrap success." U.S. president Jimmy Carter wrote, "By giving poor people the power to help themselves, Dr. Yunus has offered them something far more valuable than a plate of food—security in its most fundamental form."

At the time *Banker to the Poor* was released, Yunus wrote that Grameen's method had been "adapted to one hundred countries spanning five continents." The book, on the heels of the hundred million Microcredit Summit pledge, resulted in even further expansion, with hundreds of millions more dollars pledged for microcredit. Organizations such as FINCA, Accion, Grameen, Women's World Banking, and other stalwarts of the industry—Bangladesh's BRAC, Catholic Relief Services—received much of the support, but hundreds of new institutions sprang up, too, both to help meet the summit's goal and in response to the influx of cash. Between 1997, when the Microcredit Summit Campaign was launched, and the year 2000, over one thousand microcredit institutions claimed to reach just over twenty-three million borrowers, a number that had nearly doubled in just three years.* Thirteen million of those twenty-three million were considered the poorest of the poor; 75 percent were women. By the year 2000, USAID estimated, "there were few countries without some form of microfinance."

The figures, already spectacular, kept climbing. By 2004, the number of borrowers worldwide had reached 67 million, an increase of 45 million in just four years (and an impressive 54 million more than in 1997). The Microcredit Summit Campaign, which tracked these numbers, reported that, assuming five members per family, approximately 333 million family members had been reached in 2004.

Having achieved spectacular success in less than a decade, the Microcredit Summit Campaign gleefully reconvened. In 2005, the campaign spent $30 million on 120 different follow-up meetings, "many of them in celebration of microfinance as an accepted idea and an accomplished set of practices," observed Thomas Dichter, who worked in microfinance for decades. Vindicated, they agreed that within a decade, by 2015, microcredit organizations should reach 175 million of the world's poorest families, a near doubling of the original goal. Yunus predicted, "We will make Bangladesh free from poverty by 2030."†

The UN declared 2005 "The Year of Microcredit." In announcing the designation, Secretary-General Kofi Annan, told the General Assembly, "Microcredit is an idea whose time has come." Following the UN's lead, more governments officially endorsed microfinance. In 2006, the Microcredit Summit Campaign claimed that 133 million borrowers had been reached—a 1,123 percent increase in a nine-year period. Ninety-three

---

* From thirteen million.

† As of 2023, the latest official poverty statistics show that nearly 25 percent of the country lives below the poverty line. "Poverty & Equity Brief: South Asia: Bangladesh, April 2023," The World Bank, https://databankfiles.worldbank.org/public/ddpext_download/poverty/987B9C90-CB9F-4D93 -AE8C-750588BF00QA/current/Global_POVEQ_BGD.pdf.

million of the borrowers were "among the poorest when they took their first loan." Eighty-five percent were women.

* * *

In the 2007 book *What's Wrong with Microfinance?*, Malcolm Harper, a Brit who had been working in microfinance for decades, wrote that around 2006 he paid a visit to a man named Ali in Bogra, a large city in central Bangladesh. As they were talking, Ali looked down at his cell phone, which he had bought through Grameenphone, a new partnership between Grameen Bank and Telenor, a Norwegian telecommunications company. Thanks to the program, Bangladeshis could now own a phone—sometimes affording it with the help of a Grameen loan—and, in some cases, charge others for its use. This scenario was framed as a win-win-win: "Grameen Phone Ladies"—borrowers who bought Grameenphones with their loans, then sold phone calls—were building their entrepreneurial skills while making about $2 a day. Poor Bangladeshis who used the phones were connected to the wider world. And the Norwegian network provider Telenor could expand its reach to a poor but lucrative market.*

Grameen had launched other corporate partnerships, too. In 1998, Grameen teamed up with the agrochemical company Monsanto, a champion of the original Microcredit Summit, where Robert Shapiro, the company's chairman, had stated that "as families emerge from poverty, they can become our customers, our suppliers, our partners." Together they launched the Grameen Monsanto Center for Environment-Friendly Technologies, which aimed to test new seeds and technologies for the Bangladeshi market. Yunus dreamed that Bangladesh could "be self-sufficient in cotton production"; Shapiro thought that increased access to biotechnology meant poor countries would soon be "leapfrogging the industrial revolution and moving to a postindustrial society that is economically attractive and environmentally sustainable."

In 2010, Grameen partnered with Groupe Danone, the French food company, to create a "social business" producing fortified yogurt using

---

* In 2004, just after the program launched, Telenor's net profit after taxes was $120 million. Iqbal Quadir, "How Mobile Phones Can Fight Poverty," TEDGlobal 2005, https://www.ted.com/talks/iqbal _quadir_how_mobile_phones_can_fight_poverty.

Bangladeshi milk, then selling the finished product for just a few cents to Bangladeshi children. In addition to providing a buyer for local dairy farmers and supplying food to kids, the project allowed Danone to "tout its [Corporate Social Responsibility]," in the words of *Forbes*, and sell its products in Bangladesh. (Before the partnership, Bangladesh was, according to *Forbes*, the only country in the world "where Danone didn't sell its yogurt, water, baby food, and other products," even though nearly half the company's business was done in the developing world.) With Grameen's help, Emmanuel Faber, the company's co-chief operating officer, hoped to "take [the company's] mission into territories where we couldn't previously go." The Grameen Bank's extensive network could support marketing for the new yogurt, as borrowers could serve as both customers and agents, with Grameen yogurt sellers working on commission.

All these partnerships created even more buzz for Grameen and Muhammad Yunus, no longer a darling just of the aid industry. Microcredit was now firmly in the mainstream, as likely to be spoken about on college campuses as in corporate boardrooms.

The new obsession with the power of little loans worried some people, not least some of the delegates who had attended the Microcredit Summit that had generated all the euphoria in the first place. Some warned that putting too much emphasis on credit would obscure complicated structural reasons for poverty—everything from bad roads to extractive industries. They worried that "the world's hot idea for reducing poverty" might distract from more comprehensive solutions and wraparound social services like health care, education, and social grants. At the 1997 conference, Yoweri Museveni, the longtime controversial president of Uganda, argued that countries should first achieve universal education and vocational training, create functional roads and transport systems, and protect their own markets from cheap outside goods. "Then finally," he argued, "once you have got all of this in place, you can talk about credit." Just as USAID had argued about a decade earlier, the World Bank and United Nations agreed that for very poor people, safety nets were needed first, credit later. Even the enthusiastic *Times* editorial sprinkled in a bit of caution, warning that microcredit "cannot take the place of clean water, family planning efforts and child immunization programs. It can do little for the most desperate, those too sick or unskilled to work."

Yunus the rising star didn't disagree with some of the critiques. He recognized that there was more here, more than just what a borrower herself might be able to solve. Years later, he would say, "poverty doesn't come from the poor people themselves; poverty is imposed from outside. It's something that we have in the economic system, which creates poverty. If you [address] those problems, there's no reason why anybody should be poor." At the same time, he didn't dwell on these larger issues, either. While others warned that credit was not a "panacea," Yunus suggested it might be. His magic was in making microfinance seem at once tangible and aspirational, using phrases like "credit is a human right" and "the poor can lift themselves out of poverty" to amplify his message. Such promises were deeply moving to many readers of *Banker to the Poor* and helped to propel dramatic fundraising efforts and ever-larger goals. But they frustrated those who had begun to worry about what the popularity of high-priced loans meant for the poor people paying for them.

People like Ali. In Bogra, Ali's phone displayed a message. He read it, then told Harper, "It's quite extraordinary. The world's biggest loan shark has just got the Nobel Prize."

* * *

In December 2006, European royalty, ambassadors, and dignitaries and American celebrities filled Oslo City Hall for that year's Nobel Peace Prize ceremony. Traditional Bangladeshi dancers kicked off the celebrations. Monica Yunus, a twenty-nine-year-old soprano with the New York Metropolitan Opera, watched the performance. She was there to perform at the Nobel Peace Prize Concert, along with Lionel Richie, John Legend, and Rihanna. She was also there to congratulate her dad.

Muhammad Yunus, wearing a shiny-cheeked grin and his now famous kurta—this time, a knee-length olive green shirt under a shorter, beige-colored button-up vest—walked onstage. The Nobel Committee had decided that the 2006 Nobel Peace Prize would be shared by Yunus and the Grameen Bank he had created "for their efforts to create economic and social development from below. Lasting peace cannot be achieved unless large population groups find ways in which to break out of poverty. Microcredit is one such means."

In accepting the award, Yunus was accompanied by Mosammat Taslima Begum, who represented Grameen alongside nine other "borrowers-cum-owners," as Yunus called them. Begum had borrowed $18 to buy a goat in 1992; by 2006, she was on the bank's board. In making their decision, the Nobel Committee had stressed Grameen's focus on women, observing, "Microcredit has proved to be an important liberating force in societies where women in particular have to struggle against repressive social and economic conditions. Economic growth and political democracy cannot achieve their full potential unless the female half of humanity participates on an equal footing with the male."

Although the prize was officially shared between Yunus and Grameen, Yunus was firmly the star of the evening. He offered the centerpiece of the ceremony, the Nobel lecture. Beginning in Bengali before switching to English, Yunus told the story that by now everyone in the audience likely knew: of the $27 he lent to forty-two women, who were otherwise shackled to moneylenders, and their almost miraculous ability to pay back. As had become his trademark, the lecture was peppered with pithy, hopeful statements. "Human beings are a wonderful creation embodied with limitless human qualities and capabilities," he said. "I firmly believe that we can create a poverty-free world if we collectively believe in it. In a poverty-free world, the only place you would be able to see poverty is in the poverty museums." The quotes, particularly the one about the "poverty museums," made it into the pages of the *Washington Post*, the *New York Times*, and the *Guardian*. He received congratulations from Queen Sofia of Spain, the UN's Kofi Annan, the actor Hugh Jackman, and Princess Máxima of the Netherlands. Perhaps not surprisingly, Bill Clinton offered congratulations, too, saying, "The Nobel Committee could not have picked a more deserving recipient."

Not everyone agreed.

* * *

Just a few years before Muhammad Yunus and the Grameen Bank won the 2006 Nobel Peace Prize, Elizabeth Littlefield, then the chief executive officer

of the World Bank–affiliated Consultative Group to Assist the Poor*—
which had been set up about a decade prior to support microfinance—
wrote a letter to the Nobel Committee in Oslo. It began by acknowledging
that Muhammad Yunus was the most well-known figure in microfinance.
But Littlefield argued that despite the fame, "Grameen's contribution has
been surpassed by others who have made a more holistic contribution to
the lives of the poor." If the Nobel Committee wanted to award someone
in microcredit, she suggested they consider two other people instead: Ela
Bhatt, of India's Self-Employed Women's Association, and Fazle Hasan Abed,
of Bangladesh's BRAC. No one, Littlefield felt, had done more than Bhatt
to promote lending to women; she was, Littlefield wrote to the committee,
"the Gandhi of our times." And no one had done more than Abed to promote microfinance, tweaking the model as it expanded; BRAC was (and
remains) one of the largest NGOs in the world.

Littlefield is astutely political, having run America's Development
Finance Corporation† in the Obama administration after leaving the
World Bank. It fits her to be tempered, and her letter was firm but measured. Others are less so. One person I spoke to—who had worked in
microfinance since the 1970s—said that among insiders, Yunus was regularly referred to as "the fake. He has a golden tongue, and he doesn't
tell the truth. He stole every idea that he could possibly steal"—stole
them from small-time policymakers, colonial officers, bankers, and poor
women themselves—"and turned it around as his creative idea. Everybody knows that, but nobody talked about it because there was fear that
it would quash the movement." Another person I spoke to, an American
who had worked in microcredit policy for decades, observed Yunus "won
a Nobel Prize for thinking about how to win a Nobel Prize. He certainly
cared about [the borrowers] and tried to work with them, but what he
really was trying to do—and it was evidenced from anyone who heard
him speak—was position himself for recognition."

Nearly every microfinance advocate and funder I spoke to has an opin-

---

* In 2003 the group had shifted its name from "the Poorest" to "the Poor" to reflect concerns that small
loans couldn't help the most impoverished. Connie Bruck, "Millions for Millions," *New Yorker*, October 22, 2006, https://www.newyorker.com/magazine/2006/10/30/millions-for-millions.
† Formerly OPIC, the American government's private-sector development arm.

ion about whether Yunus was deserving of the 2006 prize. The debate could feel nitpicky and petty, and not particularly surprising given that thousands of other people had dedicated their careers to promoting the idea. Clearly Yunus had a knack for PR that others didn't; of course people felt left out. (Several people told me that when the 2006 Nobel Peace Prize was announced, Accion in particular felt slighted, given that they had started small-scale lending a decade before Grameen was officially set up and that Jeff Ashe's work had been instrumental in bringing USAID, and then other donors, on board.) But the fact is that by 2006 Yunus simply *was* more famous than Ela Bhatt or Fazle Hasan Abed or Jeff Ashe, not to mention the poor women who had been lending and borrowing from one another for centuries.

Tucked just behind the debate about whether Yunus was particularly deserving was a larger conversation about what microfinance being called a "Nobel Prize–winning" innovation might mean for small loans and small borrowers, regardless of who invented it. Those who were push-ing the self-sustaining approach, which included increasing interest rates and taking on private capital, worried that deeming microcredit a human right would open them to criticism. People would ask how a tool that would "put poverty in museums" could require costs that were triple what American credit card holders paid. Those who favored the anti-poverty framing also wrung their hands. If microfinance expanded, as it now surely would, how would there be any oversight of the growing field of lenders? Where would the money for even more expansion come from? And, even more worrisome, what if microfinance failed to live up to its promises?

Across both camps, there was broader discomfort about framing debt as absolutely, without question, a good thing. "There were a lot of peo-ple that were doubting credit," one person who worked as a manager in microcredit for years told me, "and doubting the rosy picture that Yunus was painting everywhere he went"—the high repayment rates, the claims of lifting millions out of poverty, the rhetoric of female empowerment. As Malcolm Harper tells it, his friend Ali, the Grameenphone user, was one of these dissenters, framing Yunus, with his market-rate loans, as as much of a loan shark as the lenders he was trying to displace.

But Yunus winning the Nobel quieted those critical conversations—about whether poor people should really be the target of microcredit programs, about whether women were really being empowered one loan at a time. The former microcredit manager told me that around the time of the 2006 Nobel ceremony, "We were just starting to have them, and then it was like, 'nope.'"

Layers

Old Post, Koidu, Kono, Eastern Sierra Leone

Mid-2019

ABBIE AND HER NEIGHBOR RAMATU LOOKED AT THE WEEKS THAT stretched out in front of them and saw nothing good. Abbie was still heading to Sawula with bundles of shoes, sometimes coming back to Koidu with palm oil to sell, but she was barely making her loan payments, and money for Princess's next school term was due before her LAPO debt was up. With the arrival of her new baby Mark, Ramatu had basically stopped trying with her "business," which hadn't been much to start with anyway. She was clear-eyed about the sheer lunacy of turning eighty sachets of water into money for food: how ludicrous to try to make a refrigerator work when the electricity never came, to wish customers into being when they didn't have anything to spend either.

The women needed money, and it wasn't coming. So, with a few final repayments in front of them, the women of Kochende went to a company called Capsule, a different microfinance lender. They planned to tell the loan officers the same thing they had told LAPO, about business dreams and the need for start-up cash. They would simply neglect to mention the other loan.

At the office, Abbie realized she knew several of the loan officers. They had gone to school together, before her family had run out of money and she was forced to drop out. Abbie was grateful for the connection but embarrassed for them to see her like this. If only things had been a little bit different, just a few moments of luck or connections, she felt she could have been one of them. Abbie worked up a mix of praise and guilt. "Wow, look at you, in such a big position! You look so sweet today! Remember me, from school? Remember how we used to walk together? Hey, look at me, I'm suffering now! If only I had been able to go as far as you. Look at you!"

Her old friends made sure Abbie had the correct application papers, then put the women of Kochende at the front of the line. Rather than waiting weeks to be approved, they waited just a few days.

The women each received around $70. They used some of the cash to get them through their final month of repayments to LAPO. To pay off Capsule, they took out a separate loan from another lender, A Call to Business,* and then, to pay off that loan, another, from BRAC. They had set up a short line of dominoes: this one first, paid off by that one, then the third, then the fourth.

Then the fourth. They were stuck at the last loan, from BRAC. Abbie thought maybe her friends at Capsule could help her get another loan. They put in the paperwork, each paid a "starting fee," and then waited. When Abbie and Ramatu complained about how long it was taking, "they said, 'Okay, you can bribe us if you want it to go faster,'" remembers Ramatu. "One lady said she can help us if we give her money. We would buy credit for her phone. Some days when we went there, we all pulled Le2,000 or Le5,000"—the equivalent of a few cents—"to give them a small tip. But still no loan."

"For more than six months!" says Abbie. Ramatu was annoyed by their "turning us," again and again. "We suffered so much, and they still didn't give us another loan."

Now behind on her BRAC loan—too few bottles of ginger beer in the refrigerator, too few customers to buy them—Ramatu was again taken to the police station. She called the farmer man, who bailed her out, then, after a few weeks of grumbling about it, paid off her loan. "I'm leaving microcredit," she promised, this time for good. "I said I'd never put my hand there again."

But Abbie didn't have anyone to pay off her debt. Instead, she and a few of the other Kochende women joined another group, took out another

---

* The company is now officially called actb Savings & Loans Ltd but regularly referred to as A Call to Business by microfinance borrowers. "Sierra Leone," A Call to Business, http://acalltobusiness.co.uk /sierra-leone.

loan from LAPO. "I don't want microcredit," she said. "I just don't have any other option."

* * *

A few months later, Abbie's brother and mother made the trip all the way from Sawula to Koidu. Abbie could tell even before she saw her mother's stern face that she was disappointed in her. Abbie had been inside the cell at the police station for two days by then, waiting for someone to bail her out. The officers insisted that she wasn't officially charged with anything—they were just mediating the $60 or so she still owed LAPO. If someone came with a bit of money, and if she agreed to pay in full right away, she could go. If not, she'd have to go to jail.

Abbie took the threats seriously, because she had finally learned what happened to her auntie Finda, who had disappeared a long while ago. About six months back, Abbie heard through a friend that her aunt was locked up at D.O. Barracks, Kono's main jail, about a twenty-five-minute walk from Old Post. Abbie took a motorbike taxi to the outskirts of town, hopping off behind the district's main courtroom and walking the few steps to the squat one-story prison, so low to the ground that it resembled a concrete pancake. She saw that the male side was crowded, filled with motorbike riders who had unpaid traffic tickets, construction workers accused of stealing from their boss, and several men, small in both stature and demeanor, whose faces were puffed with alcohol.

The female side was quieter but no less cold and dark. That's where she found Finda, awaiting trial for a $150 debt she owed to LAPO.

Finda had taken out a few loans to sell shoes, just like her niece. Initially, she had better luck than Abbie and found the first debt easy enough to pay off: shoes sold, loan repaid, no problem. She eventually graduated to a higher amount, taking about $300. Finda was able to pay half back before, she later told Abbie, "my luck ran out."

A LAPO loan officer took her to the police station for the rest, explaining that she had to pay or find someone who could. Finda was too embarrassed to reach out to her niece just a few minutes' walk away.

So the officers told Finda that she was being charged to court, which meant she'd be transferred over to D.O. Barracks and locked up while she awaited trial. Even years later, she wasn't sure if she had been officially charged with a crime, and if so for what. She went in front of a judge three times, who told her she was there because of the problems with microcredit. Did she have the money? No? Then she would have to go back to the cell and come back again later. She says she never had access to a lawyer or any legal advice.

Like Finda, several of the other inmates at D.O. Barracks had not been formally charged with a crime, many more not formally sentenced even if they had. Despite being steps away from Koidu's high court, a judge only presided over proceedings once every few months. If there was some hiccup—a witness didn't show up, a police officer said he was too busy to make it—the accused would go back in the cell and wait several months for a judge to come again. Many of those at D.O. Barracks had been awaiting trial for months, surviving off two paltry meals a day.

Abbie was afforded a fifteen-minute meeting with her aunt. Finda told her niece that the communal area where prisoners mingled during the day was fine enough—clean, airy, somewhat bright. She never got in any fights with other inmates, perhaps because she didn't get too close to anyone. "I spoke to everyone, but I never asked why they were in there or for how long," she later recalled. Her discretion was in part self-protection, so that no one would ask her the same. Those things, she said, she wanted to keep to herself. "But I know that there were other people there for this money business."

The cell, however, was awful, "not fit for a human." Finda slept on the concrete floor, even during the rainy season. She often felt cold. She wasn't eating enough food, not getting enough water. After several months inside, her feet and face were becoming swollen. Finda told Abbie that they were painful.

Abbie was distraught but of no real use. "I should have paid for her. She raised me. I felt so bad, she's basically my mom! But she was involved with microcredit, and I was involved with microcredit, too." Abbie learned that in exchange for a 50-cent tip for the guards, she could bring some food to her auntie. For another 30 cents, she could visit with Finda, staying for thirty minutes or so. She attempted to raise her significantly poor spirits with news of her kids, of Sawula, of the bean harvest, before the guard said, "'Okay, that's enough,' and put her back inside," remembers Abbie.

Abbie's family scrounged together about $100 for LAPO, selling whatever they could from the farm and home—not quite enough but what they could manage. They begged the microfinance manager to have mercy, let her go. It had been about a year since Finda had first been taken to the police station. Finally, after days of conversation, the manager agreed, going to the police to ask for her release. The simplicity felt cruel. Abbie had been begging for her to be let go for weeks, and now, with one wave of the hand, Finda was free.

Finda was overwhelmed with gratitude, telling Abbie over and over that she couldn't have made it without her: without the food, the clothes, the visits. After she was released, she went to the hospital three times, but her face and feet remained painful and swollen. Whenever she looked at her aunt's withered body, Abbie was overcome with shame.

Now, a few months later, Abbie's brother looked at her in the police station and told his sister "that I embarrassed the family." After he bailed her, he scolded her in the big parking lot out front. Her mother "was mad, stressed out." "They said they shouldn't be the ones to help with this." Abbie was the one in Koidu, meant to be supporting those back home. "I should have been the one helping them. I know that I really brought shame on my family."

PART 2

Trouble the Water

There is a word, an Igbo word, that I think about whenever I think about the power structures of the world, and it is "nkali." It's a noun that loosely translates to "to be greater than another." Like our economic and political worlds, stories too are defined by the principle of nkali. How they are told, who tells them, when they're told, how many stories are told, are really dependent on power.

—Chimamanda Ngozi Adichie,
"The Danger of a Single Story"

CHAPTER 9

So Much Money

NEARLY A DECADE AND A HALF SINCE FIRST STUMBLING UPON SOLIDAR-
ity groups in El Salvador, Jeff Ashe had traveled to nearly every conti-
nent to support microcredit programs. For most of that time, he says, he
remained an "utter and true believer." He was still driven by the liberation
theology he had read in his twenties, still driven by the fundamental belief
that small loans, given to poor people, were an empowering anti-poverty
solution that would pay for itself.

It was on two trips—one to Bosnia, one to Bolivia—that he started to
change his mind.

In the mid-1990s, Ashe, now an independent microfinance consultant, was sent to Bosnia and Herzegovina by Catholic Relief Services, an
international NGO based in Baltimore. He arrived just as a brutal war
was ending. One hundred thousand people had been killed. The country's
economy was in ruins; millions of people were trying to return to some
sort of semblance of normalcy. Catholic Relief Services, a major microfinance player by now, gave Ashe a broad but direct mandate: go to the
capital, Sarajevo, and help figure out how to give out microfinance loans.
This was a poor country, emerging from a war. Just as small loans had
been used in post-conflict settings in Africa and Southeast Asia, Catholic
Relief Services thought they should be used in Bosnia, too.

Ashe arrived to a city inundated with other foreign consultants and
financial managers who had been given the exact same task. "FINCA was
doing their FINCA thing, Accion was doing their thing, Freedom from
Hunger was doing their thing," Ashe recalled. He had been planning to

set up the same solidarity groups he had been championing for years, the ones based off the FEDECRÉDITO model. But now that he was there, he saw few parallels between the market vendors of San Salvador and those in Sarajevo. The economy was completely different. Bosnia and Herzegovina had a long history of state involvement in employing poor people and building critical infrastructure. Before the war, the socialist republic had a robust manufacturing sector and large state-run industries. Even though its economy was now crippled, the small-scale enterprises Ashe encountered in Sarajevo were sophisticated, run by well-educated vendors who had been engineers, professors, and scientists. The businesses were robust compared to those he had seen in Latin America or East Africa, sturdy enough to fulfill a steady stream of inventories, to hire employees. And although the country's infrastructure had been badly damaged, Ashe observed fewer obstacles compared to those small businesses faced elsewhere. Even though much had been destroyed during the war, a road network stretched across the country, there was a train system—albeit a bit unreliable and limited in scope—and the country's proximity to relatively wealthy Western Europe provided access to goods and customers that poorer countries didn't have.

Considering the situation, Ashe determined that small loans for tiny businesses were "completely inappropriate" for Bosnia and Herzegovina. "It's not what they needed. But everyone was doing it anyway." Ashe felt that FINCA, Accion, Freedom from Hunger, and Catholic Relief Services "had all taken a model they'd done with street vendors in developing countries, and just plopped it into a context where it made no sense."

Despite his mounting reservations, Ashe remained drawn to the thrill of being somewhere new. He loved learning about the lives and customs of others, loved sharing his own ideas and experiences. (In Bosnia, he even met "the king of the gypsies.") "Even though I could see the model was failing," he told me, "all of it was still such a high." More practically, he also felt stuck. Promoting and setting up solidarity groups was what he was good at, the career he had made, the way he paid his bills. Although he started to feel it was all a "boondoggle," he recognized, "my bag of tricks was limited." So, in Sarajevo, he promoted the solidarity group model anyway, suggesting a few tweaks, including supporting Bosnian versions of ROSCA, the savings and loans group he had learned about years before. (He says Catholic Relief Services disregarded his suggestions and stuck with basic microcredit.)

Disaffected but still very much within the sector, Ashe was soon asked to go on another trip, this time to Bolivia, to look at "innovations in microcredit."

By now, Accion had become famous in Bolivia for helping to set up ProDem, a nonprofit microcredit institution based in La Paz, the country's administrative capital. The lender was strikingly successful, with an expanding roster of borrowers and nearly 100 percent repayment rates. In the early 1990s, Martin Connell, a Canadian businessman and philanthropist interested in microfinance, suggested that ProDem undergo something of an experiment. Amid all the talk about the need for financially sustainable institutions, why not see if ProDem could transition to a for-profit, fully independent bank. Connell would even offer a staffer, for free, to oversee the transition.

Accion was cautious at first, worried about losing subsidized support from development funders. They became convinced when private investors began to express interest, drawn by the lender's 2.2 percent return on assets. USAID, curious to see whether financial independence was feasible—and whether, therefore, demand on donors might lessen—promised millions of dollars to the effort.

In 1992, ProDem became BancoSol, a private bank with interest rates that were one-third higher than those offered by commercial banks. BancoSol, the largest microfinance lender in Bolivia, was almost immediately applauded as an important proof of concept. In the 1998 PBS series, Accion's Maria Otero explained, "Banco Sol is a commercial bank. It has no subsidy. That has never really been done before and that is terribly important to understand because it means that you don't have to depend on donors." Although Accion had been initially reluctant about the transformation, Otero now hoped it would inspire more private interest. "Until major capital flows from big investment houses, investment firms, from big funds, into microlending programs and consequently to the poor of the third world . . . it's going to be very difficult for poverty to be eradicated," she told PBS.

The transformation of BancoSol made Bolivia, and particularly La Paz, the star of microcredit. All types of lenders suddenly opened offices across the city. When Ashe arrived and toured a market in La Paz, he realized the place was saturated. He talked to borrowers who had "on average three or four loans from different sources." On paper, that seemed to suit everyone—microcredit institutions kept their numbers high, which made them look good in the eyes of efforts like the Microfinance Summit Campaign, while also making them more appealing to funders. At the same time, borrowers had more money. But some borrowers found themselves in a vortex of debt. Ashe met borrowers who were hundreds of dollars deep, with no viable way to pay it off—unless they took out another loan.

Ashe watched, "increasingly disillusioned," as lenders aggressively sought new customers, even as overindebtedness was becoming more pronounced. He saw lenders try to steal customers from one another. To make their outreach numbers look good, "they were all counting the customers as their customers, double, triple, quadruple counting," even if one person was just taking multiple loans from different lenders. Ashe began to liken microfinance institutions in La Paz to "vultures, all around the edges of the big markets, scouring up customers"—and, much to his dismay, "all using the solidarity group methodology."

But while lenders in La Paz were competing for already overindebted customers, in rural areas, would-be borrowers such as farmers were entirely left out. "It was oversaturated, and then zero," Ashe remembers.

Ashe left Bolivia completely deflated. "It was clear this just wasn't working." His dream of empowering the poor through solidarity groups and small loans "was over." He decided it was finally time to leave microfinance.

* * *

Jeff Ashe and I met for lunch in Boston in late December 2022. Over the previous two years, we had Zoomed and spoken on the phone several times and emailed dozens more. In nearly every conversation, no matter how short, the Bosnia and Bolivia trips came up. These were clear turning points for him, moments he now ruminated on in his retirement as he tried to figure out what exactly had gone so wrong with an idea he thought would change the world.

I knew by now what he had seen and why he had found it so egregious—the overborrowing, the saturated markets. Over lunch, I told him I wanted to know *why* he thought the shift had happened, what exactly had changed to make him go from an "utter and true" believer to, just a few years later, realizing that his dream was "over."

Ashe considered my question. He paused for a few moments, in between bites of fish and chips, wiped his mouth with a napkin, and looked up. "Suddenly," he said, "there was just so, so much money."

* * *

Even with all the worries about donor scarcity, the 1997 Microcredit Summit had spurred generous support—and significant financial commitments—from the biggest names in international development. USAID, the UN, and the World Bank publicly endorsed the goal of lending to one hundred million of the world's poorest families by 2005. (The World Bank's support had actually been quietly secured nearly two years before, in the private meeting between Yunus and the bank's president, James D. Wolfensohn, arranged by David Rockefeller's daughter.) The UN-affiliated International Fund for Agricultural Development pledged 30 percent of its loan portfolio—$125 million—"to promot[ing] financial services to the poorest." The private-sector arm of the UN also pledged a third of its portfolio toward the effort. USAID, having discarded its skeptical stance, now ramped up financial support for microcredit, specifically to women and the poor.

The details of what this support entailed mattered. In 1998, a year after the summit, USAID directors declared that whatever funding they put toward microfinance needed to facilitate "institutional sustainability and financial self-sufficiency"—in other words, USAID would only fund lenders who would soon be able to pay for themselves. Rather than giving grants, which didn't need to be paid back, some funders instead offered loans, which did need to be paid back. To do so, microfinance lenders would need to find new ways to make money. This could be done in three ways: Lenders could set interest rates high enough that they could cover all costs, something that USAID now required. Lenders could convert from nonprofit to for-profit, using those profits to keep their programs running and further expand. And donors like USAID could use mechanisms like loan guarantees to encourage private capital to invest in this newly for-profit microfinance,* tapering off demand for donor resources.[†]

As an example of how this worked: USAID gave Catholic Relief Services a grant with the objective that the organization would use the money to transform the dozens of microcredit organizations it supported into for-profit financial institutions, which could then attract private capital. It also funded Accion's investments in microfinance lenders that were explicitly adopting a market-oriented approach. Emboldened by the BancoSol success, Accion was committed to "[push] the industry to be more commercial, away from its traditional philanthropic approach," in the words of one staffer. Flipping lenders for-profit became Accion's primary focus.[‡] And profitability became baked into USAID's contracts with the microlenders it supported. Chuck Waterfield worked in microfinance from the 1980s through the mid-2010s, helping to train some USAID-funded microlenders on an accounting software that helped them track their finances as they turned for-profit. USAID, he said, "would ask for the projections in my software that showed over the next five years the organization was going to reach profitability. And then they would build those figures into the contract," which could be "yanked if they weren't meeting those targets." Profitability wasn't a possibility. It was a foregone conclusion.

The goalposts had moved. The FINCAs and Accions and Grameens of the 1970s and 1980s said they were driven by ending poverty. Now, although ending poverty was still ostensibly the goal, it was just as important to cover costs and increase customers.

But even though the new objectives were clear, the details of how to reach them weren't. For one thing, there wasn't agreement on what a sustainable—let alone fair—interest rate was. Since many microfinance

---

* For example, by offering loan guarantees, a way to incentivize private lenders who might be otherwise reluctant to invest in a new, potentially unstable sector.

† For example, USAID offered loan guarantees for microcredit lenders making their first foray into capital markets—a signal to investors that this was a safe bet. "Microenterprise and U.S. Foreign Assistance," Congressional Research Service, April 12, 2001. A few years later, Congress would explicitly encourage lenders to "tap commercial sources of capital." "Microenterprise for Self-Reliance and International Anti-Corruption Act of 2000," Public Law 106–309—October 17, 2000.

‡ Maria Otero told the *New Yorker*, "Acción created the commercial model, and the commercial model is the one that works." Connie Bruck, "Millions for Millions," *New Yorker*, October 22, 2006.

lenders were not officially considered banks, they weren't regulated—national institutions and central banks had little say over what they charged. The cost of a loan could vary wildly across lenders and contexts, determined by where a microlender received its money from, how many staff a lender had, how many borrowers, and a lender's competition. Since microlenders often charged more than banks, with the rationale that it was more expensive to lend to the poor, they primarily competed with moneylenders, who famously charged an arm and a leg. Anything below 10 percent a day looked cheap by comparison.

Even so, many microfinance loans were more expensive than advertised—sometimes much more expensive. The details of how this is possible are a bit in the weeds, but they're important. Many microlenders use what's called a "flat interest rate." In this system, payments remain the same regardless of how much of a loan has been paid off. For example, if a borrower takes out $100 with a 15 percent flat interest rate, they'll pay $15 each time, whether they just took the loan or are on their last payment. Although this is called an "interest rate," flat rate essentially requires a regular monthly fee that lasts throughout the loan. By contrast, many lenders in America and Europe—and some microfinance lenders—use what's called a "*declining* balance rate." Payments are calculated as the principal is paid off. A 15 percent declining balance rate on a $100 loan means that a borrower first pays $15, then $12.75, $10.83, and so on.

This subtle difference can have a huge impact on how much someone pays—on what's called the effective, or real, interest rate. Even if a borrower in Sierra Leone and one in America are both quoted 15 percent, the Sierra Leonean may pay far more out of pocket simply because of the way her interest is calculated. Flat rate loans can wind up costing double, sometimes triple, what a declining balance loan would cost.

Recognizing that flat rates can be a boon for a lender while also nominally keeping prices low, in 1996 a World Bank consultant advised three large microfinance lenders in Bangladesh to switch their rates from declining balance to flat. Doing so would allow the companies to double their income and become self-sustaining, all while limiting sticker shock by advertising the same, relatively low interest rate.

The lenders followed this advice. As they made the switch, other lenders were incentivized to as well: if one lender charges a 30 percent declining balance rate, and another a 24 percent flat interest rate, the nominally lower flat rate appears cheaper, even though the effective interest rate will in fact cost a borrower much more. Chuck Waterfield observed a "downward spiral" in which it became standard to adopt flat interest, first in Bangladesh and then across the microfinance industry. Decades after the World Bank consultant's advice, all of the Sierra Leonean borrowers I met were charged flat interest rates. Loan officers routinely gave them three figures: how much they would get for the loan, how much they would pay in up-front "fees," and how much they would have to pay each week, a figure that remained constant regardless of how much had been paid off. Most had never been told their effective interest rates, let alone whether the lender used flat or declining balance rates. (In the United States, the Truth in Lending Act requires lenders to disclose the full cost of a loan, but there's no such regulation in Sierra Leone or in many poorer countries.) When I asked lenders why borrowers hadn't been told their real interest rates, I was told that they were too financially illiterate to understand them.

Given that there was little oversight and almost no price transparency, delegates at a 1999 follow-up meeting to the Microcredit Summit warned that lenders could hide their inefficiencies under the guise of "appropriate interest rates," even if those rates were, in fact, not very appropriate at all. Some warned that raising interest rates even further, in a bid toward financial sustainability, would leave the poorest out. Lenders could either aim for self-sufficiency or reach the most desperate, but they would have a hard time doing both.

Still, under pressure from funders who were enticed by the idea that microcredit could fund itself, and following what was becoming an industry-wide trend, organizations upped their costs to borrowers, sometimes drastically. After a Kenyan lender transitioned from nonprofit to for-profit, it charged poor borrowers *double* the rates of commercial banks. To slim budgets, lenders also cut down on other expenses like training and marketing support, programs that had previously been covered by donors and grants. That was true even as USAID and other funders recognized that additional support to borrowers, such as assistance using new technologies and accessing new markets, was essential to small businesses' success.

Lenders generally chose one of two paths: raise interest rates for the poor, or—sometimes an and/or—lend to relatively wealthier people. Some lenders began quietly shifting away from lending to poor people through groups, instead offering larger, lower-interest, individual loans to wealthier borrowers. This included men, who were considered more financially stable and more likely to have a business—the exact reason, Yunus, Hatch, Michaela Walsh, and others had argued, why they didn't need microcredit in the first place. Soon, even FINCA, an early champion of lending to women, shifted sharply toward male borrowers.

The focus on relatively upmarket loans allowed lenders to maintain large loan portfolios, lend to less risky borrowers, and escape criticism for charging usurious prices to the poor. The individual loans sometimes required collateral—a dramatic reversal from the original model pitched by Grameen, FINCA, solidarity groups, and Ela Bhatt's Self-Employed Women's Association. When lending *was* still done in groups, some borrowers actively self-selected relatively wealthy members. They left the poorest out of concern that they wouldn't be able to pay off the loan, potentially damaging future borrowing prospects for the whole group. Even at Grameen, people who didn't have previous experience with business or regular access to cash were discouraged from applying, undermining the idea that this was a way for poor people to start their own, self-made enterprise. By 2005, 40 percent of microfinance clients in Bangladesh, seen as the motherland for anti-poverty microlending, were considered nonpoor. By at least one account, by 2005, men made up half of all individual borrowers.

The poorest borrowers who remained found themselves in a particularly sticky bind. Given that the overhead—things like staff cost and office rent—on a loan was the same whether it was $20 or $200, lenders could charge much *lower* interest rates on much *larger* loans while still recouping the same cost. Put another way, the poorer the borrower, the more expensive the loan. In at least one case, poor borrowers paid *double* what wealthier microfinance borrowers paid.

RESULTS lambasted the shift to wealthier borrowers. In the late 1990s and early 2000s, it took aim at USAID after reports showed some of its spending veered away from the poorest of the poor. But others argued that perhaps the shift was not only rational—since relatively wealthy (but still poor) borrowers were also shut out from formal credit, may be better able to put the loans to good use, and could even create or expand businesses that would ultimately hire the very poor—it was also moral. With making money, or at least being self-sustaining, now a key focus, "microfinance actually *can't* reach down to the very poor," Ashe had decided. And, considering all the overindebtedness he had witnessed, he mused, "it probably shouldn't."

* * *

USAID's pro-private-sector approach was steered by Elisabeth Rhyne, who oversaw its Office of Microenterprise Development from 1994 to 1998. Rhyne prided herself on being a technocrat, not a bleeding-heart charity staffer or a charismatic leader like Muhammad Yunus. Before joining USAID, she had worked with microfinance programs in Africa. She was impressed with the basic idea of small-scale lending but found that many programs were messy and poorly run, driven more by ideology than a commitment to creating effective, long-term programs. Rhyne entered her new position at USAID with a clear vision: for-profit as the way to sustain and grow microfinance.* According to Chuck Waterfield, Rhyne "single-handedly pushed USAID to take a commercial approach. She said not a penny of that money is going to Oxfam and Freedom from Hunger, to poverty lending, it's all going for serious stuff, the BancoSols." Waterfield felt USAID's message to microfinance lenders was clear: "We'll give you money, if you convert into for-profit."

Other institutions joined USAID in advocating for this method. The European Union, CARE, the UK's international development agency, and the Inter-American Development Bank, among others, all championed

---

* In 1994, just as she was taking over at USAID, she helped to edit a book, alongside Maria Otero, the CEO of Accion, called *The New World of Microenterprise Finance: Building Healthy Financial Institutions for the Poor*. It was something of a how-to guide, outlining successful, self-sustaining programs around the world, including in Indonesia, Colombia, Kenya, and BancoSol in Bolivia.

and funded for-profit transitions. Donors supported lenders that private banks and investors were already interested in—a sign, they felt, that the industry really was becoming sustainable.

In 2002, at a follow-up meeting to the Microcredit Summit Campaign, Antonio Vives, deputy manager of the Inter-American Development Bank, envisioned that the private sector would soon command "100 percent" of the microenterprise market. He told public banks, presumably including the one he represented, "You should get out of this business because you're damaging the growth of the industry." The Consultative Group to Assist the Poor, the World Bank–supported consortium of microfinance funders and supporters, also had a "clear message," recalls Sharon D'Onofrio, who supported for-profit transitions of Catholic Relief Services microlenders. "Microfinance needs to be sustainable and the big goal here is to bring in private capital. The accepted knowledge was that donors wouldn't meet the demand, and that the private sector, not donors, should."

Even lenders in the world's poorest countries shifted tactics. As Sierra Leone's civil war was ending, at the turn of the twenty-first century, microfinance loans were subsidized. "The interest rate was way lower back then," Archibald Shodeke of the Sierra Leone Association of Microfinance Institutions told me. "There was also skills training, grants for small business, things like that." But within a few years, Shodeke says, there was a sharp turn to "sustainable microfinance approaches." Lenders were warned of funding cuts; interest rates rose. Borrowers themselves noticed that the loans were getting more expensive. Sheikh, Idrissa's uncle at Waterloo Market in the far eastern part of Freetown, remembered, "When microcredit first started, the interest was something like 5 percent. It didn't bother people." A few years later, payments increased. "At first, it was 10 percent interest. Now, sometimes it can go to 15 percent, 20 percent. Even higher." Today, the country's tens of thousands of borrowers pay a minimum of around 30 percent interest per each loan term.*

Although many funders and lenders were excited about what a self-sustaining model might offer, others had misgivings about the commercialized

---

* Which often lasts around six months but can be extended in case of late repayments.

approach, characterized by high interest rates, rapid growth, and the courting of private capital. At a follow-up meeting to the Microcredit Summit Campaign in 1999, a UN staffer warned, "If a lot of capital becomes irresponsibly available, it will create irresponsible professionals. Everyone decides 'this is fabulous, let's do it,' but they forget the disciplines to make it happen, and they destroy it very quickly."

For Catholic Relief Services' D'Onofrio, the focus on financial sustainability wasn't inherently bad. The problem was the "rate at which [funders] were trying to make this happen." After relying on grants and subsidized loans, sometimes for years, lenders had to demonstrate financial independence, often within a matter of months. In her job, D'Onofrio felt the pressure to keep "repayment rates at a hundred percent," even as interest rates were climbing higher. With a "really strong push to grow, grow, grow, you kind of sacrifice quality." There was less of a focus on how borrowers were faring, although she could see many were becoming overindebted. "It was all about building institutions," rather than supporting the borrowers themselves. "And frankly, there wasn't a lot of expertise in how to do that. The people at these large donor institutions would write these grand documents, with these big picture or conference-level kind of ideas. And then I'd say, 'Okay, send me somebody that can help me set up a branch office.' You couldn't find someone."

As they pushed to create for-profit lenders, donors were trying on a new role. Before Dale Adams and the "Spring Review," public institutions subsidized lenders with the idea that those subsidies would be passed on to borrowers, primarily in the form of lower interest rates. Now, lenders received grants, favorable loan terms, and loan guarantees with the understanding that they would use those subsidies for *themselves*, which would hold them over as they adopted a "market-based, results-oriented" approach. Money still flowed from, say, Washington to La Paz, but for markedly different purposes. This was no longer about making *borrowers* self-sufficient. It was about making sure the *lenders* were.

A Proposition

Freetown, Sierra Leone

About three-quarters through 2021

IDRISSA WAS DEEPLY SHAKEN BY THE MESS WITH THE POLICE AT THE roundabout. It was far too close a call. Feeling generally stressed and anxious, he deflected his attention away from his own responsibility in the situation—after all, he had let his license expire—directing his worries onto Aminata's loan instead. Idrissa fretted that the police could come by any day, just like they had with their neighbor Panneh. He became short with Aminata, snapping when she asked for even a few cents for sugar or bread—why couldn't she manage her own finances? One week, when she asked for about $2 to help pay off that week's debt, he yelled at her about the risk she was taking. Aminata was surprised. Although the marriage wasn't born out of love, he was always respectful, encouraging her to make her own decisions and build something that was hers alone.

Now, though, Idrissa decided he would just pay off his wife's debt himself, to rid the family of the stress. Borrowing from friends at the office, he pulled together the last $50 or so, handed it to Aminata to give to the loan officer, and washed his hands of the situation. "I advised her not to take out another loan," he remembers telling Aminata. She agreed, telling Idrissa, "I also don't want embarrassment from those people. I've decided I won't take again." In total, she had paid just over $200 for a $150 loan.

After that, to avoid the tense atmosphere at the house, Idrissa spent most evenings drinking tea and talking politics at a friend's used auto parts shop down on the main road. His absences left plenty of time for visitors at home. Kadija, the woman who sold "whatchamacallit" from her back porch to cover her daughter's private school fees and who had brought Aminata into her microcredit group, stopped by a few days after Aminata and Idrissa had agreed about wrapping up all this "microfinance wahala," as Idrissa called her loan, using the Krio word for trouble. Kadija let herself inside, taking a seat on the top step of the parlor. Aminata sat below, her knees tilted toward the ceiling.

After complimenting her on how nice the house looked and how good her yogurt was, Kadija said she had come by because she wanted to take out another loan. She needed Aminata in the group, didn't have anyone to replace her—even though Kadija's business was solid, she was far from making enough money to qualify for a larger, individual loan. Sticking to her agreement with her husband, Aminata immediately refused. No more money stress, no more worries about the police. "Please," Kadija implored, "they won't give us any money without you. We won't have a full group. Your husband, he helps you out, but the rest of us are on our own."

Recently, Kadija's husband, Abdul, had begun refusing to even pay for their daughter Ada's school fees, no matter that she was his biological child. "Maybe he thinks because I have my business now, I don't need help from him," she figured. The one time she borrowed $5 from Abdul, he demanded quick repayment, threatened that if that didn't happen "there won't be peace in the house." Kadija paid the money back, but later than he would have liked. As a result, she wore a few shiny purple bruises on her face for a week or two. The irony of having received blows from a man who worked at a women's rights organization wasn't lost on her. "But he's just a driver."

There had been trouble with her business, too. Sales of the drugs she sold had been enough to pay for daily lunch and transportation for her daughters, Rose and Ada, plus their uniforms, which needed to be replaced yearly. But recently one of her best customers had stopped coming by with his girlfriend. They used to each buy a pill of tramadol, the opiate, every day, netting Kadija an easy $2.20 by nine in the morning. Without them, the girls' transportation to and from school was gone.

She tried cutting back on expenses, making one pot of rice and stew for the family every two days. As she cooked, she privately mocked Abdul's $15-a-month contribution. With inflation, "it now costs $6 to cook every two days," she scoffed. "What's this money going to do?" But she reasoned with herself. "He only makes $100 a month. And rice is now $40 a bag.

He doesn't have much choice." She knew he was having problems with the mother of his other children, too. They'd have screaming matches over the phone about how little he gave. Sometimes, the woman showed up at their house, threatening to take everything inside. Kadija felt for her, and for Abdul. "Just leave her," she advised him. "We need peace."

Kadija was having a hard time finding that herself. One morning, she yelled at Rose when the girl dipped into leftovers for breakfast. "That stew, we're going to eat it tonight," Kadija said, slapping her hand from the pot. "You'll just have to manage. I don't have money today."

* * *

Aminata felt bad for Kadija—things with Abdul sounded stressful. She had always felt he was a wicked, cheap man, raising their rent without ever following through on his promises: to fix the water well, for example, which had been broken for as long as Aminata had lived in Two Taps. But she remained tepid about the idea of a second loan. She told Kadija about her agreement with Idrissa, and about how hard things had been for them lately: the "police business" at the roundabout, the phone calls from home. So Kadija tried a different tactic. She explained that she had already applied for the second loan anyway, including Aminata's name on the application. To start over would be too complicated, maybe require even more starting fees from a new lender. They were too far along now for her to back out.

Aminata insisted: she didn't need another loan. So, Kadija suggested something else. Aminata could take out the loan and hand over the money to Kadija. Kadija and her sister-in-law could then split it, paying back on Aminata's behalf. Aminata wouldn't have to pay a cent. All she would have to do was go to the office to tell them she wanted another loan for her yogurt business, put her initials where they told her to, and take a photo with a guarantor. Since Kadija, as leader of the group, was the one who handed the money over to the loan officer, no one would have to know.

Aminata considered Kadija's suggestion. She had been feeling more affection for her lately, not just because they had borrowed together but also because their daughters had recently become close. Aminata's daughter, Doris, loved carting Kadija's younger daughter, Ada, around Two Taps, helping her with her schoolwork and traipsing together through the neighborhood's narrow streets. And on principle, Aminata wasn't fundamentally opposed to the idea of taking out a loan for someone else. "I've heard of a lot of people who do it," she reasoned. "It happens a lot."

For example, she had recently learned something new about her neighbor Grandpa. For months, he had been telling her that one of the reasons money was so tight for him was because he was paying off a LAPO loan on behalf of a woman he had stood as guarantor for. When she ran away, overwhelmed by repayments, the responsibility fell on him.

Aminata felt bad for the old man, who was struggling to pay off the final $50 or so now that he had retired. He no longer made $65 a month as a security guard and had gone through most of his savings in the first year of "mandatory idleness," as he called it. (He claimed to have been forced out once he reached sixty.)

But Grandpa had let it slip recently that *he* had been the one to ask the woman to take out the loan—for him. He had wanted to sell used clothes but didn't think any loan officer would agree to lend to him because he was a man. With no collateral to speak of, an individual loan was out of the question.* He gave the woman "a little something" in exchange for her effort.

As far as he could tell, LAPO didn't know about the details of this transaction. He was listed as guarantor, the woman was now gone, and they just wanted their money back. The loan officers went easy on him, maybe because of his age. "They're not harassing me," he said. But he was determined to pay. Cleansing himself of the debt was a matter of duty, pride, and religion. "Islam requires that you pay off all your debts before you die. It's the honorable thing to do." Things felt more urgent as he was aging, given that in Islam, "if you die, then your family has to pay." He sold his finest suits, some shoes, and tried to slowly whittle down the remainder of the loan. "I manage," he said. "I don't worry about it. Because God is the giver. I truly have that belief."

Even if such arrangements were common, Aminata worried to Kadija

* Loans to men are usually individual loans, which, unlike group loans, do require collateral.

about what Idrissa would think. Kadija insisted that no one, not Idrissa, not Abdul, not the loan officers, needed to know about this. Aminata agreed there was little risk of the women in pencil skirts and high heels doing any significant probing. Throughout the first six-month loan, there had been no lessons, no trainings, no check-ins. The loan officer only came by Kadija's house, never to anyone else's, and only for a few minutes to collect the cash. At the top of a lined page in Kadija's repayment book, a few dates had been written by one of the loan officers. These were supposedly minutes from group meetings, but Kadija didn't remember ever having one. "Anytime the loan officer comes, she signs that. Because sometimes a white person* comes to check, and if you don't sign they'll say, 'Well, what did she pay, what did they talk about.'" The loan officers had told Kadija that "the white people can harass us" if there weren't minutes. They said their jobs were on the line. Kadija never argued. What did she care, so long as she got her loan?

* * *

In the days after stopping by her house, Kadija kept on Aminata. "She said if I don't agree, then they won't get the money. I was afraid to do it, but I felt sympathy for them." Aminata also reasoned that taking out a loan for her neighbor, who was older with better social connections, might help her out, too. Maybe Abdul wouldn't raise the rent this year. Maybe the long-promised water pump would materialize. And even though she knew there were real risks, it felt hard to take microfinance seriously. The loans seemed so fungible, as if out of thin air: given whenever the lenders felt like it, on their terms. The loan officers who came by the house seemed to write down whatever worked for them without a real consideration of what the women of Two Taps needed. They made up business names and figures that fit the demands of the white sheets they wrote on. Why shouldn't she bend the loan to fit her own needs? Aminata ultimately agreed to Kadija's request, even though she confessed, "I'm still afraid."

When Kadija approached ASA about a second loan, the women were told they'd have to give another $23 to open another account: more

---

* The managers are actually from Bangladesh, but lighter-skinned, relatively well-to-do foreigners are often referred to as "white" in Sierra Leone.

savings, more administrative fees, an "entrance fee," Kadija wasn't sure what, exactly. She found herself in a rage at the office, having figured that the process would go more smoothly with time—and realizing that she'd have to pay $46, upfront and out of pocket, since she had to cover Aminata's loan, too. Another borrower who was there recounted, "She made a mess of the place! She was yelling! She was so angry. She said, 'It's just because we're poor, that's what makes us come here. If we had money, you wouldn't ask for our money like that.'" Kadija threatened, "If you add any more fees, we won't take the loan."

The loan officer apparently knew she was bluffing. He curtly apologized, then took money for the fees anyway.

As Kadija instructed, Aminata told ASA she was taking out another loan for a "mixed" business: a little bit of drinks, a little bit of yogurt. She signed her initials on the front of a new loan book and took a photo with her guarantor, Grandpa's grandson—he in a white T-shirt, she in a blue one. She then handed the money over to Kadija. As punishment for her outburst at the office, Kadija says she received her own check two days later than the other women in the group. She laughed it off. "When I went to the office, they just kept saying, 'The system is down.'"

As Kadija had promised, the scheme stayed between the two women. Their privacy was foiled by Aminata's thin walls and Grandpa's many hours at home. He had overheard everything. Within a few days, he let the secret slip.

When Idrissa confronted Aminata, her only defense was that she couldn't deny those older than she was. He didn't speak to her until Grandpa, uncharacteristically, calmed him down. "I'm not mad. I'm not mad," Idrissa insisted, putting up his hands. "But if there's a police case, that will be on her. I won't be angry, but I will not give her any money. Not even for food."

CHAPTER 10

Like a Drug

IN THE EARLY 2000S, ELIZABETH FUNK, AN ENERGETIC TECH PROFES-sional living in the San Francisco Bay Area, heard about small loans to help poor people start their own businesses. She can't remember how, exactly; it was just sort of in the air at the time. But when she did, she felt an instant, intuitive click.

Funk was undergoing something of a life transition at the time. She had worked at Microsoft in the 1990s, helping to create Microsoft Office. She then worked at Yahoo! just as the company was going public—at the time, the third-largest initial public offering on record. She now had time and money on her hands and was energized by the opportunities her short, brilliant career had offered. She had seen how far financing and ideas and hard work could go.

Which is why microcredit made so much sense to her. "Coming from Silicon Valley, I was particularly smitten with the idea of letting people build their own way out of poverty because I'd seen the power of entrepreneurship," Funk told me over coffee in the upscale San Francisco neighborhood of Pacific Heights in the spring of 2022. "When you see that, it's like a drug." It seemed that at some fundamental level she felt she had the same essence as, say, a microfinance borrower in Mexico: both young, ambitious, hardworking women, separated only by geography and luck and proximity to wealth.*

---

* Anthropologist Erin Beck observed this sort of one-to-one assumption among other microfinance advocates and, more broadly, Westerners working in international development. She writes, "Policymakers' backgrounds . . . gave them the sense that they understood what businesses of any size

Intrigued by what she had heard about microfinance, Funk poked around, learned about Grameen, sent a $5,000 check and "a cold letter saying, 'I would really like to learn more about your organization, will somebody call me?'"

Someone soon did, and Funk was invited to a follow-up meeting of the Microcredit Summit, which she eagerly attended. There, Funk met Grameen staff, heard stories about successful small businesses and single mothers who could now comfortably take care of their kids. She also met staff from Deutsche Bank, who told her they were intrigued by the idea of investing in microfinance. It seemed promising, with its high repayment rates, its do-good image, its self-sustaining model. The high interest rates now baked into microfinance suggested potential for high profits, and if the numbers from the Microcredit Summit were to be believed, the tiny-loan industry was booming, adding millions of new customers each year. Microborrowing also had "low correlation," in the words of a Deutsche Bank memo, to mainstream financial assets or the general economy. Put another way, microcredit was unlikely to be moved by the global economy: poor people would continue to borrow no matter what. Seeing a new opportunity, in 1997 Deutsche Bank had launched a "socially motivated" microfinance fund that invested in microfinance lenders, including those who were becoming commercial. It claims to be the first bank to do so.

Investors were looking to diversify. The East Asian Miracle of the 1970s to 1990s, in which several East Asian economies recorded spectacular economic growth, as well as rising industry and wealth in China, the Indian subcontinent, and the former Soviet Union, demonstrated that there were new ventures to back and money to be made far beyond America and Europe. Economies that just a few decades before had been cut off from Western capital or seen as too risky were now rebranded, no longer "developing countries" but instead "emerging economies." Banks and private investors, eager to find new invest-

---

needed to succeed, because they could look to their own experiences as guides. . . . For example, because they had benefited from business conferences in the United States, the board [of one organization] sponsored an annual business conference for their beneficiaries, replicating an elite practice for the benefit of the poor." Erin Beck, *How Development Projects Persist: Everyday Negotiations with Guatemalan NGOs* (Durham, NC: Duke University Press, 2017), 78.

ments, began to see "an opportunity," explains Joan Trant, who worked in nonprofit microfinance before supporting commercial microlending through the International Association of Microfinance Investors. They realized, "folks at the base of the socioeconomic pyramid actually control $5.3 trillion of assets. You just have to figure out the right, cost-effective distribution channel to deliver goods and services to them. And microfinance provided that."

Soon after the follow-up Microcredit Summit meeting, Funk considered joining the Grameen Bank board, even attending one of their meetings. Funk recalls Muhammad Yunus outlining the bank's basic numbers: relatively high interest rates, low defaults, regular profits. "I said, 'but wait. You're charging a full interest rate, you're profitable. Why exactly are you *non*profit?'" (Yunus had in fact long been clear that Grameen was at least aiming to be for-profit, but that those profits were intended to be plugged back into Grameen operations and to Grameen members, not to individual private shareholders.) Funk says her "business school brain was going." (Funk has an MBA from Harvard.) She was also thinking about those she knew back in San Francisco. Several tech companies had just gone public: not just Yahoo!, but also eBay and Amazon. People in her network were now phenomenally wealthy and looking for ways to put their cash to work.

The classic approach had been philanthropic: giving grants to museums, charities, schools, and promising individuals, just as the Rockefeller Brothers Fund had done with the Grameen Bank and Women's World Banking. But Silicon Valley tycoons had come of age as concepts like social entrepreneurship—applying a business mindset, and businesses themselves, to achieving social goals—and socially responsible investing— investing in a company that has explicit social goals, but with the aim of getting your money back, if not also making a little in the process—were settling into the culture. It was now increasingly accepted that money that was invested was actually *better* than money that was free. If that money was invested well, netting not only social returns but also profits, it could generate more money, which could be used to fuel more good causes, and so on: a self-perpetuating pot of do-good cash. Silicon Valley types were also comfortable with failure. It was part of their business model, an opportunity to learn, to "pivot." If a microfinance investment went belly-up, or included an unexpected outcome, this was something to learn from, not harp on.

At the board meeting, Funk thought, "I might be able to get [Grameen] a hundred-dollar donation, but if you were to give somebody's money back, even at a zero return or one percent return, I might be able to get you a hundred *thousand* dollars. A *million* dollars."

In Funk's recollection, Yunus was unimpressed, snapping, "It's unethical to make money while doing good." She disagreed. "If my investors make a return as a byproduct, I'm okay with that. As long as your goal is growing microfinance, and you are not driven by profit, then I'm fine with my ethics." She realized later that she was essentially proposing impact investing—a sort of spin on socially responsible investing, with a focus on increasing both social and financial returns, even though this was "before the term impact investing had been coined."

Yunus's reaction was surprising, given that he and the Grameen Bank had helped to pave the way for a more commercial approach. In 1997, a piece in *Grameen Dialogue*, the newsletter of the Grameen Trust, argued that microfinance needed to "attract mainstream funds," that private-sector staff and executives needed to be recruited, that banks needed to enter the field. In an interview published in the newsletter, Yunus said, "Finding a way to get involved with the capital market itself would be a fantastic thing to do." That year, the Grameen Bank was nominated as an honorary member of the now-defunct Money Matters Institute, which aimed to create dialogue between "leaders of financial services, international institutions and policymakers in developing countries, to foster the most realistic role for private capital in the financing of genuine sustainable development."* A year later, in 1998, David Gibbons, a Yunus disciple who worked on copycat Grameen projects in Malaysia, declared on the PBS series that to expand microfinance, "we have to convince [commercial banks] this is a potentially profitable business. We can only convince them of that by helping to make profits." To help cement relationships with private capital, investors like Bill Price, who cofounded TPG Capi-

---

* Other members included the World Bank, Fidelity Investments, and State Street Corporation, one of America's "Big Three" index fund managers.

tal, one of the world's largest private equity firms, were invited to join the Microcredit Summit Advisory Board.

Funk says after her disagreement with Yunus she "obviously" didn't join Grameen's board (she says they parted ways amicably). But she couldn't shake that discussion with Deutsche Bank, or the figures Yunus had shared. She told me, "I thought, 'I'm going to prove this.' When I look at an industry and all of a sudden I see a big gaping hole, it's like, ah, man, now I have to do that. When Muhammad and everybody told me you can't do it, that's when I'm like, 'Oh, don't tell me I can't do something.'"

In 2003, Funk launched the Dignity Fund, an early microfinance investment fund that lent to microfinance companies.* The fund had "the dual goals of assisting the entrepreneurial poor to improve their lives through access to credit and generating modest investment returns for its investors," providing a third-party channel through which individuals could invest in microfinance without dealing directly with international lenders themselves. Based on research she had done, Funk believed that helping microfinance companies grow through private investment would simultaneously allow microlenders to reach more borrowers *and* charge lower interest rates at the same time. The more people lenders reached, the less it would cost per borrower, and thus the less they would have to charge.

The Dignity Fund raised nearly $6 million from family and friends, "just to see what would happen," Funk recalls. The Dignity Fund then lent that money to fourteen microfinance organizations in Mozambique, Mexico, Indonesia, Peru, India, Armenia, the Philippines, and elsewhere. Funk told investors they should expect to get their money back in a few years but gave them no sense of how much they might make on top of that. "I told them, 'I don't know what return you'll get, but it'll be better than if you gave it away.'"

She soon met others interested in investing in microfinance, who would

---

* There were several others that preceded the Dignity Fund or soon followed its establishment, including the Latin America Challenge Investment Fund, established in 1999 and offering market rate returns; MicroVest, established in 2003 and attracting a broad array of support, ranging from religious groups to accredited investors; Microcredit Enterprises, established in 2005 to offer loan guarantees for microfinance funders and below-market returns for their investors; and Developing World Markets, which offered two commercially oriented microfinance funds.

have one another over for dinner, coffee, wine, discussions. "We were like this little unofficial team of people saying, 'We don't know exactly what we're doing, but we believe in this,'" Funk recalls. Joan Trant, of the International Association of Microfinance Investors, says there was a feeling of "urgency" to get private money involved in, and expand, microfinance, especially as public donors had made it clear they wouldn't foot the bill forever. "There was no way the traditional banking system was going to serve them. There was this sense of, 'If we don't get this out there we'll lose a generation.'"

Pierre Omidyar, the founder of eBay, believed in it, too. Omidyar had started eBay in 1995 to "democratize the marketplace," so that, as the *New Yorker*'s Connie Bruck put it, "buyers and sellers would all have equal access to information and opportunity." Microcredit felt like an almost perfect parallel, another way to equalize access to capital, to unleash entrepreneurial spirit and promote free market principles.

After eBay went public, in 1998, Omidyar was worth nearly $1 billion. At first, Pierre and his wife, Pam, established a philanthropic family foundation to support microfinance and other causes—a classic grant-giving operation, akin to what the Rockefellers had done for decades. But they soon grew frustrated with nonprofit regulations. So, in 2004, they opened the Omidyar Network. Matt Bannick, a former eBay and PayPal executive who later managed the network, told me he saw it as a "philanthropic investment firm," a way to invest with a cause. Bannick says Omidyar was driven by a simple question: "Why is it when people think about doing social good, they immediately assume they have to do it with grants? Can't you also do it through investments?"* Omidyar was drawn to investing in microfinance because of the simplicity it offered. He told the *New Yorker* he was particularly taken by the idea that, after an initial injection of cash, "you're done! It's a self-sustaining, profitable model, which opens the door to reaching large numbers of people who need to be reached by this tool of access to capital."

In 2005, Pierre and Pam gave a $100 million gift to the Tufts Uni-

---

* Grants would still sometimes be used to support funders or those working in riskier environments. For example, Omidyar helped to launch BRAC in Sierra Leone and Liberia, using a mix of grants and loans.

versity endowment (the couple had met there as undergrads). Omidyar instructed that the cash be used to start a microfinance investment fund. Doing so would serve two purposes: lend money to small lenders around the world, while also making money for Tufts, which would plug profits into financial aid, research initiatives, and faculty conferences.

By this time, other niche microfinance investment outlets had opened. They were concentrated in Europe, where social investing had been pioneered by a Dutch company called Triodos, which opened in the 1980s to invest in companies that had explicit environmental goals. Taken with the idea that global capital could be funneled to the world's poorest women, and persuaded by a very persistent Michaela Walsh, Triodos soon became one of the first funders of Women's World Banking. It later funneled money into early commercial versions of microfinance in Kenya, piggybacking off earlier USAID efforts to transform one of the country's largest microfinance lenders into a commercial bank.* Government pension funds, especially in Scandinavia and the Netherlands, soon saw investing in microfinance as a way to make money for retirees while also signaling a country's commitment to global causes. Within a few years, other pension funds did the same. In 2006, TIAA-CREF, an American retirement fund that serves millions of American teachers, clinicians, and government workers, invested $100 million in microfinance through its newly launched "Social and Community Investing Department." Chuck Waterfield, who had worked in microfinance for decades and had been critical of the hard push to get microlenders to go for-profit, worried there was a fundamental tension here. Although TIAA-CREF invested in microfinance because a survey of its members "showed . . . a desire to promote human rights and economic development," Waterfield observed that "pension fund managers, as a rule, have one primary job—get the highest returns possible for their clients." TIAA-CREF members "are poor teachers, not rich people." To live as comfortably as possible, "they needed to

---

* K-REP, a Kenyan microlender, received support from USAID in the mid-1990s to transform itself from an NGO, in the words of a USAID staffer testifying to Congress in 1997, "into a bank able to leverage private investment for the benefit of poor microentrepreneurs." "Microcredit and Microenterprise: The Road to Self-Reliance," Hearing Before the Subcommittee on International Economic Policy and Trade of the Committee on International Relations, July 23, 1997.

get a high return." And that meant they needed to make money off micro-finance borrowers.

* * *

Microlenders seeking private funding—as they had been encouraged to do through the Microcredit Summit and then by donors like USAID—had another option. Rather than working with either investors or public donors, they could take on debt directly from banks. Large commercial banks within regions where microfinance was flourishing—Latin America, Southeast Asia, the Indian subcontinent—were looking to expand their customer base and, in some cases, fulfill government requirements that they facilitate lending to the poor. Some larger banks began to lend to newly transitioned microfinance banks. Some bought up newly profitable microfinance lenders. And some opened microfinance operations themselves. By the end of the twentieth century, within Latin America—where commercialized microfinance was supercharged in part thanks to the early BancoSol success and thanks to the many "emerging" economies there—commercial banks provided almost a third of microcredit. Formal financial institutions—not NGOs—provided another 50 percent.

International banks soon became interested, too.* Citigroup's charitable foundation had supported microdevelopment projects as far back as the 1960s, when it funded Accion's early work on water wells and electrification. It later worked with the Grameen Trust to start up microcredit programs in South Korea, Thailand, Indonesia, the Philippines, and Malaysia. By the turn of the century, microfinance looked profitable enough for the bank *itself*, not just the foundation, to get involved. In 2002, at a follow-up meeting of the Microcredit Summit, Victor Menezes, the senior vice chairman for Citigroup USA, said, "[We] strongly believe that [microcredit] is a commercially viable option and we really believe that this is the best way to alleviate poverty and help development around the world." Deutsche Bank, which had previously run a socially motivated microfinance fund, also opened a commercial fund, which prioritized financial, not necessar-

---

* In 1999, *The Economist* reported that "given the premium on 'socially responsible' lending, big banks are trying desperately to find ways to support microfinance." *Grameen Dialogue*, no. 41, January 2000.

ily social, returns.* In 2006, Standard Chartered announced it would funnel half a billion dollars from development finance institutions and investors down to microfinance lenders in Africa, Asia, and the Middle East. The bank saw microfinance as a "very commercially viable proposition," recalls Prashant Thakker, who launched Standard Chartered's microfinance initiative and acted as its global head for microfinance.

Investors soon had even more options when a few banks—first Citibank, then Morgan Stanley—offered microfinance collateralized loan obligations (CLOs) in the mid-aughts. Put simply, CLOs allow investors to buy debt that has been bundled together. By now, CLOs had become infamous in the American housing market, where high-risk mortgages were packaged together and sold to investors. (If you've heard of CLOs, this is probably why: the huge amount of bad debt, bundled all together, was a key ingredient in the housing and mortgage bubble that burst in 2008, bringing the global economy down with it.) The 2007 Morgan Stanley microfinance CLO bundled $110 million worth of loans to microfinance lenders in Azerbaijan, Bosnia, Kenya, Mongolia, Montenegro, Nicaragua, Peru, Serbia, and elsewhere; *Bloomberg*, covering the move, claimed that poor Nicaraguan potters would now have a chance to grow their businesses thanks to the investment. The CLO was rated, according to *Bloomberg*, "on par with debt sold by Wal-Mart Stores Inc . . . and drugmaker Eli Lilly & Co"—that is to say, Wall Street saw this as a very good investment. The debt was bought by twenty-one banks, hedge funds, insurance companies, asset managers, and mutual funds. According to the *Grameen Dialogue* newsletter, *New York Times* opinion columnist Thomas Friedman championed such microfinance CLOs. "Bundl[ing] together" microloans and selling them "on a commercial basis to the Citibanks of the world" is, Friedman thought, "how you change the world—get the big market players to do the right thing for the wrong reasons."

But those "wrong reasons" worried Sharon D'Onofrio, who worked with Catholic Relief Services, helping lenders shift for-profit. At conferences

---

* It invested on behalf of German insurance company Munich Re, Merrill Lynch, the German development bank KfW, and unnamed "Ultra-High-Net-Worth Individuals." Rocio Cavazos and Melanie Meslay, "Fund Assessment Study Microfinance Subordinated Debt Fund: VG Microfinance-Invest Nr. 1," Deutsche Bank Global Social Finance.

and fundraising events, she kept running into investors newly interested in microfinance. Although some, like Elizabeth Funk, said they were driven by financially sustainable social change, D'Onofrio saw other investors, particularly those who wanted not just to lend to microfinance companies but to buy a stake in them, glom on to "microfinance institutions because they were highly profitable, but not necessarily as a social impact." She remembers meeting one investor who was interested in microfinance because it would "offer him exposure in another currency," another because the loans were thought to be safe during economic downturns. "He started describing when the economy slows down, the microfinance institutions activities go up, because obviously more people go into the informal sector, they're unemployed, they need loans," D'Onofrio told me. She was shocked. Optimism that poverty might force more poor people to take on more debt felt starkly different from the social motivations expressed by other microfinance funders and managers she knew. For investors, it seemed, "It was all about what it would do for *them*. They were so disconnected from the clients."

D'Onofrio also began to be skeptical of those who "called themselves 'social investors.' They just *happened* to be invested in a poor country, an institution that served the poor. But they were really excited about a new 'asset class,' not the clients themselves." D'Onofrio went on, explaining, "Their expectations for returns were more than I'm getting in my retirement funds right now. And these types of investors became more and more influential." The influx of investors with their varied motivations made it difficult to know what exactly everyone was working toward. "As more and more actors became involved, microfinance became defined in ninety-nine different ways," D'Onofrio remembers. "What we were trying to achieve was not necessarily clear."

Elizabeth Littlefield, who oversaw the World Bank–affiliated Consultative Group to Assist the Poor after working with Women's World Banking, remembers "private equity investors"—with a reputation for pushing companies to quickly expand—"and social investors sitting next to each other at board meetings, pulling organizations in one direction or another." Yunus had been particularly concerned about private investors buying up equity in microfinance lenders. As partial owners, they would make more money if the lender did, and thus have an incentive to push up interest rates even higher.* Some microfinance lenders were so concerned about mission drift that they shied away from the commercialized transition, choosing to stay as little NGOs and rejecting private capital. Others leaned in. Prashant Thakker, the former global head for microfinance at Standard Chartered, says before investing in a microlender, he always tried to suss out the motivations of a microfinance company's executives, to make sure they weren't too profit-driven—no private jets, reasonable interest rates, a customer code of conduct, things like that. Over time, he told me, finding "socially minded" lenders became a struggle. "As the institutions matured and got larger, they were supported by private funding, and they sort of lost their mission."

Joan Trant of the International Association of Microfinance Investors told me that "many [investors] started out being motivated by philanthropic, humanistic objectives, but then also realized that these are investments that work." One investor told her he was drawn to microfinance because it was a risky but promising investment that could offer big rewards, akin to hedge funds, the difference being "that if I lose money, I don't feel bad because it's for a good cause." As it turns out, he didn't have much to worry about: after plugging 10 percent of his assets into the increasingly commercialized sector, he made 8 percent on loans to microlenders and expected to make 20 percent on equity investments.

Although the investor predicted that such "above-market returns are not ultimately sustainable," they became expected. Pierre Omidyar had hoped the Tufts fund would make around a 9 percent return. Although it ended up making half that, around 4.5 percent, that figure still beat out what the overall Tufts endowment itself was making. By the late aughts, Trant says the average yield on loans to microfinance institutions was around 8 percent;† equity investors, who bought a stake in a microfinance lender, were even more ambitious, targeting between 9 and 25 percent

---

* Elizabeth Funk told me that it was out of respect for this concern that the Dignity Fund only focused on lending to microfinance lenders, rather than investing through equity.

† CGAP offered a similar number: an average 7.5 percent return on equity for MFIs in 2006. Richard Rosenberg, "CGAP Reflections on the Compartamos Initial Public Offering: A Case Study on Microfinance Interest Rates and Profits," Consultative Group to Assist the Poor Focus Note no. 42, June 2007.

returns.* Chuck Waterfield says he met people at conferences who "told me secretly that their 'social' investor wouldn't put any money in unless there was a 25 percent return. If you're only making 15 percent, they won't even return your calls."

These goals seemed feasible, because microfinance lenders were doing spectacularly well. By 2007, the leading 176 microfinance institutions had an average return on equity of 17.2 percent—in many cases, much higher than what conventional banks were seeing. In 2007, Grameen sported a return on equity of 22.15 percent; BRAC, 23.27 percent; Compartamos, a microfinance company in Mexico, 57.35 percent; and Bandhan Bank in India, a whopping 131.21 percent. (As comparison, Alphabet, the parent company of Google, had just over 26 percent return on equity as of September 2022. That same year, most major U.S. industries—including chemicals, electronics, and pharmaceuticals—had far below a 50 percent return on equity.) Even microfinance companies based in regions that had been considered poor and risky, such as sub-Saharan Africa, proved they could make money. In 2012, the Nigerian lender LAPO boasted return on equity of 54 percent.

Microfinance became even more appealing when the investments seemed to weather the 2008 financial crisis. One investor told Trant that during the crash his microfinance investments were the only ones providing positive returns; Omidyar's Tufts microfinance fund made just over $13 million, a 12 percent return, in 2008. Even as collateralized loan obligations in America, with their millions of high-risk mortgages and other spectacularly overvalued debt, famously imploded, the *microfinance* CLOs remained relatively safe. Investors who had plugged money through one Deutsche Bank operation saw returns of 3.5 to 7 percent even during the crash; none lost any money. In 2008, the "Class A" investors of Elizabeth Funk's Dignity Fund saw an 8.4 percent yield. Even though some of the microfinance lenders they invested in defaulted on their obligations in the early part of 2009, by the end of the year profits had stabilized again. Throughout the height of the global recession, in 2009 and 2010, some

---

* Private investors who funneled money through Accion's for-profit investment arm were getting around 15 percent. Paul Breloff, "Accion Venture Lab: Case Narrative," *Innovations: Technology, Governance, Globalization* 10, nos. 1–2 (2015): 75–93.

lenders even paid off their debts early. It turns out the prediction had been right: the world's poor seemed to keep borrowing no matter what.

The growth in private financing for microcredit was spectacular. According to the World Bank–affiliated Consultative Group to Assist the Poor, around the world, equity investments in microfinance had grown by 60 percent *every year* from 2006 to 2010. Besides the sheer numbers, microfinance investments further popularized the idea of doing good while doing well. An investor could empower women, support entrepreneurship, and fight poverty while also making healthy returns.

By 2011, Funk considered her work done. By now, Citigroup was investing in microfinance in forty countries. Deutsche Bank was managing a $20 million microfinance investment fund on behalf of FINCA lenders, as well as an $80.6 million microfinance fund that funneled money to microfinance lenders in twenty-two countries. (Funk was on the fund's board.) A staggering $35 billion had been invested in microfinance, compared to just $15 billion when the Dignity Fund was launched a few years earlier.

Funk closed the Dignity Fund, deciding, "I'm going to get out of the way and let the elephants run." Around this time, Accion made a transition, too. It sold its microfinance investment fund, initially started with grants from USAID, to Luxembourg-based Bamboo Finance. The NGO made $105 million from the sale.

Abbie's New Home

Old Post, Koidu, Kono, Eastern Sierra Leone

2021

AROUND MIDDAY ON A WEDNESDAY, ABBIE SAT IN A DIRT COURTYARD across from her apartment. Laid out in front of her on a clean, smooth rock was a loaf of thick, chewy bread called tapa lapa and a baseball-sized avocado sliced in half. Abbie tore a piece of bread open and stuffed some of the fruit's meat inside. She bit into the sandwich over the rock that had become her new kitchen table.

Abbie was eating outside because she had been kicked out of her house. For years, she had been able to keep up with the $1.50 monthly fees the local authorities collected. She knew that $18 a year was low, even if it didn't include a toilet or running water. Some people paid $100, $200, $300 a year, for a room or two in the heart of Koidu. But her debt, and her auntie Finda's debt, had eaten up everything she had. When she fell behind on her house payments, Abbie tried negotiating a six-month grace period, enough time for her mom and her brother back in the village to help her out. The government people who collected the fees didn't want to hear it. When she was months late, "they threw my things out into the street," locking the front door with a thick, shiny silver padlock.

Her pastor and his wife took pity on her, offering that Abbie and her daughter Princess could stay in the storeroom of her beloved church. Abbie was hesitant, but they insisted. "They said I shouldn't worry about it because I'm so devoted. I go to church every Sunday, Bible study every Wednesday." The pastor showed her the space, directly across the court-yard from her old apartment. From there, she could see her old door with its shiny padlock. Built into the wall of the storeroom was a human-sized cubby. That's where she and Princess would sleep. To get up there, they had to do a little half-hop onto the ledge, butt first, then swing their legs up and over. They brought their mattress from where the government workers had thrown it in front of her apartment and placed it on the floor of the room, leaving a four-poster bed behind. The mirror had made it over, too, and most of their clothes. Abbie and Princess had to share the front parlor with a stack of chairs, a motorcycle, a speaker system, and a keyboard; Abbie would help carry the equipment across the courtyard to church every Sunday. But they could stay for free.

Abbie became obsessed with keeping the parlor clean and warm. She she used bits of bright fabrics to obscure the church's things. When she hosted visitors, she pulled a few plastic chairs from the high stack in welcome. Princess used the motorcycle as a backdrop for the selfies she took. She had her mother's wide eyes and bright smile, and spent hours forming her lips into pouty smiles, posting the photos on WhatsApp. Despite her daughter's pleadings, Abbie refused to offer anything but a blank stare in photos. "I know I'm beautiful," she protested, "but I suffer."

Abbie was sure to never cook inside, never eat there either. Anything that was too messy, too personal, had to be done elsewhere.

Abbie found herself thinking about moving back to Sawula. "It's just not working for me here," she said one afternoon from the storeroom. "I feel like I'm straining too much." She longed for a place where things were contained: where at least some food was grown nearby, where she had family she could count on, however begrudgingly. Most days in Old Post she could cobble together enough for Princess's daily lunch—around 20 cents—and transportation to and from school—30 cents, but not much else. Whenever she had enough cash to make the bike trip to the village, she would leave Princess at the storeroom for a few days, bringing along a few rubber bowls to sell and making 30 or 50 cents per sale. She would then buy palm oil to bring back to Koidu. She could get $15 for a whole container of oil, a good price, $5 more than she bought it for in Sawula. Considering the cost of the oil itself and the $3 to get there and back, she could maybe keep $2. That went to "a little bit of food that I cook. It's not very tasty, but we eat." She often only cooked every two to three days, keeping the leftover rice and stew in a big pot in the back corner of the storeroom. She and Princess would take a few bites from it a few times a day; ground cassava and banana and rice cake filled their bellies in the interim. When things got really bad, "I cry to our pastor, to give me something small." Like it had been lately. "It's been more than one month since I've had enough food to cook on the fire." Each night before bed, she and Princess "put salt in water, we drink it, and we go lay down."

When Abbie told her pastor she was thinking of moving back to the village for good, he dismissed the idea right out. "He says if I go my kid won't be able to go to school. That this is my responsibility." She wasn't convinced Princess would go as far as she wanted even if she stayed in Koidu: the girl had developed a noticeable stutter, every few words getting stuck under her tongue. She was smart enough, but the stutter made her nervous in school. She skipped some days, insisting that she had to stay in the storeroom because of an upset stomach or because her uniform wasn't clean. That didn't bode well for Abbie's dreams that Princess would get an office job one day. Still, Abbie had a feeling that God had sent her to Koidu for some reason, if not to achieve something herself then to make sure her girl could do so. "So," she shrugged, "I'm going to stick around."

The pastor told Abbie that she could stay in the storeroom for as long as she needed—this was part of God's work after all. But Abbie worried. The congregation had been growing; most Sundays, a makeshift awning made of a tarp and a few poles had to be put up, offering the overflow of worshippers a bit of shade. Speakers sat on the hard dirt, blasting the sermon throughout the neighborhood. Abbie had started getting to service early to ensure she would get a spot at the front of the church, where she could more enthusiastically sing along and raise her hands to the Lord. She wondered what the sprawling crowd might mean for the church. If it moved somewhere bigger, would the storeroom move, too?

CHAPTER 11

We Rode the Fad for as Long as We Could

FROM ITS INCEPTION, THE MICROCREDIT SUMMIT CAMPAIGN EMPHASIZED tracking the field's progress towards the ambitious goals defined at the 1997 meeting. Lenders sent in lengthy spreadsheets that tallied how many borrowers they lent to and how many were poor women. The summit, no longer just a series of meetings but now a fully staffed organization, then collated the numbers and sent out annual updates. The focus was on broad figures: whether 100 million families, then 175 million families had been reached. But despite Sam Daley-Harris's self-proclaimed "obsession" with reaching the poorest of the poor, the campaign did not track whether microfinance borrowers became less poor, or whether women borrowers became more empowered. It didn't even track the details of the loans. Lenders did not have to report the interest rates they charged, whether they offered trainings to their borrowers, or the outcome of their borrowers' businesses, not to mention their overall welfare. They did not have to report whether there was any overlap between their customers and the customers of a microfinance lender down the road. Lenders were seen as "helping to reach the goal" simply by saying they had expanded their customer base. Even if that customer paid high interest rates. Even if that customer's business failed. Even if that customer happened to be someone else's, too.

The narrow focus was in part practical: it is far easier, and far cheaper, requiring less manpower, to collate overall numbers than to look at the details behind them. Big numbers also made for great headlines. Every time a goal was reached—or, often, exceeded—provided an opportunity for a glowing press release.

The obsession with rising numbers was also part of a broader trend to take programs "to scale," a loosely defined aspiration that had become ubiquitous in both international development and business. It wasn't enough that a program reached one community, or one province, or even one country. If it worked in one place, it stood to reason that it would work elsewhere. Organizations and the donors who funded them wanted programs to expand; perpetual growth had become the main marker of success.* Funders, with an eye to efficiency, thought they would get more bang for their buck by backing already successful programs, plus start-up costs could be lowered if programs could just be copied and pasted from elsewhere. And organizations could use their reach as a sort of branding: we came up with this idea, and now it's all over the world. Sir Fazle Hasan Abed, the founder of BRAC, claimed, "Small is beautiful but scale is necessary"—a pithy statement that has become BRAC's motto and encapsulates the quiet but dramatic shift from the heady "grassroots" days of early microfinance, driven by a desire to observe and attend to individual communities' needs, to a focus on expansion that came to dominate NGOs and microlenders.

To buttress the dramatic figures, brochures and websites hinged heavily on personal anecdotes, a storytelling technique that is not unique to microfinance. Anyone who's given to any sort of charity or NGO has likely read about how that program has changed the life of a poor woman or a child, offering details about where they live, what they do, what their life was like before and after, maybe even a photo of what they look like. "Microcredit creates good anecdotes, and that's justified," Paul Rippey, an American who worked in microcredit in West Africa, told me. "When a woman has gone from being a slave to those she owes money to and then becomes independent, that *is* inspiring. On a personal level, it can keep someone going. And at an institutional level, the stories were great for fundraising." Anecdotes became crucial to explaining and celebrating microfinance's success and raising money for even further growth. The

---

* As one commentator in *Forbes* put it, the concept has "long been considered gospel." AJ Faraj, "Thinking at Scale Can Be the Secret to Sustainable Growth," *Forbes*, June 15, 2021.

stories could be dramatic: Of a man who no longer beat his wife after she became empowered through her loans and her lending group; the women who employed their husbands; the woman who could now buy sweets for all the children in the village; the mother who, despite not being able to read or write, had a son going to college. The anecdotes were often just a few sentences long and focused almost singularly on a borrower's poverty and how a small business loan helped her to escape it. Everything else—why a borrower was poor, why the economy she was working in was anemic, the details of her family life and social ties—was blurred into the periphery.

Yunus and his story of $27 to forty-two women and of Sufiya Begum and her stools had helped to pioneer this effort. He had proven that funders and policymakers were far more likely to latch on to a single story than multiple, more complicated ones. Yunus's narratives not only aimed to demonstrate the power of loans but to rectify long-held notions of the poor: that they were somehow innately destitute, somehow naturally inhabiting an immobile social position, unworthy of investment. Thanks to Yunus, "no one can look at the world's poor women solely based on their deficits and not also at their assets," Alex Counts, one of Yunus's protégés, told me. "It used to be nonsensical to say that. Now it's nonsensical to deny it."

But Yunus not only flipped long-held ideas of the poor. He also simplified them. Since poor people do not, by definition, have much money, Yunus argued that they didn't need much to make their lives much better, a kind of one-to-one argument that underlay his story of giving $27 to forty-two women and changing their lives forever. But that rationale seemed to defy what many others working in microfinance were beginning to observe: that poor people actually needed *more* money to start a successful business. Because they had so little to begin with, a few dollars here or there was more likely to be diverted to essential costs like food and health care than to a new business, and because they didn't have solid ground to stand on, poor people had to start from scratch, buying start-up materials and paying local fees that wealthier people could afford without much thought. To gather enough money to make a business successful, poor borrowers relied on multiple loans from multiple lenders. Even some microfinance "success" stories featured borrowers who were layered in debt, like those Jeff Ashe had met in the markets of La Paz, Bolivia. Take the story of Lucy Saavedra, considered a successful early borrower in the Cali, Colombia, branch of Women's World Banking. Lucy's husband, having lost his job, opened a bike repair shop. When it was broken into three months later, Lucy took out a loan to construct a workshop at their home. She then learned that other spare bike parts vendors were buying their parts on the black market. The family's prices were undercut; the business faltered. Lucy began to default on her loan, taking out others to make repayments. "Ten years later," she remembers, "we were ninety percent in debt." She considered closing the shop.

To make money, Lucy's husband migrated to Europe, and her son left school to help her in the shop. She and her children then left Cali for a cheaper town. There, with the help of remittances from her husband, still in Europe, the family got by, finally making enough to send their daughter to college.

Although the story is foregrounded by entrepreneurial efforts necessitated by unemployment, punctuated by the consequences of debt, and features a turnaround in which everything *but* credit helped the family pay off the loan—a husband who left the country for work, a son without an education—Women's World Banking offered Lucy's experience as a success. "It was amazing," recalled Clara Akerman, one of the founding trustees of WWB Cali, "because she transformed her business completely." From the perspective of WWB, Lucy survived not in spite of the loan, but because of it.

Simplistic stories told by microfinance institutions obscured broader analyses in other ways. Whenever microfinance advocates referenced the Self-Employed Women's Association, there was rarely, or perhaps just a half clause, acknowledgment of how the women became self-employed in the first place: they had lost their jobs in the wake of liberalized economic policies, which resulted in shuttered fabric factories across the Indian state of Gujarat. Microfinance group meetings were generally not seen as a place to discuss macro-level issues or to emphasize political or worker organizing. As anthropologist Erin Beck writes in her study of Guatemalan microfinance, one American organization "encourage[d] women to achieve empowerment through the market, rather than inspiring them to question its underlying structures, and to act as individuals rather than collectives."

* * *

The microfinance anecdotes that were particularly successful not only offered intimacy and simplicity and suggested empowerment but also, at the same time, suggested scale. As Phil Mader, who researches debt and development at the UK's Institute of Development Studies and has written extensively on microfinance, observes, "There are five anecdotes on a website to convince people that millions of people have done the same." But there was not much backing the assumption that if loans were working *somewhere*, they must be working *everywhere*. "There was not a lot of data around how this really was affecting people's lives," Joan Trant told me.

Part of the problem was timing. While early studies had shown spectacularly positive results that propped up claims that borrowers' incomes were increasing and women were becoming more empowered, most of this research, including Jeff Ashe's work in the 1980s, only lasted about a year and relied on a small number of respondents. That was long enough to see the short-term impacts of an injection of cash, which were likely to be positive: of course a person had more money; they had just been given some. What was missing was the broader, longer view. Little was known about whether these businesses survived after one, two, ten years, and if they did, whether those businesses actually helped a borrower and her family. And it wasn't clear if microfinance helped just a select few borrowers—those who happened to respond to a questionnaire, for example—or the average borrower. Even when Muhammad Yunus wrote *Banker to the Poor*, his core theses—that microfinance created and sustained small businesses, that it was good for children, families, and communities—had been thoroughly championed but not thoroughly tested.

Champions of microfinance did want data that considered long-term outcomes. To reach a fourth goal, "ensuring a positive measurable impact on the lives of clients and their families," the Microcredit Summit Campaign wanted to track "evidence of children going to school especially the girl child," "increase in the creation of jobs," "availability of more time for other activities," even, oddly, "increased activity in the recycling of used things." But advocates couldn't figure out how to do this in an effective way. Qualitative studies based on interviews are notoriously long and may only include just a few dozen borrowers. Quantitative studies, which focus on hard data and may include larger numbers of people, don't always easily assess immeasurable things like who makes decisions in a household. Some lenders suggested doing surveys on a client-by-client basis, assessing their profit and loss statements—an onerous process that wouldn't shine much light on how the client was faring, but simply on the health of their business. To see if clients were "empowered," microcredit employees were told to observe if borrowers had any new friends or if they felt more positively about the future. One organization suggested tracking economic change by asking staff to consider, "Are the rich getting richer and the poor getting poorer?"

All of this left a lot of room for opinion and interpretation and not a lot of clarity on the concrete effects of microfinance. Some organizations, like Freedom from Hunger and Oxfam, did try to rigorously study their programs, sometimes coming up with wildly different results. In some studies, women, particularly those who already had business opportunities, did see their incomes rise. In others, there was a weak connection between women's access to microfinance and their families being able to eat better. A nagging question emerged: If there was such disparity, and if results were so limited, was it really accurate to say that microcredit was resoundingly anti-poverty?

It wasn't clear to microfinance advocates how they could get a more comprehensive answer. So the Microcredit Summit Campaign stuck with aggregated client numbers and figures on a lender's overall financial viability "because," in the words of one participant at a 1999 follow-up meeting, "they're much easier to calculate reliably," even though those numbers "don't tell us whether our clients become less poor due to the services we provide."

That limitation was worrying. In the year 2000, the campaign declared, "[We] will have failed if 100 million families are reached, but there is little impact on the lives of the clients and their families."

* * *

By the time of the Microcredit Summit in 1997, the field of international development—at least the version launched with Truman's quest to uplift "newly awakened" nations through Western means—was about fifty years old. Governments, on their own and through institutions like the IMF and the World Bank, had pumped billions into building roads and schools, into education and health care, into microcredit, to uplift women and reduce poverty. Around the turn of the century, these institutions were stinging from a fresh round of criticism. Two books exemplified the debate. In *Dead Aid*, Zambian-born economist Dambisa Moyo argued that the $1 trillion in aid that had been plugged into Africa not only wasn't helpful. It was actually *harmful*, creating dependency, propping up inept leaders, and distorting markets. In *The White Man's Burden*, American economist William Easterly argued that Western economic policies for the world's poor had failed by hampering local institutions and economies. Both books were hugely influential, making their way into college curricula and onto talk shows. Western institutions, especially in the United States and the United Kingdom, were already sensitive to public perception that they were bloated, disconnected, and inept. To avoid a repeat of perceived failures—such as those identified in agricultural credit programs studied in the 1970s—development agencies wanted to figure out what worked and what didn't before funneling more money into "scaling up." They sought to only back programs that were deemed "proven."

In the late 1990s, some economists proposed a new way of studying development programs. Esther Duflo, Abhijit Banerjee, and several other economists helped to popularize the use of randomized controlled trials, a research method regularly used in medicine, within the social sciences. In medicine, RCTs are conducted by giving one group of people a new treatment that's being tested—say, to see whether a pill works for allergies or lowering cholesterol. That's called the "intervention arm." Another group is given a placebo, something like a sugar pill—the "control arm." Each group has whatever problem is being solved—allergies or cholesterol—but neither group knows whether they've been given the real medicine or the fake one, and the groups are divided randomly. The idea is that without knowing what they're getting, the participants won't change their behavior or be subconsciously prompted to answer one way or the other, and the randomness helps to study a wide cross section of the group being tested—not just the very old or the very young, not just women or men, but a whole range of people. Researchers can then see if the medicine is working in the intervention arm, with all other things being equal and without things like bias getting in the way.

Duflo, Banerjee, and colleagues argued that if medicines could be rigorously tested, surely development programs, which were also ultimately about saving lives, could be, too. Such study design had been used in social science research in the United States for decades, and now Duflo, Banerjee, and other economists began using it to test international development programs. Again, a group of people would be randomly assigned to an intervention—say, deworming tablets or adult literacy classes—and another, similar group of people, in the same or similar community and with the same or similar background, wouldn't receive it. After some time—often a year or several years—researchers would be able to see how the two groups fared and then determine whether the program worked.

Duflo and Banerjee both worked at MIT, bringing money, prestige, and a sense of scientific rigor to the method. With the air of clinical precision and a commitment to rigorous, longer-term research, the economists promised more sophisticated results than those produced by the methods microfinance researchers had relied on. They wouldn't just ask borrowers if they *felt* better off. They would determine if they really *were* better off. Researchers and development funders no longer just wanted to know whether microfinance was growing—it clearly was—but what lay behind those numbers. Many donors, curious about the effectiveness of their funding, became the largest supporters of development RCTs.

Although microfinance RCT results had been trickling in through the 1990s and early aughts, the first large-scale, highly publicized studies were published soon after Yunus and Grameen were awarded the 2006 Nobel Peace Prize. Many results were brutal. On the idea that microfinance would help boost small businesses, several RCTs and other studies showed that microfinance did not, as Yunus and others had claimed, increase borrowers' profits and incomes. The loans didn't even appear to increase business *revenues*, a far lower marker of success. Several studies suggested that poor borrowers were the *least* likely to see an increase in income and far more likely to wind up in debt—an understanding USAID had argued decades before, and which Muhammad Yunus and Sam Daley-Harris had flatly rejected. The borrowers who were making a profit—a minority—were more likely to be profit-making before they took out a loan, given that relatively well-off borrowers were more able to take risks, and thus more likely to invest in successful businesses. Several studies showed that, especially for poorer borrowers, the loans were actually not used for business at all, and instead spent on more pressing things like health care and school fees.

Given that the loans didn't seem to significantly help businesses, it wasn't surprising that they didn't seem to fight poverty either. For some borrowers, household consumption—one measure of wealth—actually decreased after taking a microcredit loan, with credit repayments eating into household costs. Some borrowers even cut down on basics like food. Several studies showed that the borrowers were actually *poorer* than before they took out the loan: in one, borrowers who took out a loan when they were below the poverty line ended up with *less* money than those who didn't take out a loan at all. Put another way, doing nothing, it seemed, was better than using the most acclaimed anti-poverty tool around. (Out of recognition that poor borrowers may be harmed, or at least not particularly helped, in 2003 the World Bank–affiliated Consultative Group to Assist the Poorest, created to support microfinance, made a subtle change in their name, to Consultative Group to Assist the Poor.)

And on and on. Regarding women's empowerment and its trickle-down effects on the family, a few studies demonstrated a positive impact on children going to school and on women having more decision making in the home. More often, though, studies showed no impact on either children's schooling or women's empowerment. Women did not seem to have more control over how money was used, either within their household or within their business. A few studies suggested the loans were actually associated with an *increase* in domestic violence against women. One study found that although women borrowing in groups had been pitched as a way to build female solidarity, companionship, and joint problem-solving, in reality the groups could be intensely stressful, given that members were encouraged to harass delinquent borrowers. While some studies suggested that the group model increased "social capital," others claimed it led to shaming and social exclusion.

What was striking, and hard to ignore, about the mixed, often negative results was that the studies were done in wildly different contexts: in India, where Grameen-style microfinance group lending had saturated whole communities; in Ethiopia, where microfinance lenders encouraged contraceptive use; in Morocco, where larger loans were the norm; in Bosnia and Herzegovina, a decade after the country emerged from war. Around the world, whether lenders targeted women or men or both, whether they were meant for businesses or everyday use, whether borrowers paid 12 percent interest, as was the case in Ethiopia, or 110 percent, as they did in Mexico, there was little evidence that the loans had pulled people out of poverty—or, in the words of three RCT researchers, "of transformative effects on the average borrower." At least when compared to what had been promised—poverty museums, uplifted communities, strong, steady businesses that helped the poor help themselves—microfinance had apparently failed. Still, though, as one briefing put it, "institutional outcomes were fairly strong," with revenue "increase[ing] . . . for the institution." That is, the lenders were doing well, even if the borrowers weren't.

* * *

Rather than refuting the claims and concerns, some microfinance advocates attacked the core premise of RCTs: you can't take a program that works in complicated social and economic situations and treat it as if it were a pill. Real life is messy and unexpected; sure, anecdotes can paint an overly rosy picture, but RCTs could miss the human element. How could empowerment, a nebulous concept that changed depending on a culture and community, be captured in cold, distilled trials? What if a woman didn't get richer but had a more positive understanding of herself and her role in society? Jayshree Venkatesan, who worked in Indian microfinance for years, told me that even though microfinance didn't "upend eight hundred years of patriarchy in one intervention, that doesn't mean it didn't help some people achieve their dreams." (Other academics argued that RCTs, although often critical, actually painted an overly optimistic picture, because they did not fully capture just how devastating debt and its consequences could be.)

Other critics took a broader approach, questioning why this method of study was now considered the new arbiter of success. "The anti-poverty impact evaluation craze is precariously close to inflicting an unrealistic hegemony over social change," Jonathan Lewis, founder of Microcredit Enterprises, wrote in the *Huffington Post*. "The profession's conceit is that, until an academic evaluator evaluates it, every anti-poverty program is under suspicion." Program managers worried that donors' newfound obsession with RCTs—which were being used to study everything from microfinance to animal immunization programs to police traffic stops—stymied creativity and iteration and were blind to context.

Amid the debate, microfinance advocates, as well as RCT researchers like Esther Duflo and Abhijit Banerjee, adopted a more nuanced approach. Rather than focusing on what microfinance apparently couldn't do—increase incomes, empower women, end poverty—the new suggestion was to focus instead on what it *could* do. Maybe there was a bright side to microcredit borrowers having less money: they wouldn't spend it on frivolous, unhealthy things like sweets, alcohol, cigarettes, festivals, and parties. (Casting such restrictions in a positive light resembled the moralizing lessons on "thrift" that poor people endured alongside loans in the nineteenth and twentieth centuries.) Maybe loans couldn't increase business revenue or incomes. But they could help with "consumption smoothing," a fancy way of saying helping to make ends meet. And perhaps using the loans for household costs instead of business was a good thing, an expression of the borrower's desire, a way to exert her agency. Or perhaps it indicated borrower rationality—borrowers knew that investing in food for their kids would produce a better outcome than investing in a small-scale enterprise.

The shifting narrative, that loans should be used for day-to-day consumption, made sense—except that it undercut a key rationale for high interest rates: loans could be expensive not only because borrowers would be willing to *pay* them, but because their businesses would be so successful that they could *afford* them. But what if it turned out that borrowers weren't running businesses at all, or at the very least not particularly successful ones? The rationale was further undermined by other research. While institutions like the World Bank had long promoted the idea that there were abundant investment opportunities for poor people in "emerging" economies, several studies countered that just because borrowers *could* make money, it didn't mean borrowers *would* make money—an obvious but somehow neglected point. (Just because I *could* technically open a potentially successful business in San Francisco doesn't mean that I actually *will*, or that it will be successful. There's a big jump between a *could be* and a *will be* that is contingent upon everything from specific cultural context to supply chains to a borrower's personality.) This was especially true as growing numbers of small businesses, fueled by microcredit, often competed against one another. The small-loan, high-cost, short-loan-length model that was now the norm in microfinance pushed borrowers toward cheap, easy-to-sell retail goods and away from businesses that require up-front financing but take a long time to mature, even if those businesses might ultimately make a lot more money. In Sierra Leone, this means many borrowers sell things like used clothes, imported Chinese trinkets, and fried plantains instead of investing in more substantial businesses like farming or tailoring. Poor borrowers with razor-thin margins can easily be undercut by another vendor selling the same cheap, accessible goods. How many canned tomatoes does one small community really need? How cheap do those tomatoes need to be to entice poor customers? Too much competition over a small amount of geographic and market space—too many women selling cigarettes or used clothes—has led to violent confrontations in markets saturated with microfinance, from Mexico to South Africa.

Studies found that new businesses that did succeed may require at least a year or two—or, sometimes, many years—before seeing any returns, which didn't match well with short-term, high-interest loans. And now that research showed that many loans were used for day-to-day costs that didn't result in financial returns anyway—something microfinance staffers had been noticing for years—the rationale for the high interest rates made even less sense. Jeff Ashe later reflected on the inertia of promoting a model that seemed to have outlived its usefulness. "People could see this wasn't working," he told me. "But when you're into a paradigm, into a thing that you're doing, it's really quite difficult to change gears."

* * *

Around the time that RCT results were coming out, academics, researchers, and those working in microfinance began wondering aloud not just what microfinance could and couldn't do, but also what those miraculous stories and fantastic numbers worked to obscure. In the late 1990s, Ecuador's microcredit sector boomed at the same time formal employment fell. Microfinance took off in the Republic of Georgia from the mid-1990s to the mid-aughts, while nearly two-thirds of the population was plunged into poverty. In the mid-aughts, Zimbabwe was seen as an attractive market for microcredit loans—precisely because its unemployment rate had ballooned to 60 percent. Perhaps poor people were turning to microbusinesses not because they wanted to or because it was best for the economy but because they had no other choice.

For decades, critics had warned that rosy depictions of microfinance neglected the larger economic, political, and social contexts in which borrowers' lives unfolded. At early conferences, in between presentations and funding pledges, Jeff Ashe remembers one persistent thorn in his side.

Judith Tendler was a development economist who started her career at USAID before enjoying a long tenure at MIT. Tendler studied dozens of economic development programs, often on behalf of NGOs and development institutions. As was in vogue, many of these focused on the informal sector. After years of research, Tendler was unconvinced by the focus on the small, claiming this focus came at the expense of development agencies and governments crafting policies that could enact larger, long-term structural changes. Although many of her most formative papers on the subject came out in the 1990s and early 2000s, she poked and prodded at Accion and other microfinance advocates back in the 1980s. "I remember engaging in arguments with her when I was a true believer," Ashe told me.

Tendler's basic premise was that when USAID and the World Bank and the organizations and governments they funded swung toward supporting the informal sector, they risked not only *neglecting* but *actively undermining* larger economic development efforts. With small businesses now firmly seen not only as *one* anti-poverty tool but *the* tool of choice, other state-led policy reforms—trade protectionism, industrial policy, strengthening infrastructure—fell to the wayside. The focus on the small wasn't all bad—Tendler conceded it showed "considerable learning about development" by emphasizing what occurs at the grassroots level. But unlike Yunus, who encouraged borrowers to be "self-reliant" through their own employment, Tendler thought supporting formal employment should still be the major anti-poverty approach. She felt the narrowing "represents the loss of the strategic focus . . . on employment and the growth of local industry as central to the state project of 'serious' economic development itself." In 1987, she wrote that the zeroing in was also "striking . . . given that [the informal] sector was seen, up to five years ago, as marginal, unmodern, and doomed to perish with successful growth."

Tendler also took issue with what she saw as exceptionalism for the small. As tiny firms grew—*if* they grew—informal businesses were not encouraged to abide by laws and regulations, to pay taxes, to follow labor standards. (In *Banker to the Poor* and elsewhere, Yunus railed against government regulations, which he considered unnecessarily restrictive and harmful to creative economic pursuits.) This fetishization of the small, Tendler argued, kept wages low, kept work conditions poor, and encouraged the messy side of informality, like employing children in home-bound businesses that had long, unpredictable work hours. The focus on the small also kept nascent businesses infantile, forever relegated to the informal sector, not encouraged to move beyond it.

Other economists have since argued that employment in a formal, wage-labor position is better—for an individual and an economy—than a swell of precarious small-scale businesses. "The fact is," Aneel Karnani, a professor at the University of Michigan School of Business, wrote in 2007, "most microcredit clients are not microentrepreneurs by choice. They would gladly take a factory job at reasonable wages if it were available." He pointed out that the International Labor Organization, which had first used the term "informal sector" decades before, stated that "nothing is more fundamental to poverty reduction than employment."

Even in Bangladesh, the heartland of microcredit, "it wasn't only microfinance that drove poverty reduction," Lindsay Wallace, a development economist who's worked in microfinance, told me. "There were other economic drivers influencing the economy, such as the turn to industrialization, the factories." (To be clear, that reduction had not been dramatic: by the mid-aughts, Bangladesh and Bolivia, two countries where microfinance had flourished, remained some of the poorest in the world.) In

2009, Hillary Clinton, now no longer First Lady but secretary of state—and still a champion of microfinance—told the *New York Times*, "I am also struck by every international public-opinion poll I've ever seen, that the number one thing most men and women want is a good job with a good income."

It's important to note, though, that expanding formal employment wouldn't necessarily mean expanding *female* employment, given that many women, bound by cultural norms and family responsibilities, stay at home. Sam Daley-Harris remembers Yunus telling him that some Bangladeshi women weren't allowed to touch money or go to the market. But just because there's such severe exclusion in Bangladesh doesn't mean there's exclusion everywhere. In Sierra Leone, for example, women have been the main market vendors for generations, dominating small-scale commerce across the country. In my research, nearly every moderately poor woman I met was engaged in trading of some kind. That's not to suggest there's a dynamic, feminist economy here. The women are not necessarily trading because they have some innate desire to or because it makes the most economic sense, but because there are few other options. In both Bangladesh and Sierra Leone, women are still far more likely to work in the informal sector than men, without a steady job or any benefits like pension or health care.

Beyond just focusing on formal employment, Tendler argued that the focus on the small was a feel-good distraction from the pitfalls of an increasingly globalized economy characterized by the shrinking role of the state, both as economic planner and provider of basic services. By acting as a sort of pressure valve, Tendler worried that the informal sector would "mop up" unemployment in a "trade-liberalized world," helping people to limp by without addressing the reason they had to rely on the informal sector in the first place. Programs that did have track records of reducing poverty, such as social security, expanded health care, and social safety nets, were de-emphasized in favor of "local" and "micro" programs that "distracted attention . . . from broader social policy reforms." Support for small businesses that would empower the poor was framed as a social good—a sort of privatized, micro welfare. Since the poor now had a happy alternative to formal employment, their tiny efforts would help to "keep the peace" rather than call for an expansion of the economy or broader social policy reforms.

Essentially, Tendler leaned more toward USAID's initial think-big arguments instead of the reformed, optimistic, from-the-ground-up alternative that Yunus had helped to popularize. Tendler didn't think, as some microfinance lenders argued, that poverty was primarily due to "lack of capital, lack of education, poor health conditions, and natural and man-made disasters." Tendler wanted to know what lay behind those conditions. To achieve social goals, she argued, the economy needed to grow first, something the state had proved effective in supporting in places as disparate as the United States and East Asia. She wanted large, structural changes at the top, not just small changes at the bottom—an approach that Yunus was convinced would miss the very poor. To be clear, Tendler wasn't against microcredit—in fact, she wrote several papers on how small loan programs could function better. She argued that for such programs to be successful they needed to exist alongside other reforms, from small-scale changes like marketing support for entrepreneurs to economy-wide changes that would make it easier for small businesses to survive. For her, microcredit was but one piece in a much larger puzzle.

Tendler's policy critiques were initially overshadowed by the excitement and hype about microfinance's promises. But the RCT results allowed for a shifting conversation. One of the RCTs that considered the impact of Freedom from Hunger's microcredit programs noted that there was no link between microcredit and access to health care, as Freedom from Hunger had hoped, precisely because health care remained inaccessible, inadequate, and expensive. A 2006 review for the Microcredit Summit Campaign asked, "By contending that the poorest can and do make good use of microcredit, are we letting governments off the hook for providing services, transfer payments, and other forms of assistance to the poor?" At a follow-up meeting, another participant mused, "Will we find that hundreds of millions of people of low income are accessing financial services but that tens of millions of children of primary school age are still not in school? Will we find that financial services, unthinkable in 2007, have reached some of the most remote villages of the world, but tens of thousands of children under the age of five continue to die each day from largely preventable malnutrition and disease?"

* * *

Throughout the 2000s and 2010s, as the RCTs were released, negative headlines about microfinance began to appear. In 2009, *Forbes*, reporting on two microfinance studies, remarked that they "found little impact on health, education, average consumption, women's decision making or self-reported well-being." In 2015, announcing the results of a series of microfinance studies, Innovations for Poverty Action, one of the main institutions running RCTs, put out a press release with the headline "Microcredit Doesn't Live Up to the Promise of Transforming Lives, Six Studies Show," a message that was picked up by several major media outlets such as NPR.

Journalists and academics seemed almost gleeful in discussing the poor results. Alex Counts, a protégé of Muhammad Yunus who had been involved in RESULTS congressional advocacy in the 1980s before leading the Grameen Foundation in America, felt that whether the media and researchers were reporting on microfinance's claims, or now its apparent downfall, "there was a desire for a pretty narrative driving oversimplicity." There was also the essential element of reveal. "If you find something that people don't expect, if it's contrary to what most people think, then it's like 'wow, you're really teaching us something that people don't know,'" Counts told me. That narrative trick, central to reporting on the negative RCTs, was also central to early microfinance framing: *If you think that poor people aren't creditworthy, you're wrong!* Counts describes a kind of whiplash as microfinance went from beloved to scorned. At first, politicians and donors seemed happy to support microfinance, "to say they're trying to help the poor." And then, "there was a pivot away from global support, from this being good. You wake up in five years, and the view of microfinance by politicians and philanthropy and the media had changed dramatically."

Elizabeth Littlefield, who ran the World Bank's Consultative Group to Assist the Poor, felt someone else was to blame for an overly neat narrative: Muhammad Yunus. She felt "strongly that he was oversimplifying." Rather than framing credit as an anti-poverty program or a human right or a way to empower women, Littlefield thought micro-credit should be understood as a type of finance, nothing more. These were business deals, not social programs. For-profit lenders agreed with this sentiment. "This is in a way creating wealth, more than wiping out poverty," Carlos Labarthe, the cofounder of Compartamos, a profit-able Mexican microfinance company, told the *New Yorker* in 2006. In the same article, C. P. Zeitinger, the manager of ProCredit Holding, a string of microfinance banks, said the idea of having poverty museums is "ridiculous! To claim that microfinance is going to solve poverty is a myth. From ancient Greece to today, poverty has been with us and it will occupy us forever."

Littlefield worried that Yunus's bubbly optimism left no room for honesty about the downsides of credit, which was just as likely to make poor people more vulnerable as it was to lift them out of poverty. As she saw it, a loan can be an opportunity or a trap, but it was never a human right. Writing in 2007, Thomas Dichter, who had worked in interna-tional development and microfinance for years, agreed that "the prob-lem is one of exaggerated expectations rather than with microfinance itself." He worried "there is an opportunity cost involved when so much attention is paid to one sector. Inevitably other possible answers to pov-erty reduction get less attention, especially if they seem more complex or difficult."

Of course, microfinance doesn't have to offer an either-or scenario: either you fund small businesses or you invest in macro-level economic changes; either you give loans to women who can then pay for health care or you expand public health care. But in a world of fads, short-term policy proposals, and a perceived scarcity of public resources, focusing on micro-finance *did* effectively work to distract from other solutions as well as unad-dressed structures of impoverishment. And advocates often *did* present a sort of zero-sum game: as poor borrowers became self-sufficient, they rea-soned, there would be a diminished need for broader social services and large-scale economic changes. Loans weren't pitched as a complement to more fundamental change. They were an *alternative* to it. One civil servant in Kerala, India, reportedly said—it's not clear whether in jest—"there was

no longer any need to worry about primary health care or primary education . . . because 'they now have microfinance.'"

* * *

At times, Yunus actually *had* offered a more nuanced approach about
the drivers of poverty. In his Nobel Prize acceptance speech, Yunus proclaimed that poverty "has been created and sustained by the economic
and social systems that we have designed for ourselves; the institutions
and concepts that make up that system; the policies that we pursue." He
derided American-style capitalism in which profits *must* be maximized
and economic growth is equated with corporate expansion. The early
work of Jeff Ashe, as well as Dale Adams and the "Spring Review" studies,
also focused on broader constraints: concentration of land holdings, weak
infrastructure, lack of childcare. The Bangladeshi community development
organization Proshika, which promoted "rural credit," also stressed that
"macroeconomic policy is crucial in dealing with the problems" poor people faced. Earlier research into the informal sector called for even greater
reforms: wage legislation, government purchasing of small-scale goods
and services, subsidies for food and housing. Even today, a main goal of
the Self-Employed Women's Association in India is full employment, with
benefits such as work security, income security, food security, and social
security including health care, childcare, nutrition, and shelter. (The organization's second major goal is self-reliance, with the understanding that
full employment can come from self-started efforts.) Even microfinance
stalwarts recognized the need for broader support that extended beyond
debt. BRAC, for example, offered feed and poultry immunization to some
of the chicken farmers it supported. Grameen launched programs like
Grameen Check, a fabric company that offered regular work for Bangladeshi fabric makers.

But Yunus always saw credit as the cornerstone. In 2017, Yunus said, "I
kept saying that financing is a kind of economic oxygen for people. If you
don't give this oxygen to people, people get sick, people get weak, people
get nonfunctional. The moment you connect them with the economic
oxygen, the financial facility, then suddenly they wake up, suddenly they
start working, suddenly they become enterprising." And promising

poverty museums was immensely more quotable than hashing out the sticky details about debt and its shortcomings or large-scale, multigeneration structural reform. "The media were really looking for heartwarming stories," Alex Counts told me. "Many journalists wanted to exaggerate how good this was, and we didn't do enough to say that microfinance is only part of the solution. That had some short-term benefits but also long-term costs. But we only had so much time onstage . . . and if the media and politicians were [tooting our horn] then so be it." Counts recalled one early World Bank study, which suggested that 5 percent of Grameen borrowers got out of poverty every year. "Did we make a big deal out of that [study]? You can bet we did. We rode the fad for as long as we could."

Free

Freetown, Sierra Leone

End of 2021

In the decades since she had moved to Freetown, Kadija had only traveled the approximately three and a half miles from Two Taps to the city's main beach maybe once or twice a year, on Easter or Christmas. The beach was a long stretch of golden sand outlined by a boardwalk. The city's affluent liked to exercise here, donning tight spandex and clutching sweating plastic bottles of water. As they walked, they could watch waves that were never too rough, onto which fishermen launched dugout canoes first thing in the morning.

This was Freetown's playground. On big holidays, the shoreline became packed with thousands of bodies, the sound of the waves drowned out by competing Afrobeats. The few times she went, Kadija bought a few drinks for herself and her kids, and together they strolled up and down the edge of the water, passing by people in raffia-roofed restaurants who ate from plates heavy with rice and barracuda. Kadija liked making a show of how odd it was to walk on the sand, the foreignness of being someplace so different. She'd push her feet and arms out wide to keep herself stable.

But Kadija had never been to Freetown's biggest gatherings, which took place not at public beaches but at private mansions and beach houses, where celebrants would dance to music on the edge of pools. Tickets could cost anywhere from $3 to $25, depending on the venue, crowd, food, social network, and expectations. Kadija spent each holiday listening to the steady cacophony of merriment that pumped from the big houses surrounding Two Taps. Without the money or connections to go, she would content herself by wiggling in time to the music on the concrete bench affixed to her veranda.

Now nearing forty, Kadija finally had her chance. A boy from Two Taps, whom they called Free (short for Feel Free), was throwing a launch party to celebrate his first album, something of a hip-hop, Afrobeats, and R & B blend. Free had rented a nearby mansion at the top of the hill for the evening, procuring a speaker system and a stage on which he would perform his first single. Kadija barely knew the boy but, as Two Taps' socialite and most popular bar owner, she felt ownership over the event. She encouraged everyone from the neighborhood to go. It would be a moment of collective pride and joy—and a great business opportunity. With hundreds of people there late into the night, Kadija was sure that her "stuff" would sell.

Kadija considered her finances. With her own loan, she could cover almost two of her daughter Rose's school terms. Using some of the extra $75 from half of Aminata's loan, Kadija decided she would buy two tickets—a $5.50 VIP one for her and a $3.50 regularly priced one for Rose. The girls in Rose's crew had already decided on a joint group outfit: black spandex high-waisted booty shorts, T-shirts tied up above their belly buttons, bucket hats, high socks, and athletic shoes. Her younger daughter, Ada, pouted when she learned that she wouldn't be going. Kadija didn't care that her husband, Abdul, had no interest in joining.

Kadija would use the rest of the money to buy an extra stash of her goods, setting aside a bit for Ada's school fees, which were minimal— the girl was young, and in government school. Kadija would still have enough left over for transportation to the party and back, plus a few beers at the mansion. "I never drink," she insisted. "It just makes me fall asleep. But we have to celebrate." Celebrate the burgeoning star Free, of course. But also celebrate that she finally had enough money to go to a party on the hill.

Kadija rallied her neighbors and customers, becoming something of a ticket agent. She kept a stack in her house and told every person who came by that *this* would be the event of the season, a time to celebrate how far Two Taps had come. They had their own star, Free, right here.

Also, she noted if they wanted her business that night, they knew where to find her.

When Kadija pitched the party to Aminata, her husband, Idrissa, was home.

"What does a VIP ticket get you?" he asked.

"I think you get to go upstairs," she said.

"What's upstairs?" he asked.

Kadija shrugged. "Not everyone gets to go up there."

Aminata had never been to a party like this either, not in Freetown and certainly not back in Pendembu. She gave a little clap and squeal when Kadija handed her the ticket—a normal one, no VIP—she had seen Idrissa's side-eye. "We're going to really enjoy that night!" Kadija cried, putting her arm around Aminata. Aminata's face lit up. She bounced a little bit in Kadija's embrace.

* * *

Free's party was set to begin at six o'clock sharp. At that hour, Aminata hadn't yet washed and was still in her favorite shirt: a pink racer-back she had picked up at a junks stall in town that insisted, "I can't adult today."

She was, in fact, very much adulting. As the sky darkened, Aminata hung laundry on the line outside the house, then cooked for her daughter, Doris, and Idrissa. While they ate, Aminata took a quick bucket shower, then threw on a few outfits to model for Doris. Should it be the hand-stitched dress, made of local fabric, which showed off her strong arms and fell just below her knees, mint green with lavender swirls? Or a long black stretchy one-piece? Doris liked the African print best. She thought it would match Aminata's caramel wig, which itself matched her skin perfectly. Satisfied, Doris next watched Aminata "paint her face." She put on bright blue eyeshadow, accented by baby pink metallic lipstick. Aminata stood in the corner of her parlor, repeatedly fluffing up the wig. Doris took photos of her in various poses: making a kissy face, flashing a peace sign, peering over the shoulder. "You look so beautiful, Mama!" Doris cooed.

Her neighbor Grandpa could hear the giggling from outside. He was seated on his front porch, in his usual white tank top and loose—

loosening—khaki pants, starring off into the deepening night sky. "Are you not going?" I asked. Kadija had insisted that "everyone" would be there. "Me? Going where?" It was his grandson's birthday today, but even the boy wouldn't be joining. "Where am I going to get the money for that?"

Grandpa nodded down the road toward Panneh and Mariama's place. "You think they're going, too?"

Since giving birth to a healthy baby boy, Panneh, the microfinance borrower who had been threatened with the police, had started to look much better. Her once-swollen feet had shrunk back to normal. More miraculously, she had begun to smile, even begun looking people in the eye again. She spent her days bringing her little boy from her house to her aunt Mariama's front stoop and then back home. She laughed at a twitch he had somehow developed, a little mid-hiccup freeze that lifted his lip and kept it there.

The police and a loan officer had come by right after the baby had arrived. She showed them the child, telling them, "I just gave birth. Not now." "They just went away," she said. "I'm not sure if they'll come back." In case they did, she had started selling again—just a little bit, since the demands of a young child meant she couldn't do anything substantial. For a few hours each day, Panneh walked around Two Taps with a small plastic carton filled about a quarter high with homemade sweets. In the early evenings, she replaced the sweets with a few fish balls, a little pre-dinner snack. She hoped to pay off the remaining $90 debt by the end of the rainy season.

That left no room for $3.50 party tickets. Her aunt Mariama scoffed when she thought about the event. "If I had any money, I would cook dinner tonight. I haven't eaten since the morning. No," she snapped. "I'm not going."

Aminata had recently taken to picking on Panneh. A few weeks back, Panneh had asked Aminata to take care of the baby for a few minutes while she ran a few errands. "I was watching the clock for five, ten minutes, fifteen minutes. I was worried she would leave me with him!" There was little indication this would happen; Panneh adored the child, barely left his side. But her reputation, Aminata insisted, preceded her. Given Panneh's previous history of "walking" away from problems, what made it so she wouldn't just up and leave the baby, too?

Aminata had been shifting, in ways so small to be imperceptible at first. But, measured in months, there was a noticeable change. She had begun to adopt the habits she had insisted she adamantly despised in the "Big Women" of Two Taps: the gossiping, the scheming and strategizing, the flaunting. She smiled less to some neighbors—neighbors like Panneh— and more to others, like Kadija's sister-in-law. She had gone from seeing herself as outside, righteously separate, to proudly, deservedly in.

It was the loan that did it—not the money itself, but the social connections it solidified. Aminata had learned that a central way the women of Two Taps got by was by leaning on one another. It felt thrilling that Kadija was now beholden to her. Kadija had even begun making a point of regularly stopping by to say hi, sharing a bit of food if she had extra. She complimented Aminata on her cooking, on the earrings she wore, on how smart Doris was. Aminata hadn't asked for anything from Kadija yet—she didn't feel confident enough to do that. But she hoped that with time, and favors, theirs would become a reciprocal relationship. Aminata had scratched Kadija's back, and so surely Kadija would scratch hers.

Aminata still worried about what would happen if Kadija and her sister-in-law didn't pay off the debt she had taken out for them. "It's my photo on the wall in that office. If anything happens, I'm the one who will have the problem." In her quieter moments, she expressed fears of the police, worries that were reinforced by Idrissa's muttering about how she'll be on her own if they come by.

But the risk was worth it. She had shifted from simply being in Kadija's orbit to being in her circle. Even though Aminata was in debt, she also now had power.

As she got ready for the party, Aminata clapped her hands together, smiling so hard it pushed the candy-colored lipstick into the cracks of her mouth. "Tonight is going to be a good night," she told Doris. The little girl beamed.

* * *

At the top of the hill near the mansion, Kadija took a moment to take in the sprawling city below her. From here, it seemed as though all of

Freetown was alight. The blacked-out neighborhoods below weren't visible; instead, a sparkling, calm galaxy of electrified houses dotted the hills. Kadija didn't see any shacks, didn't hear any honking, any fighting. She was up, far above Two Taps.

Once inside the mansion, near a small swimming pool the size of Aminata's house and at the base of the spiral staircase that led up to the "VIP" balcony, Kadija cracked open a can of stout she had tucked into her purse and brought out a small bag of her "stuff," which she planned to sell in one of the courtyard's many dark corners. As soon as she moved away from the lights, she was approached by a neighbor. Kadija passed him what he wanted and then pushed aside a few plastic chairs, making a small dance floor for her and Aminata.

Aminata was all pep, pushing her fists into her armpits, then pumping them up with delight. She declared each song "my favorite!" Her face soon shone with sweat. Kadija took a less energetic approach. Her hips led her body in large, round, methodical circles, a pattern interrupted every few minutes by a tap on her shoulder. Within the first hour, she had made about ten sales.

Kadija opened another can of stout. She relished the hours she had before her. Drinking, moving, dancing, smoking. This is what microfinance had given her: the freedom of enough cash to do what she wanted for one night, to know that the basics were covered but that she could still afford a few beers, a few hours away from Abdul, from the courtyard that she barely left and the worries and memories she had a hard time putting down. "I haven't felt that way in a long time," Kadija later recalled. "Getting drunk like that! I felt like I could finally relax. I see why the boy calls himself Free. That night, it really made us feel like that."

CHAPTER 12

An Opportunity

ON APRIL 20, 2007, CHUCK WATERFIELD, WHO AFTER WORKING IN microfinance for decades had become critical of the sector's move toward a for-profit approach, woke up to remarkable news.

A few years before, Waterfield had created a software program that could help microlenders build and track business plans. Although he still believed that microfinance could achieve positive social outcomes, he hoped the program would instill accounting sensibilities that would help lenders function more efficiently. One of his first clients was a Mexican lender called Compartamos, Spanish for "we share."

Compartamos had followed the same trajectory that, at this point, dominated the industry. The lender first opened in the 1990s, in the poor Mexican states of Oaxaca and Chiapas. It began as an NGO, following the teachings of Mother Teresa. Much of its funding came from a network of nonprofits called Gente Nueva. From the beginning, Compartamos focused on lending to women, not only because of the then oft-repeated claims that they were more likely to pay off their loans but also because they were the ones who happened to be around, with the men in many of the villages Compartamos targeted having gone to the United States for work. Compartamos operated as an NGO for ten years, receiving $4.3 million in grants or soft loans from international development agencies and private Mexican sources.

By 2000, Compartamos had sixty thousand borrowers. Encouraged by public efforts like the Microcredit Summit Campaign and the general excitement over "scaling up" microfinance, they wanted to expand. To raise more money, Compartamos decided to look to international private capital. It set up a regulated finance company—essentially a bank—to be overseen by the NGO. This step was encouraged by the World Bank–affiliated Consultative Group to Assist the Poor, which had given a million dollars to the organization to facilitate the shift. The International Finance Corporation, the private-sector arm of the World Bank, also invested. Accion, by now as much of a microfinance investor as a microlender itself, bought nearly $1 million's worth of stock in the new company and lent another $1 million, using money from USAID.* With the investment, Accion owned 18 percent of the new company and held a seat on its board.

The new Compartamos bank also received over $30 million in loans from public development agencies, plus around $15 million from private investors. Compartamos expanded as it had hoped, at an astounding rate of 46 percent per year from 2000 to 2006. It did this while still reporting impressive repayment rates of around 99 percent.

Then, two years after the for-profit launched and hungry for even further expansion, Compartamos issued $70 million in bonds on the Mexican securities exchange—most of which were partially guaranteed by the World Bank's International Finance Corporation. The lender also raised an additional nearly $70 million, borrowing from Mexican banks and commercial lenders. Compartamos was now firmly out of the territory of relying on public loans and government grants and into the business of raising money through the capital markets.

Compartamos now had a lot of money to pay back, which meant that borrowers still had to pay a high cost for their loans. Compartamos charged the poor women who borrowed from them an average 86 percent annual effective interest—the figure climbed to nearly 100 percent when including tax. In 2006, Compartamos's founders—Carlos Danel and Carlos Labarthe Costas, often referred to as the "two Carloses"—acknowledged that effective interest rates could even be as high as 120 percent. At the time, the median interest rate globally for microcredit institutions was roughly 30 percent, higher than an American credit card but one-fourth lower than what Comparta-

---

* The American agency had actually been interested in investing in Compartamos itself, but its lawyers were squeamish, given that it was now for-profit. So USAID funneled the money through Accion instead.

mos charged. Even within Mexico Compartamos was an outlier, charging more than most of the country's other microlenders, although there were a few notable exceptions: FINCA charged about the same, and FINCOMUN, another Mexican microlender, charged nearly 120 percent effective annual interest rate with tax. Traditional lenders—those that microcredit was meant to displace—charged anywhere from 27 to 200 percent annually.

The Carloses reasoned that the high rates were ultimately a good thing: whatever Compartamos made would be plugged back into lending, meaning more loans could go to more women. They pointed to their numbers as evidence of this rationale: by 2007, Compartamos had just over half a million borrowers, a tenfold increase in less than a decade. Even though her organization supported Compartamos, Elizabeth Littlefield, who at the time ran the World Bank's Consultative Group to Assist the Poor, had a hard time stomaching this. "Should Enrique really be paying a higher interest rate than he needs to be paying so that Rodrigo in another village can get access?"

The high interest rates weren't just plugged back into expansion—the expensive loans also fueled phenomenal profits, even for an industry that already had surprisingly high returns. In 2006, the company's return on equity was around 55 percent, *seven times* the industry average. That year, Compartamos made $57 million, with a profit margin of 23.6 percent. The price of its shares had jumped twenty-one times in just six years, from $6 million in 2000 to $126 million in 2006.

In this, Accion—an early Compartamos investor, with 18 percent of shares—saw an opportunity.

By now, Accion was focused on creating and expanding commercial microfinance lenders, a primary goal since the BancoSol conversion in Bolivia a decade before. And to do that, Accion needed cash. "Accion was always scrounging around for bits and pieces of money, and it could see that Compartamos was hugely successful," remembers Elisabeth Rhyne, who had overseen USAID's microcredit work in the mid-1990s before becoming Accion's senior vice president in 2000. "And so Accion said, 'There's a big pot of money just sitting there, and we could do so much with it. And there's plenty of people who would like to invest in Compartamos because it's a very successful organization.'" Since the chair of Accion's board also sat on the board of Compartamos, this was an easy conversation to have: Why not sell some shares? The sale would be structured so that profits would go to the original investors, like Accion, the Compartamos NGO, wealthy individuals who had invested, and the founders, the two Carloses. From its original $1 million investment, Accion thought it would get around $35 million, which it could plug back in to microlending around the world.

On April 20, 2007, Compartamos sold 30 percent of its shares on the Mexican Stock Exchange through an initial public offering, or IPO. There was immense interest. This was one of the first public sales of a microfinance company's shares, and Compartamos was a spectacularly profitable company in a country that was considered an exciting emerging economy. The sale was thirteen times oversubscribed; the price of shares went up 22 percent in the first day of trading. International fund managers and other commercial investors, primarily from outside Mexico, bought most of the shares. One banker involved in the offering told Reuters, "This is a one-of-a-kind story in the market today, which is why there is so much interest."

The sale made an incredible $450 million for its initial investors, a phenomenal three hundred–to–one return on their initial investment. Shares that Accion initially bought with $1 million were now valued at around $300 million—far, far higher than the $35 million Accion had estimated they would make. Accion retained some of its shares and took home about $135 million. The World Bank's International Finance Corporation, at the time of the sale the third-largest Compartamos shareholder, made $210 million. The NGO component of Compartamos, which also had an ownership stake, made $100 million. Private shareholders—the two Carloses, Compartamos's directors and managers, and other private Mexican investors—collectively made around $150 million. Elisabeth Rhyne was flabbergasted by the figures. "No one expected that."

* * *

When Chuck Waterfield woke to the news of the Compartamos sale on April 20, 2007, he was appalled. He fired off a long missive on a lively Yahoo! discussion group called "Microfinance Practice," filled with lenders, funders, and their critics. "I've not seen, on the order of this magnitude, such a large amount of money raised, and I've not seen such a large amount going into private and/or 'for-profit' control. Is this the future of microfinance? Is this where some other [microlenders] have already gone, and where [others] are hoping to go? Is this the 'solution to poverty'? Will microfinance become the home of the profit-maximizing investors instead of . . . to effect beneficial economic and social change?" Muhammad Yunus was also worried. Soon after the sale, in 2007, the Microcredit Summit Campaign issued a report in which Yunus said he was "shocked by the news. Compartamos's business model, and the message it is projecting in the global capital markets, is not consistent with microcredit." He publicly shamed the company for "raking in money off poor people desperate for cash."

Others felt differently. In December 2007, eight months after the sale of the Compartamos shares, Michael Chu, former CEO of Accion, published a piece in *Forbes* titled "Profit and Poverty: Why It Matters." Chu was worried that "socially conscious investors are starting to agonize over earning returns while serving the poor." Private enterprise, he argued, was the *only* way to make programs like microfinance accessible worldwide. And to raise enough money for growth—for more microfinance borrowers to be reached, and for poverty therefore to be addressed, he argued—there must be above-average returns that would attract new, large financiers. Chu had a clear message to investors: "If your objective is to roll back poverty and change the world, don't believe those that have been telling you that returns on your investment are the icing on the cake. It is the cake itself."

Chu was joined by a chorus of other supporters. Maria Otero, who worked with Accion at the time of the Compartamos sale and during the BancoSol for-profit conversion in Bolivia a decade earlier, called the offering a "phenomenal accomplishment." Dr. Steven Funk, who took an interest in commercial microfinance alongside his former wife, Elizabeth Funk, commented, "The capital markets have taken serious interest in . . . a bank that lends to the poor. By careful measure, this is reason to be excited and rejoice." One of the Carloses, Carlos Labarthe, put it most succinctly: "Before, the poor were always thought of as the problem of the private sector. But now they can be an opportunity."

* * *

In the days and weeks that followed the sale, Waterfield explained that his anguish wasn't just that Compartamos's private shareholders had made so much money in the sale, although he was "stunned" by the $450 million figure. That Accion and IFC, which both relied on public monies and both used explicit anti-poverty language, had also made millions seemed even more distasteful. Both organizations quickly retorted that they would plug whatever they made back into microfinance and other similar projects. Again, this was about expanding microfinance, not profiting from it. The Compartamos NGO said it would put its earnings into health and nutrition programs for poor Mexicans.

That wasn't good enough for everyone. Even if the profits ultimately fueled more lending, they still came from poor women paying 100 percent interest. "It's kind of like blood money," Jeff Ashe later observed. And it also left a fundamental, uncomfortable question about the role subsidies had played in propping up a bank that became hugely profitable by selling very expensive products to poor people. Is this really where global development funding, ultimately paid by taxpayers, should be going?

The Consultative Group to Assist the Poor, which had given a grant to Compartamos but had not directly invested in the lender, pointed out that subsidies had long been used to spur successful projects and business for the public good, whether that be a road, a dam, or, in this case, a lender. And banking systems around the world had been started with, and then routinely relied on, government support. Subsidies had been essential to Bolivia's ProDem, the nonprofit precursor to the famed BancoSol. Even Judith Tendler had pointed out that some of America's most profitable industries, like Silicon Valley, had been kicked off with government money.

But in the Compartamos case, the target was off. Instead of public-sector projects that would generate formal employment, the subsidies encouraged tiny businesses that may not be financially sturdy or promise employment. Compartamos borrowers might stay within the informal sector—at quite a high price—not transcend it.

Anger over the Compartamos sale and subsidies revealed a broader frustration, too. It wasn't just Compartamos that had received cheap government money, then gone commercial. Much of the microfinance sector had. Compartamos was both an outlier and emblematic. "In the beginning, all of the innovation, the creativity occurred through the NGO world," Ashe observed during one of our conversations. "Everything was built off of that." The shock at just how much a company like Compartamos could make off the backs of public subsidies made way for an outburst of anger about the broader turn in the microfinance industry. *See*, critics were saying. *This is what can happen. This is the future of microfinance.*

Although the Consultative Group to Assist the Poor didn't find anything wrong with the subsidies themselves—or, for that matter, with the commercialized approach—Elizabeth Littlefield, who headed the group at the time, felt "it was one thing to use the excess profits to grow the organization, but it went too far when those profits were instead used to pay huge dividends to shareholders." Staffers wondered whether perhaps they, as one of those early funders, should have put in some guardrails, maybe said something about those high interest rates. A sixteen-page focus note on the sale of Compartamos shares acknowledged: "Our 1996 grant of $2 million to the Compartamos NGO included no covenants about future interest rates or profit levels . . . in truth, we never gave much consideration to the possibility that Compartamos would be charging such interest rates, and generating such profits, 10 years later." Instead, they had hoped that cost to borrowers would decrease as Compartamos got more money and Mexico's microfinance sector became more competitive: in short, that the market would work. Instead, interest rates climbed even *higher* after the sale through the initial public offering, from around 100 percent effective APR to 110 percent APR. In 2012, the bank posted net profits of nearly a billion pesos. In the absence of industry standards around what constituted an acceptable interest rate and appropriate financial return, the Compartamos sale and the expensive model it was premised on "set the tone for what was expected for profitability," Sharon D'Onofrio, who had observed many microfinance lenders transition to a for-profit model, told me. "And you just couldn't get there unless you grew at an exceptional rate and you charged really high rates of interest."

Compartamos *had*, however, reached their goal of getting to one million Mexican borrowers. By 2012, 2.3 million Mexicans were taking out loans from the lender. That didn't necessarily mean their lives were better. A randomized controlled trial that considered how those borrowers fared, published in 2015, found that the company's loans had essentially no impact. Borrowing didn't help businesses or increase incomes or social status or people's ability to spend. It didn't even seem to impact their "subjective well-being." The main outcome was a "statistically significant reduction in income from government or other aid sources." Put another way, Compartamos borrowers relied less on charity and the state—a perfect neoliberal outcome.

* * *

Regardless of what one thought about Compartamos's profits and the 100 percent annual interest rates, public conversations about them threatened to further tarnish the already waning public perception of microfinance. Even those in favor of a commercialized approach worried what the company's initial public offering might do to the industry's image. Damian von Stauffenberg, executive director of MicroRate, a major microfinance rating agency, remarked that "microfinance has lost its innocence. Pre-Compartamos, microfinance was associated in the public's mind with charity; nobody questioned that this was a cause worth giving to because it helped the poor to help themselves. Compartamos has exposed a different reality—a reality of large, unbelievably profitable microfinance institutions; of international investment bankers and Wall Street investors jostling for a share of those profits; of unappetizingly high interest rates." Even Dale Adams, the Ohio State researcher who had argued for above-market interest rates as part of the "Spring Review" studies back in the 1970s, warned, "Compartamos is a festering public relations problem. It will also be a black eye for the whole microfinance industry when someone puts this on the front page of the *Wall Street Journal*, gives a speech about it on the floor of the U.S. Congress, or writes an objective article about it that is published in a major journal." Adams even called for *lowered* interest rates in the wake of the Compartamos sale—"for the first time in my professional life," he told me.

Chuck Waterfield warned that without changes, "we run the risk of the world seeing no difference between microfinance and the moneylenders we set out to displace . . . When socially responsible investors and the general public learn what is going on at Compartamos there will very likely be a backlash against microfinance. The field may find it difficult to recover if corrections are not made."

Yet despite the warnings, even after the Compartamos sale, the reputation of microfinance had the remarkable ability to rebound. Making money off a few hundred thousand poor Mexican women seemed to pale in newsworthy comparison to the financial maneuverings that fostered the global economic crisis, which began a few months later, in December 2007. Headlines moved quickly to the crash and impending recession, to rising unemployment rates, housing crises, and food shortages. Microfinance looked downright charitable in comparison. In 2008, just a few months after the Compartamos sale, *Time* magazine called microfinance one of the "ten ideas that are changing the world." In April 2009, President Barack Obama, newly sworn in, unveiled a U.S. government investment of $100 million for microcredit in the Western Hemisphere. A few months later, he gave Muhammad Yunus the Presidential Medal of Freedom. "Muhammad Yunus was just trying to help a village," Obama said, "but he somehow managed to change the world." He didn't realize that within a year, microfinance would weather another PR storm, this one far worse than the Compartamos kerfuffle. Tiny loans would soon be blamed for hundreds of deaths and a full-scale economic crisis in one of the world's largest economies.

* * *

He didn't mention this in his speech, but Obama had grown up around microcredit. His mother, Stanley Ann Dunham, had spent decades studying small-scale economic development and female empowerment programs, particularly traditional crafts in Indonesia. She took this knowledge to Bank Rakyat Indonesia, a government bank that had turned an unsuccessful agricultural credit program into a profit-making savings and loan program, one of the earliest successes of microcredit that happened in parallel to Yunus's work at Grameen. Dunham also helped the

International Labor Organization, a UN-affiliated body, outline its work in the informal sector and supported the Ford Foundation, USAID, and the World Bank's work in microcredit just as the field was expanding. In 1992, Dunham briefly joined Women's World Banking, where she helped to influence the microcredit-heavy policy platform at the 1995 United Nations Fourth World Conference on Women in Beijing, where Hillary Clinton had made her "women's rights are human rights" speech. Dunham died later that year of ovarian cancer.

Dunham fell into the Indonesia work by chance, and through love. After marrying and then divorcing Barack Obama's father, Dunham finished her undergraduate degree at the University of Hawai'i in the late 1960s while her parents helped to raise her young son Barack. She became involved in the university's East-West Center, which had been established by the U.S. Congress a few years before "to foster better relations and understandings among the peoples of the United States, Asia, and the Pacific Islands through programs of cooperative study, training, and research." Those relations were not good; at this point, the United States had already been involved in the Cold War conflict in Vietnam for half a decade. By sponsoring intellectuals from the United States and Asia, the center hoped to, in the words of John Burns, Hawai'i's territorial delegate to Congress, "engage actively in what is perhaps the most precious freedom of all—the freedom to pursue ideas."

At the center, Dunham met Lolo Soetoro, a surveyor from Java who had come to the University of Hawai'i to study geography. A few years later, they were married, and a few years after that, Dunham and Barack moved to Jakarta.

In her new home, Dunham fell in love with Indonesian handicraft. The artisans she met were mostly women, mostly rural, unable to get a loan but in need of money to expand their business. The government's Bank Rakyat Indonesia took notice, swapping subsidized agricultural credit for above-market loans to small vendors. It was hugely successful. By the 1990s, the microfinance arm of Bank Rakyat Indonesia exceeded the bank's overall profits and even made up for the bank's losses. (In fact, BRI was the first microfinance bank to have an initial public offering, in 2003, four years before Compartamos had its spectacular sale.)

Other banks in the region had begun to shift, too. In the late 1960s, as part of a populist agenda, the Indian government began requiring commercial banks to target what they called the "Priority Sector"—poor people without access to formal bank accounts. By the mid-1970s, Indian commercial banks needed to funnel 40 percent of their credit to the Priority Sector. Bangladesh and the Philippines soon had similar requirements.

To extend financial services to poor people, Indian women were encouraged to come together in groups, save together, and use those savings to on-lend to one another—essentially, form a type of saving and lending group, or ROSCA. Whereas osusus in West Africa date back at least a century, the Indian effort wasn't necessarily an organic process; many of the women were put into groups by "change agents"—often NGOs—who would "inculcate the idea of thrift and promote savings mobilization" and train them to run meetings. After successfully saving for six months, these "Self-Help Groups" would be eligible to take out loans from a bank—which in turn helped the banks reach their Priority Sector requirements. By linking the groups with banks, the program, supported by the World Bank, shortened the distance between traditional savings and formal credit. Although the banks had no choice in the matter—getting money to the poor was a government requirement—the program helped them, too: they could reach new customers without having to do the messy work of finding and vetting borrowers. In some cases, group members essentially acted as agents for a bank, encouraging other customers from their communities to pay off their loans. "Flush with cash" from Self-Help Group deposits, banks could use their new capital to on-lend to more affluent customers, who paid lower interest rates than the poor women themselves—in a way, poor people were subsidizing the more well-to-do. Given that the linkage model had been started and financed by the government and the World Bank, commercial banks had essentially received a subsidy, acquiring new customers and a new source of deposits without paying for any of the up-front costs.

By the 1990s, a few decades into the program, more than half of the country's Self-Help Groups were based in the southeastern state of Andhra Pradesh, one of the poorest in India. Its poverty soon attracted other lending programs, too. As microfinance boomed in India—with an average growth rate of 70 percent each year between 2005 and 2010—several microfinance companies opened in Andhra Pradesh. Soon, four of India's largest micro-finance institutions had their headquarters in the state. By the mid-aughts, Andhra Pradesh was referred to as the "Mecca" of microfinance. By 2005, the state was "saturated," with the government reporting that 92 percent of poor households in Andhra Pradesh had been offered a loan.

As was true elsewhere, most of the country's microlenders started out as NGOs before taking a commercial route. This was the case with the two largest lenders in Andhra Pradesh: Spandana, which as of 2007 had nearly a million borrowers in India, half of whom were in Andhra Pradesh, and the even larger SKS, whose founder, Vikram Akula—born in India but raised in the United States—had always envisioned that SKS would be a profit-making company—the only way, he thought, to effectively expand and bring capital from the West to where it was needed most. SKS was soon called the "Starbucks of Microfinance" because of its quick-turnaround, automated model, which facilitated growth rates of over 200 percent. Attracted by its impressive expansion and financial returns, American investment firm Sequoia Capital became an early shareholder, investing $11.5 million in SKS in 2007. (Sequoia is primarily known for backing Silicon Valley tech giants such as Google, PayPal, Reddit, WhatsApp, Instagram, and Zoom.) Vinod Khosla, a prominent Silicon Valley venture capitalist, was also an early investor, as was the Unitus Equity Fund, one of the first commercially focused microfinance investment funds that focused on buying shares in microfinance lenders, started by members of the Mormon church and supported by the Dignity Fund's Elizabeth Funk.

After growing its loan portfolio by a massive 300 percent in 2007 alone, in 2008, SKS raised $75 million by selling shares of its company, the largest equity investment in a microfinance company at the time. By 2010, it had raised $350 million in equity. (The now defunct Silicon Valley Bank was one investor.) SKS also sold nearly half of its loan portfolio to Citigroup. Akula, the company's CEO, said such interest at the height of the "global economic meltdown" showed "the resilience and entrepreneurial abilities of the poor not only to survive in today's economic crisis but actually to prosper because the poor are largely de-coupled from global trends"—again, that microfinance could continue to be profitable because the poor would continue to borrow even in the worst of times.

* * *

In the age of commercialized microfinance, Spandana and SKS were no longer constrained by lack of capital. Instead, they were constrained by the number of people they could lend to. From the late 1990s, USAID and other long-term donors had been pushing for microfinance institutions to lend to more borrowers, since more loan repayments would help them cover their costs and larger portfolios would be more attractive to commercial investors. It was now dogma that a lender was only successful if it was growing. But in "saturated" Andhra Pradesh, there weren't many more people who needed a loan. Hamstrung, lenders changed tactics. Instead of only searching for new borrowers, lenders also increased the size of loans, not just in the hundreds of dollars but in the thousands—a way to increase the size of a lending portfolio without necessarily having to find new customers, since borrowers could be offered multiple loans at a time. (On a 2010 panel Akula explained that the SKS model was premised on its female lenders moving up the ladder—from a $40 loan to a $400 one, taking "five, six different credit products from you.") By the mid-aughts, even though the state was deeply impoverished, the average microfinance loan in Andhra Pradesh was $1,050, nearly eight times the average amount in the rest of India. By 2010, one-third of the thirty million microfinance loans in India had been made in Andhra Pradesh. By that year, SKS had given out $3 billion in loans.

In this frenzied "quest for numbers," as one person put it, oversight became lax. "There was a big danger of rapid scaling without really caring about what happened to processes and systems," remembers Jayshree Venkatesan, who worked in microfinance in India for years. To keep their costs low while also growing their loan portfolios, loan officers, whose salaries were partially dependent on making new loans, became responsible for dozens, sometimes hundreds of clients, many of whom had taken out multiple, increasingly large loans. So long as repayments were made, they cared little what borrowers did with the loans, whether they had a loan from somewhere else, or whether they could manage more debt. Many major microcredit institutions didn't bother to verify, or even ask to see, business plans. Chuck Waterfield, who had worked with USAID microlenders, says this was not unique to India. He had observed USAID staffers advising lenders, "Don't ask borrowers what the credit is for, don't train them. Just make sure you get the money back."

Not surprisingly, all this resulted in "serious overindebtedness," Waterfield told me. Hundreds, then thousands, of borrowers in Andhra Pradesh found that they were unable to pay off their loans. In some cases, defaulters were fined every day they were late, which made repayments even more untenable.

The lack of repayments posed a new problem for loan officers: their paychecks came not only from getting loans out the door but also from maintaining high repayment rates. At Spandana, only 30 percent of staff had fixed contracts, the rest were paid based on performance. Commission and incentive-based salaries were not limited to Indian lenders. At Bank Rakyat Indonesia, the Indonesian government bank that Barack Obama's mother had worked with, a profit-sharing program was offered to bank staff. This encouraged them to expand the bank's portfolio by getting more loans out the door. Penalties were also imposed if arrears— late loans—were greater than 5 percent. The incentive-based approach had also been promoted by USAID. Years earlier, when he was training microfinance organizations, Waterfield says he observed USAID staffers tell lenders, "Pay your loan officers nothing as base salary. That will make them hold the borrowers, their families' feet to the fire, because if they don't, they won't get their bonus. They'll be sure to do it because they will have the monetary incentives. If they don't get the money back, then they're not going to get any money to feed their families." Waterfield says USAID encouraged "loan officers [to push] a borrower to take their third loan, so that they could get a bonus, and then six months later pressuring that borrower to make a repayment, to get a bonus." By the early 2000s, Waterfield says such practices were "normal." One microlender in Egypt noted that the base salaries they paid their extension officers were "insufficient to make a living." Instead, the bank offered "a lucrative monthly incentive scheme that allows them to earn up to five times their basic salary in incentives depending on their productivity," which was determined by the number of new loans, repayment rate, and number of active clients. The bank's lawyers were paid in part based on the amount of past due installments collected each month, which "encourage[d] aggressive collections." In Andhra Pradesh, stories emerged of loan officers suggesting that borrowers take out one loan to pay off another one, a way to keep both lending rates and repayment rates high. By one account, 18 percent of borrowers had taken out loans from moneylenders to pay microlenders back.* (Despite the promise that expensive, formal microfinance loans would replace informal ones, by the late 1990s and early 2000s, there was mounting research that a reliance on microfinance didn't reduce reliance on borrowing from family, friends, and moneylenders. Instead, in many cases—nearly half, in one study—microcredit loans were simply taken out *alongside* traditional forms of debt, which remained by far the leading source of credit for poor people.)

Overindebtedness might have occurred at least in part because microfinance programs were structured to facilitate repeat borrowing. Even at Grameen, one observer noted, "two weeks 'dormancy'"—that is, a borrower's time between completing one loan and taking out another—"is the normal allowed maximum period; if this is exceeded, members have to leave." Some lenders offered a stepwise approach that John Hatch had used with FINCA back in the 1980s: with each loan repayment, a borrower would become eligible for a larger loan, then a larger one, incentivizing poor people to stay on for more cash. One Egyptian program automatically approved repeat loans, whether a borrower asked for another one or not. The rinse-and-repeat method parallels the American payday loan industry, which is also marked by consistent and often overlapping loans. Mehrsa Baradaran, the law professor focused on banking, has observed that in the United States, "one large payday lender even instructs its employees on how to perpetuate the loans with a circle diagram that reflects the need for constant renewal"—a remarkably similar approach to one many microlenders had adopted.

All of this debt could be extremely stressful. Pressured by harried loan

---

* The pressures microfinance loan officers faced strike a remarkable resemblance to incentives for international development consultants, as described by Yunus in *Banker to the Poor*. "The more money officials manage to give out, the better grade they receive as lending officers. Therefore young, ambitious officers of a donor agency will choose the projects with the biggest price tag. By moving a lot of money, their name moves up the promotion ladder." Muhammad Yunus, *Banker to the Poor: Micro-Lending and the Battle Against World Poverty* (New York: PublicAffairs, 2007), 145.

officers who needed to get their money back to keep their jobs, borrowers did everything they could to pay off their loans. One borrower described being so cash-strapped that she and other borrowers shared meals, cooking in a "common pot that the neighbors shared" and splitting essentials like cooking gas and bicycles. One Bolivian borrower "split a potato into two or three pieces and gave it toasted to the children" and another "sold her sweater to have something to eat." Borrowers adopted a pattern that was remarkably similar to one that poor country governments had also learned to follow: borrow more from other lenders, cut down on spending, sell whatever is valuable.

In Andhra Pradesh, as microdebts mounted, borrowers, members of the government, and reporters claimed that loan officers, including from the largest lenders SKS and Spandana, harassed, coerced, and humiliated debtors who were behind in payment. They didn't accept an excuse, not even if a borrower had an illness or death in the family. Some loan officers reportedly stood outside borrowers' homes, yelling at them to pay and refusing to leave until they did. One reportedly put a loan overdue notice in front of a defaulter's house. Others forced borrowers to sell utensils, mobile phones, furniture, and televisions. Group members, on the hook in case of default, also began to harass one another. One loan officer even allegedly encouraged an indebted woman to sell her children into prostitution. The badgering became so intense that some borrowers left their communities.

Despite concerns of overindebtedness, microlenders in Andhra Pradesh wanted to keep expanding. And to do that, they needed even more money. Having already raised nearly $100 million in private equity, on July 28, 2010, about three years after the blockbuster Compartamos sale, SKS had its own initial public sale of shares. Although its CEO, Vikram Akula, continued to be ambitious about the company's growth, he also claimed that the initial public offering was prompted by the 2008 investment from private equity firm Sequoia Capital, which he claims included an exit clause stating that within three to five years, SKS would have to either have an IPO or be acquired. This time, the IPO was oversubscribed fourteen times, attracting Morgan Stanley, JPMorgan, and George Soros's Quantum Fund.*

Just a few months later, in December 2010, the BBC ran an article with the headline, "India's Micro-Finance Suicide Epidemic." Relying on figures from the government, the article linked eighty suicides to the stress and harassment borrowers faced from defaulting on microfinance loans. One forty-five-year-old woman featured in the story hanged herself after being unable to pay back $840 in microloans, which she had taken out to pay for one daughter's appendicitis and another daughter's pregnancy. A later investigation by the Associated Press included women who had drowned themselves—at least in one case, a woman reportedly jumped in a well with her children. Others reportedly drank pesticides. According to the AP investigation, the number of suicides was actually much higher than what the BBC had reported, estimating that two hundred people had died.

The media reports shocked readers in the West, but they weren't surprising to some working within microfinance. In the mid-1990s, borrowers facing the threat of violence from loan officers reportedly committed suicide in Bangladesh. Jeff Ashe recalls hearing "some horrendous cases with Grameen customers, and BRAC, all the darlings. I even heard about breaking someone's legs!"

Responding to the reports, the financial commissioner in Andhra Pradesh, as well as the state's human rights commission, visited borrowers. The government called the microfinance practices "barbaric," estimating that the average family who took on microdebt in Andhra Pradesh owed $660, more than half the average annual household income. Vijay Mahajan, chairman of India's Microfinance Institutions Network, told the BBC, "Multiple lending, over-indebtedness, coercive recovery practices, and unseemly enrichment by promoters and senior executives [of microcredit companies] has led to this situation."

It wasn't hard to guess which "senior executive" Mahajan was talking

---

* Whereas the Compartamos sale sold off existing shares, so that whatever was raised went to the initial investors, the SKS sale was used to create new shares, to raise money for the company to get even bigger. The $358 million made in the sale would be used to further expand lending. Muhammad Yunus, "Sacrificing Microcredit for Megaprofits," *New York Times*, January 14, 2011, https://www.nytimes.com/2011/01/15/opinion/15yunus.html.

about. The SKS sale a few months earlier, under the helm of CEO Vikram Akula, had brought even more attention to how much microfinance lenders were making and who was investing. Now, the "AP suicide crisis," as it became known, focused attention on what lay behind those profits, offering gruesome details of what a relentless quest for growth meant for some borrowers. And the hangover from the Compartamos sale a few years earlier still hadn't gone away—skeptics like Chuck Waterfield were still asking how much profit is too much and whether microfinance had lost its way.

Elisabeth Rhyne, first of USAID, then of Accion, felt the AP crisis acted as something of a pressure valve. "The anger over the suicides [was] really a way for people to express anger over the [public sale of shares]"—both Compartamos, and now SKS—and of course "the companies' profits."

It wasn't clear where to direct that anger in microfinance's increasingly expansive ecosystem. Should someone worried about microfinance be critical of investors in Luxembourg and New York? The pension fund that invested in microfinance? The pensioner herself? The journey from source of capital to borrower had become so byzantine that it worked to absolve nearly everyone of responsibility. Those who couldn't escape blame were the loan officers, offered in the media as the immediate cause of the suicides in Andhra Pradesh, with their yelling and suggestions that a woman sell her daughters into prostitution, and Vikram Akula, who had founded SKS and was CEO at the time of the IPO. Painted as ruthless and money-grabbing, Akula soon stepped down, then moved back to the United States, where he had grown up. He later tried to publish a book outlining the "inside story" of SKS. (After one thousand copies were printed, the company sued Akula for violating the confidentiality and separation agreement he signed when he left SKS.) In the book, the blame was placed on, basically, everyone else. Akula insisted that he had attempted to ensure borrower protection but that investors relentlessly pursued profits. Were it not for the sale of shares through the IPO, Akula claimed, the company would have faced bankruptcy. He also said government regulations made it difficult to transform the lender into a full-fledged bank, forcing SKS to pursue capital markets instead.

Others who defended the microfinance industry blamed local politicians for glomming together what were a few isolated incidents and hyping them into a manufactured crisis for political gain. "There was no evidence of an increase in suicide," Elisabeth Rhyne told me. "But there was an increase in linking of the suicide in the press to microfinance." Maybe government officials felt threatened because microfinance had become infinitely more successful than government-supported Self-Help Groups. While just one million Self-Help Group members across the country had taken loans, approximately thirty million microfinance loans had been made in India, an imbalance that was particularly annoying with elections on the horizon.

Those who claimed the fuss around the suicides was more about politics and PR than reality questioned whether every single one of the two hundred deaths could really be *directly* attributed to microfinance. They argued that India has a long, complicated history of suicides, particularly among rural farmers. That was true—and it was also true that those farmer suicides were deeply linked to debt. Many had taken on loans to buy basic agricultural inputs and to stay afloat after the government cut support for local agriculture and opened the market to imports. By the mid-2010s, about half of Indian farmers were in debt. From 1995 to 2015, around three hundred thousand Indian farmers committed suicide, their deaths often linked to outstanding loans and associated shame and harassment from both lenders and community members. Considering these and other suicides, at least one person within the microfinance industry crunched numbers and argued that those who took out microfinance loans in Andhra Pradesh committed suicide at a *lower* rate than the general Indian population. His argument was, "Microfinance is not killing people. It's actually saving lives."

Either way, for whatever reason and at whatever rate, the Andhra Pradesh suicides *did* happen, by all accounts. David Roodman, a measured economist who studied microfinance for years, traveled to India and interviewed some of the affected families. He didn't have a strong stance on whether microfinance, as a whole, was good or bad but did conclude that there definitely were microfinance-related suicides. Separately, the Associated Press reported that an internal SKS investigation, and an investigation commissioned by an industry group, found that SKS was at least partially responsible, linking employees to seven of the deaths.

That's not to say that politicians didn't take advantage of the crisis.

Some told borrowers their loans would be taken over by the government. Some encouraged debtors to default.

So millions did. Loan payments in Andhra Pradesh tanked, from 99.89 percent to 20 percent. Lenders, bankrupt or about to be, packed up and left. There were soon so many restrictions on what lenders could do that there was little microfinance lending done in the state at all. Citizens went from being saturated with microloans to having almost none. Politicians began giving out loans instead.

The sudden absence of money, after being awash in it, may have had serious consequences for people in Andhra Pradesh. A year after microfinance restrictions went into effect and lenders fled, economists, considering data from 150,000 households in the province, noticed a drop in consumption in the state, with a particular drop in food consumption.

All parties—journalists, the government, academics, microfinance defenders, and those horrified by the situation—focused so much on the details of the suicides themselves—Did they happen? How many exactly? How much was microfinance to blame?—that they seemed to miss the broader questions that reached far beyond Andhra Pradesh. Is it a problem that people are taking out so many loans: that a whole economy, a whole household's consumption, seems to be based on having them? Why did people need them in the first place? Mylaram Kallava, the forty-five-year-old mother who hanged herself, took out the microloans because she could not access public health care or afford private options. Just before Kallava killed herself, a federal employment program had ended. Neither she nor her husband could find regular work. Others who reportedly committed suicide relied on debt to cover education, health care, and housing expenses. One loan at a time, they were finding ways to provide what both the state and the private sector were not.

* * *

All these stories—first of lackluster, if not downright damning, RCT results, and now also of profiteering in Mexico and suicides in India—made even the most stalwart microfinance supporters think twice. In 2005, before spectacular crises made global headlines but well into internal dissent, Catholic Relief Services, which had begun working in microfinance in the 1980s, announced that the organization would pull out of their microcredit investments. They had some major concerns: about the microfinance sector's new loyalty to commercialization and high interest rates and what that meant for borrowers, as well as social strife engendered through the group lending model.

As its name implies, Catholic Relief Services is a Catholic organization. It seeks to abide by Catholic social teachings, which encourage an "option for the poor and vulnerable," "life and dignity of the human person," and "dignity of work and the rights of workers," among other principles. Those didn't seem to jibe well with a borrower in Nicaragua complaining, "'I wanted to stop after three loan cycles . . . but the loan officer told me that I could never get another loan if I stopped," or staff harassing sick borrowers for money they knew they didn't have. Kim Wilson, who was the director of the Global Microfinance Unit at Catholic Relief Services, wrote that she heard of a priest "who called out the names of tardy borrowers at the end of mass." One staffer in the Balkans was so upset about the nature of the work that she was looking for another job. "They do not see me as helping them," the staffer told Wilson, "but as an enemy." Wilson worried that "the only thing we were likely to sustain was poverty."

Still, the decision to divest from microfinance was difficult, given that some of their programs were quite profitable. A CRS fund explicitly for microcredit, "Lifelines," was doubling in size. The organization's board wrestled with the question, "Do we continue along a path of pronounced good"—even as that "good" was becoming more dubious—"or do we follow the wisdom of our principles?" Catholic Relief Services ultimately decided "that doing-well-by-doing-good had become a conceit and had outlived its usefulness." It announced that it would divest from microfinance.

Borrowers were also fed up. In 2011, dozens of women in Ouarzazate, Morocco, inspired by the Arab Spring, deliberately defaulted on their microfinance loans.

The women were poor, living in one of the poorest regions of the country. They found the interest rates, advertised at 2 to 3 percent per month but, with fees, up to 50 percent per year, untenably high. They were being harassed by loan officers. When they went to the police for help, they didn't get any.

The Moroccan debtors' strike grew, with borrowers deliberately not repaying loans to four of the country's largest microfinance companies. Fatima Zahra Elbelghiti, a Moroccan debt activist, found herself drawn to the debtors. She saw a strong parallel between demands from international creditors that the Moroccan government pay their bills, even if that meant they couldn't fund basic social programs like health care and education, and women having to cut back on food to pay their microlenders. In the women's protest, Elbelghiti read a different narrative about microfinance than the one Yunus had popularized. This wasn't about "microfinance coming to save women, to help women, to get themselves organized, to get financial stability, the whole famous story about women's empowerment," Elbelghiti told me. "No. What the women did, the movement, *that* was extraordinary."

The Moroccan strike followed a No Pago—or "I don't pay"—movement that swept Nicaragua in 2008 and 2009. The country had been an exciting place for microfinance investors and lenders, attracted by a large informal sector. Nicaragua was included in Morgan Stanley's 2007 microfinance collateralized loan obligation, a way, *Bloomberg* had promised, for poor potters to expand their businesses while investors netted steady financial returns.

But the 2008 global financial crisis—prompted, ironically, by collateralized loan obligations that focused on American mortgages—withered the country's export-oriented agricultural sector. Many of the farmers who now struggled to sell their goods had taken out microfinance loans, whose average interest rates hovered at around 33 percent, plus fees. In some cases, debtors in arrears were pursued by the courts. Broke and angry and spurred on by leftist politicians who stoked widespread defaults and dissent, thousands of borrowers defaulted.

Microfinance skeptics, especially those in the West, championed the Nicaraguan movement and other pushback from borrowers around the world. Lawyers, human rights campaigners, and journalists homed in on stories about land grabs, police involvement, and social exclusion. They hosted conferences, gave lectures, and wrote long blog posts and depressing exposés.

Some of the critical reports could have a kind of "gotcha" tone. Research-

ers tore into early microfinance studies, gleefully showing their method-
ological flaws. They pointed out how much the stories of suicidal borrowers
strayed from the Nobel Peace Prize–winning image of microfinance. The
disagreements could get personal, given that many of the dissenters had
worked in microfinance for years. After the Compartamos sale, Chuck
Waterfield battled Elisabeth Rhyne onstage at a conference; he blamed
her for the push toward commercialization at USAID years before. Hugh
Sinclair, who had worked in microfinance before writing a scathing book
about Western funders' complicity in its problems,* tore into blog posts on
San Francisco–based microfinance website Kiva and into the backgrounds
of its founders. Just as careers had been made promoting microfinance,
they now stood to be enhanced by critiquing it. Muhammad Yunus was
the easiest target, since he was the most famous, but there were complaints
from just about everyone I interviewed about just about everyone else: Jeff
Ashe, John Hatch, Michaela Walsh, all the "pioneers." Too optimistic. Not
rigorous enough. Sloppy. Too pessimistic. Too pragmatic.

It seemed that nearly everyone in microfinance—not to mention the
idea itself—went from being beloved to scorned. Sharon D'Onofrio, who
had helped Catholic Relief Services set up a self-sustaining bank in El Salvador, remembers being called into a meeting just as the organization was
reconsidering its support of microfinance. A few months before, Catholic
Relief Services had told her to make sure repayment rates were high, to
keep expanding. Now, "it was like I had invented capitalism or something.
I'm like, 'Hey guys, we all supported this five minutes ago, and now it's
become this terrible thing that you don't want to be associated with.'" She
wasn't against the pivot, understood where the organization was coming
from. "But the pendulum had *really* swung."

Others followed Catholic Relief Services' exit. Public funders, sensitive
to bad press and worried about borrower harassment and high interest
rates, didn't want to be associated with a sector whose reputation was
falling. From 2007 to 2010, a period that mapped onto both the Compartamos and Andhra Pradesh affairs, "across and among the whole international development profession, including major development institutions

---

* Hugh Sinclair, *Confessions of a Microfinance Heretic: How Microlending Lost Its Way and Betrayed the
Poor* (Oakland, CA: Berrett-Koehler, 2012).

like the World Bank and major philanthropies, they just decided it's time to move away from microfinance," remembers Elisabeth Rhyne. She watched "as more and more people [became] concerned about the industry, they left." Even the Ford Foundation, which had funded many early microcredit efforts, including helping to kick-start Grameen, quietly announced it would be ending its work in microfinance in 2015. When we spoke in 2020, Rhyne told me, "Microfinance has become almost a word that you can't use in the US."

Grameen's Alex Counts says the public rejection undermined productive conversations about how microfinance could change. The Andhra Pradesh suicides shouldn't be seen as a referendum on the entire industry. In his mind, that crisis stemmed from a particular mix of politics and profits and a peculiar history of farmer suicides, the product of just a few bad apples poisoning the barrel, an overzealous CEO, and loan officers who had gone off the rails. Instead of the death of an industry, it could be a turning point, an opportunity, something to learn from. "We were mastering things that had taken decades. We really needed more support, and smarter support, to reflect everything that we'd learned, [but] everyone was like, 'Uh, no, we're done with that.'"

The newfound dearth of public sector funders "created a vacuum," Rhyne told me—a gap that Rhyne says microfinance investors, clustered in Europe and who "remained happy with what they were seeing," were ready to fill. Kim Wilson, who helped to oversee Catholic Relief Services' microfinance programs and then its exit from small lending, soon realized that in the organization's absence, microlenders "would no longer need to juggle the Catholic Relief Services–imposed double bottom line," which required both social *and* financial returns. "They could work with a new set of board members who held a clear vision for profit." Without subsidized loans and grants from big public funders, philanthropists, and NGOs, microlenders could take on even more private debt and equity, raising more money in the capital markets. Even after the sale of SKS shares and the adjacent Andhra Pradesh suicides, nonprofit lenders converted to for-profit, hiked up interest rates, and pursued public sale of shares. Wilson worried that as public financiers retreated, all of the negative consequences that had become associated with microfinance—the borrower harassment, the high interest rates, the overindebtedness—would continue, but this time with no high expectations and no oversight whatsoever.

* * *

On January 14, 2011, four years after he and Grameen had jointly received the Nobel Peace Prize, Muhammad Yunus published an opinion piece in the *New York Times*. Despite the RCT results, the battles over Compartamos profits, the Andhra Pradesh suicides, and fears that microfinance would be essentially discarded, the industry had continued to grow—by one count, there were two hundred million microfinance borrowers as of December 2010. In many ways, this was exactly what Yunus had envisioned, what he and Sam Daley-Harris and RESULTS had pushed for a decade before. Microfinance was everywhere: funded by both banks and USAID, championed by celebrities and philanthropists, made more tangible to everyday Americans through efforts like Kiva, which promised that, with one $25 contribution, someone could "make a loan, change a life."

But Yunus's op-ed had a downtrodden tone. Under the title "Sacrificing Microcredit for Megaprofits," the piece opened with a sense of nostalgia. "In the 1970s," Yunus wrote, "when I began working [in Bangladesh] on what would eventually be called 'microcredit' one of my goals was to eliminate the presence of loan sharks who grow rich by preying on the poor . . . At that time, I never imagined that one day microcredit would give rise to its own breed of loan sharks."

Yunus worried about rising interest rates and "aggressive" marketing and loan collection tactics that had led to the debt crisis in India (he did not mention the suicides). He wrote, "Commercialization has been a terrible wrong turn for microfinance, and it indicates a worrying 'mission drift' in the motivation of those lending to the poor. Poverty should be eradicated, not seen as a money-making opportunity." He argued that "credit programs that seek to profit from the suffering of the poor" should be stripped of the title "microcredit." "Investors who own such programs should not be allowed to benefit from the trust and respect that microcredit banks have rightly earned."

Yunus didn't seem to acknowledge that he and his colleagues had been laying the groundwork for a commercial approach for years. In 2010, Dr. Steven Funk, ex-husband of the Dignity Fund's Elizabeth Funk, had a breakfast meeting with Yunus at a Microcredit Summit Campaign follow-up meeting in Kenya. Funk told Yunus he was optimistic about the commercial model, hopeful that more interest from private capital would expand borrowing opportunities and that interest rates would ultimately be pushed down through competition. He was sharply rebuked. "By this point Yunus had gotten vocal to the point of saying, making money in the space is wrong," Funk told me. "It was kind of 180 degrees from his original theories of let it blossom on its own. Now he was saying you shouldn't make more than 10 percent rate of return." Funk hoped to continue the conversation, but in his recollection Yunus told him, "You are no better than the loan sharks on the street," then stood up and left Funk to his breakfast. Funk thought, "'Yunus, where are you coming from? You yourself have been speaking this way.' He became the governor of his own success, in my opinion."

Although microfinance was portrayed as a sector divided—between those shocked by the likes of Compartamos and SKS and investors thrilled at their potential profits—in reality these two camps bolstered each other. Yunus had been influential in reframing international development not as the job of the state but one better fitted for the private sector. More specifically, he outlined a blueprint for the commercial model: by encouraging the entry of banks and private capital into microfinance, by calling for lenders to charge "sustainable" interest rates, by touting Grameen's explicit for-profit approach,* by shunning charity as paternalistic and governments as inept, by promoting the idea of "doing good by doing well" through advertising partnerships between Grameen and companies like Danone as a way for corporations to make money while addressing poverty. In a way, commercial lenders like India's SKS were exactly what Yunus had promoted. Its CEO, Vikram Akula, had essentially copied and pasted the Grameen model—a focus on women and group lending and sustainability—simply adding in foreign private capital that was keen to make a profit. The differences were subtle, but

---

* In *Banker to the Poor*, Yunus claimed that Grameen had made a profit in all but three years it had been in existence, and that it operated on "purely commercial terms" as early as 1994.

important: profit-maximizing instead of profit-making,*† private equity instead of private funding. But those distinctions became muddled as microfinance gained popularity—and, in some cases, grew so phenomenally profitable that funders were happy to look the other way.

Other early microfinance advocates also had a hard time reckoning with how they had shaped the sector. Nearly every single person I interviewed expressed regret at what microlending had become but took little personal responsibility for cultivating those changes—it seemed that everyone else had made all the mistakes. Jeff Ashe was a bit of an exception here, telling me, "I was the one in the 1980s saying, 'Wow, we can cover our costs!'" But he quickly diverted responsibility to others. "Once it was discovered that you can make money from it, then a lot of other motivations start being served. It's a sad story. It's not what I had in mind when we started this." He didn't seem to remember that he had hoped solidarity groups could be "cookie cuttered" and grow exponentially around the world—a copy-and-paste approach he later derided. He also didn't seem to acknowledge that he had suggested market-rate interest rates, which made it hard for borrowers like those he met in La Paz to pay their loans back.

Microfinance critic Chuck Waterfield thinks that Yunus felt genuine dismay at where the microfinance sector was going. "There's always this assumption, 'He can't be that good. He must be hiding something,'" Waterfield told me. But "unlike all of those who were making money off microfinance, Yunus didn't own a single share of stock in the Grameen Bank. He's an absolute utopian idealist, which is a strength and a glaring weakness. He just thinks if we all just did the right thing, none of this would have happened. He sincerely believes it." Waterfield offered a comparison:

---

* In a 2010 discussion that included Vikram Akula of SKS and Muhammad Yunus, Yunus stressed, "We are not opposed to making profit—only who makes the profit out of the poor people and how much. That is the issue. If somebody said, oh, we are a restricted profit area, we take only 1 percent profit or 2 percent profit, I said, go right ahead. No problem. But the moment you say profit, the sky's the limit." "The Tuesday Podcast: What's Better for Helping the Poor—Greed or Charity?" WBUR, September 28, 2010, https://www.wbur.org/npr/130194702/the-tuesday-podcast-what-s-better-for-helping-poor-people----greed-or-charity.

† In *Banker to the Poor*, Yunus argued that a focus on profits should infiltrate socially minded ventures to democratize capitalism. Making microfinance and similar programs profitable, while also maintaining loftier goals, would make it so that the market wouldn't be left to the purely greedy. Yunus, *Banker to the Poor*, 205–6.

Franciscan monks, at the beginning of the Renaissance, gave low-interest loans to poor people as an alternative to moneylenders. The poor borrowers would have to leave something behind as collateral; should they never show up again, that item could be sold, with proceeds used to support more lending. Local moneylenders and businessmen caught on, and pawn shops were born. "Then you've got Muhammad Yunus, who looks like a Franciscan monk in his own right, coming up with his wishful thinking and his nice idea, and then the business world snoops around and sees it, and we end up with microfinance."

* * *

In his 2011 *New York Times* op-ed, Yunus offered a course correction. He wrote, "It is possible to harness investment in microcredit and even make a profit without working through either charities or global financial markets." Yunus explained that Grameen was self-reliant thanks to savings "deposits from ordinary Bangladeshis." (He didn't mention that Grameen was only able to pay for itself nearly two decades after its official founding.) Other microfinance stalwarts like FINCA had also relied on savings for decades to fuel lending and keep themselves afloat. "More microcredit institutions should adopt this model," Yunus wrote. "The community needs to reaffirm the original definition of microcredit, abandon commercialization and turn back to serving the poor."

While some early microcredit advocates had emphasized savings, including at the Microcredit Summit, this never gained much public attention. Loans, with their promises of bootstrap success and easy alignment with a win-win framework, were far more interesting, not to mention far more profitable.

Savings reentered the conversation after it became clear—through randomized controlled trials, the Andhra Pradesh suicide crisis, and just simple observation—that a reliance on foreign-backed, high-priced debt could be harmful, or at least not particularly helpful. Several studies suggested that savings, on the other hand, seemed to be positive for borrowers: those who saved more had more money, were less reliant on debt, and spent more on food and preventative health care. There were fewer spectacular promises here, no grand suggestions that savings would launch successful businesses and end poverty. But a steady stream of savings might at least protect borrowers from financial shocks.*

Savings were good for lenders, too. If lenders could find new ways to raise capital, such as using savings to fund new loans, they could continue to expand without being at the whims of the market, bad press, and shifting governmental priorities. As lenders looked for alternative ways to raise money, savings became so essential that some microlenders instituted compulsory, or "forced" savings, requiring a borrower to put down a savings deposit before giving a loan. In some cases, a borrower would be charged a weekly savings deposit in addition to weekly loan payments. This was offered as its own sort of win-win. Borrowers would be able to squirrel away some cash, and lenders could rely on a steady stream of revenue that didn't have to come from outside sources.†

But savings requirements could effectively push up how much a borrower had to pay—by a lot. One study, done in Nigeria in 2015, showed that all told—interest rates, savings, and other fees—effective annual interest rates could reach as high as 337.4 percent (*337.4 percent!*). The median cost was a whopping 102 percent.

In the face of criticism, some companies have now removed forced savings requirements. But in Sierra Leone, they remain common. Every borrower I met was forced to make a deposit before they could take out a loan. Many didn't have enough cash to make the initial deposit, which could amount to nearly a quarter of the loan. Instead, they met the requirement by pulling from whatever money they had just been lent, for example, taking $25 from a $100 loan and keeping just $75. In practice, this slicing from the loan could make the effective loan size significantly

---

* It's remarkable that savings was pitched as an innovative idea given that poor people had been finding ways to save on their own for centuries, something Jeff Ashe learned during his early research. Many people seemed to actually prefer savings over debt. In the 1970s, Dale Adams and other "Spring Review" authors noted that even though small farmers didn't borrow often, they were actively saving and wanted other ways to do so. Even Elisabeth Rhyne, who had worked in programs that promoted credit for decades, recognized, "Poor people, every single time, if they are given the choice between taking debt versus saving money, they will choose savings."

† By 2018, in many regions, savings deposits were the largest funding source for microfinance lenders. "Global Outreach & Financial Performance Benchmark Report—2017–2018," Mix Market. Other fees help, too: in 2020 alone, BRAC made $3 million on "membership fees charged to customers, loan appraisal fee[s] charged to clients and the sale of passbooks"—that is, selling borrowers a ledger they are required to track repayments in. That year, BRAC made nearly four times as much from these fees as from grants. "Other Operating Income," BRAC International Holdings B.V. Annual Report 2020.

smaller while pushing the effective interest rates much *higher*: a borrower would have to pay back 30 percent on that $100, even if she only kept $75. Several told me they pulled from a loan to make a savings deposit at the behest of the loan officers, who suggested this as a handy way to deal with the problem of, as Ramatu in Kono put it, "needing money to get money."

Even after finding a way to fulfill the requirement, many women I met complained they didn't get their savings deposit back. Savings can be whittled down by late fees and other penalties. Whatever is left over is only given after and *if* a borrower pays off her loan in full—which, one LAPO Sierra Leone manager told me, only happens about 40 percent of the time. Because of these penalties—and because so many borrowers are late or default—in practice savings deposits can act more as collateral for a lender than active deposits for a borrower. Most of the Sierra Leonean borrowers I met, knowing that they would likely be late at least once, if not perpetually, never expected to see their savings again. Kadija told me, "They call it savings, but it's really hard to get that money back." The money lost is not marginal: enough to cover a semester of school or a quarter of annual house rent.

Microfinance institutions broadened in other ways, too. Some began offering products like death insurance. While this can protect a borrower's friends and family from having to make repayments in case she dies, it also works to protect the lender, who has fees to fall back on in case of default or death. And like savings, insurance can be compulsory, packaged together with a loan.

Some lenders instituted a grace period, giving a borrower a bit of time before her first repayment.* Some offered more refinancing options so that an overwhelmed borrower could take out another loan to help pay off the first one,† a tactic that also happened to increase a lender's repayment rates and borrowing rates in one fell swoop, making their portfolio

---

* RCTs had suggested this might allow for riskier, and therefore more high impact, investments. Dina Pomeranz, "The Promise of Microfinance and Women's Empowerment: What Does the Evidence Say?" discussion paper, Harvard Business School, 2014.

† This extension approach had been used by Grameen and later became common practice in Cambodia, one of the world's largest microfinance markets. Milford Bateman, "Microcredit in Cambodia: Why Is There So Much Support for a Failed Poverty Reduction Model?" *ISEAS Perspective* 2020, no. 134, November 25, 2020.

look healthy even though it contained borrowers who were perpetually in debt. (One person called the tactic "extend and pretend."*)

In response to critiques that the poor were unable to keep up with above-market interest rates, both BRAC and Grameen instituted subsidized programs that offered discounted loans for the poorest borrowers—a subtle but dramatic reversal of the three basic tenets of microfinance: that lending programs should never be subsidized, that market conditions should determine interest rates, and that the poor can pay a high price. The Grameen program focused on a small group of beggars—just a fraction of its estimated ten million members—who were given interest-free loans averaging around $12, as well as life insurance without any cost.

BRAC's Ultra-Poor Graduation program,† launched in 2002, offers cash grants alongside assets like livestock or equipment. Unlike its lending programs, no repayment is expected. Those in the program also receive basic social services, and training on things like water treatment and livestock rearing.

Again, the program is small compared to BRAC's overall operations. In Bangladesh alone, BRAC claimed to have nearly ten million clients as of 2023, about five times more than the 2.1 million Bangladeshi households—that's *families*, not individuals—they say they've reached through the Ultra-Poor Graduation program. And despite the emphasis on a "holistic approach" that includes social services, credit remains the core goal. After grants help the poor to stabilize, participants "graduate" to financial services, at which point the free programs and cash grants evaporate, and the poor are again left to pull themselves out of poverty. Although the World Bank's Consultative Group to Assist the Poor supported the program out of recognition that what the poor "really required" to "stabilize" their lives was food and shelter, Elizabeth Littlefield, who ran the group from 1999 to 2010, told me she also hoped governments would see the model as an alternative to welfare, a "ladder for the very poor and

---

* This resembles a practice central to America's payday lending industry, in which a loan is extended at the same time the principal is increased, making a loan that at first seemed manageable soon feel unwieldy and keeping borrowers in a cycle of debt.

† Now called the Ultra-Poor Graduation Initiative.

vulnerable," a way to help them "cover basic needs to prepare them for income generation and for eligibility for microfinance."

* * *

The most dramatic change was a call for regulation, this time from within the industry. Despite long claiming that any sort of watchdog would choke lenders' innovation and growth,* in his 2011 *New York Times* op-ed Yunus called for a "microfinance regulatory authority" in each country. In the wake of the Compartamos and Andhra Pradesh crises, many governments did institute some sort of oversight. In Andhra Pradesh, in the immediate aftermath of the suicides, the government barred microlenders from collecting payments at certain locations, such as a borrower's home or place of work. The government also set interest rate caps, which lowered the cost of loans from around 31 percent to 24 percent and banned flat interest, which had been used by about 80 percent of lenders. And they limited fees to a maximum of 1 percent, due up front. Interest rate caps were later instituted in Kenya in 2016, in Cambodia in 2017, and in Sri Lanka in 2018.

Caps, however, are easy to get around. In Cambodia, lenders have played at the edges of an 18 percent annual interest rate cap by increasing fees and savings, which has effectively raised interest rates to where they had been before: about 30 percent. Similar tactics have been used elsewhere,† such as in South Africa, where, according to one analysis, effec-

---

* In much of his writings and speeches, it seems that "regulation" was a stand-in for Yunus's fear of overreach by inept Bangladeshi officials, of whom he remained openly skeptical since his brief time as a bureaucrat in the early 1970s. Instead, Yunus advocated for self-regulation. At a 1999 follow-up meeting of the Microcredit Summit, he said: "We need some regulation, but not in the way usually you talk about it. . . . We who are in the business, let us set the rules. . . . Self-regulation is a step forward until we know there's an environment which is safe enough for us to get there and still run our business." "Final Report: 1999 Meeting of Councils, June 24–26, Abidjan, Cote d'Ivoire," Microfinance Summit Campaign.

† In some places, interest rate caps are ignored entirely. In 1997, the West African Economic and Monetary Union implemented a "Law on Usury." In 2010, usury was defined as anything over 27 percent. At least on the books, violation of the law could be penalized with up to two years in prison and a substantial financial fine. But Chuck Waterfield learned that "the usury law was known by all but understood by none." In his research, he found that half of the institutions he came across violated the law. In a 2015 post, Waterfield wrote, "Not a single [one] has been penalized for violation of the law." It was "not being enforced at all." Waterfield told me, "I can mention a half-dozen countries where the government passes price caps but does not have an enforcement mechanism. So the public and journalists assume everyone's abiding by the price caps, but nobody verifies if they are or not." Chuck Waterfield, "Advocating Transparent Pricing in Microfinance: A Review of MFTransparency's

tive annual interest rates could reach 400 percent even after an interest rate cap was instituted.

Sierra Leone's efforts, which only began a few years ago, are particularly measly. A small arm of the Bank of Sierra Leone, called the Other Financial Institutions Department, is technically responsible for overseeing microfinance lenders. But the unit, staffed by a handful of people, is essentially toothless. When I met bank officials in the summer of 2019, they made it clear that they are "in dialogue with," not regulating, microlenders. When I asked what this dialogue entailed, I was shown stacks of paper reports that had been voluntarily sent in by lenders. If a lender didn't send in an update, there was no penalty. The reports offered basic information that could be found in most annual reports, available online and in brochures: how many borrowers a lender had, the total size of outstanding loans, what percent of debtors were in arrears. There was nothing on whether borrowers had also taken out loans from other institutions, no information on the tactics lenders used to enforce repayment. Most notably, there was no oversight of interest rates or other costs. When I asked Ralph Ansumana, the director of the Other Financial Institutions Department, whether the central bank had considered instituting interest rate caps, he told me, several times, that the IMF simply wouldn't allow this. He repeated, "We have a liberalized financial system here."

In the absence of global, industry-wide standards, the country-by-country regulatory patchwork is full of holes lenders can slip through: a company working across borders can charge drastically different rates to two different borrowers who live just a few hundred miles apart, even if their incomes and socioeconomic statuses are almost exactly the same. Some regulators have focused primarily on formal financial institutions, not NGOs, leaving out some of the world's major lenders, such as BRAC. Some countries launched microfinance credit bureaus to track overlending that could bury borrowers in debt. But many lenders simply chose not to participate, rendering the bureaus inept. And many regulators didn't pay attention to subtle but important distinctions like whether an interest rate was "flat" or "declining"—small but essential details that determine how much a borrower pays.

Even if there were some sort of global norms for what has become a global industry, it's not clear who would enforce them. What is the role of foreign governments, who offer funding and write policies thousands of miles away from where loans are disbursed? What about local governments, at once encouraged to expand lending to the poor and then responsible for making sure lenders don't get out of hand? And what about equity investors in Silicon Valley, incentivized by a company's profits? As the network of financiers has expanded and funding flows become more circuitous, it has become harder to trace money, and harder still to consider who should be responsible for what behavior.

To promote some sort of uniform standards, in 2008 Accion opened the Center for Financial Inclusion, using some of the $135 million it had made through the Compartamos sale to fund the effort. (Waterfield, and many others I spoke to, saw the center as something of an attempt at salvation after the Compartamos IPO, a way for Accion to make amends for the money it made on high-priced loans. "They were embarrassed," Waterfield told me.) Accion's Elisabeth Rhyne was appointed the center's managing director—an irony, some felt, given that she had helped to put together the Compartamos sale.

The center's flagship project would be the Smart Campaign, which laid out a set of voluntary principles that lenders could choose to agree to. Participating companies could apply for a "Smart certification"—something like a fair-trade stamp for microfinance. The bar was set low. Principles included "prevent over-indebtedness, communicate prices transparently, be fair and respectful of clients." While participating lenders agreed to set prices "in a way that is affordable to clients while allowing for financial institutions to be sustainable," the Smart Campaign stopped short of actually regulating prices or setting price caps.

The Smart Campaign had deep industry ties. The newfound focus on industry self-restraint came from a meeting that Asad Mahmood of Deutsche Bank called in 2008 in the immediate wake of the pricing and abuse scandals. "Deutsche Bank was interested in the turn in the industry," Rhyne told me, not just because of the harms overborrowing and its fallout posed to borrowers but also because of associated "reputational risks." At the time, Rhyne explains, Deutsche Bank "was putting together special funds, solicit[ing] investments from wealthy and high net worth individuals and invest[ing] in microfinance institutions." These lenders were asking what Deutsche Bank and others were going to do about scandals like Andhra Pradesh. The Smart Campaign principles offered an answer.

Critics argued the Smart Campaign lacked any teeth: it was simply a feel-good effort that allowed the industry to say it was doing something while acting as a foil for tougher national regulations and more substantial industry-wide reform. Even when lenders purported to be following the principles, allegations of overborrowing, overindebtedness, and harassment continued. As of 2020, BRAC claimed to be following the Smart Campaign principles, as well as a voluntary code of conduct from the Sierra Leone Association of Microfinance Institutions. Around the same time, borrowers in Freetown and Kono claimed that BRAC used the police and court system to pressure repayments.*

* * *

There was another way to change the microfinance industry: by reforming borrowers themselves.

Something called "financial literacy" is now a regular part of the microfinance package. The idea is simple: because microfinance can be so risky, borrowers must be taught the basics of lending and saving. That knowledge will protect them from the most predatory lenders, encourage whistleblowing if there are abuses, reduce overborrowing, and encourage timely repayment of loans. What constitutes financial literacy varies widely, from toll-free phone messages that encourage borrowers not to

---

* Based on interviews with borrowers and with organizations like AdvocAid, I reported on these concerns for the *Guardian* in 2019. At the time, Bridget Dougherty, who helps to oversee microfinance for BRAC International, said BRAC had conducted an internal investigation and had "addressed this issue adequately with the staff in Sierra Leone." Mara Kardas-Nelson, "Microfinance Lenders in Sierra Leone Accused of 'Payday Loan' Interest Rates," *Guardian*, December 12, 2019. That year, Kiva, one of BRAC Sierra Leone's funders, noted it was "temporarily pausing fundraising for new loans to BRAC Sierra Leone as a result of operational issues that came to light during routine onsite monitoring. Kiva is working with BRAC Sierra Leone to resolve these issues." In 2020, Kiva "reactivated fundraising for new loans for BRAC Sierra Leone. Following operational issues discovered during a routine onsite audit, BRAC Sierra Leone management conducted satisfactory retraining with branch staff, which was confirmed by a follow-up onsite audit conducted by Kiva." "BRAC Sierra Leone," Kiva, https://www.kiva.org/about/where-kiva-works/partners/183.

take on too much debt, to loan officers teaching borrowers how to do a careful accounting of business, household, and loan costs. (In Sierra Leone, I met one loan officer who claimed to be "doing financial literacy" when he was writing out loan repayments for a borrower.) In Cambodia, one of the world's most heavily indebted countries, the government has set up a "Let's Talk Money" campaign to teach about "saving and its advantages," "the effective use of credit and debt management," and "the prevention of over-indebtedness." Maryann Bylander and Phasy Res, an American-Cambodian academic team, attended financial literacy trainings in the country. In one, conducted by a microfinance lender and paid for by USAID, microfinance borrowers watched a video clip from the "Let's Talk Money" campaign, which encouraged debtors to "make [debt] repayment your first thought, not an afterthought." The facilitator, an employee of the microfinance company, told the borrowers, "You should feel good if you had a million riel and now have nothing left over, but you've repaid your debts." Bylander and Res write that in the course, borrowers learned that overindebtedness was the result of a borrower's "poor decision making, a lack of planning, laziness, helping others too much, and/or a lack of thrift." *Her* fault, not the lender's. With its focus on individual responsibility and "moral lessons associated with creditworthiness," such as "honesty, thrift, the virtue of debt repayment," Bylander and Res saw trainings like these as a sort of "hearts and minds" of the microfinance sector.

While these programs attempt to change borrowers, financial literacy does nothing to address the basic architecture of microfinance: the high price of loans, harsh repayment tactics, and lenders' flouting of whatever regulations are on the books. Phil Mader, who studies debt and development at the Institute of Development Studies in the UK, takes issue with the premise undergirding these programs. "People say 'yes yes yes, abuse happens, that is why we need financial literacy for these people.' And I'm sick and tired of hearing that. It's a revamped version of the original story which says not only do they need financial services, we also have to teach them how to behave responsibly, and in a finance-compatible way, to see money how we see it. Rather than the other way around, saying what is it about our idea is wrong."

Ramatu Looks to God

Old Post, Koidu, Kono, Eastern Sierra Leone

2021

ALTHOUGH RAMATU HAD ALWAYS CONSIDERED HERSELF A CHRISTIAN, religion had mostly played a sporadic, and not particularly important, role in her life. She went to church a bit during the few years she lived in Freetown, right after the war, and then again for a little while after her daughter, Janet, was born. Ramatu was alone in this endeavor. Her mother expressed zero interest in attending. Her farmer friend had tried his hand at becoming a preacher decades before, caught up in admiration for a charismatic Peace Corps volunteer and pastor he wanted to emulate. He had even read the Bible inside out, could offer long quotes and interpretations in his many arguments with Ramatu. But he gave up the idea when he observed too many pastors he considered businessmen first, men of God second, if at all. "It's all about money," he mused. He hadn't been to church since.

Over the last few months, Ramatu had started to go again, this time more regularly. Every Wednesday evening and Sunday morning, she put on her best dress and shuffled the kids out the door. To show her renewed interest in God, she had taken to wearing little gold-colored crosses that hung from small hooped earrings.

The change was driven in part by proximity. A room in the back of Janet's school, just around the corner from Ramatu's house, had recently been converted into a new branch of a Freetown church. A huge picture of the main pastor, a man in Freetown, was mounted at the front. He had large shiny cheeks, arms so round they bulged in his suit jacket, and short hair that looked freshly cut. His head was tilted slightly and the photo was taken in soft light, giving him the look of a '90s R & B singer. Pastor John, the man sent to helm the new Kono outpost, was younger than the big man in the photo, with a thin body and energetic manner. Pastor John often walked through Old Post, encouraging everyone in need of a little prayer and salvation to join his congregation. Ramatu figured that included her.

Ramatu was also drawn to church because of her new baby, Mark. She had more to pray for now, both to ask for protection and to offer gratitude. Thank God the boy was relatively healthy, at the very least alive if not particularly thriving, never mind that he often seemed an unhappy child, far more ornery than easygoing Janet, who was precocious. She had learned to walk early, speak early, and now spent most afternoons splayed out on the cool gray floor of Ramatu's parlor, poring over books. Mark, on the other hand, was a spacey, sickly child. Most of his time was spent staring at whatever corner of the room he was in. He cried at the slightest provocation. Ramatu worried about his health. He was tall for his age, although not in the least bit fat, and regularly had a runny nose and upset stomach. By age two, he was still in diapers but had finally learned a few words. "Water," "mama." When he was hungry, he asked for "money."

Which Ramatu needed, too. Each day, she tallied up two lists that compiled each child's needs:

FOR JANET:
- 20 cents a day for lesson fees
- 50 cents a day for lunch
- 50 cents a day miscellaneous—books, fees, a new uniform

AND FOR MARK:
- $1.50 each for three packets of Milcolac, ready-made baby food
- 45 cents for two Pampers

Each list had an accompanying gripe. Regarding Janet's school, Ramatu moaned, "Every day it's money business. Every day! Like the other day— look, I won't lie, I didn't have money. The people at the school beat her for that, said she should never come back. I was really mad! They should really understand. I'll give it to them when I can, but when I can't they have to be patient. I'm not going to go steal something, to come and give something to a teacher. What they're doing—*that's* stealing."

As for Mark, "This child, he eats money. And he'll go to school soon. Then the responsibility will go up."

It had been nearly a year since Ramatu had taken out a loan. Despite her promise to the farmer that she would never borrow from microfinance again, in private she conceded she would consider taking another one, but only if she was offered around $200—anything less and it was so small as to be meaningless. "Even though the interest is big, I would manage. I'm not afraid of the police. I've already gone there one time, two times. If you haven't been there, you feel panicked. But now I'm used to them." But Ramatu knew that with almost no business to speak of, any loan, let alone one for $200, was unlikely to happen.

The farmer hadn't been much help recently. He'd hit an awful streak of bad luck. First, his foot had been broken when a private SUV ran over it as he was crossing a street in Freetown. He waited in the country's main hospital for nearly a month, paid hundreds of dollars, but still didn't get the operation he needed. Nearly two years later, he couldn't walk without a cane, which stunted his ability to farm and to hustle.

Newly limited in what he could do, the man had bought a motorbike for his brother to ride, to make extra cash for the family. For weeks the brother had refused to do so, worried about getting beaten up by the other younger and tougher motorcycle taxi boys, who claimed he was infringing on their turf. The brother had finally started riding, but the two were far from making their $5-a-day goal. He had begun taking on debt of his own, not from microfinance, but from a local vendor in town. It was a gentle contract: the farmer paid back when he could, with no interest. He avoided the eyes of the lender when his pockets were empty.

Finally, much of the farmer's bean crop had burned down when a neighbor set his own land alight to ready it for new plantings. In the fire's wake, the farmer mused at the brilliance of nature, remarked at the marvel that new sprouts—unplanted—had started poking through the burned stalks.

There must be some lesson about renewal here, about how everything had its own time and its own way, how, as a Kono saying went, "the sun always comes out twice." Maybe this wasn't his day, but surely tomorrow would be.

Ramatu was not hopeful.

CHAPTER 13

In the Sky

In 2019, in Homa Bay, Kenya, reports surfaced that about two dozen people had committed suicide. Every single one had something in common: they had recently defaulted on their microcredit loans.

The next year, a Kenyan senator* claimed there had been an increase in debt-related suicides in the country. In 2022, *Bloomberg* reported that in Sri Lanka, where the aggregate amount of microloans had grown more than *fifty times* from 2006 to 2020 and where interest rates could reach 220 percent,[†] an estimated two hundred microfinance debtors—all women—had committed suicide in the past three years.

For those who hoped the tweaks that had been introduced would stem the worst excesses of the sector—that interest rate caps, the Smart Campaign's voluntary code of conduct, credit bureaus, and financial literacy would quell reports of harassment and shaming—continued reports of overindebtedness and death felt disheartening. But for those who believed the sector had gone irrevocably upmarket, such stories were now expected. The now expected consequences persisted because the changes hadn't addressed the basic ingredients of the Andhra Pradesh crisis: multiple lenders competing to expand, backed by private capital, turning a blind eye to overborrowing, and aggressively pursuing repayments. Instead, those ingredients had become baked into microfinance. With reports of shaming and suicides from Kenya to Sri Lanka, it was

---

* Kipchumba Murkomen.

† This number comes from Juan Pablo Bohoslavsky, a lawyer who was the UN's independent expert on debt and human rights. He does not say whether this is annual interest or interest for the loan term.

no longer possible to claim that these stories were simply overblown by opportunistic politicians or the result of behavior by a few bad apples. This had become a global pattern, spread across decades.

Still, in the public eye the Andhra Pradesh crisis remained a worst-case example for years, thanks to the international media it garnered and its timing alongside the 2008 global financial crisis.

That is, until it was compared to Cambodia.

* * *

As was true in dozens of other countries, modern microfinance in Cambodia got its start in the wake of a crisis.

In the early 1980s, the Communist Party of Kampuchea, commonly known as the Khmer Rouge, was dissolved, after decades of repressive, bloody rule, during which millions of people were killed. As the country transitioned, NGOs, donors, foreign companies, and consultants raced to Cambodia to set up health care systems and democratic institutions, search for land mines left over from the country's civil war, and open new factories.

But Cambodia wasn't just a post-conflict—and post-Communist—country. It is also in Southeast Asia, an enticing "emerging" region. Thailand, just next door, had the world's fastest-growing economy from 1985 to 1994, with GDP increasing at 8 percent a year. (To give a comparison, America's GDP increased just 2.1 percent in 2022 and 5.9 percent in 2021.) Investors and bankers, who were by now just starting to get into microfinance, wondered if Cambodia could be next.

To help fuel a newly unleashed and hopefully burgeoning economy, by the mid-aughts, dozens of microfinance lenders had sprung up in Cambodia. Most adopted the commercialized approach now common across the sector, with NGOs morphing into for-profit companies or official banks.* As the country's economy grew—by a whopping 13.3 percent in 2005 alone—lenders got more loans out the door. Between 2004 and

---

* To give one rather typical example, KREDIT Microfinance was started by the American NGO World Relief in 1993. Oikocredit, a Dutch microfinance investment fund, later invested in KREDIT, before it was bought by Phillip Capital group, the parent company of Phillip Bank, a Singaporean-owned commercial bank operating in Cambodia since 2009. KREDIT and Phillip have now officially merged; the lender is now simply known as Phillip Bank. "Phillip Bank PLC," Oikocredit, https://www.oikocredit .coop/en/what-we-do/partners/partner-detail/11067/phillip-bank-plc.

2016, the microfinance sector expanded by roughly 45 percent *each year*. Interest rates hovered at around 20 to 30 percent annually, plus fees that could push costs up much higher.

By the mid-2010s, the country was saturated in loans—so many low-income Cambodians had taken out a microloan that there weren't many more to lend to.

So lenders took a different approach, pushing up the amount per loan as had been done in Andhra Pradesh—a way to keep loan portfolios large even if there weren't new borrowers. Loan sizes grew by 80 percent between 2015 and 2017, and then another 30 percent in 2018. (Inflation during this period was low—just 1.2 percent in 2015 and 2.5 percent in 2018—so it's not as if the loan sizes needed to increase to keep up.) As of the early 2020s, Cambodian microborrowers had on average $3,000 in debt, double the GDP per capita.*

By some accounts, Cambodians are now the most indebted people in the world. Just how much debt they have taken on is staggering. In 2020, 2.6 million Cambodians collectively owed over *$10 billion* in microfinance debt, up from just $300 million a decade earlier. The same year, one in five adults had a microloan; in some provinces, it's reportedly as high as eight out of ten.

As happens elsewhere, the loans are not necessarily being used for business. Many of the loans are used to improve a family's land, to pay for health care or a house, to pay off other loans, or to migrate to Thailand, which remains the region's economic powerhouse. Anthropologist Mary-ann Bylander, who has written extensively on microfinance in Cambodia, notes that loans are not seen as a way to radically change circumstances but "as a way to cope with the insecurities that are part of rural life."

All that borrowing brought about now-expected results. Several reports claim it's common for Cambodian borrowers to take out multiple loans, from multiple microfinance companies as well as from informal sources

---

* That would be the equivalent to Americans taking out roughly $140,000 in loans, double the country's roughly $75,000 GDP per capita. "GDP Per Capita (Current US$)—United States," World Bank, https://data.worldbank.org/indicator/NY.GDP.PCAP.CD?locations=US. Americans are not far behind, boasting an average of $96,371 in consumer debt as of 2021. Christian Zanetis, "Average American Debt," First Republic Bank, September 13, 2022, https://www.firstrepublic.com/insights-education/average-american-debt.

including moneylenders, sometimes at the behest of loan officers themselves. There are reports of Cambodian borrowers eating less food, and less quality food, and pulling their kids from school and putting them to work instead. Cambodian human rights organization LICADHO—and, separately, a group of British academics—has even suggested a link between microdebt and indentured servitude at the country's brick factories, through which factory owners agree to pay off a debt in exchange for a debtor agreeing to work. Representatives from LICADHO met kids working alongside their parents to help pay down a debt. The organization has investigated instances of children losing limbs in the country's brick factories; at least one is said to have died due to the injuries. Both child labor and debt bondage are illegal in Cambodia, as well as under international law. LICADHO claims the police and local authorities are aware of these practices.

Arguably the biggest problem in Cambodia is loss of land. Although microfinance was predicated on a collateral-free model, that has changed as the industry has shifted upmarket, toward larger individual loans. In Cambodia, any loan over $1,000 requires a land title (and many Cambodian borrowers have loans far larger than that). The use of land titles for collateral would not have been possible just a few years ago; land titles have only recently become commonplace in Cambodia. After the country transitioned from Communist rule, and following advice from the World Bank, Cambodia registered land that hadn't previously had a title or, in some cases, was communally held, giving it to individuals instead. The stated goal was to rectify historic concentration of land and democratize decision-making, since chiefs and other wealthy community members previously had a stranglehold on ownership and land use.

Land titling was also part of broader structural reforms that considered individual private property as a key driver of economic growth. If a person knew they had ownership rights, the thinking went, maybe they would be more willing to invest in a farm or build a house on that land, growing the economy as they did so. And maybe they would be willing to use that land as collateral for loans. People would then have more money to further invest—in more farms, more homes—ultimately increasing productivity and raising incomes.

All those reforms seemed to have worked in at least one way that was expected: land titling is now deeply intertwined with debt. According to Reuters, in 2020 the Cambodian Microfinance Association estimated that 60 percent of the country's microloans were collateralized by land titles. A few years earlier, LICADHO estimated that at least *one million* land titles were held by microfinance lenders—although the title officially remains in the borrower's name and as the borrower's asset, they do not have access to the title until their loan is repaid.*

Those debtors now risk losing their land. Several reports from LICADHO, as well as reporting by *Al Jazeera* and Reuters, suggest that Cambodian debtors in arrears are regularly pressured to sell their land to make payments. Sometimes, loan officers simply *suggest* selling land to get more cash. But there can be more overt coercion. LICADHO says there have been cases where a "for sale" sign has been put in front of someone's house, or a loan officer arranges a buyer. One LICADHO report included two anonymous microfinance executives who "told researchers that [microfinance institutions] regularly pressure their clients to sell land in order to repay their loans." In a 2019 video that LICADHO produced, a Cambodian borrower said he was worried that if he didn't sell the land himself, the microfinance company would sell it under cost—something a lender can't technically do without going through an onerous and expensive court process, although a Cambodian microfinance researcher I spoke with, who asked that I not use their name due to fear of reprisals, says they routinely threaten this, given that a microfinance company possesses the land title for the duration of the loan.

Flipping the notion that land titles would somehow equalize relations between local authorities and community members, borrowers also say they're pressured to sell by local chiefs, who sign off before a land title is used for collateral. According to LICADHO, some microfinance lenders reportedly pay a fee to local authorities to "help pressure payment."

---

* This practice is similar to one described—and bemoaned—by Yunus in *Banker to the Poor.* "When land is used as security, it is placed at the disposal of the creditor, who enjoys ownership rights over it until the amount is repaid." Yunus says witnessing such unequal relationships between poor borrowers and informal lenders was part of his impetus for setting up the Grameen Bank. Muhammad Yunus, *Banker to the Poor: Micro-Lending and the Battle Against World Poverty* (New York: PublicAffairs, 2007), 49.

Although the microfinance industry has accused LICADHO of cherry-picking the worst stories, these do not seem to be one-off instances. At the beginning of 2020, a survey of one thousand Cambodian households found that one in eight had to sell assets, including livestock, machinery, and land, to pay off their debt. A village chief in the province of Siem Reap told Reuters that about one third of the 134 homes in his village were up for sale or had been sold to repay debts. The Cambodian microfinance researcher told me, "The [microfinance] sector has become so large and so linked to land titles it's clear this is the biggest threat to land security in the country." The researcher described the situation—the severe overindebtedness, the land sales, and the two together—as an "impending economic disaster." One debtor, worried about losing his land to pay off a debt, told LICADHO, "We are living on the land. We do everything on the land. We are not able to live in the sky. If we sell our land, it's like selling our bodies. We have no choice left."

* * *

Despite all the negative press—in *Bloomberg, Al Jazeera,* Reuters, even in reports by the International Organization for Migration, a UN body—the Cambodian microfinance sector is well protected. Unlike in Andhra Pradesh, the Cambodian government is aligned with microlenders. Ever since long-standing prime minister Hun Sen declared 2006 the year of microfinance, the government has considered microfinance to be an important component of poverty alleviation in the country. In 2020, according to Radio Free Asia, Hun Sen* "threatened to allow banks and microfinance lenders to file complaints with the courts to confiscate borrowers' assets directly" if they didn't pay their debts, potentially risking even further land loss. "If you were to ask me the worst country to try microfinance in, Cambodia would be it," the Cambodian microfinance researcher told me. "There's no consumer protection, there's no regulation."

Cambodian lenders keep getting international financing, too. Many of the Cambodian microfinance companies accused of promoting over-indebtedness and coercive land sales have been supported by large Asian,

---

* Hun Sen was the prime minister of Cambodia from 1985 to 2023.

European, and American funders.* DEG, a subsidiary of the German government development bank KfW, has lent directly to Hattha Kaksekar Limited,† which is owned by one of the largest banks in Thailand and is one of the lenders accused of borrower harassment. The World Bank's International Finance Corporation has reportedly lent directly to AMK, one of the largest commercial microcredit lenders in the country, which has also received funding from some of Asia's largest commercial banks and European investors. The IFC also invested in other Cambodian microfinance lenders even after Human Rights Watch asked the World Bank to reconsider, given that seizures of collateral, most notably land, have become common. USAID has publicly criticized coercive land sales in the Cambodian microfinance sector, but the U.S. government still supports Cambodian microlenders, including through a bond intended to funnel about $6 million to lenders working in the country.‡ That includes LOLC Cambodia, a Sri Lankan–owned company that has been accused of harassing borrowers and encouraging them to sell land.

"I don't know how these European investors can know that there's no consumer protection and think, 'Yes, this is going to go well,'" the microfinance researcher told me. "A lot of these loans are for health care, and investors say 'That's good!' You're from Germany, how can you say that? You get free health care. Why don't you expect the same somewhere else?"

* * *

The coerced sale of land and other assets is not unique to Cambodia. The extent of the practice is dizzying. Celestine Okeke, who works with small

---

* As an example, take the Microfinance Enhancement Facility, established in 2009 by the German development bank KfW and the International Finance Corporation, the private-sector arm of the World Bank. The Enhancement Facility is managed by four investment firms, all based in Europe: BlueOrchard Finance AG, Incofin Investment Management, responsAbility Investments AG, and Symbiotics SA. According to LICADHO, "its investors include development agencies and [development] banks in Sweden (SIDA), Austria (OeDB), the Netherlands (FMO), and Germany (BMZ), as well as the IFC, the European Investment Bank, and the OPEC Fund for International Development." In total, the facility has invested $61.8 million in Cambodian microlenders. "Driven Out: One Villager's Experience with MFIs and Cross-Border Migration," LICADHO, May 2020, https://www.licadho -cambodia.org/reports/files/229DrivenOut_Briefing_ENG.pdf.
† Now known as Hattha Bank.
‡ The bond was listed on the Singapore stock exchange, with 4 percent interest. It was developed by the Impact Investment Exchange, a socially responsible lender.

businesses in Nigeria, explains that while a lender can't legally seize land or other assets in that country, "they can force you to sell the land and pay back the loan"—remarkably similar to the situation in Cambodia. One East African researcher, who didn't want to give her name because she works with lenders, told me she had seen borrowers list their household items—things like TVs, couches, and cupboards—as part of the loan approval process. The lenders can then "hold" the items while payment is forthcoming. "Sometimes they confiscate everything," she told me. "Sometimes the group members get involved. It becomes very chaotic." Another person I spoke with, who had worked in small-scale finance in Kenya, said he had seen many women's assets taken—including, literally, roofs stripped from their homes—when they defaulted on loans from the Kenya Women Microfinance Bank,* which began as an affiliate of Women's World Banking. In Uganda, one former microfinance advocate-turned-critic learned that overly indebted borrowers "had to sell off their land or domestic animals to repay the loans." If they still failed to repay, "they've had to flee to nearby islands or face horrifying prison sentences."

Jail, or the threat of it, is used against microfinance debtors from Jordan to Ghana. In 2019, I spent the summer shadowing paralegals at Advoc-Aid, a Sierra Leonean organization that works with women caught in the legal system. I went to courtrooms, police stations, and prisons across the country. All were overcrowded, packed with people arrested, awaiting trial, or serving time for what are effectively poverty-related crimes, which range from being unable to pay a traffic ticket to "loitering"—a broad term used against those the police consider "bad boys" (basically unemployed, listless young men), sex workers, and anyone who looks up to no good.

These crimes also include debt. I met dozens of people who were jailed, or were brought to the police station, when they couldn't pay off a loan. As a British colony, Sierra Leone inherited a legal system that criminalizes deceiving a creditor, but which in effect penalizes *all* debt, a tradition that reaches back centuries. In medieval England, debtors were regularly thrown into prison until their families could pay. Later, in Elizabethan

---

* Previously called the Kenya Women Finance Trust.

England, debtors could be treated as criminals if a borrower was "suf-ficiently vindictive." Penalties for infringing on imposed social order, whether nonrepayment of loans or public disorder, were a significant com-ponent of British governance both in Britain and across its colonies. In colonial Sierra Leone, people could be fined for gossiping about the gover-nor's son, for talking back, and for not following religious orders.

The British eventually recognized that the antiquated law punishing debt was confusing and outdated, and amended their own version of it. But when Sierra Leone gained independence in 1961, its laws, institu-tions, and practices weren't suddenly rewritten. Along with British-style bureaucracy, the country inherited the British legal code, by then deeply baked into the Sierra Leonean judicial system. Even today, sixty years after independence, the old colonial law that criminalizes debt, as well as doz-ens of other colonial-era laws, remain on the books.* Similar iterations of that law remain in other former British colonies, including Uganda, Tanzania, and Nigeria.

The law is specifically intended to criminalize "fraudulent" debt. What constitutes "fraud" is difficult to define, largely left up to the police offi-cer responsible for laying charges or the judge overseeing a case. Over the years, application of the law has expanded to effectively criminalize *any* type of debt, especially when it's taken by a poor person who should have "known," in the eyes of the police and judges, that they couldn't pay. (As one staffer at AdvocAid explained to me, the rationale goes: If you're poor, and you take out a loan, shouldn't you have an inkling that maybe you won't be able to pay it back?)

This includes microfinance borrowers. In my reporting, and through reports from the country's Human Rights Commission, the government-run Legal Aid Board, AdvocAid, and the Centre for Accountability and the Rule of Law, all the major microfinance lenders in Sierra Leone have been accused of going to the police, and sometimes the courts, when debtors default. Through AdvocAid, I met one woman who had spent one year and seven months awaiting trial for a $600 debt. At the High Court in Kono, I witnessed a young man receive a one-year sentence for a $60

---

* Fines also remain a key component of the justice system today, imposed for everything from public spitting to, during the Ebola epidemic, breaking curfew.

debt. I also saw people taken to traditional courts—lower courts that can't give out prison sentences, run by local authorities—for informal loans, such as those from friends or osusus. "There are people in prison in this country for about $12," Gassan Abess, who works with the Human Rights Commission, a government body, told me. Many more microfinance borrowers recalled being taken to the police, who claimed to be helping a lender "negotiate" repayment. They stayed for anywhere from several hours to several days—however long it took to come up with some cash.

* * *

In the fall of 2021, I interviewed Gabriel Eshiague in his spacious central Freetown office. Eshiague oversees the growing Sierra Leonean operations of the Nigerian lender LAPO. By 2010, decades after its founding and two years after it opened a Sierra Leonean arm, the nonprofit had some of the highest microfinance interest rates on the planet, charging up to 126 percent effective annual interest rates. More recently, LAPO had undergone a rebranding, away from classic microfinance and toward upmarket lending. LAPO now offers not just group loans but individual ones—consumer loans, education loans, transportation loans—to relatively wealthy Sierra Leoneans. When I arrived, posters of smiling, attractive, well-dressed people, their hands filled with cash, greeted me in the office's waiting area.

Eshiague was friendly and approachable, offering me a free copy of a book by the founder of the organization, Godwin Ehigiamusoe. But he was clearly very busy. Some minutes after I arrived, a few staff members hurriedly entered, looking stressed. They informed Eshiague that their lawyer was set to go to civil court to try to seize a land title from a debtor who was behind on repaying many hundreds of dollars (in addition to the criminal law on debt, assets and land can be seized through civil courts in Sierra Leone). Eshiague was calm but serious: "If he doesn't show up today, and doesn't pay, we'll take his land. If he refuses, we'll go straight to the High Court." I was surprised that Eshiague had this conversation, complete with court papers, in front of me; I had reached out to him two years earlier about allegations that LAPO takes debtors to the police and courts. When the harried staff members left, I looked at Eshiague and tilted my head in question. He offered a slight smile. "That's a lot of money," he said. "You can't just let it go."

* * *

Throughout the weeks I spent in Sierra Leonean prisons and courtrooms, I found it difficult not to see some of the proceedings I observed as absurd. Officers at the Kono High Court high-fived a man who had been accused of stealing a few farming tools after he was finally allowed to go. He had maintained his innocence and spent over a year in prison awaiting trial, only seeing a judge once. Everyone in the courtroom was giddy, gleeful that justice had been served, but I had a hard time seeing a year in prison as a victory. I think I visibly raised my eyebrows when the judge used the Queen's English in a country in which the Queen hasn't been head of state for half a century.

This feeling of absurdity, I think, came from being appalled at what people were charged with: Prosecuting a woman who was clearly dealing with mental illness for stealing a bit of food from her neighbor, locking up a man for a year for $60 he couldn't pay. It was embarrassing to see poverty on trial in such an obvious way. I felt embarrassed for the judge, for the lawyers, embarrassed that I was sitting quietly in the corner writing notes, embarrassed that anyone was taking any of this seriously. "This is a hundred-year-old, dusty law," I kept thinking to myself. One that everyone I had spoken to—every judge, lawyer, police officer—said should be changed, whenever the politicians got around to it. So what, exactly, were we doing here?

But the politicians haven't gotten around to it, and in the meantime, there are many who benefit from the law's continued use: police officers who get a "tip" for negotiating repayment, microfinance companies and other lenders who have a handy stick to use if borrowers are late. Although they seem bizarre, these trials, and the threat of them, have very real consequences for those who do go to jail and serious social stigma for those who don't. When police and loan officers came to Two Taps, Freetown, to harass pregnant Panneh about her unpaid loans, Aminata and Kadija advised her to apologize profusely and beg for more time. The police could rough her up, deny her food and water—and she was in a delicate condition. Panneh did apologize and beg, and after much yelling and enough commotion to gather a small crowd, more time was granted.

Yet even though Panneh didn't have to go to jail, the scene itself was hugely consequential. In addition to being unsure how she would pay her debt, Panneh was so ashamed, her reputation so tainted—by the debt itself and the fracas that ensued—that she left the neighborhood. She came back to Two Taps a few months later to find that her fiancé was no longer interested in having a relationship, even though she was now six months pregnant.

Panneh's soured reputation altered other relationships, too. Aminata didn't want to give her informal loans anymore, even if it just meant a bit of food or water. She didn't want to babysit her son, worried that Panneh would "run off again." Panneh mainly got by on the kindness of her uncle and by selling a few sweets on the busy main street down the road.

It can be hard to differentiate between the stresses of poverty and the consequences of microdebt. Their symptoms can look the same. Both engender strained relationships, exclusion from family and friends, stressful hopping from one payment and debt to another—be it microfinance or informal loans, worries about rental payments or school fees. Panneh suffered, in part because she already suffered, given limited social connections and little money to build on. And because there is such an intimate connection between poverty and incarceration in Sierra Leone, poor people like Panneh have all sorts of reasons they might be taken to the police—for example, selling at the wrong place at the wrong time, or for a domestic dispute. If Panneh hadn't left Two Taps because of her microfinance debt, maybe something else would have pushed her out. This may have been what Suleiman Dao, a police officer in Makeni, a town in the center of the country, was trying to get at when he told me he had "no choice" but to "criminalize" poverty. Because so many people are poor, he reasons, you can't make exceptions for it. Nearly everyone is always on the cusp of some sort of disaster.

What does seem different about the realities of everyday poverty and the consequences of microfinance is what each promises. Poverty is expected to be bad. Microfinance, on the other hand, offers hope. Hope that someone like Panneh might be able to achieve the seemingly impossible: to make her life better purely through her own ingenuity and hard work, to actualize a sort of rags-to-riches story all by herself. At the very least, these small loans are supposed to smooth out the edges of poverty. Instead, microfinance has sharpened those edges, providing yet another obstacle that Panneh must surmount. Dr. Nima Yolmo, an anthropologist who has studied microfinance in Nepal, says that it's this "aspirational component of [microfinance] that can be so troublesome." A microfinance loan has been promised to change a life, and when that life isn't changed, borrowers can experience "radical disappointment," Yolmo told me. "The promise of salvation is part of what makes people feel so bad."

Shame is central to that "radical disappointment," offering a thick, consistent glue that binds Cambodians waking up to a "for sale" sign in front of their home and Sierra Leoneans worrying that the police will show up at their doorstep. In both cases, debtors are publicly marked, indicating to the community: this person has failed. At business, at repayment, at staying within social norms. Failed at achieving something. In some cases, embarrassment itself *is* the punishment. In 2016, Elisabeth Rhyne, the former USAID, then Accion, then Center for Financial Inclusion staffer, published a piece in the *Guardian* highlighting findings from a recent survey. She noted, "In Benin and Pakistan, where regulations on microfinance are either non-existent or poorly enforced, clients spoke of providers holding customers hostage at the office, placing a defaulter in a wheelbarrow and trundling her through town, and broadcasting defaulters' names on the radio . . . The humiliation can be devastating." One person who researches the Indian microfinance industry told me, "It all starts with shame. To be in debt is shame, and that's magnified by someone sitting in your courtyard until late in the evening waiting for you to pay."

* * *

As reports of borrower harassment have become commonplace, reform efforts have winnowed. When public funders began to distance themselves from small loans in the 2010s, they distanced themselves from all things microfinance, including attempts at change.

In 2015, Chuck Waterfield closed a website he had created to track real microfinance prices, even after it had received support from Muhammad Yunus. Over the seven-year period the website existed, Waterfield and his team reviewed eighteen hundred loan products sold by 530 MFIs to fifty-two million clients, assessing things like real interest rates and hidden fees. But getting information was like pulling teeth. Waterfield estimates he had to send between thirty-one and sixty-four emails per microlender, plus another ten to twenty phone calls. (His team emailed one, Centenary Bank in Uganda, 203 times. It took nearly a year to receive any data.)

Even with all the effort, it wasn't clear what effect the website was having. Even when Waterfield pointed out that lenders were charging rates as high as 400 percent annual interest, they didn't necessarily lower their prices. He observed, "Some [lenders] have changed their prices to be more transparent (and often lower) but most have not. There were numerous [microlenders] that left their prices unchanged and a significant number who actually increased their prices, even when their prices were already on the high end of the market." Financiers weren't changing either. To Waterfield's dismay, a few years after his team demonstrated that LAPO was effectively charging as much as 144 percent APR for its long-term borrowers, the lender received a loan from the Dutch Development Bank.

There was also the question of funding the website. Waterfield told me that after a few years he simply couldn't get any more money to keep it running. Public donors didn't seem particularly interested—learning more about the problems of the industry drove them away from microfinance and toward programs that didn't have such a soured reputation—and private funders didn't have an incentive to know just how bad things could get. Lack of funding also slowed down regulations within countries, given that many governments rely on external funders to pay for review committees, policy drafting, and staff positions, or create policies in response to the promise of outside money and donor demands.

After nearly a decade of reviewing interest rates and writing long, pointed blog posts, Waterfield was burned out, no longer remotely optimistic about changes in the industry. In 2015, he wrote one last post: "Our parting advice for the industry boils down to three words: It's your turn."

In 2020, the Smart Campaign, the voluntary set of principles set up in the wake of the Compartamos and Andhra Pradesh scandals, closed. Only 135 financial microfinance institutions, out of nearly 2,000 worldwide, had been certified. Elisabeth Rhyne says the campaign was also hamstrung by funding, as public donors shied away from microfinance entirely. The bigger problem, though, was that "the investors didn't want to sign on." They claimed they had their own standards, which they would oversee. The Smart Campaign's principles have since been replaced by a "pathway" that third-party ratings agencies can use, which "describes the steps that a financial service provider can take . . . to avoid harming clients and communicate this progress to investors." (There are three steps: Commit, Improve, Report.) Even those who criticized the Smart Campaign for being toothless see this new pathway as even more inept. As of November 2023, only 309 financial service providers had signed on.

The same year the Smart Campaign closed, a separate database that included detailed information on numbers of borrowers and company profits also shut down.* Without these tools, Sugandh Saxena, who works in microfinance in India, says, "We really don't know the impact" of microfinance today "because nobody measures it anymore." "There is no independent pricing information now," adds Waterfield. "It's gone back to a complete vacuum."

* * *

It's hard to know what would have happened had more lenders been Smart certified or if stronger legislation had been put in place. Maybe microfinance would have changed. Maybe if funders like Catholic Relief Services had tried to convince other lenders of the problems with the profit-focused model, there could have been something of a reckoning, resulting in a truly reformed lending landscape.

To be clear, there have been smaller changes. Dozens of people are still trying to reform the microfinance industry, writing reports and trying to ensure lenders follow "best practices." Some lenders now offer low-interest loans for specific products, like solar lights or school fees or farming implements. Some NGOs remain focused on lending to the poorest segment of a country, offering training and other support to help them succeed. And watchdog and advocacy groups like AdvocAid have made it

---

* The MIX. Although it been created to help lenders attract more funding, it had been regularly relied upon by journalists, academics, and researchers, its data fueling many of the most critical reports on the commercialized sector.

so that publicly taking debtors to prison is a much more unseemly thing for a microfinance lender to do, although the mere threat of police stations and jail cells remains real enough for the borrowers I met, never mind that microfinance lenders, and the police and judges responsible for laying the charges and handing down sentences, have all promised change.

But there have not been broader reforms across the sector to upend the basic model on which microfinance is now built: high-priced, short-term loans with foreign financing. Such changes seem unlikely in the era of perceived donor scarcity and given that private money has been invested for decades. "From [an investor's] perspective, it's a perfect system," the Cambodian microfinance researcher told me. "You invest money, you get a return, and you call it development." There's no incentive for change, and besides, any reform that might come would be too late. "The debt levels are far far far beyond what you can fix at this point. Even the best regulations in the world" are simply inadequate. "We need to be talking debt relief."

Hugh Sinclair, who worked in microfinance before writing a controversial exposé on the industry—and then worked in microfinance again—considers the core principles of microfinance to be so inherently contradictory that even the basic model is beyond reform. "I've been trying to think about how to make microfinance work, and you just can't," he told me. "You cannot cover costs, attract private investors, and bring a service to the poor. You're trying to make someone richer by giving them an overpriced loan. Even if you offered them at 5 percent a year, it would still not work. There are only three businesses you can do: sell second-hand clothes, sell sandwiches, and wash cars."

Upending these lending systems could also radically disrupt economies and communities that have become reliant on them, as happened in the wake of the Andhra Pradesh crisis, when a drastic drop in microfinance reportedly aligned with a drop in people's food consumption. The Cambodian microfinance researcher told me, "We're talking about the stability of the economy. This is the way our citizens go to school, use health care, build homes. Since it seems we don't want to provide state services, we can't undermine any threat to that continuation of the process."

So rather than shaking the core of microfinance, the industry underwent a face-lift.

New Money

Freetown, Sierra Leone

Beginning of 2022

Aminata loved the way her body was changing. When she took her afternoon naps in the parlor, she could now comfortably rest her head on the soft underside of her bicep. Sitting on the floor, her calves no longer shone, skin flattened across the bone. Now, they blossomed around her.

People began to compliment her. "You look fresh!" Kadija said, looking her up and down on an afternoon visit. "You've gotten big!" said Grandpa. Doris, who always thought her mother beautiful, found her even more so now.

The way Aminata saw it, there were two main changes that had facilitated the weight gain: the months that had passed since her first loan, and the profits that were finally coming in from her business. Time was what she had needed, to get away from the persistence of the debt, and to build a strong enough foundation. "I'm not as stressed now, not like before," she said from her spot on the parlor floor. "My mind is at ease. I can sleep at night."

Nothing much had shifted in her day-to-day. She still made her ginger beer and yogurt every few weeks, whenever she had enough cash. She still put the wares into her fridge, hoping it would turn on. When it did, she put a bundle of cold yogurt and drinks onto her cousin Mommy's head to sell around town. Without the weekly microcredit payments, everything they made went to Aminata's cashbox. She estimated she kept around $3 a day.

With the extra money, Aminata had started cooking more regularly, every day instead of every other. She occasionally made Doris's favorite—macaroni with chunks of luncheon meat, an expensive treat given that all the ingredients were imported. She tried to keep a bit of extra prepared food around the house just in case anyone was hungry. Grandpa often still was. Every few months, he donned a dark burgundy two-piece suit, complete with wing-tip shoes. He needed to look nice when he "begged my friends for money." If he came home empty-handed after visiting SLPP politicians, he could at least count on Aminata for something to eat.

But although Aminata was now stable, her world, confined to the house, still felt too small. She continued to harbor dreams of starting a business in town but refused to take out microfinance again. "I thought about the $30 that you have to pay, before you can even get $125 or $250. You're going to struggle, to get that money back. How are you going to make that $30 they took from you? How long will that work?" So she stuck to the decision she made after her first microfinance loan: never again.

Never again for herself, at least. By now, she had agreed to take out a third loan for Kadija's group, her share this time going to Kadija's sister. This borrowing-for-others still caused Aminata some stress. "I always monitor how the weekly payments go around. I know the police will say it's criminal if anything happens." But she had relaxed into the situation. At least she knew it had worked before. "For now, they're paying, they're cooperating."

For Aminata's own aspirations, she looked to her husband, Idrissa. She knew she would never be granted a really substantial loan, one for several hundred dollars, from a microfinance company to rent her "touristic shop"—she had no collateral, nothing to make the loan officers trust that she could pay it back. But maybe Idrissa's employer would give her one. They knew him, and the fact that it was no interest would make paying it off all the easier. Idrissa nixed that outright. There was no loan big enough to cover that cost, not one that he would be eligible for, anyway. Repayments would eat up his entire paycheck.

He agreed to take out something smaller for her, $500, far more than she could get through microcredit but far less than what she wanted for the shop. She wasn't about to argue. With the cash, she set up a table at the big market in the center of town, PZ, around the corner from where her cousin Samuel sold his onions and potatoes. To secure the place, Samuel had helped her negotiate a generous but not unwieldy tip to the market chairlady. From the loan, she put aside a few weeks of fees owed to the City Council, who collected $1 daily.

Aminata chose the product she thought would be easiest to get and easiest to sell: alcohol. On her table, Aminata laid out packets of the cheap gin that made Kadija's customers punch-drunk. She mostly sold in bulk, on "trust," to those who, like Kadija, operated makeshift bars from their houses. The new business was mostly going on well, except for the guilt it produced in her. Aminata was slightly worried about rumors that the gin was so strong it could make people blind. But she thought more about how alcohol can corrode a person's days, about what a person can get up to when they feel worthless. She had seen the men asleep on Kadija's porch at ten a.m., then yelling at their wives and neighbors a few hours later, behavior she didn't want on her conscience. Her worries were way-laid by the fact that, on a good day, about $250 could pass through her hands, about $20 she could keep after she paid off her suppliers and the City Council. Morality aside, she found it was easy to pay back the $100 she owed to Idrissa's employer each month.

"I'm starting to sell," she said. "Little by little."

* * *

Now grown in body and spirit, Aminata took the trip she had been avoiding for those three years, seven months: back to Pendembu. She finally had the cash to go home, with enough left over to bring some essentials from the city. There would no longer be the threat of talk that she had gotten thin and sick in Freetown, that she must not be doing as well as her family said she was. Now, over four years after she had initially left the village, she was finally ready.

She had waited long enough. Her mother had grown weaker in the past months, still with an unexplained illness that whittled her body down. She was barely able to work and had defaulted on her most recent micro-finance loan. Aminata's sister, who lived in Adonkia, a village twenty minutes outside Freetown, had recently taken out her own microfinance loan, ostensibly to grow her business selling rocks from a quarry off the highway. Instead, she sent the cash to Pendembu, to help her mother pay down the debt.

Aminata arrived back home to find her mother in the local missionary hospital, the best in the region. She had been given no clear diagnosis that she could understand but was told she'd have to come back regularly for treatment. Work was out of the question. Her father would keep on with his traditional medicine trade, but the police now knew where he sold and had started asking him for a little something to let their eye slip past him. On occasion, they still confiscated his herbs and pills. Aminata swore that the officers then sold the things themselves.

Aminata promised she would send what she could once she was back in Freetown, to which her mother nodded wordlessly. Her family needed something substantial, more than just the remittances she and Idrissa promised to give and then struggled to deliver. Not just tens or even hundreds of dollars, but thousands.

* * *

Idrissa agreed with Aminata that they needed more money. He was no longer simply annoyed that his salary had stayed the same all these years, regardless of how much he worked or how expensive things were. He was insulted. He had begun repeating the same phrase. "Drivers are the backbone of the organization. Without us, how are they going to get anywhere? We're the hardest working. And we don't get anything. No respect!"

Idrissa wanted to try something new, something that gave meaning to his days. For months, he and a neighbor, a powerful man in the local branch of the APC political party whom everyone knew as "Chairman," had discussed setting up a tea shop around the corner from the man's used auto parts shop. They were certain it would be a profitable business. There would be little overhead—through his connections, Chairman could secure land and get a small shack built, basically for nothing—and a lot of cash moving through, given that the city's motorbike riders and poda poda drivers and day laborers regularly started their day with a strong cup of ataya, a type of Chinese gunpowder tea popular across West Africa.

After work, they would have another cup, or two or three, while discussing football, politics, work, the situation back home. Idrissa figured they could use the profits from the tea stall for the things the neighborhood lacked and that Abdul, the landlord, never seemed to deliver: another water pump, a disaster fund, perhaps a paved road. For Idrissa, this was about proving that a community could make it on its own, a source of pride and responsibility. The project would also prove essential to Chairman's political organizing, another place to host visitors and hold meetings, an example of his ability to get things done.

A small but sturdy shack now stood near Chairman's auto shop, with a roof and four walls. The only thing to finish was the floor, still made of dirt. Neighborhood men had already begun stopping by for a cup of tea and conversation in the mornings.

Recently, Idrissa had a new idea about how to use the profits, one he gleaned by watching Aminata and her problems with the loans. He and Chairman could set aside a pot of money for women to borrow from, interest free. All an applicant would need is a guarantor; no collateral, no group. A committee, overseen by Chairman and Idrissa, would determine who got how much, for what, and what the terms would be.

The plan came with the risk of favoritism. Idrissa had made his political affiliations well known; Grandpa's wife, for example, wouldn't expect to be at the top of the list of recipients, given the family's alternate political choices. And it didn't seem inconceivable that Chairman might use the loans to further exert influence, a kind of thinly veiled cash-for-votes. There were many stories of this happening before, particularly in the lead-up to election time. In fact, Julius Maada Bio's government had recently launched the Munafa Fund, which offered shockingly low-interest loans—below bank rates—to small businesspeople across the country. Almost immediately, there were rumors of premade lists in SLPP strongholds, that those on the list were funded overnight. When I asked one Freetown trader whether she had considered applying for a loan through the fund, she told me, "That money is not for everyone. It's political money. You have to know someone to get it."

Idrissa didn't worry about the politics of his new idea. He wanted to focus on the bigger picture. "We want this instead of microfinance," he explained. Rather than being beholden to someone from outside, this could be a way for women to invest money from their own community.

Still, he remained adamant that his wife shouldn't take another loan on her own, no matter the source. Never mind that Idrissa was hundreds of dollars in debt to the organization he worked for. The difference, he insisted, was that repayments were automatically taken from his paycheck. He didn't have to put anything aside in a cashbox, then check to see if he had enough, so there was little risk of default. Another distinction, unuttered, is that these loans were under his purview. Idrissa could choose to give money to his wife. Or he could choose not to.

* * *

Aminata didn't pay much mind to Idrissa and his tea stall. After her trip to Pendembu, she decided she needed someone who would think big, strategically. No more of this few hundred dollars here or there.

As soon as Aminata returned to Two Taps, she walked straight over to Mohamed's. The man lived a few houses over and had been Idrissa's best friend ever since they had both moved to the neighborhood decades ago. The two were regarded as the smartest men in Two Taps. They both spoke and read Arabic and English, teaching the languages to whoever wanted to learn. They regularly discussed global events: whether there was any rationality in America's January 6 insurrection, the coup in Guinea, the crisis in Afghanistan.

But although Idrissa was smart, and had graduated from high school, Mohamed was even sharper. Even though he didn't have his high school graduation certificate, Mohamed had learned to use a computer. He could surf the Web and type long papers that included elaborate charts and graphics. He spent his days at an Internet café in the center of Freetown, hammering out ideas for projects he wanted to start. He pulled from what he saw around him: programs from big international NGOs, with their promises of upliftment and empowerment and sustainable solutions, not to mention millions of dollars that seemed just waiting to be used. He had seen firsthand what such organizations could do. Mohamed had been born with a club foot so pronounced that moving had been a slow, painful, and noticeable affair for most of his life. As a young man, he had become active with the Sierra Leone Union on Disability Issues, a local NGO that sometimes worked with bigger foreign ones. He successfully advocated to get surgery at a special hospital run by a private organization four hours outside Freetown. The operation had straightened the foot somewhat. Not perfect, but workable. Sometimes, he experienced shooting pains in his hip so severe that he was laid up in bed for days. Aminata would bring him food and medicine then, encouraging him to wait it out. "You just have to bear it," she would say.

Working long hours at the Internet café, Mohamed had come up with dozens of ideas he thought an NGO might want to fund: a dog-training vocational program; a soap-making program; pig-rearing; an antitribalism organization that would fight sectarian violence in Sierra Leone, complete with a jingle and listening circles just like those that sprang up during Ebola. To make any of these a success, all he needed was a bit of cash, which seemed achievable. He had seen the NGOs' SUVs, their multistoried offices, the mansions their foreign staff lived in. He estimated he needed $10,000 at least, maybe up to $40,000, to get one of his ideas off the ground.

Aminata knocked on his door. She told him she wanted him to focus on an idea he had been nurturing for years: to train disabled people to be farmers in the north, near where Aminata's family was. She knew he had been told by a few NGO staff and people in government offices that in theory it was a good idea. It ticked off all the right boxes. It helped the marginalized, was "green," worked toward the Sustainable Development Goals. But no promises. They would maybe get back to him later, but this wasn't their priority for now.

Except for that one man, at one government agency, who said he could put the proposal forward if Mohamed could hand over $1,000, something of a thank-you and tip and starting fee. Doing so, the man promised, would make the project eligible for a $30,000 grant.

Mohamed huffed—where was he going to get $1,000? But Aminata thought the man's request reasonable. It fit with the lessons she had learned from microfinance: First, that social connections are essential, a lesson gleaned from Kadija working her network. Second, that bribes work—that you had to have money to get money. Several microlending cycles in, she and the other women in the Two Taps group still understood that the only reason they had received any money at all was because they were willing to give something in advance. That it was called a "start-up fee" was only semantics. The message was clear: if you didn't pay, you were never going to get anywhere.

Aminata proposed a plan. She and Mohamed could team up, him finessing the proposal to incorporate the broader community—including her family—and she working to tap into her substantial family network in Freetown, raising money needed to slick the necessary palms. They would call the project "Village Sufferers," "because we're trying to reduce the suffering in the village," she explained. "We want to change their life." It could be Mohamed's big break and what Aminata needed to start something real for her family.

Mohamed appreciated her enthusiasm. But he didn't particularly understand why she needed to go this route. Unlike him, she had easy access to money. He had listened to her complain about microfinance, sympathized with her fear of the police and the stress that regular repayments caused. But he had also felt a twinge of jealousy. He had told her and Idrissa, "Do you know how hard it is for a disabled person to get a loan? They look at us, and they think, 'You can't work hard.' But disabled people can work! They can do farming. They can do trading. They can ride kekes. If I had the chance, I'd take out microfinance. I'd be afraid," he said, then shrugged. "But I need money."

CHAPTER 14

It's Not Microfinance.
It's Financial Inclusion

IN 2011, AMERICAN ANTHROPOLOGIST ERIN BECK OBSERVED A CHANGE made by Namaste, an American-backed microlender she had been following for years. Perhaps responding to the crises in India and Mexico and the waning reputation of microfinance internationally, Namaste had revised its mission statement. Beck wrote in her 2017 book on microfinance in Guatemala that the statement "contains no mention of loans at all," even though loans to women were still at the heart of its work. Even its founder, who had explicitly set up a microcredit NGO, no longer considered Namaste to be primarily a lender. Instead, the organization now claimed to "directly contribute to women's economic empowerment by providing business development programs and analytics that increase the business profits of low-income entrepreneurs."

This new, hazy language, of business assistance not poverty alleviation, analytics not loans, had been slowly percolating in the sector for a while. A few years after the initial Microcredit Summit Campaign, back in 1997, the U.S. Congress declared it was working not just to fund small loans but to build "a more inclusive financial sector" worldwide. In 2004, as the commercialized model was taking off, USAID claimed its work had now shifted away from microfinance to "three key objectives: mobilizing private capital, promoting digital financial services, and championing inclusive financial services." In 2006, Robert Annibale, who headed up Citi Microfinance, talked "not about reducing poverty but about 'financial inclusion,'" according to Connie Bruck of the *New Yorker*. "Hopefully,"

Annibale said, "one day, 'microfinance' will kind of go away, and we'll talk about who's providing financial services to whom."

The definition had already undergone an expansion, first from micro-credit, with a focus on loans, to microfinance, with a focus on savings and insurance products, and now to the far broader "financial inclusion," which encompassed not just loans but savings, not just savings but insurance, not just insurance but mobile payments and digital loans—essentially, any financial service that targets a poorer person, anywhere from Kenya to California. (As it sounds, mobile payments are sent through mobile phones, and digital lenders offer credit digitally, mostly through mobile phones but also online.) Helpfully, discarding the term "microfinance" also allowed for the negative associations to go away with it. And expanding away from poverty lending and toward the "missing middle" who have "limited access to capital," as Citi described it—that is, focusing on relatively wealthy businesses and people, a target group USAID had advocated for decades before—offered more investment opportunities, more ways to help. Lindsay Wallace, a development economist who has worked with the Mastercard Foundation and the UK's international development agency, felt that the broadening was largely positive, "about recognizing that microfinance was only suitable to some clients." The poor maybe weren't the best to lend to, and it seemed that other people needed financial services, too. Just as Esther Duflo and Abhijit Banerjee and others suggested that microfinance could support "consumption smoothing," Wallace hoped that a broader array of financial services would help poor people to manage "inflows and outflows" by mixing and matching a variety of financial tools to meet their needs—just the way an American might rely on a credit card, a mortgage, cash, and a bank account on any given day. Accion also supported the change. The organization considered the shift from microfinance to the broader notion of financial inclusion a "moral imperative."

With the shift came even more new language. "Very small loans" have been largely replaced by "financial services." "Women" had long ago been replaced by "entrepreneurs," who were now replaced by "the unbanked"—literally, anyone without an official, formal financial account, which as of 2022, amounted to around 1.5 billion people, according to the World Bank.

I first came across the word "unbanked" in a USAID document from the 1970s. It came up again thirty years later, in 2005, when staffers trying to convince Citigroup to launch its microfinance business division argued that the "unbanked" offered a significant untapped customer base. In the words of one venture capitalist, the unbanked represent a "tremendous market opportunity." (Citi Microfinance was later rebranded Citi Inclusive Finance, then again Citi Social Finance.) With each new customer, banks can not only claim to be meeting a fundamental need but expand their reach. "There's all this talk about reaching 'underserved populations,'" says Phil Mader, who researches debt at the Institute of Development Studies. "But there are massive genuine material interests for the financial industry to open up a new client base for themselves."

While "financial inclusion" for the "unbanked" sounds expansive and hopeful, it boils down to getting poor people some sort of basic financial service—loans, bank accounts, savings accounts, a phone that can transfer money. Although there are suggestions that financial inclusion "may alleviate"—not end—"poverty and inequality," the World Bank offers a strikingly mundane outline of the new goals: that "individuals and businesses have access to useful and affordable financial products and services that meet their needs . . . delivered in a responsible and sustainable way." That's a much more toned down aspiration than ending poverty or empowering women. And that measured tone is deliberate. After seeing the reputation of microfinance rise and fall so spectacularly, "as an industry, it was unsaid, but *basically* said, 'let's not promise something again,'" Sugandh Saxena, who works with India's Microfinance Institutions Network, told me. "What we are doing is efficient financial services for the poor. This is what we aim for, this is our objective. The narrative changed completely. There is far less of a focus on impact."

But the key architecture underpinning microfinance remains. Again, numbers drive the push to "bank the unbanked." As was true with the framing around microcredit, an absence of something—first, loans, now, financial services—suggests that it must, necessarily, be desired and needed.

Accion, forever a chameleon, changed with the times. In a 2015 paper, Paul Breloff, an Accion staffer, wrote, "Accion has long stood for the idea that it's possible to have a greater social and economic impact by working with markets rather than against them." He pointed out that Accion was a key driver of the "commercialized approach" in microfinance, "once seen as controversial by some . . . now prevalent in social enterprise, impact investing, philanthropy, and even government aid programs."

Now, to "spur innovation in financial inclusion," Accion invested in early "financial inclusion start-ups," just as they had invested in commercial microfinance before. In 2012, Accion Venture Lab was launched, a "venture capital" arm of the nonprofit that would "promot[e] better financial services to more people at the base of the pyramid." Accion's vision was to "build a financially inclusive world, where everyone has access to high-quality, affordable financial services."

Breloff headed the $10 million Venture Lab. He had previously worked at the Indian lender SKS, which had been heavily criticized for its practices in Andhra Pradesh. His job there was "to turn SKS into a distribution channel to the BOP"—that's short for "base of the pyramid"—"for all sorts of products, a one-stop shop for rural India. In addition to financial products like credit and insurance, we provided solar lights, water purifiers, cell phones, lower-priced fast-moving consumer goods, and even primary school education," a mash-up of privatized basic services. (He does not mention SKS's alleged role in the AP suicide crisis, calling the company a "world-class" microlender.)

Accion Venture Lab's first investment was in a company that allowed people to buy "e-content"—games and apps—with prepaid phone credit, which Accion curiously argued "would be enormously valuable to the unbanked." It later invested in Varthana, which gives loans to "affordable private schools" in India, and DemystData, which helped financial institutions tap into a person's data to find new "unbanked" customers. Accion Venture Lab also invested in Konfio,* a Mexican lender that, as of 2020, offered average interest rates of around 30 percent, mostly to much higher

---

* Accion Venture Lab is just one of several investors pumping money into the remodeled "financial inclusion space." Michael Chu, who, in the wake of the Compartamos sale, encouraged social investors to see their financial return as "the cake itself," later cofounded IGNIA, a venture capital firm in Mexico focused on the "emerging middle class and low-income populations." "Michael Chu: Senior Lecturer of Business Administration," Harvard Business School Faculty & Research, https://www.hbs.edu/faculty/Pages/profile.aspx?facId=261321. As it happens, IGNIA also invested in Konfio. "Companies," IGNIA, https://igniaunlocked.mx/portfolio-4-col/.

income borrowers: the average loan size was $25,000, for businesses that were already up and running and needed a boost.

Although Konfio's customer base was quite different from Muhammad Yunus's initial forty-two women, the language Accion used to justify the investment is almost verbatim to that used to justify microfinance decades before. Accion claimed that the borrowers need new lending options, since their only other alternative is moneylenders, who charge over 100 percent. This rationale didn't make a lot of sense given that even larger microfinance loans had, by now, been common in Mexico for decades, something Accion knew well given its history investing in Compartamos years before. Besides, Konfio borrowers quoted in a story in the *Financial Times* said their alternative was not moneylenders but banks.

But this sort of justification is not an anomaly. In many press releases, industry reports, and news articles about financial inclusion and banking the unbanked, Yunus's original story, or a version of it, is centrally included in the opening paragraphs. Although the goal has become more concentrated and feasible, the narrative remains intensely hopeful. Accion claims that accessing financial services can "make or break whether someone will be able to take advantage of an opportunity . . . or absorb a financial shock . . . Evidence also shows that financial inclusion is positively correlated with growth and employment at the macro level." Queen Máxima of the Netherlands, a longtime supporter of microfinance, is now the UN Secretary-General's Special Advocate for Inclusive Finance for Development. She supports financial inclusion not only because it's "pro-growth," since countries "will have a higher GDP once you have a fully financially included population," but also "pro-poor, which means that it reduces inequality, and that's something that is always really interesting."

There's a remarkable cyclicality that runs through the history of microfinance. First, a repackaging of old concepts and ideas—osusus, credit unions—as the world's new anti-poverty tool, and now a similar repackaging of those same basic tools through financial inclusion, a term that is at once more optimistic and less ambitious while ultimately retaining the core tenets of microfinance: that what the poor need are financial tools above all else, and that they must pay for those tools. The newest iteration at once hearkens back to early efforts by USAID to focus on wealthier borrowers rather than Yunus's "anti-poverty" lending approach, while stripping that approach of its substance. While USAID initially advocated for a state-led safety net for the poor and generous package of supportive services for small businesspeople, financial inclusion pitches access to financial services as the primary end goal through which all other aims can be achieved. Just as Yunus argued that once a poor woman has a loan she can take care of herself and her family, the rationale now goes that once a person has a mobile bank account, they can access whatever the market has to offer: health care, education, housing. In both framings, life is simply better once finance is involved. Phil Mader, the debt researcher, considers the increasing reliance on financial tools in international development the "financialization of poverty."

* * *

At the same time that "financial inclusion" efforts use familiar arguments, familiar programs, and rely on familiar idealism, microlenders themselves are embracing this new, broader language. Like Namaste in Guatemala, many have rebranded themselves as being in the business of broadly supporting the "unbanked," even though lending remains at their core.* "It's not like there was a movement away" from the microfinance model, explains Elisabeth Rhyne, "so much as there was a shift of language." Mader told me, "If you talk about microfinance, then everyone goes, 'oh yeah, yes we made a mistake with microfinance and now we're doing something else, we're doing financial inclusion.' It's just the newest iteration." Besides, he points out, "Who would be for financial *exclusion*?"

Borrowers easily see past this reframing. Erin Beck, the anthropologist who noticed Namaste's language change in Guatemala, observed that "while Namaste's donors, policymakers, and leaders have accepted this rebranding, the women whom the NGO targets have not." She wrote,

---

* Yunus seems to have predicted this. In a 1997 interview with Alex Counts, Yunus said, "Tomorrow Grameen Bank may not exist, but credit for the poor will remain. It will flourish. It is an irreversible process. People now know that the poor are credit worthy. Efficient organizations that are aggressive will continue to arise in Bangladesh as well as in other countries." *Grameen Dialogue*, no. 31, July 1997.

"They continue to view Namaste as roughly equivalent to other [micro-lenders] operating in the area."

* * *

Digital lenders like Mexico's Konfio are at the forefront of the newer, broader financial inclusion era, with digital lending promising to reach millions of people, offering financial support in just a few seconds. There are several stories about how digital lending got its start, but the most widely known takes place in Kenya in 2007. That year, the British development agency and Safaricom, the country's largest telecommunication company, came up with a faster way for microfinance lenders to collect payments, not through loan officers but by using mobile phones. Soon, everyday Kenyans started using the technology not only to pay back their creditors, as had been expected, but to send money from one person to another: say, $50 from a son working in Nairobi to his mom back home. Safaricom realized it could charge a small fee for the service, and the idea of "mobile money" stuck, and since then, Kenya has become the ground zero for these other digital finance programs. By 2010, more people had subscribed to the service than had a bank account.

Those who had funded early mobile money efforts, as well as supporters of microfinance, such as the Consultative Group to Assist the Poor and the Gates Foundation, figured it would be an easy transition from digital money to digital loans. They reasoned that transactions done by cell phone could be done more cheaply and efficiently than in brick-and-mortar microfinance offices. With fewer personnel to hire, and fewer buildings to rent, costs could come down. Rather than having loan officers check business plans, algorithms could determine a person's creditworthiness and consider how much interest to charge. Today, mobile lenders rely on data like how quickly phone calls are returned, how often someone calls their mother, and how much prepaid credit they have on their phone. Konfio uses "more than 5,000 biographical, social and financial data points," pulling from a borrower's cell phone data and social media to determine a person's creditworthiness, a model that facilitates loans disbursal within twenty-four hours. In some cases, a potential borrower doesn't need to show proof of income, or a job, or even attempts at starting a small business to get a digital loan. Milford Bateman, a British academic who's written extensively about microfinance and is a vocal critic, says the low threshold "means that everybody and their dog can now have microcredit."

Since the Kenyan mobile money system was created in 2007, both mobile money and digital lending have expanded exponentially, not just in Kenya but also in poor and middle-income countries where microfinance is also popular, including the Philippines, Bangladesh, India, and Mexico. But Kenya remains the heartland of digital finance. According to one 2019 report, 86 percent of all Kenyan consumer loans between 2016 and 2018 were issued digitally, with 77 percent of all Kenyan borrowers having taken *only* digital loans. One mobile loan company, GetBucks Kenya, saw a growth of 447 percent in just two years, from 2017 to 2019. Loans can range from a few bucks to thousands of dollars, depending on the lender and the borrower. Digital lenders generally target a different type of person than the microfinance borrowers Muhammad Yunus spoke about: not impoverished, entrepreneurial women but someone who already has some disposable income and something to quickly spend it on and, of course, a mobile phone. In many cases, lenders target young men. In Kenya, journalists report that digital loans have become common for sports betting. Given the loans' easy access and the addictive nature of betting, it's a combination that can spin debtors into a hole very quickly.

They often find they have a lot to pay back. Despite the promise that digital lending would be cheaper, what with the limited staff and office costs, Chuck Waterfield estimates that effective annual interest rates can reach a whopping 250 percent—more than double what Compartamos charged, to much criticism, in the 2000s. The digital lender Branch, which was started in 2015 by Matt Flannery, one of the founders of the San Francisco–based microlending site Kiva.org, charges anywhere from 1.7 to 17.6 percent monthly interest. Although some loans only last two months, others last a year, with interest rates of 22 to 229 percent annually. (Branch also operates in Tanzania, India, and Nigeria.)

The high rates, despite the relatively low cost to do business, may be due to the fact that digital lenders have been spectacularly successful fundraisers, often backed by investors who expect a profit. Branch has raised several hundred million dollars from investors including Andreessen Horowitz, a venture capital firm based in Silicon Valley; Foundation Capital, another venture capital firm; TLG Capital, which believes "that commercial and social returns can, and should, go hand in hand"; and the World Bank's International Finance Corporation, among others. In 2019, Branch partnered with Visa to "offer preferential loan terms to merchants in . . . Africa . . . who accept Visa on mobile phones." In announcing the partnership, a vice president at Visa said, "Our partnership with Branch provides Visa a key distribution mechanism to reach people that were previously out of reach and help shape the future of microfinance," adding, "we believe financial empowerment is an essential passport out of poverty." In 2023, Branch also bought a microfinance bank in Kenya.

The original Kenyan digital payments service, M-PESA, is reported to be the most profitable service offered by Safaricom, itself one of the most valuable companies in East Africa. Safaricom also offers digital loans that cost up to 90 percent annual interest (the official monthly rate is 7.5 percent, but that rate doubles if it's not paid off in one month). It also has an ownership stake in a separate digital loan company, which offers annual interest rates of around 150 percent. M-PESA recently partnered with Visa to offer a "virtual" credit card; MasterCard is also expanding into digital payments in the Middle East and Africa. Dozens of other banks and private firms have also invested in other microfinance and digital lenders.

Borrowers who do fall behind on repayments—roughly 40 percent, by one estimation*—have been subject to a slick new type of harassment that hinges on a familiar tactic: shame. Debtors in arrears reported having text messages sent to their contacts, tattling that their friend or family member is behind on payments. (It's important to note that a similar approach has been reportedly used by the Kenyan government as recently as 2019, when they threatened to publicly post photos of students who were behind on loan payments to the Kenyan Higher Education Loans Board.) While companies like Branch say they condemn harassment of debtors, online

---

* A 2019 report from the Center for Financial Inclusion estimated that between 2016 and 2018, 2.2 million Kenyans couldn't pay back a digital loan. The majority had taken out multiple loans. "Making Digital Credit Truly Responsible," Center for Financial Inclusion, September 25, 2019, https://www.centerforfinancialinclusion.org/making-digital-credit-truly-responsible.

reviews of Skywave Management, a debt collection agency that has reportedly been contracted by the company, include complaints of repeated calls, text messages, and threats even after debts are paid off. Kenya's Credit Reference Bureau, originally pitched as a solution for debtors because it would help to prevent overborrowing, has become a problem for overindebted borrowers of all stripes—those who take out classic microfinance loans, digital loans, even loans from the government. Those in arrears can end up on a "debtors list," sometimes for reasons they don't understand and without a clear pathway to have their name removed, even long after debts are paid. Being on the list can limit other borrowing opportunities and impact job prospects, as some employers require clearance from the Credit Reference Bureau before hiring.

* * *

Sugandh Saxena, of India's Microfinance Institutions Network, worries that now-familiar public shaming can become even more pronounced when a loan is made without an actual person involved. In traditional microfinance, a loan officer would go to a borrower's house, "they would see that the borrower has just one room and few clothes, maybe a small TV, and that's it, you know? So as a loan officer, at some point, in your mind, you think that you don't want to hurt that person. But with digital, there's almost no connection with the customer." That change could be a good thing: there's no loan officer to knock on your door, sit in your living room all night, or suggest you throw yourself in a well with your children. But it also means there's no one to know the details of a borrower's situation: why they might be struggling, the specifics of their case, no one to decide they're not going to report them to the Credit Reference Bureau. "Digital lenders can charge something like 600 percent and they don't mind," Saxena told me. "They don't realize that for such a small amount you are making somebody a defaulter forever."

In 2019, one of Kenya's largest newspapers reported that a twenty-five-year-old man hanged himself after being reported to the bureau for defaulting on a mobile loan of about $30. There were also reports of suicides linked to digital loans in India at the height of the coronavirus pandemic. Jayshree Venkatesan, who worked in microfinance for years, reflected, "It's such an

echo of the Andhra Pradesh crisis." Instead of yelling outside a borrower's house or posting a sign in their front yard, "they're actually calling and
messaging people in your phone book, and saying, 'You know, X, Y, Z has
borrowed and is not repaying.' It's that shame that's leading to suicides."

Chuck Waterfield, the microfinance critic who set up the pricing website that closed in 2015, also sees many similarities between digital lending
in places like Kenya and the oversaturated microfinance sectors in India,
Bolivia, Mexico, Bosnia, and elsewhere: a lot of borrowing, pushed by lenders with a lot of money and an appetite for growth, and harsh consequences
when repayments aren't forthcoming. He's determined that the problems
of microfinance have not been solved but diluted, spread across a wider
variety of products. He predicts, "It's all going to fall apart. It's all going be a
total mess. Governments should be stepping in to stop it before it happens."

For the most part, they're not. Because digital lenders are not considered banks *or* microfinance lenders, they fall outside the remit of both the
central banks and whatever microfinance regulations may exist, even voluntary ones. They are often not subject to interest rate caps. Because the
digital lending field is moving so quickly and is concentrated in countries
that often do not have robust technology regulation, there is little oversight
over how the data lenders have access to it or how it is used or stored—those
decisions are left to the discretion of the companies and their funders. Phil
Mader worries: "There's a whole new area of consumer protection issues
that we don't even have a handle on, even in this country"—he's from the
UK—"much less in these less developed countries. The poorly regulated
emerging financial markets of Africa have become an experimentation
field to try out products that they would never be allowed to try out elsewhere. The amount of experimentation you can do in Africa is stunning
compared to what you can do in Europe. And the insights that mobile
phone providers have into people's everyday financial lives in Kenya are
incredible." (In 2019, the Kenyan government, recognizing the country
has become something of a ground zero for financial inclusion programs
including digital lending, passed a data protection bill that required companies to protect a borrower's data and not use punitive repayment methods, although thousands of cases of abuse have still been reported.) At
the same time, with watchdog efforts like Chuck Waterfield's website and

the Smart Campaign now closed, it's very difficult to get information on digital lenders themselves. "There's no transparency in profitability, portfolio quality, anything," says Saxena, of India's Microfinance Institutions Network. "There's no information about anything."

In 2022, a blog post from Accion's Center for Financial Inclusion, which continued even after the Smart Campaign was shut down, tepidly warned that while "innovative entrants" might offer "improved services and product designs," that might come at the expense of "treating clients with respect and understanding." Sharon D'Onofrio, formerly of Catholic Relief Services, put it more bluntly. She worries that borrowers may now have some anonymity, but in return they might be stripped of their humanity.

Some of those who were supportive of microfinance, even of the broader goals of financial inclusion, are deeply skeptical of digital lending. Elisabeth Rhyne, who retired in 2019 after leading Accion's Center for Financial Inclusion for years, thinks "the FinTech"—that's financial technology—"borrowing models are worse than microfinance ever was. The interest rates are higher and the default rates are much higher. There are good FinTech lenders out there, but the norm is worse." She's particularly worried about Silicon Valley money backing the ventures, which "expects much higher returns, with the fiction of social motivation." In our conversations, she described digital lending as a kind of commercialized microfinance on steroids. Even though some critics of the microfinance industry have been deeply skeptical of Rhyne and the Smart Campaign, she feels they really were doing their best to help lenders and funders learn from mistakes and rectify them. Now, she worries that lenders don't even have to operate under the pretense of doing better. She thinks the general sense is, "Unless the regulators are telling me what I can and can't do, I'm going to do what I want." The new framing of "inclusion" has allowed for a scrubbed-clean image without doing any of the work of change.

* * *

Over a decade since Citigroup's Robert Annibale talked about financial inclusion, nearly three-quarters of adults in developing countries have some sort of formal financial account. But there's limited evidence that those who have been financially included are, as hoped, more resilient. A

2022 study from the Center for Financial Inclusion considered whether people in Colombia, Bolivia, Peru, Myanmar, and Cambodia who had access to financial tools fared better during COVID. Researchers found: it depends. A person's buoyancy was heavily determined by the specifics of their situation: their job, their family network, how much they had saved, how savvy they were. Basically, their well-being depended on how well they were doing otherwise, not on their access to financial services. In fact, borrowers who had managed to stay afloat during the pandemic did so mostly *without* financial services. They reduced business stock, fired employees, sold their assets, cut down on food. Few borrowed to get by, but if they did, many chose informal lenders over formal ones.

The study did make clear that financial tools did *not* help the *poorest* people surveyed, specifically those living below the poverty line—results that resembled those from microfinance studies conducted over a decade earlier, which showed that those who were already wealthier generally fared better, and those poorer more likely to be harmed.

Even though the authors concluded with an optimistic tone—"it appears that financial inclusion did indeed boost some borrowers' resilience in the wake of the pandemic, and we found no indications that financial inclusion reduced the resilience of any borrowers"—the Center for Financial Inclusion was concerned. Later that year, another paper from the group pointed to "a sway of new research" that showed "while access to finance is growing globally, financial health and well-being are stagnating or even declining."

The authors determined that part of the problem is the hidden fees that eat into whatever little money these newly banked people have. But the bigger issue is structural. Food and other goods are getting more expensive; climate disasters are expected to push millions of people into poverty each year; and medical expenses, now the biggest financial worry for both men and women in every region in the world, are rising. Borrowers in Cambodia, many now financially included, still struggle to get their crops to market because of troubled infrastructure. And even if they do, they don't make much, as crop prices have plummeted. While many financial inclusion advocates suggest that bank accounts and debit cards are a way for poor people to pay for life's necessities, few advocate for those necessities to be cheaper.

I'll be the first to say that a bank account is important to my life. I use it almost every day, and how much money I have in it is one marker of my success or failure, a source of stress or relief. But there are so many things outside of that bank account that determine its contents: my background, my job, my husband's job, how much I pay for health care, the city I live in, the housing policy that determines my rent, the work I do, my family's history and economic well-being. The bank account reflects the confines and privileges of my life, but it did not make any of it.

So it's not so much that the goal of financially including people is inherently bad, although there is much money to be made from their inclusion. Someone having a debit card instead of cash or being able to send money to a relative hundreds of miles away can be hugely helpful in many situations. But if the goal of these programs is to make people's lives better, as some still claim it is, the approach remains way off. If more people are going into more debt to cover basic expenses—things like water, health care, education—should that really be considered a success? Just because a person is now "financially included," that tells us little about the texture, and stresses, of a debtor's daily life.*

Phil Mader of the Institute of Development Studies isn't surprised that groups like the Center for Financial Inclusion find themselves baffled when things like bank accounts and savings programs don't seem to address greater issues of wealth inequality and inadequate public services. "There is some really strong willingness to believe that financial services are the key to solving so many people's problems. I would never idolize [financial services] as anything that's saved me from any calamity, but we're saying they can save the poor by shortening the length from Wall Street to these people. We've never lived in such a finance-saturated era. It's like the development sector has found a hammer and then everything is a nail.

"Think about if digital loans were offered as a replacement for social services in your country," he continued. "Would that be good enough?"

---

* For a U.S. comparison, historian Keeanga-Yamahtta Taylor has called the focus on extending high-priced housing and financial schemes to marginalized Americans "predatory inclusion." Sean Illing, "The Sordid History of Housing Discrimination in America," *Vox*, May 5, 2020, https://www.vox.com /identities/2019/12/4/20953282/racism-housing-discrimination-keeanga-yamahtta-taylor.

It's Easier and It's Harder

Sukudu, Kono, Eastern Sierra Leone

2021

ABBIE DIDN'T KNOW WHERE EXACTLY TO FIND HER AUNT FINDA. WHEN she was released from D.O. Barracks, her aunt was debt-free but penniless and frail. She was also deeply embarrassed. After her year in jail, Finda didn't want to go back to Sawula or Koidu or anywhere anyone might know her. "She was so ashamed," remembers Abbie. Abbie also felt embarrassed for—maybe even by—her aunt. Embarrassed that debt had taken over Finda's life, embarrassed that she hadn't been able to do anything about it, even a little embarrassed that Finda didn't turn out to be a good enough businesswoman to pay off all the microcredit fees. When friends asked after Finda, Abbie just told them that she was gone.

It was easier to start over somewhere where Finda could be anonymous. Abbie heard that her aunt was in Sukudu, a mining town about an hour and a half by motorbike from Koidu, heard that she carried gravel out of artisanal, informal mines for a living, that she worked for someone everyone called Pastor, that she lived someplace called Waga Street.

But Abbie had never actually been to Sukudu herself. She didn't know this Waga Street, this Pastor, didn't have Finda's number, didn't know who her aunt was staying with. To find her, she would just have to go and ask.

* * *

In the 1950s, at the beginning of Sierra Leone's diamond rush, Sukudu was a large, chaotic boomtown, where thousands of diggers scrounged through the dark red earth. Within a decade, the most plentiful deposits had been picked through. Miners left, the value of homes that had been built with diamond money sharply declined, and the area resembled, in the words of one writer, a "war ravaged village." A few hundred people stayed on to sort through what was left.

Today, Sukudu is surrounded by dozens of small-scale, artisanal mines producing gold and diamonds. Deep, ugly gashes have been dug into the ground, oozing water and mud. Were you to see the village from above, it would look as if an unforgiving, energetic ice cream scoop had been blindly taken to the earth.

Abbie arrived in Sukudu late morning, thrilled to see the tall minarets from the town's main mosque swirl above the red and green of the earth after the hours on the back of a motorbike. She immediately began to search for her auntie. She asked a group of men sitting on a broad veranda, then the proprietor of a tea stall, a pharmacist, a woman pumping water from a well and another selling bread, if they had heard of a woman named Finda, "the one they call Krio Mammi, that skinny one." All furrowed their brow, took a moment to answer, then insisted they hadn't. No one smiled. Abbie went on like this for two hours, the same refrain said to anyone who would listen. "I'm looking for a woman named Finda, the one they call Krio Mammi, that skinny one." Exhausted, she took a break for lunch—a stale piece of bread—at the tea stall. She rested her elbows on her knees and grumbled, "I can't even find my mother." The bread seller looked up. "Your mother? Why didn't you say so? Follow me."

The woman guided Abbie to a pit at the edge of town. It wasn't very deep, or wide—a person could probably walk around it in just a few minutes. There was only one water pump at the top of the hole, lazily spitting out red mud. It was midafternoon by the time Abbie and the woman arrived, and no one seemed to be working. A few women milled around a hut made from raffia. Abbie asked, "Do you know Finda, the woman they call Krio Mammy, that skinny one?"

"She just left," a woman said flatly, then turned back around.

Abbie blurted out, "I'm her daughter!" and the woman softened. "She just left, moments ago, down that road. Go get her!"

Abbie hopped back on the bike. A minute or so later, she spotted a small figure, pushed up to the bushes on the side of the road that hugged the jungle. Finda wore a lapa patterned with overlapping triangles of yellow, pink, and navy, a yellow T-shirt, and small hoop earrings. She carried a small bucket on her head. As she walked, she sucked the fruit out of a small hole she had torn into the flesh of a bright yellow mango the size of a baseball. When she turned at the sound of the bike, the mango's meat showed through a gap-toothed smile, which she offered to Abbie. Finda jumped on the back of the bike, hugging her arms around her niece's waist. She directed them toward the end of Waga Street, where a few kids ran toward the banana plants that hemmed the outer edge of town.

Finda's room sat off a porch that was perched atop a set of crumbling but sturdy mud brick stairs. She rented from a kind landlady who lived in the main house, which was cool and spacious and mainly devoid of furniture. Finda's room, on the other hand, was small, hot, and dark. For a window, there was a hole banged out of the clay wall. It looked and smelled as if animals used to live there. The room had a few pieces of clothing, a notebook, and a bed, but none of the trappings that Ramatu, or even Abbie, had—no pictures on the walls or handbags, no chairs, no mirror, no frilly ceiling hangings, no fabric. It looked more like camp than a home.

When she was not mining for Pastor, Finda spent most of her time on one of the two long wooden benches on the porch, trading stories with the landlady, who sold nuts and lollipops while complaining about her husband, who generally wore a scowl. On this day, she greeted him briefly when he arrived home in the afternoon, then looked back toward the water in the bucket on the ground before her, which had turned purple from the nuts she was cleaning. Finda picked one up, examined it, and nibbled.

"Life is easier and harder in Sukudu," Finda told her niece. Easier in that the air is cooler and the place quieter, the water colder and sweeter, so fresh you can drink it directly from the well, although some say it's been poisoned by decades of mining. Pastor is kind enough—"he makes a point not to yell because he feels sorry for us. Today I was grumbling, my back hurt, everything hurt, and he said, 'Okay, you can go.'" He still offered her regular pay, $2 for a full day.

Finda was grateful for the steadiness of the work, difficult as it was. No matter what she did, or how her body felt, if she showed up and showed a bit of effort, she got paid. There were no sales to make. No haggling to be done. No calculations. No microcredit repayments. No bad luck.

But Sukudu was harder in that her body constantly hurt from all the carrying and stooping; she bought pain medicine almost every day. Her health had never recovered from her time in the cell. "They gave me medicine at the hospital, but it didn't really make it better." The doctors told her to eat healthy, to build up her body, which she found difficult to do. It was all but impossible to get fish all the way out here. She had seen none in the rivers, and by the time the little bony ones from Koidu made it to Sukudu, the price reached 20 or 50 cents for one the size of your middle finger. And good luck finding chicken, which mostly came all the way from the United States or Brazil.

Still, Finda was grateful that the village offered a cloak of anonymity, big enough to cover her shame. Even though she was far from kin—she hoped to send money to her kids whenever she was able to save enough—there was something comforting in knowing that "there are so many people here who are running from microfinance," explained Finda. "That's why all those people you asked were trying to hide me. We just say we don't know the person if a stranger asks for them." The landlady pointed to a slight figure walking quickly down the road. "See that woman who just passed by? She's also here because of all"—hand wave—"this."

Musu, another member of Abbie's Kochende microfinance group, had long wondered whether Yabom, the woman whose kids she now took care of, had gone to the nearby town of Peyima, just down the river from Sukudu, after she called her from the police station so many years earlier. Since then, Musu had only been in touch with Yabom's family once, to see if they could help take care of the children. They begged her to keep them in Koidu, for school, they said, and didn't offer information on where Yabom was. Musu heard she was maybe in Peyima, maybe in the main prison in Freetown, maybe at D.O. Barracks, where Finda had been, but she didn't push. The family was poor, far poorer than she and her husband could imagine. She felt embarrassed for even having asked. As the kids became integrated in her family, Musu felt a growing sense of pride: it was something of a blessing, a sign of her own relative prosperity, to be able to take on someone else's burdens and not complain about it. Or at least not complain too much. "Ask about her for me!" Musu had shouted to Abbie with a cheeky smile as she left Koidu that morning. They both knew she wouldn't.

Abbie did want to see someone else, though, someone she knew was also "hiding" here from microcredit: Adama, the rock breaker whose abs had turned into a washboard and whose hands were cut and swollen from working in the quarry outside the mine in Old Post, who had also been part of Kochende.

Back in Koidu, Adama found that even when she had a spectacular day, breaking rocks at the quarry then selling something like twenty buckets for $1 each, all her money went to caring for her kids. She barely had anything left over, let alone enough to pay down the microfinance debt. A few months into her loan and already struggling, Adama was in a motorbike accident. When the bike fell on her, it made a gash that ran up and down her calf. She couldn't work for weeks.

As her debt "climbed on her," as Adama described it, her children started working in the quarry, too. The youngest ones mostly toddled around, carrying just a few rocks to their mother. Only her eldest daughter was strong enough to do anything substantial. But the girl had to stop working when she became visibly pregnant. Adama blamed herself for the situation. "She didn't have money for school, that's why she went to that man." Even after the baby was born, Adama had a hard time looking her daughter in the eye.

"I kept trying, at the quarry, but those people just kept harassing me," Adama recalled. She says she was taken to the police station by BRAC, spending the night there. Then, "one day Mr. Bah, the manager"—from LAPO this time, she had taken out nearly half a dozen loans from different lenders—"he took me to the office and kept me there the whole day. He let me go at four p.m. and said he'd come tomorrow for the money."

By the time the sun rose the next morning, Adama had left Koidu, leaving her kids with a neighbor in Old Post. "I decided to escape. I left my children. I just ran away." She now lived a few blocks away from Finda in Sukudu. "I came here because they say you can make more money and because here I just have to pay for myself. When I'm in town, my kids are always asking for this and that. Money for school fees, money for transport, food." She tssked. "Always money, always money. It's too much. That's what made me leave them there. I need rest. When I'm there, they torment my heart. When I wake up in the morning, and my kids can't eat, I feel awful. Here, I'm just taking care of myself, little by little. I'm managing."

Her leg still pained her from the bike accident, but she didn't have the money she needed to buy regular painkillers. Because of the injury, she could only work a few days a week at another local mine on the other side of Sukudu, hauling buckets of mud and sludge up a steep, slippery hill to a boss who spent his days sitting under a large umbrella that protected him from the sun. "I've been here four or five months, but I can't save any money." Adama's previously flat belly had softened a bit with the intermittent breaks.

One day fed into another, and another. The longer Adama stayed away, the harder it seemed to go back to Koidu. Her children's costs were mounting in her absence. Her youngest daughter hadn't been in school for nearly a year because the fees hadn't been paid. Abbie let Adama's kids eat with her sometimes, if she and her daughter Princess had anything left over. "When I cook rice, I'll give it to them. But she left five children! It's too much." Sometimes, Adama's neighbors would call, telling Adama, "My children are suffering. They say, 'You ran away from this money, and you left them behind.'"

She did try to visit when she could. She was most excited to see her granddaughter, who was turning out to be a beautiful child despite the circumstances, with fine, silky hair clustered at the crown of her head. "My baby!" Adama would say, squishing the little girl's face right up to her own. "I haven't seen you in ages. Did you miss me? I missed you. How are you? Kiss your granny, kiss your granny." The baby looked neither pleased nor displeased with the affection. She stared at her grandmother's pursed mouth, giving it a tap with her hand. Adama often worried that the little girl cried so much. The baby was skinny in the way an adult body is skinny: her neck elongated, arms sloped down at the elbow, sleek calves. She retained a belly, but only because her body wasn't long enough yet for it to go anywhere.

Abbie tssked and cooed and tried to comfort Adama, switching between encouragement—"You can bear it!"—and condemnation of the microfinance managers, "those people, they are so wicked!" Mostly, she sympathized. "It's too much, it's too difficult for her." Abbie truly felt sorry for the woman. "I know it isn't easy. Because I know that if she was able to make it, she wouldn't have left the children and gone to the village. She told me before she left, she said, 'Things here are really stressing me.'" But she also felt conflicted about all this leaving. She resented Adama's ability to just pick up and go, while "we, we stay! When we find a little bit of money, we pay."

Abbie was glad to see that Adama was all right—not thriving, but all right. She was far more concerned about Finda. Her aunt hadn't yet decided whether to consider Sukudu home or a stopover. "I don't know how long I'll be here." Finda shrugged. "It's up to God." Seated on the front porch next to her landlady, Finda confessed she'd been toying with taking out microcredit again. She wanted to start a business. She had some ideas: maybe sell shoes again, maybe sell some of those brightly colored buckets that were sold all over Koidu. Something that could add to the bit that Pastor gave each day.

Abbie was startled. "You really think you can pay? You really want that?" Her landlady piled on the discouragement. "You'd have to sell way too quickly. You won't be able to manage it."

Finda gave a little gurgle of a laugh. She looked embarrassed to be chastised by these younger women, embarrassed to consider a loan like the one that had landed her in prison. But she was getting old—the mining work could only go on for so long, even with Pastor's kindness. She didn't see many other options. Finda shrugged, then looked down at the porch before taking another bite of the nut. She was grateful it was known to stem hunger, because it wasn't clear where dinner would come from.

Around the four p.m. call to prayer, three kittens played in the late afternoon shade made by the roof of the house across the street. Abbie decided it was time to leave. It would be dark soon, and Princess was waiting for her back home.

Finda escorted her niece back to the main road. The two walked arm in arm down Waga Street, back toward the well-stocked pharmacies that lined the main street. "Because of all the mining?" Abbie asked Finda, who nodded, then called to everyone, "This is my daughter. If she ever comes again, let her go straight to my house!" The two women giggled, inviting stares.

At the end of the road, Finda bought a fresh round of injectable pain medicine. The pharmacist took her money, telling her to come back for the shot after the sun went down to avoid dizziness in the heat.

Abbie grabbed her aunt by the shoulders, promising to come back soon, then hoisted herself on the bike. As it took off, Finda became a whirl of color, her thin arm raised in goodbye. From the back of the bike's long black seat, Abbie waved back, little wisps of hair blowing behind her like she was a movie star.

Just outside town, Abbie looked up to see a flock of swallows. They dipped toward the earth, then arced back toward the sky. "It's beautiful here," she said. "Maybe I'll come, too."

Conclusion

We will not accept aid for the underdeveloped countries as "charity." Such aid must be considered the final stage of a dual consciousness—the consciousness of the colonized that *it is their due*, and the consciousness of the capitalist powers that effectively *they must pay up*.

— FRANTZ FANON, *THE WRETCHED OF THE EARTH*

I WANT TO GIVE YOU AN UPDATE ON THE PEOPLE WHO ARE INCLUDED IN these pages.

Up until the spring of 2023, Aminata was still selling alcohol at PZ, Freetown's main market. She stopped when a group of men associated with the ruling Sierra Leone People's Party took sticks to the stalls of women associated with the opposition All People's Congress. Aminata lost all her goods in the looting. She and the other market women decided to wait it out for a few months, should there be more trouble in the lead-up to the June 2023 election. The election *was* marked by violence and "statistical inconsistencies"—a nice way of saying potentially stolen by Julius Maada Bio, who, as of June 2023, entered his second term as president. A few weeks later, Aminata gave birth to her first child, a healthy baby boy. Her husband, Idrissa, and adopted daughter, Doris, who was nine when the boy was born, are thrilled to welcome him to the household.

Aminata's efforts at gathering $1,000 to help Mohamed net a government contract petered out: her relatives were reluctant to keep contributing as Sierra Leone's economy plunged even further into crisis. Idrissa still works as a driver for the same NGO. He says the tea stall he started with a friend is going well, but he doesn't give details.

During a terrible fight, Kadija's husband threatened to kick out her elder daughter, Rose. Kadija responded, "If he kicks her out, he kicks me out, too." She left Two Taps and moved across town, to be closer to her sister.

Without her covered patio and parlor, Kadija no longer had a safe place to sell her stuff. So she resorted to her first vocation: hairstyling. To start, she took out another microfinance loan, borrowing from a different lender on the other side of Freetown and leaving her old debts behind. She still complains about the fees and the interest rate but feels lucky to borrow at all: with inflation reaching the highest level it has in years and the country's currency depreciating by 60 percent in 2022 alone, lenders are warier than ever.

To avoid violence in the lead-up to the 2023 presidential election, and to avoid the farmer man who would not stop pursuing her, Ramatu has moved from Old Post to another part of Koidu. For months, she did not tell the farmer where she was living, even as she continued to rely on whatever money he could part with. He even helped her buy a few bags of rice, which she sold by the cup from her new front parlor. At first, Ramatu sold maybe half a dozen cups each day, making a few cents each time. But as inflation rose, so did the cost of rice. Even when she did sell, Ramatu found it harder to pull together enough money to buy a full bag. It soon became harder to find customers, too, as people turned to locally grown cassava to get by. Ramatu knows she's no great businesswoman. But the rice business was actually a good idea, and one that was going well, until much larger forces got in the way.

In 2022, Ramatu gave birth to another son. The boy is lively and healthy, fatter and more smiley than her first son, Mark, who keeps getting sick with colds and stomach bugs thanks to his playing in dirty water that runs through her neighborhood ("It's like shit," she told me). She has high hopes for her youngest son. The day the boy was born was a fortuitous one in Kono. It was the beginning of the presidential election season; while Ramatu was in labor, the president visited town and gave a speech at the hospital where she gave birth. Thanks to his being around, "there was light for twenty-four whole hours that day! The whole day! That's how I know that he'll be lucky."

Abbie still has one foot in Koidu, another back in her village, grow-ing beans and hot pepper. Her daughter Princess, now much taller than her mother, is in high school. Abbie is determined to stay in Koidu until Princess graduates. Abbie's aunt Finda is still mining for Pastor in Sukudu. Adama, the rock breaker, is still there, too. Both see their children intermittently.

The women in Kono still have not seen or heard from Yabom, the microfinance borrower who fled from the police station years ago.

Jeff Ashe lives in Cambridge, Massachusetts, where he's been based since he moved back to the United States in the 1990s. In his first few years home, he set up Working Capital, an American small lending oper-ation. At its core, the model was essentially the same as FEDECRÉDITO's: small business owners in Florida, Delaware, Massachusetts, New Hamp-shire, Maine, Rhode Island, and Vermont could get a loan if they joined a solidarity group, just as millions of others had done around the world.

But there were a few key differences. Borrowers received intensive support and business training, something some lenders had done in the early years of microfinance but which had largely fallen off when such programs were deemed too expensive. Working Capital capped annual interest rates at 12 percent, a figure that was determined when Work-ing Capital learned that a Vermont anti-usury law wouldn't let them go any higher. Whereas some microlenders had encouraged governments to remove interest rate caps, or ignored them entirely, here, Working Cap-ital adhered to regulation, adopting the rate as their own. Rather than encouraging loan after loan, as had become the norm in many micro-credit institutions, many Working Capital members took out one, maybe two loans, then bowed out. Without a steady stream of lending, it was clear the institution wouldn't be sustainable (it was transferred in 1999 to Accion, who discarded the solidarity group model and gave individual loans instead). But it was hoped the borrowers' businesses would be.

The research Ashe did in the early 1980s on savings and loan groups—the ROSCAs—stayed with him. As he became disillusioned with inter-national microfinance, he became convinced that ROSCAs were *the* alternative model. People solving their own problems with little outside meddling could "flip the paradigm" and offer "real financial inclusion at a tiny fraction of the cost." Ashe thought "it would have such an enormous impact that it could revolutionize the whole field." In our conversations, Ashe described his advocacy on this as something of an attempt at absolution, a way to steer microfinance back to its grassroots origins.

Now in his eighties, Ashe remains a true believer in this alternative approach. For years, Ashe led a program called Saving for Change at the international NGO Oxfam, which tried to set up and support ROSCAs around the world.* Now, as part of a course he teaches on microfinance at Columbia University's School of International and Public Affairs, he encourages students to research versions of ROSCAs used by immigrant communities in the United States. Ashe has even written a book on savings groups.† When we last spoke, Ashe's newest idea was to have leaders of existing savings groups train leaders of new ones; an outside organization could coordinate and pay a small stipend for the training.

I never found Ashe particularly clear on why an outside organization would need to be involved, given that the whole idea is that ROSCAs are organic and uniquely local. When I pushed, I always got the same explanation, which never really felt like a satisfactory answer: that ROSCAs were already bigger than microfinance, and therefore if a development organization wanted to really help, they should focus here.‡ But he was never clear on what an outside organization could offer that the local communities couldn't do themselves. Despite acknowledging that one of his biggest life lessons is learning just how complicated outside interventions can be, it seems that Ashe remains, at his core, an interventionist,

---

* Several other nonprofits have set up similar initiatives, including Catholic Relief Services and Freedom from Hunger, two previous champions of microfinance. These efforts have been bolstered by results from randomized controlled trials that savings groups can—as the name implies—increase savings, and sometimes increase assets and business investment. Across Sierra Leone, NGOs now set up osusu-style groups, offering training and sometimes materials—things like a cashbox, ledgers—even though osusus predate these NGOs by at least a century. These financial services are sometimes attached to other services, like health care or education. In some cases, ROSCAs are encouraged to charge interest on loans to make the approach more "sustainable."
† Jeffrey Ashe with Kyle Jagger Neilan, *In Their Own Hands: How Savings Groups Are Revolutionizing Development* (Oakland, CA: Berrett-Koehler Publishers, 2014).
‡ When I asked one of Ashe's contemporaries—another microfinance advocate turned critic—about Ashe's insistence on outside support, he shrugged and said, "I'm not really sure," noting that outsiders might "muck it up." In the late 1990s, the anthropologist Parker Shipton warned, "Osusu groups are functioning comparatively well, though the resources they muster are limited; and in the end the best way of helping them might be to leave them alone." Parker Shipton, "How Gambians Save and What Their Strategies Imply for International Aid," Policy Research Working Paper Series 395, World Bank, Agriculture and Rural Development Department, April 1990.

energized by the thrill of being involved in something far beyond himself. "I've been behind a couple of big movements, from the Peace Corps to Accion," he told me. "You can always feel a little bit of a ripple, then suddenly the energy shifts and takes over. Somebody's got to start it."

John Hatch, the founder of FINCA, has lived in Santa Fe, New Mexico, since he retired from the organization in 2007. In our conversations, he was deeply critical of FINCA's move toward a more commercialized approach, although he remains a member of the board. His wife, Mimi, whom he met at the RESULTS "Hands Across America" event in the 1980s, passed away in 2016. Hatch now spends much of his free time traveling and writing. The last time we spoke, he was working on a memoir.

Although he has left RESULTS, Sam Daley-Harris remains involved in grassroots-style, policy-focused advocacy, helping other organizations adopt the RESULTS approach. He has been particularly involved in climate activism. Although he laments the turn to a commercial microfinance model, he remains staunchly supportive of Muhammad Yunus and still strongly believes that microfinance loans should solely focus on the poorest (and still resents USAID and other large development funders for suggesting otherwise).

In 2011, Muhammad Yunus resigned as managing director of the Grameen Bank after a prolonged battle over whether he was required to leave given that he had surpassed the mandatory retirement age for a government-affiliated post. Many of the people I spoke to say he was pushed out not because he was seventy but by Prime Minister Sheikh Hasina, who felt threatened by Yunus's significant global profile and political ambitions. (The government also pointed to a critical 2011 documentary* to claim Yunus had mismanaged funds at Grameen.) Now in his eighties, Yunus remains based in Bangladesh, despite facing continued political attacks from the Bangladeshi government.†

Although Yunus is still seen by many to be the father of microfinance,

---

* *The Micro Debt*, directed by Tom Heinemann.

† In 2022, while I was researching this book, Prime Minister Hasina claimed that Yunus worked to cancel a World Bank loan for a bridge, an allegation for which there is no public evidence. "'Dr. Yunus Blocked Padma Bridge Funds,'" Prothomalo, May 18, 2022, https://en.prothomalo.com/bangladesh /politics/dr-yunus-blocked-padma-bridge-funds. Sam Daley-Harris, Alex Counts, and others continue to publicly voice support for Yunus amid these allegations.

he has continued to distance himself from the sector. As part of a 2022 investigation into commercial microfinance banks, Yunus told *Bloomberg,* "The concept of microcredit was abused by some and turned into profit-making enterprises for owners of microcredit institutions. Many went in the inevitable direction of loansharking. I felt terrible that microcredit took this wrong turn." (At the time the *Bloomberg* report was published, the Grameen Foundation website still declared, "Moving from a 'funding' model to a sustainable 'financing' model enables a win for investors and a permanent escape from poverty.") Yunus's more recent public efforts focus on the broad concept of "social business," the idea that businesses that are motivated not just by profit but also by social objectives can "solve the world's most pressing problems."* Yunus has continued to champion the idea that there is an entrepreneur in each poor person. In 2017 he told the *Guardian,* "There are roughly 160 million people all over the world in microcredit, mostly women. And they have proven one very important thing: that we are all entrepreneurs."

After her years working at USAID, then Accion, Elisabeth Rhyne left her position heading up the Center for Financial Inclusion in 2019. Although she is critical of FinTech lending models, such as digital lending, she remains a consultant in the now-broadened "financial inclusion" sector, trying to rein in some of its worst excesses.

Chuck Waterfield now spends his time tending goats—nine of them when we spoke, all dwarf goats. (He joked, "It's microdairy.") He makes "fancy goat cheese" for himself and his friends, which he serves with honey from his own bees. He wrote his last article on microfinance in 2016, when he criticized the sale of an NGO's microfinance operations to a company that grew out of the South African payday lending industry. He's stayed away ever since.

---

* This is not a new campaign for Yunus. In his 1998 book, *Banker to the Poor,* he wrote, "Social-consciousness-driven enterprises can be formidable competitors. . . . I believe that if we play our cards right, social-consciousness-driven enterprises can do very well in the marketplace." Muhammad Yunus, *Banker to the Poor: Micro-Lending and the Battle Against World Poverty* (New York: PublicAffairs, 2007), 206. In his 2006 Nobel Peace Prize lecture, Yunus predicted, "Almost all social and economic problems of the world will be addressed through social businesses. Health care for the poor, financial services for the poor, information technology for the poor, education and training for the poor, marketing for the poor, renewable energy—these are all exciting areas for social businesses." Muhammad Yunus, "Nobel Lecture," The Nobel Prize.

Michaela Walsh, who helped to found Women's World Banking, still lives in New York City, a place she has called home for well over fifty years. Now in her eighties, Walsh still volunteers when she can, speaking to young people about her early days in microfinance and mentoring them on their careers while also catching the occasional jazz show. She cowrote a history of Women's World Banking, *Founding a Movement: Women's World Banking, 1975–1990*, which was published in 2012.

Ela Bhatt, the founder of the Self-Employed Women's Association in Gujarat, India, passed away in 2022 at the age of eighty-nine. Her life was celebrated in Indian media, the *New York Times*, the *Wall Street Journal*, the *Financial Times*, and by the Elders—a group of "senior statesmen, peace activists and human rights advocates" founded by Nelson Mandela—who called her a "powerful and forceful advocate for voiceless and marginalized people across the world." SEWA is now made up of 2.5 million women. It still considers itself a trade union, still follows Gandhian principles, and is still driven by two goals: full employment and self-reliance.

The microfinance sector has continued to grow, with a few key players, often foreign owned or financed, dominating major markets like Cambodia. Although subsidized government grants have waned, U.S. government support for small-scale lending, particularly through loans and loan guarantees, has continued.* While exact numbers of borrowers are harder to come by now that microfinance watchdogs and tracking websites have closed, as of 2018, one estimate suggested that about 140 million people had a microfinance loan. Those who advocate for broader "financial inclusion" will offer even more staggering figures—the World Bank estimates that 1.2 billion people opened a bank account between 2011 and 2017. The concept continues to pick up speed. Before he took over as World Bank president in

---

* For example, in 2019, then president Donald Trump signed the Women's Entrepreneurship and Economic Empowerment Act, which required that 50 percent of USAID resources for Micro, Small, and Medium Enterprises target the "very poor"—language that Sam Daley-Harris and Muhammad Yunus might be pleased with. "U.S. Agency for International Development Micro, Small and Medium-sized Enterprise: Fiscal Year 2020 Results Report to Congress," https://mrr.usaid.gov/docs/MSME_Results_Report_FY2020.pdf. Although the narrative continues to focus on lending-as-female-empowerment, the actual percentage of women included has decreased, sometimes dipping far below 50 percent. As recently as 2016, USAID still said that 98 percent of borrowers pay back their loans. Development Credit Authority, USAID, updated September 8, 2016, https://www.usaid.gov/what-we-do/economic-growth-and-trade/development-credit-authority.

June 2023, Ajay Banga headed up MasterCard. His efforts at the company "included partnerships with governments and banks to issue MasterCard branded debit cards to millions of individuals" in order to advance financial inclusion. Even before Banga's tenure, the World Bank claimed "financial inclusion is a key enabler to reducing poverty and boosting prosperity."

After collateralized loan obligations, CLOs, gained a reputation for helping to blow up the international economy in 2008, microfinance-oriented CLOs went quiet, too, despite their strong performance in the midst of the global recession. They've since come back. In 2019, J.P. Morgan partnered with responsAbility Investments AG, a Swiss-based "international impact asset manager" best known for facilitating microfinance investments. They put together a $175 million CLO that would fund nearly six million microfinance borrowers as well as other small and medium enterprises (SMEs). A press release described the deal as a way for microfinance companies to "access global capital markets," while a "range of investors" could "contribute to financial inclusion in developing countries, earn a commercial return, and diversify their exposure across multiple borrowers and geographies."

Microfinance IPOs—initial public offerings—like the ones Compartamos and SKS undertook have also continued. In 2018, Bandhan Bank, an Indian microlender, sold shares through an IPO that was fifteen times oversubscribed. Its shareholders have included the American investment fund Fidelity Investments and French banks BNP Paribas and Société Générale, as well as some of India's richest men. In July 2018, ASA International, which has a large footprint in Sierra Leone, became Europe's first publicly listed microfinance institution. It secured a £313 million valuation on the London Stock Exchange. Meanwhile, Compartamos, still overseen by the two Carloses, has continued to grow. As of 2022, it was one of Mexico's most profitable microfinance lenders and the largest microfinance lender in Latin America (it now has operations in Peru as well as Mexico). As of December 2022, its shareholders included Goldman Sachs Asset Management, BlackRock Fund Advisors, and the Vanguard Group, one of the world's leading investment companies. Compartamos also still receives loans from public funders, including the U.S. government and the Inter-American Development Bank.

Impact investing, a concept that in many ways got its start through microfinance, with Yunus arguing that businesses be dually motivated by profits and by social returns and early microfinance investment funds attempting to put this principle into practice, has increased in popularity. While Alex Counts, founder of the Grameen Foundation, estimates that just a few years ago nearly half of impact investing focused on microfinance, today those investments have expanded to broader environmental, social, and governance—ESG for short—goals. Today you'll be hard pressed to find a business or investor, from bespoke hat companies to ExxonMobil to the asset management firm BlackRock, which doesn't claim it's in the business of changing the world by seeking "triple bottom line" returns: good for people, planet, and profits.

Elizabeth Funk, who started the Dignity Fund in 2005, is proud of how broad the concept has become. She thinks the reframing of everything as an investment can help individuals and investors reconsider where their money is going and what exactly it's doing in the world: "Do I want to invest in this bottle of Coke? Or do I want to invest in pulling carbon from the atmosphere?" Others see the unspecific goals associated with microfinance investing as a warning. Matt Bannick, who helped eBay's Pierre Omidyar make early microfinance investments through his Omidyar Network, worries that the lack of clear-cut impact measurements means that everyone can claim they're doing good, without offering details about what exactly it is they're doing. He thinks the lack of specificity allows for a sort of "impact washing. Once you say you're an impact investor, it's assumed you must therefore be having an impact, without actually having to measure what that impact is." Bannick sees the microfinance industry's obsession with "inputs not outputs," as exemplified by the Microcredit Summit Campaign's tracking of how many borrowers there were but not necessarily how they were doing, as a lesson. You should not measure your success by how much money you put in, but on real-life, tangible results.

In 2019, Esther Duflo, Abhijit Banerjee, and Michael Kremer, another early RCT adopter, won the Nobel Prize in Economics "for their experimental approach to alleviating global poverty." Thanks to their work on randomized controlled trials, the committee noted, "We now have a large number of concrete results on specific mechanisms behind poverty and specific interventions to alleviate it." As with Yunus's Nobel Peace Prize, this success has been met with criticism. Those who implement and rely on RCTs have been accused of experimenting on the poor, searching for obvious solutions that would be considered the bare minimum in wealthier countries (do we really need a study to determine that clean water is good?), and withholding basic services like health care or education programs from one community to prove that they work in another. What about the basic principles driving medical RCTs, like "do no harm"—are those being practiced here, too?

Ironically, some of these questions are remarkably similar to those raised about microfinance, the reputation of which randomized controlled trials helped to complicate. Are the numbers really as good as they claim to be? Does it make sense to promote "scale" once something has been "proven" through an RCT, ignoring the specifics of a particular context? Is this truly the gold standard, or just the tool that has become the most popular? (One critic has called the dominance of RCT "more a matter of faith than science.") Several critics have similarly suggested that RCTs promote one-off, low-cost micro-solutions that act as a salve for poverty rather than longer, broader, more complex socioeconomic changes that might fundamentally address it.

* * *

Throughout the last few years, I've had several occasions where someone has asked me, "So, what do you think? Is microfinance a good thing? Or, is microfinance *definitely* bad?"

I've never had a particularly good answer. After years of getting to know the women in Kono and Freetown, I honestly don't have a strong sense of how *they* would answer that question. I asked these women, and dozens of others I met during this research, whether they wanted microfinance companies to leave Sierra Leone—whether life would be better off without them. Aminata, who had other options through her husband, was the only one who gave an emphatic answer: yes, life would be better without microfinance. (Many of the legal experts I interviewed said yes, too—Gassan Abess, a representative from the Human Rights Commission, insisted that he wished microfinance had never come to Sierra Leone, that it was ruining families and communities. He has become so disturbed by women going to the police and jails because of unpaid debt that he has begun intervening directly, negotiating with microfinance companies or police officers, in addition to advocating for the law to change.) But nearly every other woman gave an equally insistent no: we can't manage without these tiny loans. If companies were going to leave, one woman told me, "we would beg them to stay."

This was confusing, given that I'd spent countless hours listening to borrowers complain about high-priced loans, confusing conditions, constant repayments, and their inability to make ends meet. So, I asked this woman why she would beg microfinance companies to stay. It was simple: "Because we need money."

The women in Freetown and Kono have incredibly sophisticated understandings of what debt can do. A loan might plunge them further into poverty, might mean jail time, or might help them get by in some new way, although not one that will substantively change their situation. Still, that getting by can really help. As Isabelle Guérin, a senior research fellow at the French Institute of Research for Development, observes, there's a kind of emancipation in choosing to take out debt, an exertion of agency, of knowing the risks and choosing to take them anyway. More tangibly, there's simply the freedom that comes with more money, even if it might mean less freedom (and money) later. Even though some of the women I met—Panneh in Two Taps, Finda in Sukudu—say they are markedly worse off now than before they took on microdebt, they still cannot conceive of life without it. Because, right now, they do have to pay for health care and education. Without larger structural issues being addressed, they must find a way to get by.

Women are terrified of the loans and their consequences. And they are also terrified of life without them.

So, if someone asks if microfinance works, I give them an answer I think that someone like Finda may offer. I'll say, on the one hand, that microfinance is the reason she went to jail, but also, on the other, that she'd take out another loan if given the chance, considering the reality of her life, hemmed in by poverty and its ramifications. She'd like that loan to be large enough to do something substantial with, and with low enough rates to be able to pay it back, but she knows that's unlikely. (In part as a response to concerns about the consequences of microfinance, dozens of microfinance-affiliated programs, often relying on grants or domestic funding rather than the capital markets, do offer longer-term, lower-interest loans. These are sometimes coupled with other supports like training and social programs; RCTs have shown such lending schemes to be more effective in helping borrowers meet their daily needs and less likely to plunge them into debt. However, these programs remain small and often geographically concentrated. The women I met in Sierra Leone, where the commercial model still dominates, did not have access to them.) I'll say that women like Finda have found a way to survive, to "manage," in their words, relying on social connections and turns of fate to smooth out terrifying situations (I watched one woman, arrested for debt, casually walk out of a police station in the heat of the afternoon, after everyone else had fallen asleep). For Abbie, and Ramatu, and Aminata, microfinance is remarkably unremarkable: just another source of debt woven into a complex tapestry of lending and borrowing, an expensive daily burden they've learned to live with.

But just because a person can, somehow, cope with 40 percent interest rates to pay for her child's education or cover groceries, does that mean they should? The women are clear that there is nothing special, nothing beautifully self-perpetuating or emancipatory, about the actual *lending* part of microfinance. Because the loans are too small and too expensive to start a business with, and because Sierra Leone's economy is so hostile that most small businesses die, what microfinance offers is cash. It just so happens that the cash comes with the baggage of high interest rates, visits from the police, and potential shame from families and communities.

So why not just cut to the chase. If randomized controlled trials and by now thousands of observations demonstrate that at best microfinance offers a way to "smooth consumption," why not offer cash without all the conditions, without requiring someone to make up a business idea and rack up layers of debt just so they can feed their family?

Giving cash to a poor person is an idea that's radical in its simplicity, and easily open to criticism, especially from those who don't believe in a free lunch or think it must somehow be spoiled, or who balk at a program that can't pay for itself. But it's an idea that's picking up steam.

In 2012, GiveDirectly was launched. As the name suggests, the organization sends money directly to people who need it, no expectations or strings—no interest rates or fees—attached. The money does not need to be repaid. People do not have to claim to be using it for a business or some other earmarked purpose. Using the now-ubiquitous RCTs, GiveDirectly claims that people who have received the money spend it on health care, irrigation systems, tin roofs, school fees, and water. One study claims that, two years after roughly $500 was given, researchers found "sustained increases in assets"—people had more stuff, things like farming tools and water tanks. Another study found that giving around $500 increased children's growth, because their families could afford more and better food. A few found that cash transfers increased income in a community, both considering those who directly received money as well as the people around them, given that the community had more cash in circulation.

In addition to one-off cash transfers, GiveDirectly is also trying out a universal basic income program, which offers a regular, baseline "income": a small amount of cash each month given to poor adults in parts of Kenya, Malawi, and Liberia.* That idea is gaining traction more broadly. Universal basic income has been tried in communities as varied as Stockton, California, and among two thousand unemployed people in Finland. Studies have found that regular cash transfers can improve mental and physical health and financial stability.

This isn't a book on cash grants or universal basic income, so I won't give a definitive answer or offer a stance here (especially since I can't seem to give one for microfinance). Researching this book has been an education in afterthoughts and unintended consequences. If I've learned anything in writing these pages, it's that distilling deeply complicated problems into bite-size solutions is a great way to make a big mess, often without meaning to.

That said, having spent several years with these women, I can say that the basic premise of giving cash to poor people makes a lot of sense. Poor

---

* The Omidyar Network, a key supporter of microfinance in the 2000s, has backed the program, stating, "It is clear that cash transfers have an important role to play in alleviating poverty and empowering people." The Omidyar Network, "Why We Invested: GiveDirectly's Basic Income Experiment," GiveDirectly, February 7, 2017, https://www.givedirectly.org/why-we-invested-givedirectlys-basic-income-experiment/?gclid=Cj0KCQjwiIOmBhDjARIsAP6YhSWNnkJXY6LLdc5LPda2JM8OgAdt954S3TZWO2EryV6J2zsxYVROD3AaApaMEALw_wcB.

people are, by definition, poor in that they don't have money. Rather than taking a more circuitous route, encouraging people to make up businesses they know may never get off the ground and charging them interest rates many will not be able to afford, it's logical to give them a main thing they're lacking. And because there's no expectation of repayment, there's no money to be made here, no risk of the "slippery slope" that so many microfinance managers fell down when they went from worrying about covering costs to making money. Private equity investors and commercial banks wouldn't get involved, because there would be no reason, no incentive, for them to do so. Money might still be given from outside a community, but then it would stay firmly inside, not sent back to funds in Luxembourg or Geneva.

Of course, for this to be about helping people to not just get by, but to get by a lot *better*, larger structural issues would have to be addressed, too. If inflation is 30 percent, as it is in Sierra Leone as I write,* simply giving people more cash to pay for increasingly more expensive things isn't going to do much. Even if a person suddenly has an extra cow, or a new way to pay for schools, that doesn't mean the milk from the cow will get to market or that school fees won't keep going up or that the education will be quality.† Without other substantial, structural changes, universal basic income and cash grants could easily replicate a main problem with microfinance: focusing on the small, on the individual, on material inputs as *the* answer to poverty distracts from larger societal-level solutions. (If everyone has a loan to pay for doctors' visits, why try to make those free?) Some libertarians‡ have latched onto universal basic income precisely *because* it could further diminish the role of the state.

It seems clear—I'd argue even more obvious than giving a poor person money—that building comprehensive public social systems is the long-term answer, albeit one that is complex, expensive, and time-consuming, with changes made over generations, not months or years. But given that

---

* July 2023.

† Notably, the positive results from the experiment in Stockton were diminished during the coronavirus pandemic. A study author remarked, "Five hundred dollars a month is not a panacea for all social ills." Jeanne Kuang, "Stockton Guaranteed Income Study Finds Pandemic Damped Positive Results," *CalMatters*, April 12, 2023, https://calmatters.org/california-divide/2023/04/california-guaranteed-income/.

‡ Peter Thiel is a major proponent.

poverty and its consequences already stretch across generations—with children losing their mothers to jail or going to work with them to help pay off their family's loans—I'd wager that it's worth finding a more comprehensive solution, on a moral, political, and economic level, even if that's a much harder road to follow.* Rather than leaving each person to fight for themselves in deeply constrained economies, legal systems, and societies that make it almost impossible for that person to succeed, we should commit to building systems that take care of a whole person, not just the aspect that is most easy, convenient, or "cost-effective" to address.

Talking about long-term changes in the tax code and social safety nets and trade systems is a far different approach from the one Muhammad Yunus took. His greatest brilliance was not in coming up with microcredit—it seems he never really did anyway, at least not in the way that most of us have learned the story. His brilliance is as a storyteller, weaving elegant narratives that promise profound change in a complicated world. When many of us feel, perhaps increasingly, in our own bubble, the notion of helping others through a simple mechanism offers an optimism that evades much of our daily experience, in which the magnitude of the world's troubles feels both intangible and intractable. We feel we can't change systemic racism, can't undo hundreds of years of unequal wealth accumulation, can't turn back global inequality, a consequence of colonialism and extraction. (We can't even figure out how to properly recycle plastic.) The idea that simply by giving a loan to people who have found themselves in a more precarious situation we can at the very least express our desire for something different is an understandably powerful one.

But it's not an optimism I attempted to replicate in these pages. This book is certainly critical, maybe even caustic at times. But for me, there is a different sort of optimism in this critique. I *do* think we should discard overly simplistic narratives and solutions that dominated at least some pockets of international aid in the twentieth century. I *do* think

---

* And again, it doesn't have to be an either-or: either give cash or consider longer-term solutions that get at the heart of poverty. When universal basic income was tried in Finland, that cash was offered *on top* of a robust social safety net that includes free health care and education. Instead of being spent on school fees or doctors' visits, the income was used on better food, house repairs—even on starting new businesses. Alex Matthews, "Finland's Answer to Universal Basic Income," DW.com, May 30, 2020, https://www.dw.com/en/does-finland-show-the-way-to-universal-basic-income/a-53595886.

the focus should be on the bigger, harder, longer things. I understand that it can feel defeatist to talk about the structural underpinnings of poverty: things can feel so bad, inequality so deeply entrenched, it can be hard to imagine another way. But we must be honest about the change that is needed and how much has already changed. The world isn't fixed. It is created, the result of policy decisions, individual choices, rhetoric made and believed in. Microfinance was not an inevitable development fad, nor was the broader outsourcing of social and political problems to the private sector. Rather, such "solutions" are a product of the histories, people, and ideas described in these pages. When we appreciate this manufacturing, and don't assume predetermination, then we can begin to imagine and create meaningful change, stepping forward more confidently, more cautiously, and clear-eyed, able to recognize and learn from our mistakes, able to understand that the needle does move, just never as quickly or as easily as neat stories would have us believe.

The biggest lesson from this book is that it's important to question how these stories are constructed and consider the political, economic, and historical forces that inform them and shape individuals, institutions, and policy fads. If microfinance proponents had slowed down, taking the time to learn more about the context and social complications they were wading into and examining the roots of their own beliefs and perspectives, perhaps some of the most severe consequences could have been avoided. Instead, they adopted a narrow vision, neglecting broader history, culture, and politics that ultimately inform how small loans function in people's lives. Intervening in another person's life requires profound hubris. Taking time to quietly sit with the complexity such interventions demand should be lauded, not seen as too onerous, specific, or ineffective.

Such interrogation can be done on a much smaller scale, too. If you do want to continue to support microfinance, or cash transfers, or anything else for that matter, do your research. Look up not just the interest rate but the *effective* interest rate—including fees and penalties and type of calculations used—to learn what a person is being charged. If it's not listed, ask for it. If you don't get a response, do so publicly, and do it again and again. Look at who is funding the organization you want to support. Look at what their objectives are. Look at the laws in the countries where they work. Read a bit about the economic, political, and cultural history of that place—see this not just as an obligation but as an exercise in curiosity. Research what legal aid organizations exist there and see what they say about microfinance. Learn about what your government's stance is and why they have taken that stance (USAID documents are surprisingly easy to access, even those going back several decades). In addition to interrogating what a program says it can do, consider what that picture obscures, what might be done instead.

Doing this makes it so that microfinance is not the quick-fix, feel-good solution it's been offered to be by organizations such as Kiva, whose website says, "make a loan, change a life." But impacting someone else's life *should* take time. You, as the funder, deserve to know where your money is going and how it's being used. The borrower deserves the best possible conditions, too.

If you are looking to support organizations that assist people caught up in Sierra Leone's criminal justice system, AdvocAid focuses specifically on women and girls and has done much to help publicize how debt and other crimes of poverty can unjustly land women in police stations and prisons. The Center for Accountability and the Rule of Law has worked closely with AdvocAid on efforts to decriminalize petty crimes and focuses on both men and women. Prison Watch Sierra Leone is a watchdog organization that regularly monitors the country's prison conditions. All three provide free legal advice and support to impoverished Sierra Leoneans. I am grateful to have learned from all of them while researching this book.

Notes

Gone: Old Post, Koidu, Kono, Eastern Sierra Leone

2 **Those who first lived:** "The Diamond Story in Sierra Leone," Penn State College of Earth and Mineral Sciences, accessed August 3, 2023, https://courseware.e-education.psu .edu/courses/earth105new/content/lesson11/09.html.

2 **most of the miners:** "Appendix 2: Submission to the TRC. National Forum for Human Rights Submission to the TRC," https://www.sierraleonetrc.org/downloads/Appendix2 _Submissions.pdf.

3 **But it was undesirable:** Septimus Senessie, "Mining Company Blast Destroys Homes in Eastern Sierra Leone," *Politico SL*, April 23, 2013, https://www.politicosl.com/node/1153.

Introduction

7 **This was the early 2000s:** UNAIDS and the World Health Organization, "AIDS Epidemic Update: December 2004," accessed July 20, 2023.

8 **"for their efforts to create":** NobelPrize.org, "Press Release," October 13, 2006, https: //www.nobelprize.org/prizes/peace/2006/press-release/.

8 **In 2010 alone:** Jan P. Maes and Larry R. Reed, "State of the Microcredit Summit Campaign Report 2012," Microcredit Summit Campaign: A Project of the RESULTS Educational Fund, 2012.

9 **largest Ebola outbreak in world history:** "2014–2016 Ebola Outbreak in West Africa," Centers for Disease Control and Prevention, https://www.cdc.gov/vhf/ebola/history/2014-2016 -outbreak/index.html.

11 **multibillion-dollar industry:** Aarti Goswami, Goswami Borasi, and Vineet Kumar, "Microfinance Market by Provider (Banks, Micro Finance Institute (MFI), NBFC (Non-Banking Financial Institutions), and Others) and End User (Small Enterprises, Micro Enterprises, and Solo Entrepreneurs or Self-Employed): Global Opportunity Analysis and Industry Forecast, 2021–2030," Allied Market Research, October 2021, https://www.alliedmarketresearch.com /microfinance-market-A06004.

14 **a sprawling city:** "Freetown Population 2023," https://worldpopulationreview.com /world-cities/freetown-population.

15 **the poorest countries in the world:** "Sierra Leone," World Food Program, accessed July 15, 2023, https://www.wfp.org/countries/sierra-leone.

Chapter 1: Twenty-Seven Dollars to Forty-Two Women

19 **when Bill Clinton:** Jann S. Wenner, Hunter S. Thompson, William Greider, and P. J. O'Rourke, "Bill Clinton: The Rolling Stone Interview," *Rolling Stone*, September 17, 1992.

19 **Yunus and Clinton had met:** Muhammad Yunus, *Banker to the Poor: Micro-Lending and the Battle Against World Poverty* (New York: PublicAffairs, 2007), 175–76.

19 **later gutting:** Alana Semuels, "The End of Welfare as We Know It," *The Atlantic*, April 1, 2016.

19 **during the early '90s recession:** Jennifer M. Gardner, "The 1990–91 Recession: How Bad Was the Labor Market?" *Monthly Labor Review*, June 1994.

19 **Famously, his unofficial:** "It's the Economy, Stupid," *Harvard Political Review*, October 17, 2012, https://harvardpolitics.com/its-the-economy-stupid/.

19 **In their meeting:** Wenner et al., "Bill Clinton: The Rolling Stone Interview."

20 **the second-largest:** "How Our Endowment Works," Ford Foundation, https://www.fordfoundation.org/news-and-stories/videos/how-the-ford-foundation-uses-grants-to-tackle-inequality/how-our-endowment-works/.

20 **heading the Economics Department:** Yunus, *Banker to the Poor*, 33.

20 **having spent his childhood:** Yunus, *Banker to the Poor*, 3.

20 **Yunus grew up well-to-do:** Yunus, *Banker to the Poor*, 3–4.

21 **But otherwise he kept:** Yunus, *Banker to the Poor*, 10.

21 **but it was his mother:** Yunus, *Banker to the Poor*, 5–6.

21 **Yunus was a bright student:** Yunus, *Banker to the Poor*, 15–20.

21 **By one estimation:** Jason Hickel, "How Britain Stole $45 Trillion from India," *Al Jazeera*, December 19, 2018, https://www.aljazeera.com/opinions/2018/12/19/how-britain-stole-45-trillion-from-india.

21 **Sick of exploitation and colonial rule:** Rund Abdelfatah, Ramtin Arablouei, Asma Khalid, et al., "Road to Partition," *Throughline*, December 15, 2022.

22 **the Bangladeshi independence movement:** "Sheik Mujibur Rahman Declares Region Independent Republic," ABC, March 26, 1971.

22 **"My choice is":** Yunus, *Banker to the Poor*, 21.

22 **According to a piece in *Time* magazine:** Ishaan Tharoor, "Forty Years After Its Bloody Independence, Bangladesh Looks to Its Past to Redeem Its Future," *Time*, December 16, 2011.

22 **Back in America, Yunus helped:** Yunus, *Banker to the Poor*, 25–28.

23 **and hundreds of thousands of Bangladeshis had been killed:** "Bangladesh: War of Liberation," Mass Atrocity Endings, World Peace Foundation, https://sites.tufts.edu/atrocityendings/2015/08/07/bangladesh-war-of-liberation/.

23 **In the course of the conflict:** "BANGLADESH: Mujib's Road from Prison to Power," *Time*, January 17, 1972.

23 **"By the time the war":** Yunus, *Banker to the Poor*, 29.

23 **A few months later, in early 1972:** Yunus, *Banker to the Poor*, 33.

23 **Foreign engineers and policymakers:** "Bangladesh-ADB: 40 Years of Development Partnership," Asian Development Bank, 2013, https://www.adb.org/sites/default/files/publication/30426/bangladesh-adb-40-yrs-dev-partnership.pdf.

23 **One academic framed international efforts:** Naomi Hossain, "The Geopolitics of Bare Life in 1970s Bangladesh," *Third World Quarterly* 42, no. 11 (November 2, 2021): 2706–23.

24 **The billions in aid:** National Archives, "Marshall Plan (1948)," September 28, 2021, https://www.archives.gov/milestone-documents/marshall-plan.

24 **The World Bank, only recently set up:** World Bank, "History," https://www.worldbank.org/en/archive/history.

24 **A sister organization, the International Monetary Fund:** "The IMF in History," International Monetary Fund, https://www.imf.org/en/About/Timeline.

24 **That left a huge gap:** "Decolonization of Asia and Africa," Office of the Historian, U.S. Department of State, https://history.state.gov/milestones/1945-1952/asia-and-africa.

24 **despite the Indian subcontinent:** Maria Abi-Habib, "The Forgotten Colonial Forces of World War II," *New York Times*, September 3, 2020.

24 **in his 1949 inauguration address:** "Point Four: Background and Program (International Technical Cooperation Act of 1949)," Committee on Foreign Affairs, July 1949, https://pdf.usaid.gov/pdf_docs/Pcaac280.pdf.

25 **Highly planned projects:** Michelle Murphy, *The Economization of Life* (Durham, NC: Duke University Press, 2017), 17–29.

25 **Through the Marshall Plan:** National Museum of American Diplomacy, "The Marshall Plan," https://diplomacy.state.gov/online-exhibits/diplomacy-is-our-mission/development/the-marshall-plan/.

25 **Truman considered it essential that:** "Point Four: Background and Program."

26 **unimpressed with international development:** Yunus, *Banker to the Poor*, 142–45.

26 "perennial management problems": Yunus, *Banker to the Poor*, 38.

26 "the assumption is that": Yunus, *Banker to the Poor*, 144.

27 neither the time nor the ability: Yunus, *Banker to the Poor*, 38.

27 Lackluster, paper-pushing: Yunus, *Banker to the Poor*, 142–45.

27 His job at: Yunus, *Banker to the Poor*, 33.

27 the United States pushing: "The Green Revolution: Accomplishments and Apprehensions," address by the Honorable William S. Gaud, Administrator, Agency for International Development, Department of State, March 8, 1968.

27 On top of that instability: Caf Dowlah, "The Politics and Economics of Food and Famine in Bangladesh in the Early 1970s—with Special Reference to Amartya Sen's Interpretation of the 1974 Famine," *International Journal of Social Welfare* 15, no. 4 (October 2006): 344–56.

27 worsened by floods: "Entitlement Failure," *Encyclopedia Britannica*, https://www .britannica.com/science/famine/Entitlement-failure.

27 Yet again, Yunus: Yunus, *Banker to the Poor*, vii.

27 International support also sputtered: "Bangladesh Fears Thousands May Be Dead as Famine Spreads," *New York Times*, November 13, 1974.

27 Poor, landless rural: Amartya Sen, *Poverty and Famines: An Essay on Entitlements and Deprivation* (Oxford: Clarendon Press, 1981).

27 Over a million: Howard LaFranchi, "From Famine to Food Basket: How Bangladesh Became a Model for Reducing Hunger," *Christian Science Monitor*, June 18, 2015, https: //www.csmonitor.com/USA/Foreign-Policy/2015/0617/From-famine-to-food-basket-how -Bangladesh-became-a-model-for-reducing-hunger.

27 Yunus says it was his mother: Yunus, *Banker to the Poor*, 5.

28 "dread my own lectures": Yunus, *Banker to the Poor*, viii.

28 "I am going to go": Sam Daley-Harris, "At the Knee of Muhammad Yunus: Stories of Hope and a New Way of Seeing the World," unpublished essay.

28 In 1976, in a village called Jobra: Yunus, *Banker to the Poor*, 45–50.

29 At Oslo City Hall: "The Nobel Peace Prize Award Ceremony and Concert 2006," Nobelprize.org, https://www.nobelprize.org/ceremonies/the-nobel-peace-prize-award-ceremony-and-concert -2006/.

29 "I offered . . . $27": Muhammad Yunus, "Nobel Lecture," The Nobel Prize.

30 "I am not in the money business": Yunus, *Banker to the Poor*, 50.

30 multiyear effort: Yunus, *Banker to the Poor*, 50–113.

32 the government would become the majority owner: Yunus, *Banker to the Poor*, 117–19.

Restless: Freetown, Sierra Leone

34 rebels attacked towns across the north: Lansana Fofana, "RELIGION BULLETIN-SIERRA LEONE: Italian Priest Abducted," Inter Press Service News Agency, November 22, 1998.

34 When they entered her village: "Sierra Leone: List of Extremely Violent Events Perpetrated During the War, 1991–2002," Sciences Po Mass Violence and Resistance—Research Network, January 20, 2016, https://www.sciencespo.fr/mass-violence-war-massacre-resistance /en/document/sierra-leone-list-extremely-violent-events-perpetrated-during-war-1991-2002 .html.

Chapter 2: An Epiphany

41 bananas became one of: "Bananas in Costa Rica," Observatory of Economic Complexity, https://oec.world/en/profile/bilateral-product/bananas/reporter/cri.

41 monopolize commercial banana growing: Miguel Guevara, "The History and Impact of the United Fruit Company in Costa Rica," *Grow Jungles*, October 29, 2021, https: //growjungles.com/united-fruit-company-in-costa-rica/.

41 worker repression and bloody coups: Olúfémi O. Táíwò, "When the United Fruit Company Tried to Buy Guatemala," *The Nation*, December 7, 2021, https://www.thenation .com/article/economy/united-fruit-guatemala/.

41 "banana republics": Guevara, "The History and Impact of the United Fruit Company in Costa Rica."

42 **"fragmented, awkward and slow"**: "John F. Kennedy: Special Message to the Congress on Foreign Aid," March 22, 1961.

42 **not particularly popular**: John Norris, "Kennedy, Johnson and the Early Years," *Devex*, July 23, 2014, https://www.devex.com/news/sponsored/kennedy-johnson-and-the-early-years -83339.

42 **now referred to as USAID**: "USAID History: About Us," U.S. Agency for International Development, February 10, 2023, https://www.usaid.gov/about-us/usaid-history.

42 **which would become America's**: "USAID and PL–480, 1961–1969," Office of the Historian, U.S. Department of State, https://history.state.gov/milestones/1961-1968/pl-480.

42 **"The economic collapse of"**: "John F. Kennedy: Special Message to the Congress on Foreign Aid," https://www.presidency.ucsb.edu/documents/special-message-the-congress -foreign-aid-1.

42 **"serve, shoulder to shoulder"**: "Peace Corps," JFK Library, www.jfklibrary.org/learn /about-jfk/jfk-in-history/peace-corps.

42 **"created an atmosphere"**: Interview with Eric Chetwynd.

43 **"organiz[e] the community"**: "Description of Peace Corps Volunteer Service: John Hatch—Peace Corps Volunteer—Colombia," Peace Corps.

44 **hoping that loans and bank accounts would offer**: Dale W. Adams, "The Birth of a New Paradigm in Rural Finance: AID's Role," USAID, May 11, 2011, 9.

44 **fund investment from the bottom up**: John Sanbrailo, "Draft for Discussion: USAID Private Sector Programs: An Overview 1961–2014," Annual General Meeting USAID Alumni Association, Private Sector Engagement Panel, October 24, 2014.

45 **"to do economic development"**: "Timeline: Founding," DAI, https://www.dai.com /who-we-are/history.

45 **the reason his home country**: Walter Rodney, *How Europe Underdeveloped Africa* (Washington, DC: Howard University Press, 1981).

45 **the Black Panthers'**: "The Black Panther Party Mutual Aid," People's Kitchen Collective, http://peopleskitchencollective.com/panthers-mutual-aid.

45 **out-of-the-box thinkers**: Charles H. Hession, "E. F. Schumacher as Heir to Keynes' Mantle," *Review of Social Economy* 44, no. 1 (1986): 1–12.

46 **"man must be given"**: "A Praxis in Participatory Rural Development," Proshika brochure, n.d., 11.

46 **There were reports**: "A Praxis in Participatory Rural Development," 4–5.

46 **a phenomenal failure**: "Alliance for Progress and Peace Corps, 1961–1969," Office of the Historian, U.S. Department of State, https://history.state.gov/milestones/1961-1968 /alliance-for-progress.

46 **"a cleverly managed"**: Thomas Sankara, 1987 speech at the Organization of African Unity.

46 **as Kwame Nkrumah**: Kwame Nkrumah, *Neo-Colonialism: The Last Stage of Imperialism* (New York: International Publishers, 1976).

46 **"The origins of the debt"**: Eric Toussaint and Damien Millet, *Debt, the IMF, and the World Bank: Sixty Questions, Sixty Answers* (New York: Monthly Review Press, 2010), 206.

47 **"Must we starve"**: "Stop Starving the World's Poor to Pay Debts," *Los Angeles Times*, September 25, 1989.

47 **the U.S. Foreign Assistance Act**: "Foreign Assistance Act of 1961," Public Law 87–195; approved September 4, 1961.

47 **shift "away from"**: "USAID History: Celebrating 60 Years of Progress," USAID, https: //www.usaid.gov/about-us/usaid-history.

47 **found himself wondering**: *Volunteer: The Magazine of the Peace Corps*, No. 5, May–June 1970, https://web.archive.org/web/20110718173107/http://historyofthepeacecorps.org /primarysources/19700501%20Volunteer%20May-Jun.pdf.

48 **developed a strong critique**: *Volunteer: The Magazine of the Peace Corps*.

48 **start an international "self-help group"**: Interview with Terry Holcombe.

48 **"start[ed] their own lives"**: Accion brochure.

48 **"rather critical of"**: *Volunteer: The Magazine of the Peace Corps*.

48 **An early promotional video**: "Accion en Venezuela," https://www.youtube.com/watch ?v=JzG9QlaiSz8.

48 **not seen as agents:** *Volunteer: The Magazine of the Peace Corps.*
48 **Social Responsibilities of the Businessman:** Howard R. Bowen, *Social Responsibilities of the Businessman* (Iowa City: University of Iowa Press, 2013).
49 **a hold in Latin America:** Interview with Terry Holcombe.
49 **General Motors, Ford, Mobil Oil:** Accion brochure.
49 **Its board of directors:** Accion brochure.
49 **"Gee, maybe I'm learning":** "WMC intvw complete," https://www.youtube.com/watch?v=7_il_dxOtDY.
49 **"money directly to the community":** Interview with Terry Holcombe.
49 **"informal sector":** "USAID's Contribution to Microfinance: From Microfinance to Financial Inclusion," prepared by Anicca Jansen for the Office of Microenterprise and Private Enterprise Promotion, October 2014.
49 **up to 70 percent:** "USAID's Contribution to Microfinance."
50 **sometimes fractious cities:** Interview with Eric Chetwynd.
50 **asked USAID to create:** "USAID's Contribution to Microfinance."
50 **the butcher, the baker:** Accion, "Bruce Tippett: The Father of Microfinance," Medium.com, March 26, 2015, https://medium.com/@Accion/the-father-of-microfinance-20feb3bd6dfd.
50 **One American researcher observed:** Simon Fass, "The Economics of Survival: A Study of Poverty and Planning in Haiti," U.S. Agency for International Development, October 1980.
50 **"people's economy":** Yunus, *Banker to the Poor*, 207.
51 **"ephemeral opportunities":** Keith Hart, "Kinship, Contract, and Trust: The Economic Organization of Migrants in an African City Slum," in Diego Gambetta, ed., *Trust: Making and Breaking Cooperative Relations* (New York: B. Blackwell, 1988), 176–93.
51 **"Microeconomic theory . . . is incomplete":** Muhammad Yunus, *Banker to the Poor: Micro-Lending and the Battle Against World Poverty* (New York: PublicAffairs, 2007), 150, 207.
51 **"in the barrios":** Interview with Terry Holcombe.
51 **"Accion was there first":** Accion, "Bruce Tippett."
52 **all men:** Interview with Pedro Paes Leme.

Back Home: Old Post, Koidu, Kono, and Sawula, Kono, Eastern Sierra Leone

55 **spring of 2014:** "2014–2016 Ebola Outbreak in West Africa," CDC, March 17, 2020, https://www.cdc.gov/vhf/ebola/history/2014-2016-outbreak/index.html.
58 **Lift Above Poverty Organization:** "LAPO Microfinance Company SL Limited," https://lapo-sl.org/.

Chapter 3: Copycats

61 **"confirm":** "Small Enterprise Approaches to Employment for the Urban Poor," prepared by Michael Farbman, Office of Urban Development Bureau for Development Support Agency for International Development, U.S. Department of State, June 1978, 8.
61 **Did lending to small businesses:** "Small Enterprise Approaches to Employment for the Urban Poor," 1.
61 **"beatniks were morphing":** Jeff Ashe, "My First 50 Years in the Development Trenches," unpublished essay, April 2018.
62 **"campesinos revolucionarios":** Ashe, "My First 50 Years in the Development Trenches," 8.
62 **the loans were short-term:** Dale W. Adams, "*Progress with Profits: The Development of Rural Banking in Indonesia.* By Richard H. Patten and Jay K. Rosengard. San Francisco: Institute of Contemporary Studies Press, 1991. xix, 114 pp." *Journal of Asian Studies* 51, no. 3 (August 1992): 715–16.
63 **"shocked by the poverty":** Mehrsa Baradaran, *How the Other Half Banks: Exclusion, Exploitation, and the Threat to Democracy* (Cambridge, MA: Harvard University Press, 2015), 66.
63 **Filene was equally distressed:** "Federal Credit Union Act," MyCreditUnion.Gov, https://mycreditunion.gov/financial-resources/calendar-events/federal-credit-union-act.
63 **German cooperative movement:** Baradaran, *How the Other Half Banks*, 66.
63 **alternative to high-priced moneylenders:** "Federal Credit Union Act."
63 **spoke with President Theodore Roosevelt:** Baradaran, *How the Other Half Banks*, 66–67.

63 **several influential journalists:** "Federal Credit Union Act."
63 **in 1908:** "Our Story," St. Mary's Bank, https://www.stmarysbank.com/nav/about-us/history/our-story.
63 **opened in Manchester, New Hampshire:** "Federal Credit Union Act."
63 **"common good":** Baradaran, *How the Other Half Banks*, 65–68.
64 **"needs of the poor":** Baradaran, *How the Other Half Banks*, 94–95.
63 **across many other movements:** Baradaran, *How the Other Half Banks*, 66, 78–97.
65 **a variety of names:** F. J. A. Bouman, "ROSCA: On the Origin of the Species / ROSCA: Sur l'origine du phenomène," *Savings and Development* 19, no. 2 (1995): 117–48.
65 **began documenting:** William R. Bascom, "The Esusu: A Credit Institution of the Yoruba," *Journal of the Royal Anthropological Institute of Great Britain and Ireland* 82, no. 1 (1952): 63–69.
65 **promote monetization:** Interview with Bill Maurer.
65 **promote credit unions internationally:** Dale W. Adams, "The Birth of a New Paradigm in Rural Finance: AID's Role," written for USAID, May 11, 2011, 9.
66 **"Unless the basic savings habits":** Clifford Geertz, "The Rotating Credit Association: A 'Middle Rung' in Development," *Economic Development and Cultural Change* 10, no. 3 (April 1962): 241–63.
66 **grown since the 1960s:** Bouman, "ROSCA: On the Origin of the Species."
66 **what is now Nigeria:** Bascom, "The Esusu."
66 **In Sierra Leone:** Bouman, "ROSCA: On the Origin of the Species."
66 **Goods, labor, and favors:** David Graeber, *Debt: The First 5,000 Years* (Brooklyn, NY: Melville House, 2011).
66 **people prefer:** Parker Shipton, "How Gambians Save and What Their Strategies Imply for International Aid," Policy Research Working Paper Series 395, The World Bank, Agriculture and Rural Development Department, April 1990.
67 **relied on chiefs:** Padraic X. Scanlan, *Freedom's Debtors: British Antislavery in Sierra Leone in the Age of Revolution* (New Haven, CT: Yale University Press, 2017).
67 **fat leeches:** Milford Bateman, "De-industrialization and Social Disintegration in Bosnia," in Thomas Dichter and Malcolm Harper, eds., *What's Wrong with Microfinance?* (Rugby, Warwickshire, UK: Practical Action Publishing, 2007), 200.
67 **largely don't exist:** Parker MacDonald Shipton, *Credit Between Cultures: Farmers, Financiers, and Misunderstanding in Africa* (New Haven, CT: Yale University Press, 2010), 117.
68 **seen as "inferior":** Scanlan, *Freedom's Debtors*.
68 **"was an integral part":** Bill Maurer, *How Would You Like to Pay? How Technology Is Changing the Future of Money* (Durham, NC: Duke University Press, 2015), 132.
68 **the insistence on formal credit:** Scanlan, *Freedom's Debtors*.
68 **Across the Indian subcontinent:** Interview with Nima Yolmo.
68 **which fellow group members:** Kathleen Stack, "Freedom from Hunger Stories: Nepal: The Origin Story," unpublished essay, November 5, 2020.
68 **loan from a group fund:** Muhammad Yunus, *Banker to the Poor: Micro-Lending and the Battle Against World Poverty* (New York: PublicAffairs, 2007), 65.
68 **Nicolas Lainez explains:** Nicolas Lainez, "The Contested Legacies of Indigenous Debt Bondage in Southeast Asia: Indebtedness in the Vietnamese Sex Sector," *American Anthropologist* 120, no. 4 (December 2018): 671–83.
69 **"prone to amnesia":** Erin Beck, *How Development Projects Persist: Everyday Negotiations with Guatemalan NGOs* (Durham, NC: Duke University Press, 2017), 22.
70 **came from Rochac Zaldaña:** Correspondence with Milagro Maravilla.
70 **unequal countries in the world:** James Nelson Goodsell, "Rich-Poor Gap Drives El Salvador Toward Civil War," *Christian Science Monitor*, February 25, 1980.
70 **"Coffee Republic":** "A Coffee Republic," *Encyclopedia Britannica*, https://www.britannica.com/place/El-Salvador/A-coffee-republic.
70 **lost access to traditional farms:** Augustine Sedgewick, *Coffeeland: One Man's Dark Empire and the Making of Our Favorite Drug* (New York: Penguin Press, 2020).
71 **to quash a revolt:** "Jan. 22, 1932: La Matanza ('The Massacre') Begins in El Salvador," Zinn Education Project, https://www.zinnedproject.org/news/tdih/la-matanza/.
71 **tens of thousands:** "The Eclipse of the Oligarchs," *New York Times*, September 6, 1981.

71 **were Indigenous people:** "Jan. 22, 1932: La Matanza ('The Massacre') Begins in El Salvador."

71 **FEDECRÉDITO was founded:** Correspondence with Milagro Maravilla.

Easy Money: Freetown, Sierra Leone

73 **boasting nearly:** ASA Microfinance Sierra Leone, https://sierraleone.asa-international .com/.

74 **nominally free:** "FQSE—Free Quality School Education," Ministry of Basic and Senior Secondary Education, Sierra Leone, https://mbsse.gov.sl/fqse/.

74 **lowest in the world:** "Poorest Countries in the World 2023," World Population Review, https://worldpopulationreview.com/country-rankings/poorest-countries-in-the-world.

75 **only one quarter:** "Education," UNICEF Sierra Leone, https://www.unicef.org/sierraleone /education.

75 **48 percent:** "Literacy Rate, Adult Total (% of People Ages 15 and Above)—Sierra Leone," World Bank, https://data.worldbank.org/indicator/SE.ADT.LITR.ZS?locations=SL.

Chapter 4: Cookie Cutter

80 **"chang[e] their lives":** John R. Beardsley, "Program for Investment in the Small Capital Enterprise Sector PISCES Phase I: Assisting the Smallest Economic Activities of the Urban Poor," Final Workshop Report, Accion, April 29, 1980, 17–18.

80 **Across all the projects studied:** Eric Chetwynd Jr. and William R. Miner, "Pioneering in International Urban Development, Creating USAID Policies and Programs, 1970–1982: A Case Driven History of Urban Development," Technical Assistant Program, U.S. Agency for International Development, 2018.

81 **"Green Revolution":** "The Green Revolution: Accomplishments and Apprehensions," address by William S. Gaud, Administrator, Agency for International Development, March 8, 1968.

81 **formed the bedrock:** Interview with Dale Adams.

82 **"Spring Review of Small Farmer Credit":** Dale Adams, "The Birth of a New Paradigm in Rural Finance: AID's Role," USAID, May 11, 2011.

82 **massive defaults:** Susan Johnson and Ben Rogaly, "Microfinance and Poverty Reduction," Oxfam UK and Ireland and ACTIONAID, 1997.

83 **to poor farmers:** Adams, "The Birth of a New Paradigm in Rural Finance."

83 **White Highlands:** Parker MacDonald Shipton, *Credit Between Cultures: Farmers, Financiers, and Misunderstanding in Africa* (New Haven, CT: Yale University Press, 2010), 32–33.

83 **no quiet agricultural revolution:** Adams, "The Birth of a New Paradigm in Rural Finance."

84 **staffers at development agencies:** Interview with Eric Chetwynd.

84 **again left out:** Gita Sen and Caren Grown, *Development, Crises, and Alternative Visions: Third World Women's Perspectives* (New York: Monthly Review Press, 1987).

84 **"do not reach [them]":** Statement by Patricia Hutar, Head, U.S. Delegation to the World Conference for International Women's Year, June 25, 1975.

84 **"women's work":** Sen and Grown, *Development, Crises, and Alternative Visions.*

85 **Foreign Assistance Act was amended:** Women in Development, Progress Report to Members of AID Senior Operations Group, U.S. Agency for International Development, Department of State, June 17, 1976, https://pdf.usaid.gov/pdf_docs/PNAAC668.pdf.

85 **"a vital human resource":** Department of State, Agency for International Development, "Integration of Women into National Economies," Annex A, September 16, 1974, in Women in Development, Progress Report to Members of AID Senior Operations Group, U.S. Agency for International Development, Department of State, June 17, 1976, 15.

85 **By the late 1970s:** "Sec. 113. Integrating Women into National Economies," U.S. Foreign Assistance Act as amended by sec. 108 of the International Development and Food Assistance Act of 1977.

85 **growing concerns about overuse:** Michelle Murphy, *The Economization of Life* (Durham, NC: Duke University Press, 2017).

85 **empowering them to be economic actors:** "To Our Credit: Bootstrap Banking and the World," PBS, September 1998.

86 **United Nations conference on women:** "World Conference of the International Women's Year, 19 June–2 July 1975, Mexico City, Mexico," United Nations, https://www.un .org/en/conferences/women/mexico-city1975.

86 **an ambitious young woman:** Michaela Walsh, Shamina de Gonzaga, and Lilia Clemente, *Founding a Movement: Women's World Banking, 1975–1990* (New York: Cosimo Books, 2012).

87 **envisioned as a union for self-employed women:** "To Our Credit: Bootstrap Banking and the World."

87 **"committee to organize":** Walsh et al., *Founding a Movement.*

88 **Bangladeshi academic Lamia Karim:** Lamia Karim, *Microfinance and Its Discontents: Women in Debt in Bangladesh* (Minneapolis: University of Minnesota Press, 2011).

88 **An early video:** *Nazma,* International Fund for Agricultural Development, n.d.

88 **"It is the women":** "Sewa Founder Ela Bhatt Passes Away at the Age of 89," Young Turks | CNBC-TV18, https://www.youtube.com/watch?v=Ge3YYEhJ0HA.

88 **remarkably good fundraisers:** Erin Beck, *How Development Projects Persist: Everyday Negotiations with Guatemalan NGOs* (Durham, NC: Duke University Press, 2017), 9.

88 **"women's groups":** Shipton, *Credit Between Cultures.*

89 **"welfare queen":** "The Truth Behind the Lies of the Original 'Welfare Queen,'" *All Things Considered,* NPR, December 20, 2013.

89 **"of dependency":** "Radio Address to the Nation on Welfare Reform, August 1, 1987," Ronald Reagan Presidential Foundation and Institute.

89 **market forces:** Adams, "The Birth of a New Paradigm in Rural Finance."

89 **"does nothing as well":** "A Time for Choosing Speech, October 27, 1964," Ronald Reagan Presidential Library and Museum.

89 **services privatized:** Sheldon Danziger and Robert Haveman, "The Reagan Budget: A Sharp Break with the Past," *Challenge* 24, no. 2 (May–June 1981): 5–13.

89 **revved up:** Elisabeth Rhyne, "The PISCES Project—Helping Small Enterprises Swim Upstream," USAID's Microfinance Consortium, May 1, 2014.

90 **"predominant 'private sector'":** "USAID's Contribution to Microfinance: From Microfinance to Financial Inclusion," prepared by Anicca Jansen for the Office of Microenterprise and Private Enterprise Promotion, USAID, October 2014.

90 **"market-based principles":** "Celebrating Sixty Years of Progress," USAID, https:// www.usaid.gov/who-we-are/usaid-history.

90 **"bootstrap development":** Beck, *How Development Projects Persist,* 2.

90 **"Enterprise":** Shipton, *Credit Between Cultures.*

90 **structural reasons for poverty:** Sen and Grown, *Development, Crises, and Alternative Visions.*

91 **played a role:** Adams, "The Birth of a New Paradigm in Rural Finance."

91 **some of the key claims that Reagan made:** Muhammad Yunus, *Banker to the Poor: Micro-Lending and the Battle Against World Poverty* (New York: PublicAffairs, 2007), 205–11.

91 **told PBS:** "To Our Credit: Bootstrap Banking and the World."

91 **microcredit training manual:** Shirley Buzzard and Elaine Edgcomb, eds., "Monitoring and Evaluating Small Businesses: A Step by Step Guide for Private Development Organizations," PACT, 1987, 66.

91 **the publication QZ:** Eshe Nelson, "Nobel Winner Muhammad Yunus Wants Two Financial Systems—One for the Rich and One for the Poor," *QZ,* October 20, 2018, https: //qz.com/1430076/nobel-winner-muhammad-yunus-wants-two-financial-systems-one-for -the-rich-and-one-for-the-poor.

92 **"realistic interest rates":** Adams, "The Birth of a New Paradigm in Rural Finance."

92 **Borrowers were mostly:** Marjorie Lilly, "A Report on the Third in a Series of PISCES Workshops: June 13, 1984, Washington, DC," Cambridge, MA, Accion International/AITEC.

92 **as much as 40 percent:** Chetwynd and Miner, "Pioneering in International Urban Development, Creating USAID Policies and Programs, 1970–1982," 181.

92 **improved cohesiveness:** Lilly, "A Report on the Third in a Series of PISCES Workshops."

92 **borrowers' self-esteem:** Jeff Ashe, "The PISCES II Experience: Local Efforts in Micro-Enterprise Development, Volume I," Agency for International Development, April 1985, 134.

92 **cover operating costs:** "A.I.D. Microenterprise Development Program: Report to the U.S. Congress," U.S. Agency for International Development, March 30, 1990.

92 **"nothing ever happens":** Interview with Elisabeth Rhyne.

93 **"Poverty is solved":** Tom Heinemann, "The Micro Debt," *NRK Brennpunkt*, 2011.

Kochende: Old Post, Koidu, Kono, Eastern Sierra Leone

96 **mining boomtown:** David Clive King, "Diamond Mining Settlements in Central Kono District, Sierra Leone," thesis submitted for the degree of Doctor of Philosophy of the University of London, January 1979, 233.

Chapter 5: The Poorest of the Poor

98 **Hands Across America:** John Hatch, "Impossible Love," unpublished memoir.

98 **"We Are the World":** Tyler Coates, "Why Hands Across America Is So Vital to Jordan Peele's *Us*," *Esquire*, March 21, 2019, https://www.esquire.com/entertainment/movies/a26883876/hands-across-america-us-movie-explained/.

98 **officially ascribed:** Kathryn Reid, "1980s Ethiopia Famine: Facts, What's Changed, How to Help," World Vision, November 3, 2022, https://www.worldvision.org/disaster-relief-news-stories/1980s-ethiopia-famine-facts.

98 **$60 million:** Tina Benitez-Eves, "Behind the Song Lyrics: 'We Are the World,'" *American Songwriter*, March 7, 2022, https://americansongwriter.com/behind-the-song-lyrics-we-are-the-world/.

98 **6.5 million:** Coates, "Why Hands Across America Is So Vital to Jordan Peele's *Us*."

98 **numbers had swelled:** Peter Dreier, "Reagan's Legacy: Homelessness in America," Shelterforce, May 1, 2004, https://shelterforce.org/2004/05/01/reagans-legacy-homelessness-in-america/.

99 **The film:** *Nazma*, International Fund for Agricultural Development.

100 **"16 Decisions":** "Grameen Bank's Sixteen Decisions," Village Volunteers.

100 **video claimed:** *Nazma*.

100 **picking up steam:** Muhammad Yunus, *Banker to the Poor: Micro-Lending and the Battle Against World Poverty* (New York: PublicAffairs, 2007), 112–27.

100 **video proclaimed:** *Nazma*.

100 **"never seen":** Sam Daley-Harris, "At the Knee of Muhammad Yunus: Stories of Hope and a New Way of Seeing the World," unpublished essay.

100 **Even though RESULTS:** Sam Daley-Harris, *Reclaiming Our Democracy: Healing the Break Between People and Government* (Philadelphia: Camino Books, 1994), 107–251.

101 **"fit that bill":** Interview with Alex Counts.

101 **working on legislation:** Daley-Harris, *Reclaiming Our Democracy*, 113–14.

101 **firmly on board:** Interview with Elisabeth Rhyne.

102 **In 1986:** Daley-Harris, *Reclaiming Our Democracy*, 109.

102 **"very ambitious Buddha":** Interview with Paul Rippey.

102 **without the Grameen Bank:** Daley-Harris, *Reclaiming Our Democracy*, 114.

102 **spoke to Congress:** "Lending to Microenterprises: Direct Assistance to the Small Economic Activities of the Poor," testimony presented to the House Banking Committee, the House Select Committee on Hunger, by Jeffrey Ashe, Senior Associate Director, ACCION International, February 25, 1986.

102 **USAID worried:** Interview with Eric Chetwynd.

103 **fund bigger loans:** Daley-Harris, *Reclaiming Our Democracy*, 112–19.

103 **"to the poor directly":** Yunus, *Banker to the Poor*, 149.

103 **RESULTS-backed:** Daley-Harris, *Reclaiming Our Democracy*, 112–19.

103 **"ridiculous":** Interview with Elisabeth Rhyne.

104 **"they can't run a business":** Daley-Harris, *Reclaiming Our Democracy*, 121.

104 **separate social programs:** "USAID's Contribution to Microfinance: From Microfinance to Financial Inclusion," prepared by Anicca Jansen for the Office of Microenterprise and Private Enterprise Promotion, USAID, October 2014.

104 **"unsound, and contrary":** Daley-Harris, *Reclaiming Our Democracy*, 121.

105 **"I'm an economist":** Daley-Harris, *Reclaiming Our Democracy*, 120–24.

105 **an appropriations bill earmarked:** Daley-Harris, *Reclaiming Our Democracy*, 124–25.

105 **FINCA was awarded a multimillion-dollar grant:** Interview with John Hatch.

105 **were married:** Hatch, "Impossible Love."
106 **A leftist coalition:** Olivia Bell, "Poverty and Gender Inequality in Post-War El Salvador," *Global Majority E-Journal* 4, no. 1 (June 2013): 27–39.
106 **military, which received training:** Raymond Bonner, "America's Role in El Salvador's Deterioration," *The Atlantic*, January 20, 2018.
106 **one hundred thousand:** Bell, "Poverty and Gender Inequality in Post-War El Salvador."
106 **"death squads":** "Report of the UN Truth Commissioner on El Salvador," United Nations Security Council, April 1, 1993.
106 *cul de sac*: Hatch, "Impossible Love."

The City Hustle: Freetown, Sierra Leone
107 **By 2023:** "Sierra Leone," World Factbook, https://www.cia.gov/the-world-factbook /countries/sierra-leone/.
108 **donors like USAID:** "Sierra Leone: Global Health," USAID, https://www.usaid.gov/sierra -leone/global-health.
108 **surprisingly low official infection rates:** Mara Kardas-Nelson, "A Faint Spectre in Sierra Leone: Covid-19," Global Health Now, Johns Hopkins Bloomberg School of Public Health, April 20, 2021, https://globalhealthnow.org/2021-04/faint-specter-sierra-leone -covid-19.
113 **world's largest and oldest:** "10 Facts About BRAC, the World's Largest NGO," Borgen Project, https://borgenproject.org/10-facts-about-brac/.
113 **Originally Bangladeshi:** Ian Smillie, *Freedom from Want: The Remarkable Success Story of BRAC, the Global Grassroots Organization That's Winning the Fight Against Poverty* (Sterling, VA: Kumarian Press, 2009).
113 **across the country:** "BRAC Microfinance Sierra Leone Limited," https://bracinternational .org/brac-microfinance-sierra-leone/.
114 **which forbids:** "Interest (riba)," Islamic Relief Worldwide, https://islamic-relief.org /interest-riba/.

Chapter 6: Bees
116 **Freedom from Hunger:** Interview with Kathleen Stack.
116 **nearing 70 percent:** "1999 Meeting of Councils, June 24–26, Abidjan, Cote d'Ivoire, Final Report," Microfinance Summit Campaign, 1999, 48.
116 **"I can":** "Women's Empowerment Impact Review," Freedom from Hunger.
117 **extended to repayment:** Muhammad Yunus, *Banker to the Poor: Micro-Lending and the Battle Against World Poverty* (New York: PublicAffairs, 2007), 58–72.
117 **in Mexico City:** Michaela Walsh, Shamina de Gonzaga, and Lilia Clemente, *Founding a Movement: Women's World Banking, 1975–1990* (New York: Cosimo Books, 2012).
117 **cockfights:** "Indonesia's Badan Kredit Kecamatan (BKK)," *Daily Yomiuri*, February 10, 1995.
117 **"destitute mother":** Yunus, *Banker to the Poor*, 72.
118 **millions of borrowers:** Interview with Kathleen Stack.
118 **Grameen Trust:** Yunus, *Banker to the Poor*, 155–63.
118 **United States, Europe, Australia, Japan:** "Letters to the Editor," *Grameen Dialogue*, no. 31, July 1997.
118 **Women's World Banking:** Walsh et al., *Founding a Movement*.
119 **"bees" who "trans-pollinated their ideas":** Parker MacDonald Shipton, *Credit Between Cultures: Farmers, Financiers, and Misunderstanding in Africa* (New Haven, CT: Yale University Press, 2010), 180.
119 **friends in Bangladesh's finance ministry:** Yunus, *Banker to the Poor*, 117–19.
119 **Katalysis Partnership:** "About Us," Namaste, https://namastedirect.org/about-us/.
119 **They shared drinks:** Erin Beck, *How Development Projects Persist: Everyday Negotiations with Guatemalan NGOs* (Durham, NC: Duke University Press, 2017), 67–68.
120 **official government entourage:** Interview with Elizabeth Littlefield.
120 **Sékou Touré:** Interview with Paul Rippey.
120 **private institutions:** Susan Johnson and Ben Rogaly, "Microfinance and Poverty Reduction," Oxfam UK and Ireland and ACTIONAID, 1997.

120 **had been integral:** Nicola Banks, David Hulme, and Michael Edwards, "NGOs, States, and Donors Revisited: Still Too Close for Comfort?" *World Development* 66 (February 1, 2015): 707–18.

121 **"sweethearts":** Banks et al., "NGOs, States, and Donors Revisited."

121 **By the early 1990s:** Beck, *How Development Projects Persist*, 45.

121 **over three million:** "India," Indian Center for Not-for-Profit Law, https://www.icnl .org/resources/civic-freedom-monitor/india.

121 **lobby on behalf of:** Interview with Elisabeth Rhyne.

121 **"professional":** Aksartova, "Why NGOs?"

121 **"crisis of confidence":** Lester M. Salamon, "The Rise of the Nonprofit Sector," *Foreign Affairs*, July 1, 1994.

122 **"Structural Adjustment Programs":** "Structural Adjustment Programmes," United Nations Economic and Social Commission for Western Asia, https://archive.unescwa.org /structural-adjustment-programmes.

122 **reduced financial regulation:** Ngozi Okonjo-Iweala and Philip Osafo-Kwaako, "Nigeria's Economic Reforms: Progress and Challenges," Brookings Institution, March 2007.

122 **reduced price guarantees:** Eric Toussaint, "IMF: Inhuman at the Micro and Macro Levels," Committee for the Abolition of Illegitimate Debt, February 27, 2020, https:// www.cadtm.org/IMF-Inhuman-at-the-micro-and-macro-levels.

122 **Basic services:** F. E. Ogbimi, "Structural Adjustment Is the Wrong Policy," *African Technology Forum* 8, no. 1, http://web.mit.edu/africantech/www/articles/PlanningAdjust .htm#1.

122 **fill the void:** Ian Gary, "Confrontation, Co-operation or Co-optation: NGOs and the Ghanaian State During Structural Adjustment," *Review of African Political Economy* 23, no. 68 (June 1996): 149–68.

122 **half of all new:** Peter Hall-Jones, "The Rise and Rise of NGOs," Public Services International, May 2006.

122 **education services in Kenya:** Beck, *How Development Projects Persist*, 45.

122 **about a third:** Sada Aksartova, "Why NGOs? How American Donors Embraced Civil Society After the Cold War," *International Journal of Not-for-Profit Law* 8, no. 3 (May 2006).

122 **charging for services:** Salmaan Keshavjee, *Blind Spot: How Neoliberalism Infiltrated Global Health* (Oakland: University of California Press, 2014).

122 **half of all NGO revenue:** Hall-Jones, "The Rise and Rise of NGOs."

122 **The country faced:** Ogbimi, "Structural Adjustment Is the Wrong Policy."

123 **"sharp increase":** "Lift Above Poverty Organization (LAPO)," Kiva.org, https:// www.kiva.org/about/where-kiva-works/partners/20#LAPOupdate.

123 **"in place of social security":** Yunus, *Banker to the Poor*, 228–30.

123 **primarily to access:** J. D. Von Pischke, "*Methodenstreit* and Sustainability in Microfinance: Generalizations Describing Institutional Frameworks," in Thomas Dichter and Malcolm Harper, eds., *What's Wrong with Microfinance?* (Rugby, Warwickshire, UK: Practical Action Publishing, 2007), 125.

124 **Such groups:** Aksartova, "Why NGOs?"

124 **$100 million:** Milford Bateman, "De-industrialization and Social Disintegration in Bosnia," in Dichter and Harper, *What's Wrong with Microfinance?*, 207.

124 **proclaimed, "self-employment":** "Declaration and Plan of Action," Microcredit Summit, February 2–4, 1997.

124 **a bill passed:** "H.R.4073—To amend the Microenterprise for Self-Reliance Act of 2000 and the Foreign Assistance Act of 1961 to increase assistance for the poorest people in developing countries under microenterprise assistance programs under those Acts, and for other purposes," 107th Congress (2001–2002).

124 **ease often painful transitions:** "Microcredit Summit +5, November 10–13, 2002, New York City, Final Report," Microcredit Summit Campaign, 49.

125 **"Communist Professor":** Yunus, *Banker to the Poor*, 97–204.

125 **tell the *Guardian*:** Miriam Cosic, "'We Are All Entrepreneurs': Muhammad Yunus on Changing the World, One Microloan at a Time," *Guardian*, March 28, 2017, https:// www.theguardian.com/sustainable-business/2017/mar/29/we-are-all-entrepreneurs -muhammad-yunus-on-changing-the-world-one-microloan-at-a-time.

125 **Mexican farmers struggled:** Michael Pollan, "A Flood of U.S. Corn Rips at Mexico. Under Free Trade, Small Farmers and the Nation's Ecology Are Suffering," *Los Angeles Times,* April 23, 2004.

125 **as an answer:** Milford Bateman, *Why Doesn't Microfinance Work? The Destructive Rise of Local Neoliberalism* (London: Zed Books, 2010).

126 **in the wake of severe flooding:** Yunus, *Banker to the Poor,* 138.

126 **the expansion in microlending:** S. M. Rahman, "A Practitioner's View of the Challenges Facing NGO-Based Microfinance in Bangladesh," in Dichter and Harper, *What's Wrong with Microfinance?*

126 **reportedly opened:** Todd S. Purdum, "Bengali Women Are Candid with Hillary Clinton," *New York Times,* April 4, 1995.

127 **"cost-effective job creation":** "Microcredit Creates Jobs," *Grameen Dialogue,* no. 39, July 1999.

127 **hundreds of millions:** "A.I.D. Microenterprise Development Program Report to the Congress," U.S. Agency for International Development, March 30, 1990.

127 **meeting arranged by:** Sam Daley-Harris, "At the Knee of Muhammad Yunus: Stories of Hope and a New Way of Seeing the World," unpublished essay.

127 **then met Michaela:** Interview with Michaela Walsh.

127 **contributed to:** Yunus, *Banker to the Poor,* 164.

127 **"personally, absolutely":** Daley-Harris, "At the Knee of Muhammad Yunus."

127 **a group of donors:** "CGAP: 20 Years of Financial Inclusion Progress," CGAP, https://www.cgap.org/blog/series/cgap-20-years-financial-inclusion-progress.

128 **Even though agriculture:** Malcolm Harper, "Microfinance and Farmers: Do They Fit?" in Dichter and Harper, *What's Wrong with Microfinance?*, 83–84.

128 **mostly neglected:** Dale Adams, "The Birth of a New Paradigm in Rural Finance: AID's Role," USAID, May 11, 2011.

128 **rebrand themselves:** Shipton, *Credit Between Cultures,* 185.

128 *away* **from other programs:** Joanna Ledgerwood, *Microfinance Handbook: An Institutional and Financial Perspective* (Washington, DC: World Bank, 1999).

128 **discarded a broad focus:** Greg Chen and Stuart Rutherford, "A Microcredit Crisis Averted: The Case of Bangladesh," CGAP Focus Note, no. 87, July 2013.

128 **offered additional services:** Richard Morse, Anisur Rahman, and Kersten L. Johnson, eds., *Grassroot Horizons: Connecting Participatory Development Initiatives East and West* (Rugby, Warwickshire, UK: Practical Action Publishing, 1995).

128 **"everyone needs a loan":** Paul Rippey, "Everyone Needs a Loan . . . ," SavingsRevolution, http://www.savings-revolution.org/homepage/2018/6/11/everyone-needs-a-loan.

Chapter 7: New Goals

134 **had lunch:** Muhammad Yunus, *Banker to the Poor: Micro-Lending and the Battle Against World Poverty* (New York: PublicAffairs, 2007), 175–76.

134 **"the most important":** Mehrsa Baradaran, *How the Other Half Banks: Exclusion, Exploitation, and the Threat to Democracy* (Cambridge, MA: Harvard University Press, 2015), 162.

134 **net early funding:** Yunus, *Banker to the Poor,* 112–13.

134 **Two of South Shore's:** Yunus, *Banker to the Poor,* 175–76.

134 **"economic basket cases":** Jann S. Wenner, Hunter S. Thompson, William Greider, and P. J. O'Rourke, "Bill Clinton: The Rolling Stone Interview," *Rolling Stone,* September 17, 1992.

135 **specifically in his home state of Arkansas:** "Bill Clinton on the Microcredit Summit Campaign," Microcredit Summit Campaign, https://www.youtube.com/watch?v=6_HI4YleK8E.

135 **"pocket of poverty":** Milford Bateman, "The Power of a Dollar," *Jacobin,* November 11, 2015, https://jacobin.com/2015/11/microcredit-muhammad-yunus-bono-clinton-foundation-global-poverty-entrepreneurial-charity.

135 **"firebrand feminist":** Pat Morrison, "Time for a Feminist as First Lady?" *Los Angeles Times,* 1992.

136 **shoulder-length:** "On This Day: Secretary Clinton's 1995 United Nations Speech— 'Women's Rights Are Human Rights,'" Clinton Foundation, https://www.youtube.com/watch?v=L7evFMipVZE.

136 **"are women's rights":** Hillary Rodham Clinton, "Read Hillary Rodham Clinton's 'Women's Rights' Speech from 1995," *The Atlantic*, September 1, 2020, https://www.theatlantic.com /politics/archive/2020/09/read-hillary-rodham-clintons-womens-rights-speech/615733/.

136 **conference declaration:** "Beijing Declaration and Platform for Action: Beijing+5 Political Declaration and Outcome," UN Women, 1995.

136 **rallying cry:** "Women's Rights," Amnesty International, https://www.amnesty.org/en /what-we-do/discrimination/womens-rights/.

136 **"highly successful":** "First Lady Hillary Rodham Clinton Remarks for the United Nations Fourth World Conference on Women," September 5, 1995.

136 **which Clinton attended:** Hillary Rodham Clinton, "Read Hillary Rodham Clinton's 'Women's Rights' Speech from 1995."

136 **"Credit Corner":** "Snapshots from Beijing: Women's Economic Rights Take Center Stage," Women's World Banking, September 14, 2015, https://www.womensworldbanking .org/insights-and-impact/snapshots-from-beijing-womens-economic-rights-take-center -stage/.

137 **TV clips:** "BANGLADESH: HILLARY & CHELSEA CLINTON VISIT UPDATE," AP Archive, https://www.youtube.com/watch?v=rfXV803Lo2c.

137 **age thirteen:** Todd S. Purdum, "Bengali Women Are Candid with Hillary Clinton," *New York Times*, April 4, 1995.

137 **Oval Room:** Sam Daley-Harris, "At the Knee of Muhammad Yunus: Stories of Hope and a New Way of Seeing the World," unpublished essay.

137 **"power dining destination":** Tierney Plumb, "Longstanding Power Dining Destination the Oval Room Has Closed for Good," *Eater DC*, November 10, 2020, https://dc .eater.com/2020/11/10/21559069/oval-room-closing-fine-dining-white-house-d-c.

137 **"platform for action":** "Snapshots from Beijing."

137 **"will flourish":** "Hillary Clinton—4th World Conference for Women Speech," AmericanRhetoric.com, https://www.youtube.com/watch?v=6V9mHmeK7XM.

137 **half dozen:** Daley-Harris, "At the Knee of Muhammad Yunus."

137 **Millennium Development Goals:** "Introduction: 2000–2015," UN Documentation: Development, https://research.un.org/en/docs/dev/2000-2015.

138 **pull together a "microcredit summit":** Susan Davis and Vinod Khosla, "Taking Stock of the Microcredit Summit Campaign: What Worked and What Didn't Work 1997–2006? What Is Needed 2007–2015?" Microcredit Summit Campaign.

138 **agreed to be honorary cochair:** Interview with Sam Daley-Harris.

138 **one hundred million:** Sam Daley-Harris, *Reclaiming Our Democracy: Healing the Break Between People and Government* (Philadelphia: Camino Books, 1994), 244–45.

139 **40 percent annual growth:** "State of the Microcredit Summit Campaign Report 2001," Microcredit Summit Campaign.

139 **was again warned:** Daley-Harris, *Reclaiming Our Democracy*, 244–45.

139 **not ideal customers:** Interview with Sam Daley-Harris.

139 **February 1997:** Daley-Harris, "State of the Microcredit Summit Campaign Report 2007."

139 **"macro idea":** "#tbt: The 1997 Microcredit Summit, Where It All Began," Microcredit Summit Campaign, https://mcsummit.wordpress.com/2015/06/04/tbt-the-1997 -microcredit-summit-where-it-all-began/.

139 **"is a human right":** "1997 Microcredit Summit," Grameen, http://www.grameen.com /category/microcredit-summit-1997/.

139 **Women *must* be:** "Declaration and Plan of Action," Microcredit Summit, February 2–4, 1997.

140 **more unusual participants:** Participant list, Microcredit Summit, February 2–4, 1997.

140 **back in the 1980s:** Jake Samuelson, "Bob Annibale: Banker to the Banker of the Poor?" *Next Billion*, https://nextbillion.net/bob-annibale-banker-to-the-banker-of-the-poor/.

140 **as global inequality increased:** Jason Hickel, *The Divide: A Brief Guide to Global Inequality and Its Solutions* (London: William Heinemann, 2017).

140 **"shareholder primacy":** Sheelah Kolhatkar, "The C.E.O. of Anti-Woke, Inc.," *New Yorker*, December 12, 2022.

141 **good while doing well:** Latapí Agudelo, Mauricio Andrés, Lára Jóhannsdóttir, and Brynhildur Davídsdóttir, "A Literature Review of the History and Evolution of Corporate

Social Responsibility," *International Journal of Corporate Social Responsibility* 4, no. 1 (January 22, 2019): 1.

141 **"productive work":** "Microcredit Summit Report," Microcredit Summit Campaign.

142 **$21 billion:** Daley-Harris, "State of the Microcredit Summit Campaign Report 2007."

142 **Not just to reach the poorest:** Daley-Harris, *Reclaiming Our Democracy*, 244.

142 **still relied on:** "Microcredit and Microenterprise: The Road to Self-Reliance," Hearing Before the Subcommittee on International Economic Policy and Trade of the Committee on International Relations, July 23, 1997.

142 **only 26 of the 481:** "Reaching Down and Scaling Up: Meeting the Microenterprise Development Challenge," U.S. Agency for International Development, Microenterprise Results Reporting for 1997.

142 **"independence from":** Judith Tendler, "Small Firms, the Informal Sector, and the Devil's Deal," *IDS Bulletin* 33, no. 3 (July 2002).

142 **special act of parliament:** "The Tuesday Podcast: What's Better for Helping the Poor—Greed or Charity?" WBUR, September 28, 2010, https://www.wbur.org/npr/130194702/the-tuesday-podcast-what-s-better-for-helping-poor-people----greed-or-charity.

143 **over $150 million:** Connie Bruck, "Millions for Millions," *New Yorker*, October 22, 2006.

143 **mid-1990s:** Shahidur Khandker, Baqui Khalily, and Zahed Khan, "Is Grameen Bank Sustainable?" Human Resources Development and Operations Policy Working Papers, World Bank, February 1994.

143 **reiterated at the summit:** "Declaration and Plan of Action."

143 **"Ten P's":** "Vote of Thanks from H. E. Dr. Jamo, the Ambassador of Mozambique," in "Report on the Southern Africa Region Microcredit Summit (SARMS)," Lusaka, Zambia, September 22–25, 1998.

143 **had started to do:** Greg Chen and Stuart Rutherford, "A Microcredit Crisis Averted: The Case of Bangladesh," CGAP Focus Note, no. 87, July 2013, https://www.cgap.org/sites/default/files/Focus-Note-A-Microcredit-Crisis-Averted-July-2013.pdf.

143 **expansive umbrella:** Interview with Sam Daley-Harris.

143 **Delegates did agree:** "Declaration and Plan of Action."

144 **"of the planet":** Daley-Harris, "State of the Microcredit Summit Campaign Report 2007."

144 **"truly historic occasion":** Daley-Harris, *Reclaiming Our Democracy*, 245.

Traffic Fines: Freetown, Sierra Leone

147 **over one thousand:** "Fernando Moleres: 'Merciless Justice,'" Prison Photography, https://prisonphotography.org/tag/pademba-road-prison/.

148 **inflation hit:** "Sierra Leone: Inflation Rate from 1988 to 2028," Statista, https://www.statista.com/statistics/1044774/inflation-rate-in-sierra-leone/.

Chapter 8: Nope

150 **"hot idea":** "Opinion: Micro-Loans for the Very Poor," *New York Times*, February 16, 1997.

150 **during a congressional hearing:** "Microcredit and Microenterprise: The Road to Self-Reliance," Hearing Before the Subcommittee on International Economic Policy and Trade of the Committee on International Relations, July 23, 1997.

151 **Indira Gandhi Prize:** *Grameen Dialogue*, no. 41, January 2000.

151 **To Our Credit:** "To Our Credit: Bootstrap Banking and the World," PBS, September 1998.

151 **"This business approach":** "Declaration and Plan of Action," Microcredit Summit, February 2–4, 1997.

151 **exuberant claims:** "Microcredit Summit +5, November 10–13, 2002, New York City, Final Report," Microcredit Summit Campaign.

152 **Banker to the Poor:** Muhammad Yunus, *Banker to the Poor: Micro-Lending and the Battle Against World Poverty* (New York: PublicAffairs, 2007), ix.

152 **new institutions sprang up:** "Reaching Down and Scaling Up: Meeting the Microenterprise Development Challenge," U.S. Agency for International Development, Microenterprise Results Reporting for 1997.

153 **Between 1997:** "Empowering Women with Microcredit," Microcredit Summit Campaign Report 2000.

153 **USAID estimated:** "USAID's Contribution to Microfinance: From Microfinance to Financial Inclusion," prepared by Anicca Jansen for the Office of Microenterprise and Private Enterprise Promotion, October 2014.

153 **By 2004:** Susan Davis and Vinod Khosla, "Taking Stock of the Microcredit Summit Campaign: What Worked and What Didn't Work 1997–2006? What Is Needed 2007–2015?" Microcredit Summit Campaign.

153 **"in celebration of":** Thomas Dichter, "Introduction," in Thomas Dichter and Malcolm Harper, eds., *What's Wrong with Microfinance?* (Rugby, Warwickshire, UK: Practical Action Publishing, 2007), 5.

153 **175 million of the world's poorest families:** Sam Daley-Harris, "State of the Microcredit Summit Campaign Report 2007," Microcredit Summit Campaign.

153 **"free from poverty":** Ansel Karnani, "Microfinance Misses Its Mark," *Stanford Social Innovation Review*, Summer 2007.

153 **"The Year of Microcredit":** "Introduction: 2000–2015," UN Documentation: Development, https://research.un.org/en/docs/dev/2000-2015.

153 **"whose time has come":** Dina Pomeranz, "The Promise of Microfinance and Women's Empowerment: What Does the Evidence Say?" Discussion Paper, Harvard Business School, 2014.

153 **officially endorsed microfinance:** Davis and Khosla, "Taking Stock of the Microcredit Summit Campaign."

153 **In 2006:** Sam Daley-Harris, "State of the Microcredit Summit Campaign Report 2007."

154 **Ali looked down:** Malcolm Harper, "Microfinance and Farmers: Do They Fit?" in Dichter and Harper, *What's Wrong with Microfinance?*, 83.

154 **sometimes affording it:** Judy Mann, "Partnership Takes Bioscience to Bangladesh," *Washington Post*, July 3, 1998.

154 **$2 a day:** Iqbal Quadir, "How Mobile Phones Can Fight Poverty," TEDGlobal 2005, https://www.ted.com/talks/iqbal_quadir_how_mobile_phones_can_fight_poverty.

154 **teamed up with:** Mann, "Partnership Takes Bioscience to Bangladesh."

155 **words of *Forbes*:** Helen Coster, "Danone and Grameen Bank: Partners in CSR and Marketing," *Forbes*, May 21, 2021, https://www.forbes.com/sites/csr/2010/05/21/danone -and-grameen-bank-partners-in-csr-and-marketing/.

155 **Some warned that:** Daley-Harris, "State of the Microcredit Summit Campaign Report 2007."

155 ***Times* editorial:** "Opinion: Micro-Loans for the Very Poor."

156 **"imposed from outside":** Diana Drake, "5 Truths About Microfinance," Wharton Global Youth Program, October 3, 2018, https://globalyouth.wharton.upenn.edu/articles /social-impact/5-truths-microfinance/.

156 **"world's biggest loan shark":** Harper, "Microfinance and Farmers: Do They Fit?", 83.

156 **Monica Yunus:** "Metropolitan Opera Soprano Monica Yunus, Daughter of 2006 Nobel Peace Prize Winner, to Perform at Nobel Concert Dec. 11, 2006, in Oslo, Norway," Top40-charts.com, December 7, 2006, https://top40-charts.com/news.php?nid=29012.

156 **"for their efforts":** "Press Release," Nobel Peace Prize, 2006, https://www.nobelprize.org /prizes/peace/2006/press-release/.

157 **"borrowers-cum-owners":** "Muhammad Yunus Nobel Lecture," Nobel Peace Prize, 2006.

157 **to buy a goat:** "Muhammad Yunus," World Summit of Nobel Peace Laureates, http: //www.nobelpeacesummit.com/muhammad-yunus/.

157 **"important liberating force":** Daley-Harris, "State of the Microcredit Summit Campaign Report 2007."

157 **"a more deserving recipient":** "Bill Clinton on the Microcredit Summit Campaign," Microcredit Summit Campaign, https://www.youtube.com/watch?v=6_HI4YleK8E.

158 **wrote a letter:** Elizabeth Littlefield correspondence with the Norwegian Nobel Institute, April 10, 2002.

Layers: Old Post, Koidu, Kono, Eastern Sierra Leone

164 **Many of those:** Interview and review of court documents with Kemoh Kandeh, paralegal at the Legal Aid Board's Kono office.

Chapter 9: So Much Money

169 **One hundred thousand people:** "Bosnia and Herzegovina, 1992–1995," United States Holocaust Memorial Museum, https://www.ushmm.org/genocide-prevention/countries /bosnia-herzegovina/case-study/background/1992-1995.

170 **long history:** "Economy of Bosnia and Herzegovina," *Encyclopedia Britannica*, https: //www.britannica.com/place/Bosnia-and-Herzegovina/Economy.

171 **Accion was cautious at first:** Interview with Elisabeth Rhyne.

171 **2.2 percent return:** "To Our Credit: Bootstrap Banking and the World," PBS, September 1998.

171 **curious to see:** "USAID's Contribution to Microfinance: From Microfinance to Financial Inclusion," prepared by Anicca Jansen for the Office of Microenterprise and Private Enterprise Promotion, October 2014.

171 **ProDem became BancoSol:** "To Our Credit: Bootstrap Banking and the World."

171 **the largest microfinance lender in Bolivia:** "Remarks by the First Lady at the Microcredit Summit," White House Office of the Press Secretary, February 3, 1997, https: //clintonwhitehouse5.archives.gov/WH/EOP/First_Lady/html/generalspeeches/1997 /19970919-16145.html.

173 **spurred generous support:** Muhammad Yunus, *Banker to the Poor: Micro-Lending and the Battle Against World Poverty* (New York: PublicAffairs, 2007).

173 **The World Bank's support:** Sam Daley-Harris, "At the Knee of Muhammad Yunus: Stories of Hope and a New Way of Seeing the World," unpublished essay.

173 **pledged 30 percent:** Sam Daley-Harris, "State of the Microcredit Summit Campaign Report 2007," Microcredit Summit Campaign.

173 **now ramped up:** "USAID's Contribution to Microfinance."

173 **USAID now required:** "Functional Series 200—Programming Policy: AIDS Chapter 219 Microenterprise Development," Partial Revision Date: March 10, 2021, USAID.

174 **how this worked:** Interview with Sharon D'Onofrio, January 4, 2020.

174 **market-oriented approach:** Raimar Dieckmann, "Microfinance: An Emerging Investment Opportunity. Uniting Social Investment and Financial Returns," Deutsche Bank Research, December 19, 2007.

174 **was committed to:** Paul Breloff, "Accion Venture Lab: Case Narrative," *Innovations: Technology, Governance, Globalization* 10, nos. 1–2 (2015): 75–93.

174 **Accion's primary focus:** Breloff, "Accion Venture Lab: Case Narrative."

176 **"downward spiral":** Chuck Waterfield, "Advocating Transparent Pricing in Microfinance: A Review of MFTransparency's Work and a Proposed Future Path for the Industry," MFTRansparency.org, July 15, 2015, https://www.mftransparency.org/wp-content/uploads /2015/08/MFTransparency-Advocating-Transparent-Pricing-in-Microfinance.pdf.

176 **Truth in Lending Act:** "Truth in Lending," Office of the Comptroller of the Currency, https://www.occ.treas.gov/topics/consumers-and-communities/consumer-protection/truth -in-lending/index-truth-in-lending.html.

176 **"appropriate interest rates":** "1999 Meeting of Councils, June 24–26, Abidjan, Cote d'Ivoire, Final Report," Microfinance Summit Campaign.

176 **Lenders could:** Vijay Mahajan, "From Microcredit to Livelihood Finance," in Thomas Dichter and Malcolm Harper, eds., *What's Wrong with Microfinance?* (Rugby, Warwickshire, UK: Practical Action Publishing, 2007), 243.

176 **Kenyan lender transitioned:** Parker MacDonald Shipton, *Credit Between Cultures: Farmers, Financiers, and Misunderstanding in Africa* (New Haven, CT: Yale University Press, 2010), 188–89.

177 **was essential:** "Reaching Down and Scaling Up: Meeting the Microenterprise Development Challenge," U.S. Agency for International Development, Microenterprise Results Reporting for 1997.

177 **more financially stable:** Jonathan Morduch, "How Statistics Shaped Microfinance," New York University and Institute for Advanced Study, November 17, 2016.

177 **even FINCA:** Interview with Sharon D'Onofrio.

177 **sometimes required collateral:** Susan Johnson and Namrata Sharma, "'Institutionalizing Suspicion': The Management and Government Challenge in User-Owned Microfinance Groups," in Dichter and Harper, *What's Wrong with Microfinance?*, 50, 61.

177 **left the poorest out:** Paul Mosley and David Hulme, "Microenterprise Finance: Is There a Conflict Between Growth and Poverty Alleviation?" *World Development* 26, no. 5 (May 1, 1998): 783–90.

177 **discouraged from applying:** Fabrizio Felloni, Hans Dieter Seibel, and Andres Cornejo, "Mainstreaming Grameen Banking in Philippines," in Malcolm Harper and Sukhwinder Singh Arora, eds., *Small Customers, Big Market: Commercial Banks in Microfinance* (Warwickshire, UK: ITDG Publishing, 2005), 32.

177 **By 2005:** S. M. Rahman, "A Practitioner's View of the Challenges Facing NGO-Based Microfinance in Bangladesh," in Dichter and Harper, *What's Wrong with Microfinance?*, 194.

177 **poor borrowers paid *double*:** Malcolm Harper, "What's Wrong with Groups?" in Dichter and Harper, *What's Wrong with Microfinance?*, 38.

178 **veered away from:** Sam Daley-Harris, *Reclaiming Our Democracy: Healing the Break Between People and Government* (Philadelphia: Camino Books, 1994), 246.

178 **not only rational:** Mahajan, "From Microcredit to Livelihood Finance," in Dichter and Harper, *What's Wrong with Microfinance?*

178 **Other institutions joined USAID:** Harper et al., eds., *Small Customers, Big Market*, 133, 149, 181–82, 205, 211.

179 **Antonio Vives:** "Microcredit Summit +5, November 10–13, 2002, New York City, Final Report," Microcredit Summit Campaign.

180 **UN staffer warned:** "To Our Credit: Bootstrap Banking and the World."

180 **"market-based, results-oriented":** Erin Beck, *How Development Projects Persist: Everyday Negotiations with Guatemalan NGOs* (Durham, NC: Duke University Press, 2017), 55.

180 **making sure the *lenders* were:** Kim Wilson, "The Moneylenders Dilemma," in Dichter and Harper, *What's Wrong with Microfinance?*, 98.

Chapter 10: Like a Drug

187 **third-largest initial public offering:** Yahoo! Finance, "This Day in Market History: The Yahoo! IPO," April 12, 2018, https://finance.yahoo.com/news/day-market-history-yahoo-ipo-160806008.html.

188 **"low correlation":** Raimar Dieckmann, "Microfinance: An Emerging Investment Opportunity. Uniting Social Investment and Financial Returns," Deutsche Bank Research, December 19, 2007.

188 **in 1997 Deutsche Bank:** Rocio Cavazos and Melanie Meslay, "Fund Assessment Study Microfinance Subordinated Debt Fund: VG Microfinance-Invest Nr. 1," Deutsche Bank Global Social Finance February 2015.

188 **the East Asian Miracle:** Nancy M. Birdsall et al., *The East Asian Miracle: Economic Growth and Public Policy*, A World Bank Policy Research Report (Washington, DC: World Bank Group, 1993).

188 **eager to find new investments:** "355: The Giant Pool of Money," *This American Life*, May 9, 2008.

189 **MBA from Harvard:** Elizabeth Funk, "About Elizabeth Funk, CEO and Founder of Dignity Capital," Medium.com, November 16, 2018, https://medium.com/@Elizabeth-FunkCA/about-elizabeth-funk-ceo-and-founder-of-dignity-capital-1df6730dc7de.

190 **in *Grameen Dialogue*:** *Grameen Dialogue*, no. 31, July 1997.

190 **David Gibbons:** "To Our Credit: Bootstrap Banking and the World," PBS, September 1998.

190 **cement relationships:** Interview with Steven Funk.

191 **"dual goals":** Letter to Dignity Fund investors, March 25, 2011.

191 **fourteen microfinance organizations:** "Profile of Microfinance Institutions Funded (Data as of 12/31/2008)," Dignity Fund.

192 **"democratize the marketplace":** Connie Bruck, "Millions for Millions," *New Yorker*, October 22, 2006.

192 **worth nearly $1 billion:** Jennifer Sullivan, "Investor Frenzy over eBay IPO," *Wired*, September 24, 1998.

192 **grew frustrated:** Interview with Matt Bannick.

192 **opened the Omidyar Network:** "Turning Breakdowns into Breakthroughs: How Omidyar Network Is Contributing to Systems Change," Omidyar Network, July 13, 2022, https://omidyar.com/turning-breakdowns-into-breakthroughs-how-omidyar-network-is-contributing-to-systems-change/.

192 **"you're done!":** Bruck, "Millions for Millions."

193 **serve two purposes:** Alexandra Bogus, "Tufts Microfinance Fund Sees Strong Returns in Fiscal Year 2008," *Tufts Daily*, April 6, 2009.
193 **concentrated in Europe:** Interview with Elisabeth Rhyne.
193 **Triodos:** Interview with Michaela Walsh.
193 **later funneled money into:** Simon Pfanner, "MICROCAPITAL BRIEF: Triodos Sells 14.5% Equity Stake in K-rep Bank of Kenya to Existing Shareholders Centrum Investment, K-rep Group," *MicroCapital*, November 29, 2014, https://www.microcapital.org /microcapital-brief-triodos-sells-14-5-equity-stake-in-k-rep-bank-of-kenya-to-existing -shareholders-centum-investment-k-rep-group/.
193 **especially in Scandinavia:** Interview with Joan Trant.
193 **TIAA-CREF:** "TIAA-CREF Launches $100 Million Global Microfinance Investment Program," *Philanthropy News Digest*, September 21, 2006, https:// philanthropynewsdigest.org/news/tiaa-cref-launches-100-million-global-microfinance -investment-program.
194 **Large commercial banks:** Harper et al., eds., *Small Customers, Big Market*, 1–6, 59–63, 209–15.
194 **within Latin America:** Erin Beck, *How Development Projects Persist: Everyday Negotiations with Guatemalan NGOs* (Durham, NC: Duke University Press, 2017), 54.
194 **Citigroup's charitable foundation:** Accion, "Bruce Tippett: The Father of Microfinance," Medium.com, March 26, 2015, https://medium.com/@Accion/the-father-of -microfinance-20feb3bd6dfd.
194 **worked with the Grameen Trust:** *Grameen Dialogue*, no. 39, July 1999.
194 **Victor Menezes:** "Microcredit Summit +5, November 10–13, 2002, New York City, Final Report."
195 **Standard Chartered announced:** "Foundations Turn to Microfinance to Fight Poverty," *Philanthropy News Digest*, May 3, 2006.
195 **"commercially viable proposition":** Interview with Prashant Thakker.
195 **Morgan Stanley microfinance CLO:** Neil Unmack, "Morgan Stanley Sells CLO to Fund Nicaraguan Potters," *Bloomberg News*, May 31, 2007.
195 **Thomas Friedman:** *Grameen Dialogue*, no. 41, January 2000.
197 **shied away from:** Interview with Joan Trant.
197 **9 percent return:** Bruck, "Millions for Millions."
197 **still beat out:** Interview with Joan Trant.
198 **between 9 and 25 percent:** Interview with Joan Trant.
198 **return on equity:** Dieckmann, "Microfinance: An Emerging Investment Opportunity."
198 **Alphabet:** "Alphabet ROE 2010–2022 | GOOG," https://www.macrotrends.net/stocks /charts/GOOG/alphabet/roe.
198 **most major U.S. industries:** "Return on Equity by Sector (US)," NYU Stern School of Business, January 2022, https://pages.stern.nyu.edu/~adamodar/New_Home_Page/datafile /roe.html.
198 **LAPO boasted return:** Chuck Waterfield, "Advocating Transparent Pricing in Microfinance: A Review of MFTransparency's Work and a Proposed Future Path for the Industry," MFTransparency.org, July 15, 2015, https://www.mftransparency.org/wp-content/uploads /2015/08/MFTransparency-Advocating-Transparent-Pricing-in-Microfinance.pdf.
198 **one Deutsche Bank operation:** "Global Social Investment Fund: Global Commercial Microfinance Consortium I," Deutsche Bank Community Development Finance Group.
199 **paid off their debts early:** "Dignity Fund 2009 Impact Report," Dignity Fund.
199 **on behalf of FINCA lenders:** "FINCA Microfinance Fund B.V.," https:// impactyield.com/funds/finca-microfinance-fund-b-v.
199 **$80.6 million:** Ben Thornley and Daniel Brett, "Case Study: Deutsche Bank Global Commercial Microfinance Consortium 1," November 2013.
199 **on the fund's board:** "Elizabeth Funk," Dignity Capital, https://web.archive.org/web /20220122041028/https://dignitycapital.squarespace.com/efunk.
199 **$35 billion:** Letter to Dignity Fund investors, March 25, 2011.
199 **made $105 million:** Isabella Steger, "Microfinance Growing in Attraction to Private-Equity," *Wall Street Journal*, November 18, 2012.

Chapter 11: We Rode the Fad for as Long as We Could

203 **sent in lengthy spreadsheets:** Jonathan Morduch, "How Statistics Shaped Micro-finance," New York University and Institute for Advanced Study, November 17, 2016.

203 **annual updates:** "State of the Microcredit Summit Campaign Report 2001," Microcredit Summit Campaign.

204 **"Small is beautiful":** Greg Chen, "Looking Ahead in 2023: Scaling Beautifully," BRAC, January 30, 2023, https://bracupgi.org/news-updates/policy/scaling-beautifully-2023/.

205 **could be dramatic:** Sam Daley-Harris, "At the Knee of Muhammad Yunus: Stories of Hope and a New Way of Seeing the World," unpublished essay.

205 **long-held notions:** Abhijit Banerjee and Esther Duflo, *Poor Economics: A Radical Rethinking of the Way to Fight Global Poverty* (New York: PublicAffairs, 2011).

206 **Lucy Saavedra:** Michaela Walsh, Shamina de Gonzaga, and Lilia Clemente, *Founding a Movement: Women's World Banking, 1975–1990* (New York: Cosimo Books, 2012), 62–64.

206 **Erin Beck writes in:** Erin Beck, *How Development Projects Persist: Everyday Negotiations with Guatemalan NGOs* (Durham, NC: Duke University Press, 2017), 78.

207 **women were becoming more empowered:** "Empowering Women with Microcredit," Microcredit Summit Campaign Report 2000.

207 **not thoroughly tested:** Ansel Karnani, "Microfinance Misses Its Mark," *Stanford Social Innovation Review*, Summer 2007.

207 **a fourth goal:** Sam Daley-Harris, *Reclaiming Our Democracy: Healing the Break Between People and Government* (Philadelphia: Camino Books, 1994), 244.

207 **wanted to track:** "Report on the Southern Africa Region Microcredit Summit (SARMS)," Lusaka, Zambia, September 22–25, 1998, Microcredit Summit Campaign.

208 **suggested doing:** Shirley Buzzard and Elaine Edgcomb, eds., "Monitoring and Evaluating Small Businesses: A Step by Step Guide for Private Development Organizations by Members of the Small Enterprise Evaluation Project," PACT, 1987.

208 **their incomes rise:** "Economic Capacity and Security Impact Review," Freedom from Hunger.

208 **weak connection:** "Ghana Nutrition Impact Study," Freedom from Hunger.

208 **"calculate reliably":** "1999 Meeting of Councils, June 24–26, Abidjan, Cote d'Ivoire, Final Report," Microcredit Summit Campaign.

208 **"will have failed":** "Empowering Women with Microcredit."

209 **Dead Aid:** Dambisa Moyo, *Dead Aid: Why Aid Is Not Working and How There Is a Better Way for Africa* (New York: Farrar, Straus and Giroux, 2009).

209 **White Man's Burden:** William Easterly, *The White Man's Burden: Why the West's Efforts to Aid the Rest Have Done So Much Ill and So Little Good* (New York: Penguin Press, 2006).

209 **"proven":** Sanjay Reddy, "Economics' Biggest Success Story Is a Cautionary Tale: Field Experiments Now Dominate Development Economics—Often at the Expense of the World's Poor," *Foreign Policy*, October 22, 2019.

210 **increase borrowers' profits and incomes:** Abhijit Banerjee, Esther Duflo, Rachel Glennerster, and Cynthia Kinnan, "The Miracle of Microfinance? Evidence from a Randomized Evaluation," *American Economic Journal: Applied Economics* 7, no. 1 (January 2015): 22–53.

211 **relatively well-off:** "Microcredit: Impact and Promising Innovations," Abdul Latif Poverty Action Lab, https://www.povertyactionlab.org/policy-insight/microcredit-impacts-and-limitations.

211 **more pressing things:** S. M. Rahman, "A Practitioner's View of the Challenges Facing NGO-Based Microfinance in Bangladesh," in Thomas Dichter and Malcolm Harper, eds., *What's Wrong with Microfinance?* (Rugby, Warwickshire, UK: Practical Action Publishing, 2007), 195.

211 **didn't seem to fight poverty:** Banerjee et al., "The Miracle of Microfinance?"

211 **actually decreased:** Justin Sandefur, "The Final Word on Microcredit?" Center for Global Development, January 22, 2015, https://www.cgdev.org/blog/final-word-microcredit.

211 **household costs:** Kathleen E. Odell, "Measuring the Impact of Microfinance: Looking to the Future," Grameen Foundation USA, 2015.

211 **actually *poorer*:** Vijay Mahajan, "From Microcredit to Livelihood Finance," in Dichter and Harper, *What's Wrong with Microfinance?*, 245.

211 **subtle change:** Connie Bruck, "Millions for Millions," *New Yorker*, October 22, 2006.

211 **trickle-down effects:** Sandefur, "The Final Word on Microcredit?"

211 **showed no impact:** "Microcredit: Impacts and Promising Innovations."

211 **more control:** "Impact Review: Teaching Entrepreneurship," Freedom from Hunger.

211 *increase* **in domestic violence:** Manuela Angelucci, Dean Karlan, and Jonathan Zinman, "Microcredit Impacts: Evidence from a Randomized Microcredit Program Placement Experiment by Compartamos Banco," *American Economic Journal: Applied Economics* 7, no. 1 (January 1, 2015): 151–82.

211 **intensely stressful:** "What Does the Evidence Tell Us?" Microfinanceandworldhunger .org, 2016, http://microfinanceandworldhunger.org/2013/06/wrap-up-of-the-evidence-project -what-the-evidence-tells-us/.

211 **shaming and social exclusion:** Dina Pomeranz, "The Promise of Microfinance and Women's Empowerment: What Does the Evidence Say?" Harvard Business School, Discussion Paper, February 2014.

212 **different contexts:** Sandefur, "The Final Word on Microcredit?"

212 **out of poverty:** "Microcredit: Impacts and Promising Innovations."

212 **"transformative effects":** Sandefur, "The Final Word on Microcredit?"

212 **"institutional outcomes":** "Impact Review: Teaching Entrepreneurship."

213 **"evaluation craze":** Jan P. Maes and Larry R. Reed, "State of the Microcredit Summit Campaign Report 2012," Microcredit Summit Campaign.

213 **being used to study:** "Randomly Controlled Trials of Public Policy," Institute for Public Policy and Social Research, Michigan State University, http://ippsr.msu.edu/public -policy/michigan-wonk-blog/randomized-controlled-trials-public-policy.

213 **festivals, and parties:** Banerjee et al., "The Miracle of Microfinance?"

213 **moralizing lessons:** Mehrsa Baradaran, *How the Other Half Banks: Exclusion, Exploitation, and the Threat to Democracy* (Cambridge, MA: Harvard University Press, 2015).

213 **"consumption smoothing":** Daryl Collins, Jonathan Morduch, Stuart Rutherford, and Orlanda Ruthven, *Portfolios of the Poor: How the World's Poor Live on $2 a Day* (Princeton, NJ: Princeton University Press, 2009).

213 **borrower's desire:** Banerjee et al., "The Miracle of Microfinance?

213 **borrower rationality:** "Microcredit: Impacts and Promising Innovations."

213 *could* **make money:** Dichter and Harper, *What's Wrong with Microfinance?*

214 **pushed borrowers toward:** Milford Bateman, "Microcredit in Cambodia: Why Is There So Much Support for a Failed Poverty Reduction Model?" *ISEAS Perspective*, no. 134, November 25, 2020.

214 **violent confrontations:** Milford Bateman, *Why Doesn't Microfinance Work? The Destructive Rise of Local Neoliberalism* (London: Zed Books, 2010).

214 **before seeing any:** Vijay Mahajan, "From Microcredit to Livelihood Finance," in Dichter and Harper, *What's Wrong with Microfinance?*, 247.

215 **worked to obscure:** Malcolm Harper and Sukhwinder Singh Arora, eds., *Small Customers, Big Market: Commercial Banks in Microfinance* (Warwickshire, UK: ITDG Publishing, 2005), 131, 180, 239.

216 **"represents the loss":** Judith Tendler, "Undoing the Poverty Agenda and Putting It Back Together: Social Policy, Economic Development, or What?" June 2006, https://media .entopanlab.it/storage/achii/media/judith-tendler/2000-2011/tendler_file1C2A_6-6-06.pdf.

216 **"as marginal":** Judith Tendler, "The Remarkable Convergence of Fashion on Small Enterprise and the Informal Sector: What Are the Implications for Policy?" December 3, 1987, https://media.entopanlab.it/storage/achii/media/judith-tendler/1980-1989 /Remarkable_Convergence_12_87.pdf.

216 **exceptionalism for the small:** Judith Tendler, "Small Firms, the Informal Sector, and the Devil's Deal," *IDS Bulletin* [Institute of Development Studies] 33, no. 3 (July 2002).

216 **Aneel Karnani:** Aneel Karnani, "Microfinance Misses Its Mark," *Stanford Social Innovation Review* 5, no. 3 (Summer 2007): 34–40.

216 **poorest in the world:** Alexander Cockburn, "The Myth of Microloans," *The Nation*, October 19, 2006.

217 **"struck by":** Mark Landler, "A New Gender Agenda," *New York Times*, August 18, 2009.

217 **to touch money:** Daley-Harris, "At the Knee of Muhammad Yunus."

217 **dominating small-scale commerce:** Akintola J. G. Wyse, *The Krio of Sierra Leone: An Interpretive History* (Washington, DC: Howard University Press, 1991).

217 **far more likely:** "Gender Inequality in Bangladesh: Engaging Men and Boys to Close the Gap," Concern Worldwide, February 28, 2022, https://www.concern.net/news/gender-inequality-in-bangladesh-closing-the-gap.

217 **"mop up":** Tendler, "Small Firms, the Informal Sector, and the Devil's Deal."

217 **"distracted attention":** Tendler, "Undoing the Poverty Agenda and Putting It Back Together."

218 **"keep the peace":** Tendler, "Undoing the Poverty Agenda and Putting It Back Together."

218 **"lack of capital":** Beck, *How Development Projects Persist*, 78.

218 **miss the very poor:** Muhammad Yunus, *Banker to the Poor: Micro-Lending and the Battle Against World Poverty* (New York: PublicAffairs, 2007), 212.

218 **remained inaccessible:** "Freedom from Hunger," Givewell.org, https://www.givewell.org/international/charities/freedom-from-hunger.

218 **"By contending":** Susan Davis and Vinod Khosla, "Taking Stock of the Microcredit Summit Campaign: What Worked and What Didn't Work 1997–2006? What Is Needed 2007–2015?" Microcredit Summit Campaign.

218 **"Will we find":** Sam Daley-Harris, "State of the Microcredit Summit Campaign Report 2007," Microcredit Summit Campaign.

219 **"found little impact":** "How to Measure Microfinance's Social Impact," *Forbes*, December 2, 2009.

219 **Doesn't Live Up:** Alex Counts, "Microfinance and the Backlash," *Stanford Social Innovation Review*, November 8, 2022, https://ssir.org/books/excerpts/entry/microfinance_and_the_backlash.

219 **NPR:** Nurith Aizenman, "You Asked, We Answer: Can Microloans Lift Women Out of Poverty?" NPR, November 1, 2016, https://www.npr.org/sections/goatsandsoda/2016/11/01/500093608/you-asked-we-answer-can-tiny-loans-lift-women-out-of-poverty.

220 **told the *New Yorker*:** Bruck, "Millions for Millions."

220 **Writing in 2007:** Malcolm Harper, "What's Wrong with Groups?" in Dichter and Harper, *What's Wrong with Microfinance?*, 1–6, 41.

220 **in Kerala, India:** Malcolm Harper, "Some Final Thoughts," in Dichter and Harper, *What's Wrong with Microfinance?*, 258.

221 **Yunus proclaimed:** "Muhammad Yunus Nobel Lecture," Nobel Peace Prize, 2006.

221 **broader constraints:** Eric Chetwynd Jr. and William R. Miner, *Pioneering in International Urban Development, Creating USAID Policies and Programs, 1970–1982: A Case Driven History of the Office of Urban Development*, Technical Assistance Bureau, U.S. Agency for International Development, 2018.

221 **"macroeconomic policy is crucial":** Richard Morse, Anisur Rahman, and Kersten Johnson, *Grassroot Horizons: Connecting Participatory Development Initiatives East and West* (Rugby, Warwickshire, UK: Practical Action Publishing, 1995), 89.

221 **Earlier research:** Simon Fass, "The Economics of Survival: A Study of Poverty and Planning in Haiti," U.S. Agency for International Development, October 1980.

221 **a main goal:** "About Us," SEWA, https://www.sewa.org/about-us/.

221 **"economic oxygen":** Diana Drake, "5 Truths About Microfinance," Wharton Global Youth Program, October 3, 2018, https://globalyouth.wharton.upenn.edu/articles/social-impact/5-truths-microfinance/.

Chapter 12: An Opportunity

229 **Oaxaca and Chiapas:** "The Implications of Increased Commercialization of the Microfinance Industry: What Can We Learn from the Discussions That Followed the Compartamos IPO?" MFI Solutions.

229 **Mother Teresa:** Gavin Finch and David Kocieniewski, "Big Money Backs Tiny Loans That Lead to Debt, Despair and Even Suicide," *Bloomberg*, May 3, 2022, https://www.bloomberg.com/graphics/2022-microfinance-banks-profit-off-developing-world/.

229 **From the beginning:** Connie Bruck, "Millions for Millions," *New Yorker*, October 22, 2006.

229 **To raise more money:** Richard Rosenberg, "CGAP Reflections on the Compartamos Initial Public Offering: A Case Study on Microfinance Interest Rates and Profits," Consultative Group to Assist the Poor, Focus Note no. 42, June 2007.

230 **was encouraged by:** Interview with Chuck Waterfield.

231 **55 percent:** "Banco Compartamos," Social Enterprise Case Series, Social Enterprise Institute, Northeastern University, 2010, https://www.northeastern.edu/sei/wp-content/uploads/2011/10/Banco_Compartamos.pdf.

231 **$57 million:** Noel Randewich, "UPDATE 2—Mexican Microlending Bank Surges in Market Debut," Reuters, April 20, 2007, https://www.reuters.com/article/mexico-compartamos-idUSN2025193920070420.

231 **with a profit margin:** Rosenberg, "CGAP Reflections on the Compartamos Initial Public Offering."

231 **18 percent of shares:** Milford Bateman, *Why Doesn't Microfinance Work? The Destructive Rise of Local Neoliberalism* (London: Zed Books, 2010), 143–44.

232 **$35 million:** Interview with Elisabeth Rhyne.

232 **bought most of the shares:** Rosenberg, "CGAP reflections on the Compartamos Initial Public Offering."

232 **"one-of-a-kind":** Randewich, "UPDATE 2—Mexican Microlending Bank Surges in Market Debut."

232 **$450 million:** Chuck Waterfield, "Advocating Transparent Pricing in Microfinance: A Review of MFTransparency's Work and a Proposed Future Path for the Industry," MFTransparency.org, July 15, 2015, https://www.mftransparency.org/wp-content/uploads/2015/08/MFTransparency-Advocating-Transparent-Pricing-in-Microfinance.pdf.

232 **$1 million:** Finch and Kocieniewski, "Big Money Backs Tiny Loans That Lead to Debt, Despair and Even Suicide."

232 **$135 million:** Rosenberg, "CGAP Reflections on the Compartamos Initial Public Offering."

232 **International Finance Corporation:** Randewich, "UPDATE 2—Mexican Microlending Bank Surges in Market Debut."

232 **$210 million:** Finch and Kocieniewski, "Big Money Backs Tiny Loans That Lead to Debt, Despair and Even Suicide."

232 **Private shareholders:** Bateman, *Why Doesn't Microfinance Work?*, 143–44.

232 **long missive:** Chuck Waterfield comments on Compartamos IPO, posted on the Microfinance Practice Yahoo! discussion group on April 23, 2007.

233 **"shocked by the news":** Sam Daley-Harris, "State of the Microcredit Summit Campaign Report 2007," Microcredit Summit Campaign.

233 **"raking in":** Chris Monasterski, "Muhammad Yunus Challenges Compartamos Bank," World Bank Blogs, Private Sector Development Blog, October 1, 2007, https://blogs.worldbank.org/psd/muhammad-yunus-challenges-compartamos-bank.

233 **"Profit and Poverty":** Michael Chu, "Profit and Poverty: Why It Matters," *Forbes*, December 20, 2007, https://www.forbes.com/2007/12/20/michael-chu-microfinance-biz-cz_mc_1220chu.html?sh=5ab789ed7c16.

233 **"phenomenal accomplishment":** Daley-Harris, "State of the Microcredit Summit Campaign Report 2007."

233 **"excited and rejoice":** Daley-Harris, "State of the Microcredit Summit Campaign Report 2007."

233 **"an opportunity":** Bruck, "Millions for Millions."

234 **"stunned":** Chuck Waterfield comments on Compartamos IPO.

234 **expanding microfinance:** Daley-Harris, "State of the Microcredit Summit Campaign Report 2007."

234 **poor Mexicans:** Rosenberg, "CGAP Reflections on the Compartamos Initial Public Offering."

235 **sixteen-page focus note:** Rosenberg, "CGAP Reflections on the Compartamos Initial Public Offering."

235 **110 percent APR:** Manuela Angelucci, Dean Karlan, and Jonathan Zinman, "Microcredit Impacts: Evidence from a Randomized Microcredit Program Placement Experiment by Compartamos Banco," *American Economic Journal: Applied Economics* 7, no. 1 (January 1, 2015): 151–82.

235 **posted net profits:** "Resolutions with Regard to the Appointment or Reelection, as the Case May Be, of the Members of the Board of Directors and the Certification of Their Independent Status," Compartamos.

236 **2.3 million:** Manuela Angelucci, Dean Karlan, and Jonathan Zinman, "Win Some Lose Some? Evidence from a Randomized Microcredit Program Placement Experiment by Compartamos Banco," Working Paper 19119, National Bureau of Economic Research, June 2013.

236 **the industry's image:** Daley-Harris, "State of the Microcredit Summit Campaign Report 2007."

237 **Chuck Waterfield warned:** Chuck Waterfield comments on Compartamos IPO.

237 *Time* **magazine:** Bateman, *Why Doesn't Microfinance Work?*

237 **$100 million:** Reuters Staff, "US Unveils $100 Mln Microfinance Fund for Americas," Reuters, April 18, 2009, https://www.reuters.com/article/americas-summit-microfinance -idUSN1833100020090418.

237 **Medal of Freedom:** "Remarks by the President at the Medal of Freedom Ceremony," The White House, August 12, 2009.

237 **Dunham also helped:** "Spotlight on Alumni: EWC Alumna Ann Dunham—Mother to President Obama and Champion of Women's Rights and Economic Justice," East-West Center, October 12, 2012.

238 **briefly joined:** "Stanley Ann Dunham's Legacy," Stanley Ann Dunham Scholarship Fund, https://stanleyanndunhamfund.org/stanley-ann-dunham/.

238 **East-West Center:** "About," East-West Center, https://www.eastwestcenter.org/about.

238 **"to pursue ideas":** "Origins," East-West Center, https://www.eastwestcenter.org/about -ewc/origins.

238 **exceeded the bank's:** *Grameen Dialogue*, no. 41, January 2000.

238 **four years before:** Iyanna Holmes, "MICROCAPITAL STORY: SKS Microfinance Raises $75.4 Million in Equity Capital Transaction Led by Sandstone Capital," Microcapital .org, November 14, 2008, https://www.microcapital.org/microcapital-story-sks-microfinance -raises-754m-in-equity-capital-in-transaction-led-by-sandstone-capital/.

239 **"Priority Sector":** Hugh Manahan, "Private Equity Investments in Microfinance in India," *Michigan Business & Entrepreneurial Law* 4, no. 2 (2015).

239 **similar requirements:** Interview with Prashant Thakkar.

239 **commercial banks had essentially received a subsidy:** R. Srinivasan, "Canara Bank, Alanganallur Branch, Madurai District, Tamil Nadu, India," in Malcolm Harper and Sukhwinder Singh Arora, eds., *Small Customers, Big Market: Commercial Banks in Microfinance* (Warwickshire, UK: ITDG Publishing, 2005), 90–91.

239 **more than half:** "Case Study 2—Andhra Pradesh, India: Participation in Macroeconomic Policy Making and Reform," World Bank, March 2003.

239 **As microfinance boomed:** Bateman, *Why Doesn't Microfinance Work?*, 132–33.

240 **"Mecca" of microfinance:** Prabhu Ghate, "Learning from the Andhra Pradesh Crisis," in Thomas Dichter and Malcolm Harper, eds., *What's Wrong with Microfinance?* (Rugby, Warwickshire, UK: Practical Action Publishing, 2007), 163.

240 **nearly a million:** Raimar Dieckmann, "Microfinance: An Emerging Investment Opportunity. Uniting Social Investment and Financial Returns," Deutsche Bank Research, December 19, 2007.

240 **whose founder:** "Vikram Akula, SKS Microfinance Pvt. Ltd., 1998 Global Fellow," Echoing Green, https://fellows.echoinggreen.org/fellow/vikram-akula/.

240 **the only way:** "The Tuesday Podcast: What's Better for Helping the Poor—Greed or Charity?" WBUR, September 28, 2010, https://www.wbur.org/npr/130194702/the-tuesday -podcast-what-s-better-for-helping-poor-people----greed-or-charity.

240 **$11.5 million:** Tamal Bandyopadhyay, "Vikram Akula's Inside Story of SKS Microfinance Will Remain Untold," *Mint*, June 18, 2018, https://www.livemint.com/Opinion /PmUdeo7PRC2aPIXy625wCM/Vikram-Akulas-inside-story-of-SKS-Microfinance-will -remain.html.

240 **Vinod Khosla:** Megha Bahree, "A Big Split over Microfinance," *Forbes*, October 1, 2010.

240 **started by:** Interview with Elizabeth Funk.

240 **300 percent in 2007 alone:** Holmes, "MICROCAPITAL STORY: SKS Microfinance Raises $75.4 Million in Equity Capital Transaction Led by Sandstone Capital."

240 **$75 million:** Erika Kinetz, "Micro-Lender's Own Probe Links It to 200 Suicides," Associated Press, February 24, 2012.

240 **$350 million in equity:** "The Tuesday Podcast: What's Better for Helping the Poor?"

240 **said such interest:** Holmes, "MICROCAPITAL STORY: SKS Microfinance Raises $75.4 Million in Equity Capital Transaction Led by Sandstone Capital."

241 **From the late 1990s:** "Reaching Down and Scaling Up: Meeting the Microenterprise Development Challenge," U.S. Agency for International Development, Microenterprise Results Reporting for 1997.

241 **the SKS model was:** "The Tuesday Podcast: What's Better for Helping the Poor?"

241 **By the mid-aughts:** Manahan, "Private Equity Investments in Microfinance in India."

241 **one-third:** Soutik Biswas, "India's Micro-Finance Suicide Epidemic," BBC News, December 16, 2010, https://www.bbc.com/news/world-south-asia-11997571.

241 **$3 billion in loans:** "The Tuesday Podcast: What's Better for Helping the Poor?"

241 **"quest for numbers":** Ghate, "Learning from the Andhra Pradesh Crisis," 167.

241 **loan officers, whose salaries:** Waterfield, "Advocating Transparent Pricing in Microfinance."

241 **So long as repayments were made:** Fabrizio Felloni, Hans Dieter Seibel, and Andres Cornejo, "Mainstreaming Grameen Banking in Philippines," in Harper and Arora, *Small Customers, Big Market*, 32.

242 **defaulters were fined:** Ghate, "Learning from the Andhra Pradesh Crisis," 169.

242 **their paychecks:** Waterfield, "Advocating Transparent Pricing in Microfinance."

242 **only 30 percent:** Narasimhan Srinivasan, "Weathering the Storm II: A Case Study of Spandana," Center for Financial Inclusion, November 9, 2020, https://www.centerforfinancialinclusion.org/weathering-the-storm-ii-a-case-study-of-spandana.

242 **At Bank Rakyat Indonesia:** *Grameen Dialogue*, no. 41, January 2000.

242 **Penalties were also imposed:** Hans Dieter Seibel, "The Microbanking Division of Bank Rakyat Indonesia: A Flagship of Rural Microfinance in Asia," in Harper and Arora, *Small Customers, Big Market*.

242 **One microlender in Egypt:** Craig F. Churchill, "Moving Microfinance Forward: Ownership, Competition and Control of Microfinance Institutions," The MicroFinance Network, 1998.

243 **By one account:** Ghate, "Learning from the Andhra Pradesh Crisis," 166.

243 **nearly half:** S. M. Rahman, "A Practitioner's View of the Challenges Facing NGO-Based Microfinance in Bangladesh," in Dichter and Harper, *What's Wrong with Microfinance?*

243 **microfinance didn't reduce reliance:** Rahman, "A Practitioner's View of the Challenges."

243 **by far:** Interview with Nima Yolmo and Bill Maurer.

243 **"two weeks 'dormancy'":** Malcolm Harper, "What's Wrong with Groups?" in Dichter and Harper, *What's Wrong with Microfinance?*, 42.

243 **a stepwise approach:** Irina Aliaga and Paul Mosley, "Microfinance Under Crisis Conditions: The Case of Bolivia," in Dichter and Harper, *What's Wrong with Microfinance?*, 123.

243 **One Egyptian program:** Cathryn Carlson, "Microfinance at Banque du Caire, Egypt," in Harper and Arora, *Small Customers, Big Market*, 125.

243 **"one large payday lender":** Mehrsa Baradaran, *How the Other Half Banks: Exclusion, Exploitation, and the Threat to Democracy* (Cambridge, MA: Harvard University Press, 2015), 111.

244 **One borrower described:** Aliaga and Mosley, "Microfinance Under Crisis Conditions."

244 **loan overdue notice:** Ghate, "Learning from the Andhra Pradesh Crisis," 169.

244 **harassed, coerced, and humiliated:** Kinetz, "Micro-Lender's Own Probe Links It to 200 Suicides."

244 **Having already raised:** Holmes, "MICROCAPITAL STORY: SKS Microfinance Raises $75.4 Million in Equity Capital Transaction Led by Sandstone Capital."

244 **the IPO was oversubscribed:** Finch and Kocieniewski, "Big Money Backs Tiny Loans That Lead to Debt, Despair and Even Suicide."

245 **the headline:** Biswas, "India's Micro-Finance Suicide Epidemic."

245 **A later investigation:** Kinetz, "Micro-Lender's Own Probe Links It to 200 Suicides."

245 **reportedly committed suicide:** David Hulme, "Is Microdebt Good for Poor People? A Note on the Dark Side of Microfinance," in Dichter and Harper, *What's Wrong with Microfinance?*, 20.

245 **Responding to the reports:** Ghate, "Learning from the Andhra Pradesh Crisis," 164–65.

245 **told the BBC:** Biswas, "India's Micro-Finance Suicide Epidemic."

246 **publish a book:** Bandyopadhyay, "Vikram Akula's Inside Story of SKS Microfinance Will Remain Untold."

246 **made it difficult:** Bahree, "A Big Split over Microfinance."

247 **While just one million:** Vijay Kulkarni, "Microfinance Through Self-Help Groups—Case Study of State Bank of India," in Harper and Arora, *Small Customers, Big Market*, 69–70.

247 **long, complicated history:** Janos Chiala and Vinith Xavier, "India's Sugarcane Farmers: A Cycle of Debt and Suicide," *Al Jazeera*, April 3, 2017, https://www.aljazeera.com/features/2017/4/3/indias-sugarcane-farmers-a-cycle-of-debt-and-suicide.

247 **a measured economist:** David Malin Roodman, *Due Diligence: An Impertinent Inquiry into Microfinance* (Washington, DC: Center for Global Development, 2012).

247 **the Associated Press reported:** Kinetz, "Micro-Lender's Own Probe Links It to 200 Suicides."

247 **take advantage of:** Manahan, "Private Equity Investments in Microfinance in India."

248 **99.89 percent:** Waterfield, "Advocating Transparent Pricing in Microfinance."

248 **packed up:** Srinivasan, "Weathering the Storm II: A Case Study of Spandana."

248 **Politicians began:** Biswas, "India's Micro-Finance Suicide Epidemic."

248 **a drop in consumption:** Dinesh Unnikrishnan, "Microfinance Crisis Leads to Loss of 35,000 Jobs," *Mint*, October 21, 2013, https://www.livemint.com/Companies/99un1M17pdKE1O6BOAB1qJ/Microfinance-crisis-leads-to-loss-of-35000-jobs.html.

248 **Just before:** Biswas, "India's Micro-Finance Suicide Epidemic."

248 **relied on debt:** Chiala and Xavier, "India's Sugarcane Farmers."

249 **announced that the organization:** Kim Wilson, "The Moneylender's Dilemma," in Dichter and Harper, *What's Wrong with Microfinance?*, 97.

249 **Catholic social teachings:** "Catholic Social Teaching Principles," Catholic Relief Services, https://www.Catholic Relief Services.org/resource-center/CST-101.

249 **didn't seem to jibe well:** Wilson, "The Moneylender's Dilemma," 97–98, 100–104.

249 **women in Ouarzazate, Morocco:** Interview with Fatima Zahra Elbelghiti and Nathan Legrand.

250 **No Pago:** Garrett Jaso, "Weathering the Storm II: A Case Study of Financiera FAMA," Center for Financial Inclusion, February 26, 2021, https://www.centerforfinancialinclusion.org/weathering-the-storm-ii-a-case-study-of-financiera-fama.

252 **Ford Foundation:** Darren Walker, "Moving the Foundation Forward," November 8, 2015, https://www.fordfoundation.org/news-and-stories/stories/posts/moving-the-ford-foundation-forward/.

252 **"would no longer need":** Wilson, "The Moneylender's Dilemma," 107.

252 **Even after the sale:** Interview with Sugandh Saxena.

253 **by one count:** Dina Pomeranz, "The Promise of Microfinance and Women's Empowerment: What Does the Evidence Say?" Discussion Paper, Harvard Business School, 2014.

253 **"make a loan, change a life":** Kiva, https://www.kiva.org/.

253 **Yunus's op-ed:** Muhammad Yunus, "Sacrificing Microcredit for Megaprofits," *New York Times*, January 14, 2011.

255 **offered a comparison:** "Pawning," *Encyclopedia Britannica*, https://www.encyclopedia.com/history/encyclopedias-almanacs-transcripts-and-maps/pawning.

256 **offered a course correction:** Yunus, "Sacrificing Microcredit for Megaprofits."

256 **were far more interesting:** Interview with Elisabeth Rhyne.

256 **savings, on the other hand:** Pomeranz, "The Promise of Microfinance and Women's Empowerment."

257 **337.4 percent:** Björn Bernhardt, Anselm Dannecker, Gods'man Attah, Brock Hoback, and Steffen Ulrich, "Loan Pricing of Nigerian Microfinance Banks: Survey & Methods of Assessment," GIZ's Pro-Poor Growth and Promotion of Employment (SEDIN) Programme, August 2015.

259 **ten million members:** "Grameen Bank," https://grameenbank.org/.

259 **basic social services:** Greg Chen and Stuart Rutherford, "A Microcredit Crisis Averted: The Case of Bangladesh," CGAP Focus Note, no. 87, July 2013.

259 **In Bangladesh alone:** "Microfinance," BRAC, https://www.brac.net/program/microfinance/.

259 **2.1 million:** "Putting the Furthest Behind First," BRAC Ultra-Poor Graduation Initiative, https://bracupgi.org/.

259 **"graduate":** Jan P. Maes and Larry R. Reed, "State of the Microcredit Summit Campaign Report 2012," Microcredit Summit Campaign.

260 **Yunus called for:** Yunus, "Sacrificing Microcredit for Megaprofits."

260 **interest rate caps:** Manahan, "Private Equity Investments in Microfinance in India."

260 **flat interest:** Waterfield, "Advocating Transparent Pricing in Microfinance."

260 **played at the edges:** Finch and Kocieniewski, "Big Money Backs Tiny Loans That Lead to Debt, Despair and Even Suicide."

261 **400 percent:** Waterfield, "Advocating Transparent Pricing in Microfinance."

262 **set of voluntary principles:** "Client Protection Principles," Center for Financial Inclusion.

263 **claimed to be following:** BRAC International Holdings B.V. Financial Report 2020.

263 **voluntary code of conduct:** "Microfinance Institutions (SLAMFI) Apprise Bank Governor on Its Activities," *Awoko Newspaper*, May 30, 2019, https://awoko.org/2019/03/30/sierra-leone-news-microfinance-institutions-slamfi-apprise-bank-governor-on-its-activities/.

264 **"Let's Talk Money":** Tanwi Kumari, "Client Perspectives on Consumer Protection: Analysis of a Client Survey in Cambodia," Center for Financial Inclusion, https://content.centerforfinancialinclusion.org/wp-content/uploads/sites/2/2020/08/Analysis-of-a-Client-Survey-in-Cambodia.pdf.

264 **Maryann Bylander and Phasy Res:** Maryann Bylander and Phasy Res, "'If You Fall, Stand Up Again': The Moral Nature of Financial Literacy in the Global South," *Development and Change* 52, no. 1 (January 2021): 26–53.

Chapter 13: In the Sky

269 **had committed suicide:** Sushovan Dhar, "Let Us Unite Against Micro-Credits and Illegitimate Debt," Committee for the Abolition of Illegitimate Debt, March 4, 2020, https://www.cadtm.org/Let-us-unite-against-micro-credits-and-illegitimate-debt?debut_tous_articles_auteur=10#pagination_tous_articles_auteur.

269 **claimed there had been an increase:** Ndungu Gachane, "Murang'a Man Hangs Self over Sh3,000 Mobile App Loan," *Nation*, June 29, 2020, https://nation.africa/kenya/counties/muranga/murang-a-man-hangs-self-over-sh3-000-mobile-app-loan-177764.

269 **reported that in Sri Lanka:** Finch and Kocieniewski, "Big Money Backs Tiny Loans That Lead to Debt, Despair and Even Suicide."

269 **fifty times:** Gavin Finch and David Kocieniewski, "Big Money Backs Tiny Loans That Lead to Debt, Despair and Even Suicide," *Bloomberg*, May 3, 2022, https://www.bloomberg.com/graphics/2022-microfinance-banks-profit-off-developing-world/.

270 **during which millions:** "Cambodia," University of Minnesota Holocaust and Genocide Studies, https://cla.umn.edu/chgs/holocaust-genocide-education/resource-guides/cambodia.

270 **world's fastest-growing:** Pasuk Phongpaichit, "The Thai Economy in the Mid-1990s," published online by Cambridge University Press, October 21, 2015, https://www.cambridge.org/core/books/abs/southeast-asian-affairs-1996/thai-economy-in-the-mid1990s/B70142D54BD845B789060B2A8C534420.

270 **a comparison:** "GDP Growth (Annual %)—United States," World Bank, https://data.worldbank.org/indicator/NY.GDP.MKTP.KD.ZG?locations=US.

270 **13.3 percent:** "GDP Growth (Annual %)—Cambodia," World Bank, https://data.worldbank.org/indicator/NY.GDP.MKTP.KD.ZG?locations=KH.

270 **Between 2004 and 2016:** Daniel Rozas, "Inexorable Growth in Cambodia: Like a Rolling Stone?" Mimosa, May 9, 2016, https://mimosaindex.org/inexorable-growth-in-cambodia-like-a-rolling-stone-2/.

271 **country was saturated:** "Collateral Damage: Land Losses and Abuses in Cambodia's Microfinance Sector," LICADHO, August 2019.

271 **Inflation during this period:** "Inflation, Consumer Prices (Annual %)—Cambodia," World Bank, https://data.worldbank.org/indicator/FP.CPI.TOTL.ZG?locations=KH.

271 **had on average:** Hema Bansal, "Land Seizures and Reported Abuses in Cambodia: CFI Responds," Center for Financial Inclusion, October 15, 2019, https://www.centerforfinancialinclusion.org/land-seizures-and-reported-abuses-in-cambodia-the-center-for-financial-inclusion-responds.

271 **most indebted people:** Interview with Jeff Ashe.

271 *$10 billion:* Bansal, "Land Seizures and Reported Abuses in Cambodia."

271 **$300 million:** "Collateral Damage: Land Losses and Abuses in Cambodia's Microfinance Sector."

271 **one in five:** Finch and Kocieniewski, "Big Money Backs Tiny Loans That Lead to Debt, Despair and Even Suicide."

271 **eight out of ten:** "Collateral Damage: Land Losses and Abuses in Cambodia's Microfinance Sector."

271 **to pay for health care:** "Driven Out: Microfinance Debt and Cross-Border Migration," LICADHO, May 5, 2020, https://www.licadho-cambodia.org/video.php?perm=88.

271 **pay off other loans:** "Collateral Damage: Land Losses and Abuses in Cambodia's Microfinance Sector."

271 **or to migrate to Thailand:** "Driven Out: Microfinance Debt and Cross-Border Migration."

271 **"as a way":** Maryann Bylander, "Credit as Coping: Rethinking Microcredit in the Cambodian Context," *Oxford Development Studies* 43, no. 4 (October 2, 2015): 533–53.

272 **loan officers themselves:** "Driven Out: One Village's Experience with MFIs and Cross-Border Migration."

272 **There are reports:** Dannet Liv, "Study of the Drivers of Over-Indebtedness of Microfinance Borrowers in Cambodia: An In-Depth Investigation of Saturated Areas," Cambodia Institute of Development Study, 2013.

272 **British academics:** K. Brickell, L. Parsons, N. Natarajan, and S. Chann, *Blood Bricks: Untold Stories of Modern Slavery and Climate Change from Cambodia*, Royal Holloway University of London, 2018.

272 **microdebt and indentured servitude:** "Built on Slavery: Debt Bondage and Child Labour in Cambodia's Brick Factories," LICADHO, December 2016.

272 **requires a land title:** Interview with Cambodian microfinance researcher.

272 **Cambodia registered land:** Howard Stein, Faustin P. Maganga, Rie Odgaard, Kelly Askew, and Sam Cunningham, "The Formal Divide: Customary Rights and the Allocation of Credit to Agriculture in Tanzania," *Journal of Development Studies* 52, no. 9 (May 2, 2016): 1306–19.

273 **According to Reuters:** Matt Blomberg and Mech Dara, "Land to Lose: Coronavirus Compounds Debt Crisis in Cambodia," Reuters, September 21, 2020, https://www.reuters .com/article/us-cambodia-finance-loans-idUSKCN26C02S.

273 *one million* land titles: "Collateral Damage: Land Losses and Abuses in Cambodia's Microfinance Sector."

273 **reports from LICADHO:** "Driven Out: One Village's Experience with MFIs and Cross-Border Migration."

273 **as well as reporting:** Blomberg and Dara, "Land to Lose."

273 **"for sale":** "Collateral Damage: Land Losses and Abuses in Cambodia's Microfinance Sector."

273 **loan officer arranges:** Interview with Cambodian microfinance researcher.

273 **two anonymous microfinance executives:** "Collateral Damage: Land Losses and Abuses in Cambodia's Microfinance Sector."

273 **2019 video:** "Video: Selling Land to Repay MFI Debt," LICADHO, August 19, 2019, https://www.licadho-cambodia.org/video.php?perm=84.

273 **routinely threaten:** Interview with Cambodian microfinance researcher.

274 **At the beginning of 2020:** Blomberg and Dara, "Land to Lose."

274 **"impending economic disaster":** Interview with Cambodian microfinance researcher.

274 **"We are living":** "Video: Vicious Cycle of Debt," LICADHO, August 8, 2019, https: //www.licadho-cambodia.org/video.php?perm=82.

274 **International Organization for Migration:** Maryann Bylander, "Debt and the Migration Experience: Insights from South-East Asia," International Organization for Migration, 2019.

274 **Hun Sen "threatened":** "NGOs Stand by Reporting on Abuses in Cambodia's Loan Sector After Lenders Demand 'Corrections,'" Radio Free Asia, July 16, 2020, https:// www.rfa.org/english/news/cambodia/loans-07162020130948.html.

275 **owned by one of the largest banks in Thailand:** Bank profile, Hattha Bank, https: //hatthabank.com/about/bank-profile.

275 **lent directly to AMK:** "Worked to Debt: Over-Indebtedness in Cambodia's Garment Sector," LICADHO, June 2020.
275 **and European investors:** "AMK Microfinance of Cambodia Secures $15 Million Loans from Belgian Investment Company," *Khmer Times,* July 15, 2023, https://www .khmertimeskh.com/501324458/amk-microfinance-of-cambodia-secures15-loans-from -belgian-investment-company/.
275 **Human Rights Watch asked:** "Cambodia: Micro-Loan Borrowers Face Covid-19 Crisis," Human Rights Watch, July 14, 2020, https://www.hrw.org/news/2020/07/14/cambodia -micro-loan-borrowers-face-covid-19-crisis#.
275 **publicly criticized:** Finch and Kocieniewski, "Big Money Backs Tiny Loans That Lead to Debt, Despair and Even Suicide."
275 **a Sri Lankan–owned company:** Shareholder structure, LOLC (Cambodia) Plc., https: //www.lolc.com.kh/en/share_holders.
276 **affiliate of Women's World Banking:** Washington K. Kiiru and Glenn D. Pederson, "Kenya Women Finance Trust: Case Study of a Micro-Finance Scheme," World Bank, December 1997.
276 **In Uganda:** Paul Rippey, "Princes, Peasants and Pretenders: The Past and Future of African Microfinance," in Thomas Dichter and Malcolm Harper, eds., *What's Wrong with Microfinance?* (Rugby, Warwickshire, UK: Practical Action Publishing, 2007), 114.
276 **Jordan:** Rana F. Sweis, "Microloans, Seen as Salvation for Poor Women, Trap Many in Debt," *New York Times,* April 8, 2020.
276 **Ghana:** Interview with Appiah Kusi Adomako.
276 **reaches back centuries:** David Graeber, *Debt: The First 5,000 Years* (Brooklyn, NY: Melville House, 2011), 233.
277 **infringing on imposed social order:** Akintola J. G. Wyse, *The Krio of Sierra Leone: An Interpretive History* (Washington, DC: Howard University Press, 1991).
277 **amended their own version:** "The Theft Act 1968," *Journal of Criminal Law* 33, no. 1 (January 1969): 63–72.
277 **Similar iterations:** Interview with Jami Solli.
277 **criminalize *any* type of debt:** Interview with Simite Lavaly.
278 **126 percent:** Neil MacFarquhar, "Banks Making Big Profits from Tiny Loans," *New York Times,* April 13, 2010.
281 **a piece in the *Guardian*:** Elisabeth Rhyne, "Do Lenders Make Clear the Risks of Microfinance Loans?" *Guardian,* March 17, 2016, https://www.theguardian.com/global -development/2016/mar/17/microfinance-loans-do-lenders-make-clear-risks.
281 **"starts with shame":** Interview with Sushovan Dhar.
281 **Chuck Waterfield closed a website:** Chuck Waterfield, "Advocating Transparent Pricing in Microfinance: A Review of MFTransparency's Work and a Proposed Future Path for the Industry," MFTransparency.org, July 15, 2015, https://www.mftransparency.org/wp-content /uploads/2015/08/MFTransparency-Advocating-Transparent-Pricing-in-Microfinance.pdf.
282 **In 2020, the Smart Campaign:** "The Smart Campaign," Center for Financial Inclusion, https://www.centerforfinancialinclusion.org/about/what-we-do/the-smart-campaign.
283 **"pathway":** "Client Protection Pathway," Cerise+SPTF, https://cerise-sptf.org/client -protection-main/.
283 **a separate database:** "MIX," Center for Financial Inclusion, https://www.centerfor financialinclusion.org/about/what-we-do/mix.

New Money: Freetown, Sierra Leone
289 **the Munafa Fund:** Abdul Rashid Thomas, "President Bio Unveils Le100 Billion Enterprise Development Fund for Struggling Businesses," *Sierra Leone Telegraph,* February 13, 2021, https://www.thesierraleonetelegraph.com/president-bio-unveils-le100-billion -enterprise-development-fund-for-struggling-businesses/.

Chapter 14: It's Not Microfinance. It's Financial Inclusion
293 **a change made by Namaste:** Erin Beck, *How Development Projects Persist: Everyday Negotiations with Guatemalan NGOs* (Durham, NC: Duke University Press, 2017), 74.
293 **U.S. Congress declared:** "Microenterprise for Self-Reliance and International Anti-Corruption Act of 2000," Public law 106–309—October 17, 2000.

293 **USAID claimed its work:** "USAID's Contribution to Microfinance: From Microfinance to Financial Inclusion," prepared by Anicca Jansen for the Office of Microenterprise and Private Enterprise Promotion, USAID, October 2014.

293 **Robert Annibale:** Connie Bruck, "Millions for Millions," *New Yorker*, October 22, 2006.

294 **negative associations:** Interview with Peter Bartlett.

294 **"moral imperative":** Paul Breloff, "Accion Venture Lab: Case Narrative," *Innovations: Technology, Governance, Globalization* 10, nos. 1–2 (2015): 75–93.

294 **1.5 billion:** "COVID-19 Boosted the Adoption of Digital Financial Services," World Bank, https://www.worldbank.org/en/news/feature/2022/07/21/covid-19-boosted-the-adoption-of-digital-financial-services.

295 **USAID document from the 1970s:** "Small Enterprise Approaches to Employment for the Urban Poor," prepared by Michael Farbman, Office of Urban Development Bureau for Development Support, Agency for International Development, U.S. Department of State, June 1978, 13.

295 **trying to convince Citigroup:** Bruck, "Millions for Millions."

295 **one venture capitalist:** Mehrsa Baradaran, *How the Other Half Banks: Exclusion, Exploitation, and the Threat to Democracy* (Cambridge, MA: Harvard University Press, 2015), 174.

295 **was later rebranded:** "Social Finance," Citi, https://www.citigroup.com/global/our-impact/strengthening-community/social-finance.

295 **"may alleviate":** Eduardo Polloni-Silva, Naijele da Costa, Herick Fernando Moralles, and Mario Sacomano Neto, "Does Financial Inclusion Diminish Poverty and Inequality? A Panel Data Analysis for Latin American Countries," *Social Indicators Research* 158, no. 3 (2021): 889–925.

295 **the World Bank offers:** "Financial Inclusion," World Bank, https://www.worldbank.org/en/topic/financialinclusion.

295 **forever a chameleon:** Breloff, "Accion Venture Lab: Case Narrative."

296 **a Mexican lender that:** Jude Webber, "Fintech Offers Lifeline for Crisis-Hit Mexican Businesses," *Financial Times*, May 12, 2020.

297 **Accion claimed:** "Case Study: Konfio Innovates in Digital Lending for Mexican SMSEs," Accion, August 28, 2018, https://www.accion.org/konfio-innovates-in-digital-lending-for-mexican-msmes.

297 **the *Financial Times*:** Webber, "Fintech Offers Lifeline for Crisis-Hit Mexican Businesses."

297 **"make or break":** Breloff, "Accion Venture Lab: Case Narrative."

297 **Queen Máxima:** "H.M. Queen Máxima of the Netherlands," UN Secretary-General's Special Advocate for Inclusive Finance for Development, https://www.unsgsa.org/.

297 **"pro-growth":** "H.M. Queen Máxima of the Netherlands: Building a Financially Inclusive World," Financial Health Network, January 2022, https://finhealthnetwork.org/podcast/h-m-queen-maxima-of-the-netherlands-building-a-financially-inclusive-world/.

298 **"while Namaste's donors":** Beck, *How Development Projects Persist*, 75.

299 **the British development agency:** Dina Pomeranz, "The Promise of Microfinance and Women's Empowerment: What Does the Evidence Say?" Discussion Paper, Harvard Business School, 2014.

299 **than had a bank account:** Bill Maurer, *How Would You Like to Pay? How Technology Is Changing the Future of Money* (Durham, NC: Duke University Press, 2015), 11.

299 **had funded early mobile money:** Interview with Elizabeth Littlefield.

299 **"more than 5,000":** Jan Bellens, "How Banks Can Play a Stronger Role in Accelerating Financial Inclusion," EY, April 25, 2018, https://www.ey.com/en_ua/trust/can-inclusive-banking-drive-economic-growth-in-emerging-markets.

299 **within twenty-four hours:** "Case Study: Konfio Innovates in Digital Lending for Mexican MSMEs."

299 **need to show proof:** Interview with Milford Bateman.

300 **According to one 2019 report:** "Making Digital Credit Truly Responsible," Center for Financial Inclusion, September 25, 2019, https://www.centerforfinancialinclusion.org/making-digital-credit-truly-responsible.

300 **GetBucks Kenya:** "MyBucks Annual Report 2019."

300 **common for sports betting:** Jonathan W. Rosen, "How Mobile Money Supercharged Kenya's Sports Betting Addiction," *MIT Technology Review*, April 14, 2022.

300 **The digital lender Branch:** "How It Works," Branch, https://branch.co/how-it-works.

301 **several hundred million:** Sarah Hansen, "Mobile Lending App Branch Partners with Visa, Announces $170 Million in Fresh Funding," *Forbes*, August 7, 2019.

301 **from investors including:** "TLG Invests in Branch Nigeria," TLG Capital, November 2018, https://tlgcapital.com/tlg-invests-in-branch-nigeria/.

301 **"that commercial and social":** "TLG Capital," https://tlgcapital.com/.

301 **Branch partnered with Visa:** Hansen, "Mobile Lending App Branch Partners with Visa, Announces $170 Million in Fresh Funding."

301 **"Our partnership with Branch":** "Branch International Raises $170M Series C Financing, Led by Foundation Capital and Visa," *Business Wire*, April 8, 2019.

301 **bought a microfinance bank:** Kenn Abuya, "What Is Branch Pro, and Why Is the Lender Keen on Becoming a Full-fledged Neobank?" *TechCabal*, June 5, 2023, https://techcabal.com/2023/06/05/branch-is-transitioning-to-a-neobank/.

301 **the most profitable service:** Paula Gilbert, "M-Pesa Remains Safaricom's Most Profitable Service," *Connecting Africa*, July 13, 2022, https://www.connectingafrica.com/author.asp?section_id=761&doc_id=778966.

301 **valuable companies in East Africa:** Victor Oluwole, "Safaricom Ranked the Most Valuable Firm in East Africa by Market Cap," *Business Insider Africa*, November 22, 2021, https://africa.businessinsider.com/local/markets/safaricom-ranked-the-most-valuable-firm-in-east-africa-by-market-cap/dj5wj00.

301 **Safaricom also offers:** "Financial Report FY2020," Safaricom.

301 **"virtual" credit card:** Adriana Nunez, "Visa Brings Virtual Cards to M-Pesa Users to Capitalize on Africa's Payment Digitization," *Insider Intelligence*, June 3, 2022.

301 **MasterCard is also:** Adriana Nunez, "Mastercard Signs New Deals to Capitalize on Payments Digitization in the Middle East and Africa," *Insider Intelligence*, May 25, 2022.

301 **roughly 40 percent:** Interview with Jami Solli.

301 **reportedly used by the Kenyan government:** Nancy Agutu, "Helb to Publish Names, Photos of Defaulters from 1975 to Date," *The Star* (Kenya), November 18, 2019.

302 **Kenya's Credit Reference Bureau:** Interview with Crystal Simeoni.

302 **"debtors list":** Interview with Jami Solli.

302 **twenty-five-year-old man:** Ndungu Gachane, "Murang'a Man Hangs Self over Sh3,000 Mobile App Loan," *Nation*, June 29, 2020, https://nation.africa/kenya/counties/muranga/murang-a-man-hangs-self-over-sh3–000-mobile-app-loan-177764.

303 **passed a data protection bill:** Kenn Abuya, "Kenya's Data Protection Commissioner Takes Aim at Loan Apps," *Techcabal*, May 16, 2023, https://techcabal.com/2023/05/16/kenyas-data-protection-commissioner-takes-aim-at-loan-apps/.

304 **a blog post from:** Paul DiLeo, "Slow-Motion Extinction? Or Can Impact Investors Reinvigorate Pro-Poor Financial Inclusion?" Center for Financial Inclusion, November 1, 2022, https://www.centerforfinancialinclusion.org/slow-motion-extinction-or-can-impact-investors-reinvigorate-pro-poor-financial-inclusion.

304 **nearly three-quarters:** "Financial Inclusion."

305 **2022 study:** Till Bruckner, "Does Financial Inclusion Boost Borrowers' Resilience? Three Lessons from the Pandemic," Center for Financial Inclusion, November 14, 2022, https://www.centerforfinancialinclusion.org/does-financial-inclusion-boost-borrowers-resilience-three-lessons-from-the-pandemic.

305 **Later that year:** Leora Klapper and Pia Roman Tayag, "Responsible Finance and Its Role in Improving Financial Resilience and Well-Being," Center for Financial Inclusion, October 27, 2022, https://www.centerforfinancialinclusion.org/responsible-finance-and-its-role-in-improving-financial-resilience-and-well-being.

305 **as crop prices:** Chhum Chantha, "As Farmers Are Hit by the Fall of Mung Bean Prices, the Ministry of Agriculture Calls for the Promotion of All Products," *Cambodianess*, July 15, 2023, https://cambodianess.com/article/as-farmers-are-hit-by-the-fall-of-mung-bean-prices-the-ministry-of-agriculture-calls-for-the-promotion-of-all-products.

It's Easier and It's Harder: Sukudu, Kono, Eastern Sierra Leone

307 **In the 1950s:** David Clive King, "Diamond Mining Settlements in Central Kono District, Sierra Leone," thesis submitted for the degree of Doctor of Philosophy of the University of London, January 1979.

309 **it's been poisoned:** King, "Diamond Mining Settlements in Central Kono District, Sierra Leone."

310 **finding chicken:** "Poultry Meat in Sierra Leone," OEC, https://oec.world/en/profile/bilateral-product/poultry-meat/reporter/sle.

Conclusion

315 **"statistical inconsistencies":** Reuters, "Sierra Leone Election Observers Flag 'Statistical Inconsistencies,'" CNN, June 21, 2023, https://www.cnn.com/2023/06/30/africa/sierra-leone-polls-controversy-intl/index.html.

316 **60 percent in 2022:** "Macroeconomic Context," World Bank in Sierra Leone, https://www.worldbank.org/en/country/sierraleone/overview.

319 **resigned as managing director:** Alastair Lawson, "How Grameen Founder Muhammad Yunus Fell from Grace," *BBC News*, April 5, 2011, https://www.bbc.com/news/world-south-asia-12734472.

320 **Yunus told *Bloomberg*:** Gavin Finch and David Kocieniewski, "Big Money Backs Tiny Loans That Lead to Debt, Despair and Even Suicide," *Bloomberg*, May 3, 2022, https://www.bloomberg.com/graphics/2022-microfinance-banks-profit-off-developing-world/.

320 **Grameen Foundation website:** "Our Family of Organizations," Grameen Foundation, https://grameenfoundation.org/about-us/the-grameen-family.

320 **broad concept of "social business":** "Yunus Social Business," https://www.yunussb.com/.

320 **he told the *Guardian*:** Miriam Cosic, "'We Are All Entrepreneurs': Muhammad Yunus on Changing the World, One Microloan at a Time," *Guardian*, March 28, 2017, https://www.theguardian.com/sustainable-business/2017/mar/29/we-are-all-entrepreneurs-muhammad-yunus-on-changing-the-world-one-microloan-at-a-time.

321 **"powerful and forceful":** "The Elders Mourn the Passing of Ela Bhatt," The Elders, November 2, 2022, https://theelders.org/news/elders-mourn-passing-ela-bhatt.

321 **It still considers itself:** "About Us," SEWA, https://www.sewa.org/about-us/.

321 **140 million:** Upamanyu Lahiri, "How to Boost Microfinance in the United States," Council on Foreign Relations, August 22, 2022, https://www.cfr.org/blog/how-boost-microfinance-united-states.

321 **1.2 billion:** "Financial Inclusion: Overview," World Bank, https://www.worldbank.org/en/topic/financialinclusion/overview.

322 **"included partnerships with":** Sunil Gupta, Rajiv Lal, and Natalie Kindred, "MasterCard: Driving Financial Inclusion," Harvard Business School Case 515–035, October 2014 (revised June 2016).

322 **the World Bank claimed:** "Financial Inclusion," World Bank, accessed April 13, 2023, https://www.worldbank.org/en/topic/financialinclusion.

322 **J.P. Morgan partnered:** "responsAbility Closes USD 175 Million Microfinance Securitization," July 17, 2019, https://www.responsability.com/en/press-releases/responsability-closes-usd-175-million-microfinance-securitization.

322 **In 2018, Bandhan Bank:** "Initial Public Offer of Bandhan Bank Oversubscribed 15 Times on Last Day of Issue," IndiaTV, March 19, 2018, https://www.indiatvnews.com/business/news-initial-public-offer-of-bandhan-bank-oversubscribed-15-times-on-last-day-of-issue-433423.

322 **Its shareholders have included:** "Shareholding Pattern as of August 5, 2020," Bandhan Bank.

322 **In July 2018:** "Private Equity Players Eye Microfinance Institutions," Bassiouni Group, September 26, 2018.

322 **As of 2022:** "General Information," Gentera, https://www.gentera.com.mx/gentera/relacion-con-inversionistas/informacion-general.

322 **its shareholders included:** "Compartamos SAB DE CV," https://www.marketscreener.com/quote/stock/COMPARTAMOS-SAB-DE-CV-8686421/company/.

322 **public funders:** "Citi, DFC and JICA Announce $70 Million in Financing to Support Women-Owned Small Businesses in Mexico," Citi, March 29, 2021, https://www.citigroup.com/global/news/press-release/2021/citi-dfc-and-jica-announce-70-million-in-financing-to-support-women-owned-small-businesses-in-mexico.

322 **Inter-American Development Bank:** "IDB Invest Supports Micro and Small Companies in Mexico Through Compartamos," IDB, June 2, 2022, https://www.idbinvest

.org/en/news-media/idb-invest-supports-micro-and-small-companies-mexico-through
-compartamos.

323 **dually motivated by:** Muhammad Yunus, *Banker to the Poor: Micro-Lending and the Battle Against World Poverty* (New York: PublicAffairs, 2007), 208.

323 **won the Nobel Prize in Economics:** "Press Release," The Nobel Prize, October 14, 2019, https://www.nobelprize.org/prizes/economic-sciences/2019/press-release/.

324 **clean water is good:** John M. Colford Jr., Timothy Wade, Sukhwinder Sandhu, et al., "A Randomized, Controlled Trial of In-Home Drinking Water Intervention to Reduce Gastrointestinal Illness," *American Journal of Epidemiology* 161, no. 5 (February 17, 2005): 472–82, https://doi.org/10.1093/aje/kwi067.

324 **some of these questions:** Sanjay G. Reddy, "Economics' Biggest Success Story Is a Cautionary Tale: Field Experiments Now Dominate Development Economics—Often at the Expense of the World's Poor," *Foreign Policy*, October 22, 2019.

327 **GiveDirectly claims:** "Research at GiveDirectly: Published Randomized Controlled Trial Studies," GiveDirectly, https://www.givedirectly.org/research-at-give-directly/.

327 **GiveDirectly is also trying:** "Universal Basic Income Study," GiveDirectly, https://www.givedirectly.org/ubi-study/.

327 **Finland:** Alex Matthews, "Finland's Answer to Universal Basic Income," DW.com, May 30, 2020, https://www.dw.com/en/does-finland-show-the-way-to-universal-basic-income/a-53595886.

327 **Studies have found:** Jeanne Kuang, "Stockton Guaranteed Income Study Finds Pandemic Damped Positive Results," *CalMatters*, April 12, 2023, https://calmatters.org/california-divide/2023/04/california-guaranteed-income/.

328 **30 percent:** "Inflation, Consumer Prices (Annual %)—Sierra Leone," World Bank, https://data.worldbank.org/indicator/FP.CPI.TOTL.ZG?locations=SL.

328 **Some libertarians:** Alyssa Battistoni, "The False Promise of Universal Basic Income," *Dissent*, Spring 2017.

331 **Kiva, whose website says:** Kiva, https://www.kiva.org/.

Acknowledgments

I've learned that writing a book is at once excruciatingly solitary and deeply, often invisibly, communal. Over the last few years, I've relied on hundreds of people, many who will never know that or how they have contributed: authors whose work I have learned from and who have inspired me; the random people I've met at bars or over dinner who have unknowingly helped me to challenge or refine my ideas; friends and family who listened to me speak about this more than I'd like to admit (or, I'm sure, they would have cared to), offered encouragement when I felt overwhelmed, and kept me feeling supported and happy throughout the process. I'm deeply grateful to the many people who listened to early iterations of ideas for this book, and those who read early drafts, including students at the UC Berkeley Graduate School of Journalism, Ngozi Cole, Orla Adams, Anne Erickson, Lin Nelson, and especially Peter Kardas, for his hawk-eyed edits. Thank you to Jenn Kahn, Michael Pollan, and Edward Wasserman for believing in my ability to tackle this subject, and to the UC Berkeley Human Rights Center for getting this project off the ground with financial and research support. Big thanks to Alexa Koenig and Andrea Lampros for their guidance, Janine Graham for her dedicated research, and Lesley Cosme Torres, Imran Malik, Katie Licari-Kozak, Brett Simpson, Freddy Brewster, Sasha Hupka, Noah Baustin, Jesse Bedayn, Anne Daugherty, Elena Neale-Sacks, Thomas Brouns, Isabella Bloom, Isabella Fertel, Ari Sen, Sabrina Kharrazi, and Michelle Pitcher for their additional research. Milagro Maravilla provided exceptional research on the history of FEDECRÉDITO and El Salvador's small lending movements. The International Women's Media

Foundation's Howard G. Buffett Fund for Women Journalists, Investigative Reporters and Editors, Logan Nonfiction Program, Mesa Refuge, Richard J. Margolis Award, and the Blue Mountain Center all provided invaluable support, for which I am immensely grateful. A huge thank-you to Adam Hochschild for helping to refine the early idea and encouraging me to pursue this—I am so impressed by your seemingly endless patience and mentorship to so many young writers; we cannot thank you enough. Biggest love to Sienna Kuykendall and Londiwe Gamedze for keeping me sane in the Bay and a big thank-you to Page Street for offering a beautiful, peaceful writing space.

Deep appreciation for Wendy Strothman and Sara Bershtel, who got this book off the ground and steered it in the right direction, and the entire team at Holt, particularly Anita Sheih, Zoë Affron, Hannah Campbell, Carolyn O'Keefe, Laura Flavin, Sonja Flancher, and my immensely able and steady editor, Serena Jones—your enthusiasm and confidence buoyed me.

Thank you to the Sierra Leonean market vendors, shopkeepers, and the odd police officer and judge who let me sit in the corner and take notes for hours, often asking the stupidest questions. Kumba Tekuyama, Umaru Sheriff, Principal Turay, Sherry Bangura, David Kpakiwa, and Elizabeth Musa continue to be essential guides and friends. This book would not have been possible without Signe Roelsgaard Nielson, who helped me to see my ignorance about the way microfinance functioned in Sierra Leonean society so many years ago, and AdvocAid for hosting me and sharing their research in the summer of 2019. Special thanks to Rebecca Wood, Ayo Max-Dixon, Nenny Kargbo, Namsa Thoronka, Julie Sesay, Faith Bangura, Josephina Hinga, Joseph Bangura, Patrick Steven, and Fatmata Lamarana Bah for their hospitality, insights, transparency, and kindness. Thanks to the staff at the Human Rights Commission, particularly Gassan Abess, who met with me numerous times over my visits, provided invaluable context and information, and always kept in touch in the interim. Thanks to the Legal Aid Board, particularly Claire Carlton-Hanciles and Kemoh Kandeh, who provided frank observations and didn't seem to mind me tagging along, even last-minute. Thank you to Bankolay Turay for supporting research, and for your insights, at the Legal Aid Board and in prisons.

I have the greatest respect for the many people who shared their stories with me for this book, offering intimate personal history and insight and hours and hours of their time. Although not every single one is named in these pages, their ideas and experiences have all informed what is included here. I am immensely grateful for the dozens of women who trusted me enough to let me into their shops and living rooms, allowing me to observe their daily lives and ask them simple, sometimes obtrusive, things. Their children, husbands, and neighbors were equally patient. Their warmth and hospitality are gifts that I do not take lightly, and I will continue to carry these with me. I'm sure I have made errors in telling their stories, but I hope I have done them at least some measure of justice.

My parents, Lin Nelson and Peter Kardas, in many ways shaped this book before I even knew I wanted to write it, encouraging me to pursue questions and my love for writing for as long as I can remember. Thank you for years of guidance, advice, feedback, and many conversations over warm meals.

Raphael Frankfurter is my heart, my steadiness, the one who sharpens my brain and my conscience, demanding more of me and the world in the gentlest of ways. I am grateful every day for our partnership.

Index

Page numbers in *italics* refer to maps.

About the Author

Mara Kardas-Nelson is an independent journalist who focuses on international development and inequality. Her award-winning work has appeared in the *New York Times*, the *Nation*, NPR, the *Guardian*, the *Mail & Guardian*, and elsewhere. Mara has also spent years working in global health, including with Partners in Health, Médecins Sans Frontières, and South Africa's Treatment Action Campaign. Originally from the United States, she has lived in Canada, South Africa, and Sierra Leone. Her time in different parts of the world informs the questions she asks and how she frames her stories.

—